THE BEST OF THE BROWNIES' BOOK

The Brownies' Book
JANUARY, 1920
One Dollar and a Half a Year
Fifteen Cents a Copy

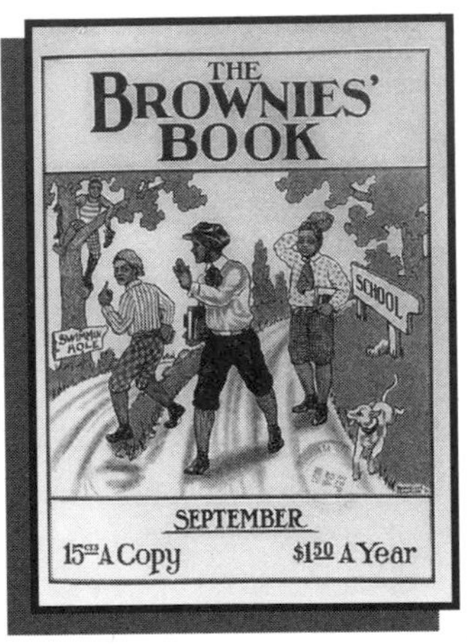
THE BROWNIES' BOOK
SCHOOL
SEPTEMBER
15cts A Copy
$1.50 A Year

The Brownies' Book
$1.50 A YEAR
September, 1920
15 CTS. A COPY

The Brownies' Book
JUNE, 1921
$1.50 A YEAR
15cts. A COPY

THE BROWNIES' BOOK
FOR MAY 1921

The BROWNIES' BOOK
EASTER
$1.50 A YEAR
APRIL-1920
15 CTS A COPY

THE IONA AND PETER OPIE LIBRARY OF CHILDREN'S LITERATURE

The Best of The Brownies' Book

Edited by Dianne Johnson-Feelings

Introduction by Marian Wright Edelman

Oxford University Press
New York

Acknowledgments

I extend my thanks to Nancy Toff and her staff at Oxford University Press for their enthusiasm about this project and to Robert O'Meally for his thoughtful editorial advice. I also wish to thank Loraine Machlin for her wonderful design. Catherine (Missy) Lewis has my sincere appreciation for being the ideal research assistant.

Oxford University Press

Oxford New York
Athens Auckland Bangkok Bombay
Calcutta Cape Town Dar es Salaam Delhi
Florence Hong Kong Istanbul Karachi
Kuala Lumpur Madras Madrid Melbourne
Mexico City Nairobi Paris Singapore
Taipei Tokyo Toronto
and associated companies in
Berlin Ibadan

Published by Oxford University Press, Inc.,
198 Madison Avenue, New York, New York 10016

Design: Loraine Machlin
All photographs from the collection of the Library of Congress except for those on pages 300, 333, 334, and 347, which are from the collection of the Schomburg Center for Research in Black Culture, the New York Public Library, Astor, Lenox, and Tilden Foundations .

Library of Congress Cataloging-in-Publication Data
The best of the Brownies' book / edited by Dianne Johnson-Feelings.
p. cm. — (The Iona and Peter Opie library of children's literature)
ISBN 0-19-509941-9
1. Afro-American children. 2. Afro-Americans—Juvenile literature. [1. Afro-Americans.]
I. Johnson-Feelings, Dianne. II. Brownies' Book. III. Series.
E185.86.B48 1995
973'.0496073—dc20 95-17677
CIP

1 3 5 7 9 8 6 4 2

Printed in the United States of America
on acid-free paper

CONTENTS

Part 3

Everyday Living: Growing Up in 1920

Part 4
TELL ME A STORY

Part 5
FOR ALL LITTLE FOLK: AN INTERNATIONAL COMMUNITY

Part 6

For the Children of the Sun

This book is for a new generation of Brownies

Richard Ross, Jr., Taelor Marie Johnson, and Niani Feelings

Ailea and Sierra Stites
Jonelle Francis
Chymere Hayes
James Daniel Irby, III
Rufus Carl Gordon, III
Candace Smith

Verbena and Lauren Soodoo
Jasmine and Kendra Little
Lee Young
Paul Fletcher-Hill
Lynn Poe
Julian Marshall
Seth and Sarah Gilliard
Theodore and Miriam Rollock
Olaoluwa, Ifeoluwa, and Adeoluwa Afolayan
Lauren, Rachel, and Mariah Smith
Shalaine and Desmond Archie
Heather and Erica Wright and A. J. Wiggs
The grandchildren of Bob and Carol Bowman
Luke Green
Pierre, Sebastian, Cecile, and Adrian Goud-Le Grain

The Children of Holly Hill, South Carolina

INTRODUCTION

Marian Wright Edelman

Childhood reading is what led me to believe that the whole world was mine to explore, and that no one could limit me—or any child—to only a small part of it. *The Brownies' Book* gave many "colored" or "Negro" children, as we then were called, that same sense of boundless possibility.

I grew up with more books and magazines in our home than clothes or luxuries, and I'm grateful for that. Surrounding me from very early childhood were names like Gandhi, Benjamin Mays, Howard Thurman, W. E. B. Du Bois, and Langston Hughes. My Daddy valued reading almost as much as prayer, service, and work. The only time he would not assign chores for my brothers and sister and me was when we were reading—so we read a lot!

At the time there were things I'd rather have been doing—swimming or skipping rope or reading magazines of *my* choosing (Daddy once caught me reading a spicy, forbidden *True Confessions*, which I had slipped inside a news magazine). But I know now that reading helped instill in me a sense of life that transcends the artificial boundaries of race, class, gender, and material things. Despite the messages of worthlessness I got from living in the segregated, small-town South of my youth, reading exposed me to the intellectual giants of my race. And that has provided a life-long layer of insulation against the ugly voices of doubt, racism, and hatred.

Looking over this anthology from *The Brownies' Book*, I'm struck by the wealth of self-love and self-respect the magazine afforded its young readers. Going out into their 1920 world, black children faced every sign, symbol, slogan, and slight needed to convince them they were second best, at best. But reading an essay by Langston Hughes or Nella Larsen, answering a quiz about the contributions of heroes and heroines of their race, reading profiles of their forebears, and seeing children who looked like them in photos and drawings was a strong antidote.

Also striking to me is that *The Brownies' Book* really *wasn't* a children's magazine. It was a magazine for parents and children to read together, to learn from together, and to spark their thoughts and dreams and desire for more knowledge. It was another means by which the African-American family was drawn together and strengthened.

I hope you will read *The Best of The Brownies' Book* with *your* family. I hope you will be proud of the great cultural legacy African-American writers and artists of the 1920s and 1930s have left for you to enjoy. During this period—the Harlem Renaissance—creative works by black pioneers in literature, art, music, theater, and dance reflected the beauty and diversity of African-American life. They set a standard for artistic excellence that Americans of all races learned to respect.

The Best of The Brownies' Book is a gift of love. Turn each page and begin to dream. Your life is filled with possibility. Reach high, look forward, and never give up. The world is waiting for you!

PREFACE

Dianne Johnson-Feelings

The Brownies' Book was a magazine for children that was published every month for 24 months, from January 1920 through December 1921. But the idea for it was expressed first in the pages of *The Crisis*, the official magazine of the National Association for the Advancement of Colored People, which W. E. B. Du Bois edited from 1910 to 1936. An announcement of its coming appeared in August 1919. And an article about the editors' and publishers' inspiration appeared in October 1919, the annual "Children's Number." When *The Brownies' Book* was just an idea, and then when it became a real publication, one of the most important things about the magazine was that it was for a very special group of readers—"the Children of the Sun." That was the editors' name for all African-American children. But the young people who read *The Brownies' Book*—"brownies"—were probably children of NAACP members. In 1920, African Americans were often called Negroes or colored people, terms you will see in this book. But remember that no matter what name was used, the magazine was designed especially for young people whose ancestors were from the continent of Africa.

There were three people who worked very hard to create *The Brownies' Book*. One of them was W. E. B. Du Bois, who was born in Massachusetts in 1868 and died in Ghana, West Africa, in 1963. He was a scholar, professor, and writer who was educated at fine schools: Fisk University, Harvard University, and the University of Berlin. He was one of the founders of the NAACP, an organization that was committed to making the lives of African Americans better through ending legal segregation, the system that supported separation of the races and inferior treatment of African Americans.

The business manager of *The Brownies' Book* was Augustus Granville Dill, who held the same position with *The Crisis*. He was a 1908 graduate of Harvard University and a professor of the social sciences at Atlanta University.

Jessie Fauset was the literary editor in 1920 and the managing editor in 1921. Like Du Bois and Dill, she was well educated. She held degrees from Cornell University and from the University of Pennsylvania, and she studied at the Sorbonne in Paris. Today, she is well known and

The Brownies' Book

Announcement is made of the publication beginning in November of a Monthly Magazine for Children

DESIGNED FOR ALL CHILDREN,
BUT ESPECIALLY FOR *OURS*.

It will be a thing of Joy and Beauty, dealing in Happiness, Laughter and Emulation, and designed especially for Kiddies from Six to Sixteen.

It will seek to teach Universal Love and Brotherhood for all little folk—black and brown and yellow and white.

Of course, pictures, puzzles, stories, letters from little ones, clubs, games and oh—everything!

One Dollar a year ***Ten Cents a copy***

W. E. B. DuBois, Editor
A. G. Dill, Business Manager

ADDRESS:
The Brownies' Book, 2 W. 13th Street, New York City

respected for the books she wrote for adults. And in fact, as literary editor of *The Crisis* from 1919 through May 1926, she played a role in encouraging other African-American writers as well.

The annual literary contests sponsored by *The Crisis* played an important part in nurturing what is now referred to as the Harlem Renaissance—a time when many black writers, artists, philosophers, and entertainers were part of a community of creative energy centered in Harlem, a largely African-American neighborhood in New York City. The Renaissance began during the same period that *The Brownies' Book* was in existence—a period when black Americans, especially those of the middle class, were critical of the nation but optimistic that change could occur.

This was the atmosphere in which Du Bois, Dill, and Fauset decided to create *The Brownies' Book*. They wanted African-American children and young adults to know about the history and achievements of Negro people. They wanted Negro children to know that even though black people in America had endured many struggles, they also had achieved many goals. For them, it was important to have a magazine that taught black children about the lives of other black people, because most of the other children's magazines, movies, schoolbooks, and picture books in 1920 portrayed black people as being ugly and rarely, if ever, doing anything important.

The Brownies' Book assured the children of the sun that their mothers and fathers, teachers and preachers, writers and artists, neighbors and friends, at home and across the oceans, were intelligent and creative. Many people helped *The Brownies' Book* to accomplish this. For example,

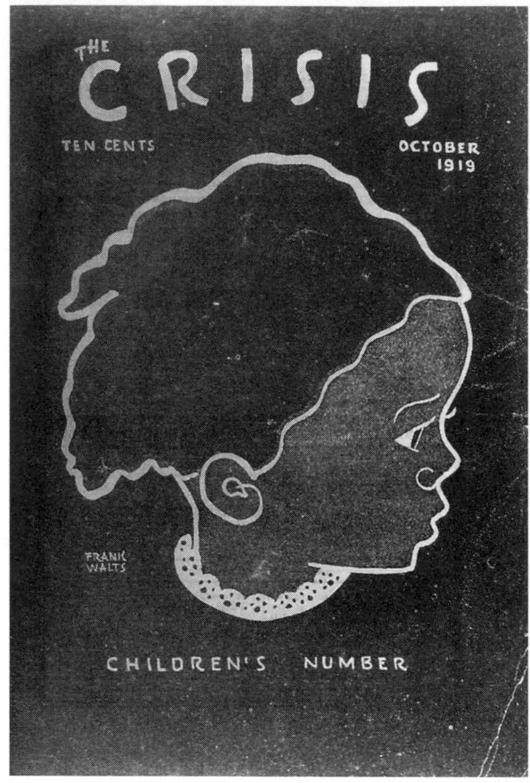

every issue of the magazine included stories. Some of them were folktales. Some took place in the real world and some in fantasy worlds. Many people wrote and sent in stories and poems and illustrations, and from those Jessie Fauset chose the ones that would appear in each issue. Sometimes the writers were adults who are now well known for writing for other adults, such as Nella Larsen (who signed her submissions with her married name, Nella Larsen Imes). Others were teachers. Others were writers who, as far as we know, never wrote for any other magazine or published any books. Sometimes, the writers were young readers of the magazine. Among them was Langston Hughes, who began to write for *The Brownies' Book* when he was a young man just finishing high school. He contributed stories, poems, and games to *The Brownies' Book*. You might have read his poetry or his recently republished *Popo and Fifina*, the novel he wrote about 10 years later with Arna Bontemps.

Not only did *The Brownies' Book* feature stories, games from around the world, and poetry, it also included several other sections that readers could look forward to with every issue. One of these sections was "The Judge," which was written by Jessie Fauset. The judge was an adult who had conversations with children about all kinds of things: their parents, their behavior, their friends, their schoolwork, and much more. "The Jury" was the column in which letters from young readers like you were printed. When you read some of their letters, you will see what was important to African-American children then and what they liked about *The Brownies' Book*. In "The Grown-Ups' Corner" you would have read the letters of the parents of the "brownies." They wrote often because they were pleased with the magazine. On the "Little People of the Month" pages, you will read about the accomplishments of young people from all over the country, including learning to play musical instruments and winning contests, and you will see photographs of them, too.

Besides the photographs, other beautiful artwork filled the pages of *The Brownies' Book*. Most of the illustrations were created by Negro artists. This was important to the editors of the magazine because they were proud of this art, and they wanted young people to know that they could be artists when they grew up. In fact, the editors wanted the young readers to dream about being many things: doctors, writers, musicians, teachers, athletes, actors, inventors, scientists, parents, and anything else they wanted to be. To encourage these dreams, each issue of the magazine included the stories of people, famous and not famous, who accomplished much with their lives. The editors also encouraged children by suggesting books they could read to help them know more about history and to prepare for the future.

Each issue of *The Brownies' Book* also had a section called "As the Crow Flies" in which the children of the sun learned about current events in America and all over the world. This was an important part of the magazine because the editors wanted the readers to know that they were part of a very big world with many different countries and many different kinds of people, all with their own ways of doing things. And even though *The Brownies' Book* was created especially for African-American children, the editors wanted it "to teach Universal Love and Brotherhood for all little folk—black and brown and yellow and white." This could happen only if young people around the world knew something about each other. The brownies learned about their friends around the world through stories and games and even letters from children in other places who read *The Brownies' Book* too.

Perhaps as you read *The Best of The Brownies' Book*, just a sample of what appeared each month, you will feel as if you are a "true brownie"—a regular reader of the magazine more than 75 years ago. For in many ways, you might not be so different from those of the 1920s who were called "the Children of the Sun."

NOTABLE CONTRIBUTORS TO THE BROWNIES' BOOK

W. E. B. DU BOIS

William Edward Burghardt Du Bois was one of the most forcefully influential thinkers, writers, and political leaders of the 20th century. For several of that century's decades, Du Bois (who pronounced the name "Du Boyce") was the most important spokesperson for African Americans; he embodied the group's determination to shake off the legacy of slavery, to attain broad intellectual and cultural achievement, to rise.

Born February 23, 1868, in Great Barrington, Massachusetts, young Du Bois felt a sharp sense of his responsibility as a black American of talent. Even in high school, where he was the only black student, he took a position as a correspondent for a New York newspaper and urged blacks to develop self-help projects and to take political action. As an undergraduate at all-black Fisk University in Nashville, Tennessee, his commitment to black leadership broadened and deepened. He later wrote that blacks he met in the South "seemed bound to me by new and exciting ties." These African-American connections were confirmed by work during the summers, when he taught school in one of Tennessee's remote valleys.

From Fisk, Du Bois went to Harvard, where he received a second B.A. degree, studied under the philosophers William James and George Santayana, became the first African American to earn a Ph.D. (with a prize-winning dissertation on the slave trade to America), and then went on to Germany for further study.

Though he held a variety of teaching positions throughout his life—at various points he taught Greek, Latin, German, English, economics, and history—Du Bois's career as a writer most profoundly confirmed his having, as he said in a personal essay while at Harvard, "something to say to the world." His second book was *The Philadelphia Negro* (1899), the first scientific study of the race problem in the United States. He wrote many other books, including autobiographies, novels, and scholarly essays on the role of blacks in the history of the world.

By far his most significant book was *The Souls of Black Folk* (1903). Partly a reminiscence, partly an analysis, partly a political statement, it stands as one of the most powerful works of the modern era. *Souls* offers definitions of blackness that serve us well today.

For example, Du Bois observes that to be black in America (and one might add, to be an American of whatever ethnicity) is to face a double identity. As an African American, he wrote, "one ever feels his two-ness—an American, a Negro, two souls, two thoughts, two unreconciled strivings, two warring ideals in one dark body."

Throughout his career, Du Bois stayed in touch with as wide an audience as possible through his books and also through his vital associations with magazines and journals. All told, he founded five periodicals: the *Moon Illustrated Weekly*, *Horizon*, *Phylon*, *The Crisis*, and *The Brownies' Book*.

As writer, editor, and publisher, Du Bois kept in mind his original design of transforming the political fortune of blacks in the United States. But he also felt strongly that the black scholar/artist should move beyond the writing table to take direct political action. Here again he took the lead. In 1905 he founded the Niagara Movement, whose purpose was to fight American racism and segregation. In 1908 he was among those who founded the National Association for the Advancement of Colored People (NAACP), which became the premier organization for black rights advocacy in the country.

Because of his longstanding commitment to the idea that black people all over the world share a common bond, Du Bois is often called the "Father of Pan-Africanism." He became an internationally influential figure, a champion for black rights on a global scale. In 1963, he died in Accra, Ghana, having renounced his U.S. citizenship in favor of his new homeland in Africa. At the March on Washington, where Martin Luther King, Jr., made his "I Have a Dream" speech, it was announced that W. E. B. Du Bois, "the Old Man" who had inspired so much progressive action and who was well-known to the new generation of black leaders, was gone.

AUGUSTUS GRANVILLE DILL

Augustus Granville Dill, born in 1881, was the business manager of *The Crisis*, the magazine of the NAACP, during part of the period when W. E. B. Du Bois was the editor. Dill had once been Du Bois's student at Atlanta University and had worked with him on such publications as *The College-Bred Negro American* (1910), *The Common School and the Negro American* (1911), *The Negro American Artisan* (1912), and *Morals and Manners among Negro Americans* (1914). Dill was educated at Harvard, graduating in 1908. He taught for a while at Atlanta University, succeeding Du Bois in the sociology department, but he eventually moved north because of his interest in the NAACP. Committed to the education of African-American children, Du Bois and Dill formed Du Bois and Dill Publishers in order to produce *The Brownies' Book*, but it closed when the magazine was halted for economic reasons. In addition to the magazine, however, the company released Elizabeth Haynes's book *Unsung Heroes* (1921), a collection of biographical profiles about outstanding African Americans.

Dill was multitalented. He was the organist for his church and was known for wearing a chrysanthemum in his buttonhole. Although Dill and Du Bois eventually terminated their business alliance, Du Bois would later praise Dill for his skill and hard work through difficult times. Augustus Granville Dill retired to Louisville, Kentucky, where he died on March 8, 1956.

JESSIE REDMON FAUSET

For many years Jessie Redmon Fauset was considered a minor literary figure of the Harlem Renaissance of the 1920s and 1930s. Fortunately, her place in the history of African-American culture is now being reevaluated by critics and literary historians who recognize that her influence on black culture of that time was considerable.

Born in Camden County, New Jersey, Jessie Redmon Fauset was the daughter of an African Methodist Episcopal minister. An honor student in high school, Fauset was awarded a scholarship to Cornell University. She graduated in 1905 and was elected to Phi Beta Kappa, the prestigious academic honor society. After teaching Latin and French in Washington, D.C., for 13 years, Fauset continued her studies at the Sorbonne in Paris and earned a master's degree in French at the University of Pennsylvania in 1919.

Fauset wrote both fiction and poetry but is best known today for her four novels, *There is Confusion* (1924), *Plum Bun* (1929), *The Chinaberry Tree* (1931), and *Comedy: American Style* (1933). All of these works concerned the sometimes very perplexing lives of black Americans of relatively privileged status. *Plum Bun*, the most celebrated of Fauset's works, centers around the lives of two African-American sisters who grew up in a middle-class home. One of the sisters is light-skinned enough to pass for white, and, for a time, does so, but she can never forget her links to the black neighborhood that nourished her and needs her talents. Perhaps Fauset's greatest significance as a novelist is that she took the formulas and stereotypes of her day—including those of light-skinned heroines passing for white—and made them complex and human characters. She is a very important figure in African-American literature and in the emerging field of black feminist writing.

Fauset knew firsthand the difficulties of being gifted, black, and female. Though in the 1920s she tried hard for a position as an editor in a New York publishing company (even offering to work at home to avoid the problem of integrating the all-white world of big-league publishing), she received no such job and was forced to content herself with secondary school teaching for most of her professional life.

Jessie Fauset deserves more recognition than she is generally given for her influential work as an editor. She worked as literary editor with W. E. B. Du Bois at *The Crisis* from 1919 to 1926 and later became a contributing editor. And for the two-year life of *The Brownies' Book*, she served as literary editor, also writing many signed and unsigned essays, poems, stories, and biographies and editing the work of many other writers. At both *The Crisis* and *The Brownies' Book*, she was a mentor to authors who later became well known, such as Claude McKay, Countee Cullen, Langston Hughes, and Jean Toomer. Because she did so much for other writers, Langston Hughes identified her as one of the most significant influences on the literature of the Harlem Renaissance.

LANGSTON HUGHES

The most prolific and perhaps the most celebrated of black writers, Langston Hughes had a rich and diverse literary career. The first serious black American writer to support himself by his writings (and his recitations) alone—without an academic post or "day job" of any steady sort, Hughes lived by the pen. Before his death, he had presented his audience with novels, plays, short stories, essays, autobiographies, books of poems, television scripts, songs, picture books, newspaper columns, and anthologies of many kinds.

Hughes particularly gloried in his youthful readers, for whom he wrote many poems and stories. He also wrote five books specifically for children that appeared in a series of "Firsts" tailor-made for children: *The First Book of Negroes* (1952), *The First Book of Rhythms* (1954), *The First Book of Jazz* (1955), *The First Book of the West Indies* (1956), and *The First Book of Africa* (1960).

The Opie Library of Children's Literature, of which *The Best of The Brownies' Book* is a part, has brought into print *The First Book of Rhythms* (now called *The Book of Rhythms*), based in part on his experience as a teacher at Chicago's Laboratory School for Children; *The Sweet and Sour Animal Book*, a previously unissued A-B-C book in poetic form; *Popo and Fifina*, a novel for children coauthored with Hughes's long-time friend and collaborator Arna Bontemps; and *Black Misery*, an ironic picture book with one-liners about such black predicaments as this one: "Misery is when you are not supposed to like watermelon, but you do!" Widely known as "the poet laureate of Harlem," Hughes was also the poet laureate of the young.

Born in Joplin, Missouri, on February 1, 1902, James Langston Hughes was elected class poet in elementary school and in 1916 first read a poem in public during the school's graduation exercises. His family moved to

Cleveland, Ohio, where he attended Central High School and served, in his senior year, as yearbook editor.

In 1921, Hughes taught English in Mexico, where he had moved to join his father, who had left the family. While there he published his first prose piece, a dramatic sketch called "In a Mexican City" in *The Brownies' Book* (included in this volume) as well as the now-classic poem "The Negro Speaks of Rivers" in *The Crisis*. In 1921, too, he entered Columbia University but his wanderlust let him remain there only for one year. (Later in the decade he would complete his B.A. degree at Lincoln University.)

In the early 1920s, Hughes signed on as a boat's steward and traveled to the Azores, the Canary Islands, and Africa. Before returning to the United States to join his mother in Washington, D.C., he took a freighter to Paris, Genoa, and other points in Europe. His second autobiography, *I Wonder as I Wander* (1956), was rightly named.

In the mid-1920s, Hughes began to receive recognition as a poet. He won important prizes in 1925, and the following year published his first volume of poetry, *The Weary Blues*. Some of this collection evoked in wonderful ways the sound and sense of blues music.

Hughes's poetry was later published in the books *Fine Clothes to the Jew* (1927), *The Dream Keeper and Other Poems* (1932), *Shakespeare in Harlem* (1942), *Fields of Wonder* (1947), *One-Way Ticket* (1949), *Montage of a Dream Deferred* (1951), *Ask Your Mama: 12 Moods for Jazz* (1961), and *The Panther and the Lash* (1967).

Beginning in 1943, Hughes created a fictional character named Jesse B. Simple, whose name indicated something of his philosophy for survival. This character, whose narratives and comments on the American scene were first captured in Hughes's weekly column in the *Chicago Defender*, an African-American newspaper, won for Hughes the widest audience he had ever known. More than any thing else Hughes wrote, the Simple pieces reached a mass black audience. With caustic, bluesy wit and unsparing irony, Simple spoke his mind in a lingo and from a standpoint that Harlem and other similar communities recognized as their own.

By the time of his death in 1967, Hughes was widely celebrated as one of the principal writers of the Harlem Renaissance of the 1920s and 1930s and as an American writer of extraordinary skill and vision: one of the century's key voices. His reputation as such has been exalted by the appearance of *The Complete Poems of Langston Hughes* (1995), edited by Arnold Rampersad, and by Rampersad's prize-winning two-volume biography, *The Life of Langston Hughes* (1986, 1988).

NELLA LARSEN IMES

As recent scholarship has demonstrated, Nella Larsen Imes (who generally used the professional name of Nella Larsen) was a tremendously skillful and powerful novelist of the Harlem Renaissance. Born in Chicago on April 13, 1891, Larsen was an intensely private woman, one whose personal history has remained obscure. We do know that she attended primary schools in Chicago and spent a year at Fisk University. In 1912, she entered the Lincoln Hospital Training School for Nurses in New York City, graduating in 1915. Her nursing career eventually took her from New York back to the South, again to Fisk, then later to Tuskegee Institute in Alabama, where she was a nurse, administrator, and teacher. She then moved back to New York, which seemed a more fitting place for her restless and lively nature. Larsen was able to return to the Lincoln Training School to work as a supervising nurse. In 1919, she married physicist Elmer S. Imes. After 1922, she took courses in library science and eventually became a children's librarian at the New York Public Library.

Her closeness with books, the concerns of her childhood and youth, and the active social scene of Harlem fostered Larsen's writing aspirations. From her earliest publications in the "Playtime" section of *The Brownies' Book* ("Three Scandinavian Games" in June 1920 and "Danish Fun" in July 1920) to her farewell piece, "The Author's Explanation" (*Forum*, April 1930), Larsen was part of the exciting, productive literary activity of the Harlem Renaissance.

In addition to essays and reviews she published two acclaimed novels, *Quicksand* (1928) and *Passing* (1929). Both these novels address the situation of black women who feel oppressed both by the violence of white racism and by the punishing limits of middle-class Negro society. These broad themes come to life in *Quicksand*, whose scenes and characters seem drawn from Larsen's experiences at southern black colleges and in Harlem.

As a writer, Larsen herself got off to quite a promising start in Harlem, which seemed to offer the wider world that she, like her heroines, desired. She received spirited encouragement from Walter White, the chief executive of the NAACP, and from Carl Van Vechten, the photographer and writer who was a tireless promoter of African-American artists and intellectuals. Larsen's literary efforts gained a wider field of recognition when *Quicksand* won the prestigious Harmon Foundation Award for "distinguished achievement among Negroes" and when Larsen won a Guggenheim Fellowship—the first time that honor had ever been granted to a black American.

In 1930, after allegations of plagiarism (which she and her editor steadfastly denied), Nella Larsen Imes gave up her literary career and returned to nursing. She was found dead in her Manhattan apartment on March 30, 1964.

ARTHUR HUFF FAUSET

Arthur Huff Fauset, the half-brother of Jessie Redmon Fauset, was born in 1889 in Flemington, New Jersey. An anthropologist and folklorist, he earned his B.A., M.A., and Ph.D. degrees from the University of Pennsylvania. He was a teacher and principal in the Philadelphia public schools from 1918 to 1946. Though he is not as well known as other figures of the Harlem Renaissance, he was quite visible in the social, political, and academic activities of the time.

Fauset's research and scholarship focused on black people of Nova Scotia, the American South, Philadelphia, and the West Indies. A gifted and multifaceted writer of stories, folktales, essays, articles, and reviews, he published widely in the African-American journals *Opportunity*, *The Crisis*, *Fire!*, *Black Opals* (which he helped launch), and *The Brownies' Book*. He also wrote biographies of Sojourner Truth and Booker T. Washington and *For Freedom: A Biographical Story of the American Negro* (1927). He died in Philadelphia on September 2, 1983.

LAURA WHEELER WARING

Laura Wheeler Waring, born in Hartford, Connecticut, in 1887, was a painter, illustrator, and educator. She studied at the Pennsylvania Academy of Fine Arts (1918–24) and the Grand Chaumiere, Paris (1924–25). Waring's artistic work received much favorable critical attention, and she was in demand as a portrait painter and as an illustrator for periodicals. Her portrait subjects include W. E. B. Du Bois, Jessie Fauset, James Weldon Johnson, and Marian Anderson. Her art was exhibited at the Art Institute of Chicago (1933), Howard University (1937, 1939), the American Negro Exposition (Chicago, 1940), the Corcoran Gallery in Washington, D.C., and the Smithsonian Institution (1933). She died in Philadelphia on February 3, 1948.

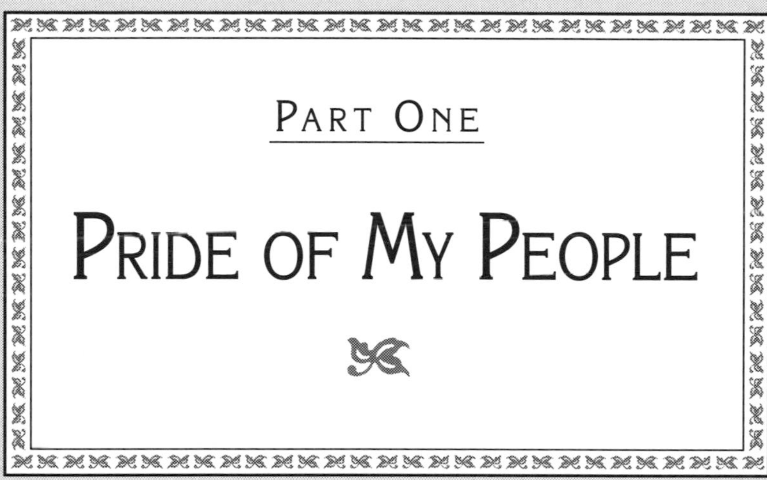

PART ONE

PRIDE OF MY PEOPLE

The creators of The Brownies' Book were very proud of being African American—or colored, or Negro, as they said at that time. And they wanted to communicate this sense of pride to young people. They wanted the readers to know about all of the things that people of African descent accomplished that made the world a better place. And they wanted them to recognize that each one of them and their own family members had many things to feel proud about too, that their skin color had nothing to do with how valuable they were as people.

In order to share information about Negro accomplishments, they regularly published selections that addressed the issue of pride directly. One story in this section, for example, is about a little girl of failing pride who thought that she would be happier with blonde hair than with her own curly black hair. Sometimes "The Judge" column addressed the greatness of the continent of Africa, which is the theme, too, of the play "The King's Dilemma."

Very often children and parents wrote letters to the magazine that talked about why they liked to read it. One reason they mentioned over and over again was that it was important to them, young and old, to see—in writing and in photographs and artwork—African-American people who were using their lives to help other African-American people. The grown-ups and the children often said that they also wanted to honor the memory of the black people who lived and suffered during slavery and earlier, in Africa.

As Jessie Fauset says in her poem "Dedication," for too long children had not been able to find poems and stories and songs and history books that depicted the pride that they felt in their communities. The contributors to The Brownies' Book were trying to change this. They knew that if children were educated about the experiences and histories of their own people, later it would be easier for them to appreciate the diverse people and cultures around the world.

DEDICATION

Jessie Fauset

To Children, who with eager look
Scanned vainly library shelf and nook,
For History or Song or Story
That told of Colored Peoples' glory—
We dedicate *The Brownies' Book*.

THE JURY

Could you take time to suggest a small library for me? Or if you couldn't, do you know anybody who could? I want to know a great deal about colored people. I think when I finish school I shall go to Africa, and work there in some way. If I decide to do this I ought to know a great deal about our people and all the places where they live, all over the world, don't you think so? My father is always saying that a great many wonderful things are going to happen to Negroes within the next twenty-five years, and I want to be able to understand and appreciate them.

George Max Simpson, *Toronto, Canada*

Dear Mr. Editor:
My Mother says you are going to have a magazine about colored boys and girls, and I am very glad. So I am writing to ask you if you will please put in your paper some of the things which colored boys can work at when they grow up. I don't want to be a doctor, or anything like that. I think I'd like to plan houses for men to build. But one day, down on Broad Street, I was watching some men building houses, and I said to a boy there, "When I grow up, I am going to draw a lot of houses like that and have men build them." The boy was a white boy, and he looked at me and laughed and said, "Colored boys don't draw houses."

Why don't they, Mr. Editor?

My mother says you will explain all this to me in your magazine and will tell me where to learn how to draw a house, for that is what I certainly mean to do. I hope I haven't made you tired, so no more from your friend,

Franklin Lewis, *Philadelphia, Pa.*

Dear Sir:
I am writing to ask you to refer me to some books on the Negro. I want to learn more about my race, so I want to begin early. I am twelve years old and hope to, when I am old enough, bend all of my efforts for the advancement of colored people.

I want to subscribe for *The Crisis*, but I don't want to subscribe until I go to Covington, Ky., where I go to school. . . .

I hope some day that all detestable "Jim-Crow" cars will be wiped out of existence, along with all prejudice, segregation, etc.

Eleanor Holland, *Wilberforce, Ohio*

Sometimes in school I feel so badly. In the geography lesson, when we read about the different people who live in the world, all the pictures are pretty, nice-looking men and women, except the Africans. They always look so ugly. I don't mean to make fun of them, for I am not pretty myself; but I know not all colored people look like me. I see lots of ugly white people, too; but not all white people look like them, and they are not the ones they put in the geography. Last week the girl across the aisle from me in school looked at the picture and laughed and whispered something about it to her friend. And they both looked at me. It made me so angry. Mother said for me to write you about it.

Alice Martin, *Philadelphia, Pa.*

THE GROWN-UPS' CORNER

I have been waiting with some interest for the appearance of *The Brownies' Book*, but I understand the printers' strike has delayed it. I am sure you have many good plans in mind for our children; but I do hope you are going to write a good deal about colored men and women of achievement. My little girl has been studying about Betsy Ross and George Washington and the others, and she says: "Mamma, didn't colored folks do anything?"

When I tell her as much as I know about our folks, she says: "Well, that's just stories. Didn't they ever do anything in a book?" I have not had much schooling, and I am a busy woman with my sewing and housekeeping, so I don't get much time to read and I can't tell my little girl where to find these things. But I am sure you know and that now you will tell her.

My husband worked in a munitions plant during the war and there were a few foreigners there. He said they often spoke of some big man in their country, but didn't seem to know about any big colored men here. And he said that when he came to think of it, he didn't know much about anybody but Booker T. Washington and you and Frederick Douglass.

Our little girl is dark brown, and we want her to be proud of her color and to know that it isn't the kind of skin people have that makes them great.

Bella Seymour, *New York City*

THE JUDGE

"My teacher wants to know which is the greatest continent," said Billikins.

"America," answered Billy promptly.

"Why?" asked the Judge.

"O, well—it just is, everybody knows that."

"I should certainly say Europe," said William.

"Why?" asked the Judge again.

"Because it's the center of the greatest civilization the world has known—the leader in Art and Science and Industry, and governs most of the world."

"Nevertheless, I should say Asia," said Wilhelmina, "because it is the oldest and wisest—the mother of all religion, the home of most men, the mother of races and the originator of human culture."

"And I," said the Judge, "would say Africa."

They all stared at him.

"Are you joking?" asked Billy.

"No."

"But you don't really mean it," protested William.

"I suppose," pouted Wilhelmina, "that you're just saying Africa because we are all of African descent. Of course—"

"Do I usually lie?" asked the Judge.

"No-o oh no!—but how on earth can you say that Africa is the greatest continent? It is stuck way in the back of the Atlas and the geography which Billy uses devotes only a paragraph to it."

"I say it because I believe it is so. Not because I want to believe it true—not because I think it ought to be true, but because in my humble opinion it is true."

"And may we know the reasons?" said William.

"Certainly: they are seven."

("O Master, we are Seven," chanted Wilhelmina.)

"*First:* Africa was the only continent with a climate mild and salubrious enough to foster the beginnings of human culture.

"*Second:* Africa excels all other continents in the variety and luxuriance of its natural products.

"*Third:* In Africa originated probably the first, certainly the longest, most vigorous, human civilization.

"*Fourth:* Africa made the first great step in human culture by discovering the use of iron.

"*Fifth:* Art in form and rhythm, drawing and music found its earliest and most promising beginnings in Africa.

"*Sixth:* Trade in Africa was the beginning of modern world commerce.

"*Seventh:* Out of enslavement and degradation on a scale such as humanity nowhere else has suffered, Africa still stands today, with her gift of world labor that has raised the great crops of Sugar, Rice, Tobacco and Cotton and which lie at the foundation of modern industrial democracy."

"Gee!" said Billy.

"Don't understand," wailed Billikins.

"Few people do," said the Judge.

"I was just wondering," mused Wilhelmina, "who the guys are that write our histories and geographies."

"Well, you can bet they're not colored," said William.

"No—not yet," said the Judge.

"Do they tell lies?" asked Billy.

"No, they tell what they think is the truth."

"And I suppose," said Wilhelmina, "that what one thinks is the truth, is the truth."

"Certainly not," answered the Judge. "To tell what one believes is the truth is not necessarily to lie, but it is not consequently true."

"Then one can tell falsehoods and not always lie."

"Certainly."

"I'm going to try that," said Billy.

"I wouldn't," warned the Judge. "You see it's this way: there are lots of things to be known and few to know them. Our duty is therefore not simply to tell what we believe is true, but to remember our ignorance and be sure that we know before we speak."

THE JURY

Today I happened to be casually glancing over the magazines on the shelf of our school library and saw a copy of *The Brownies' Book*. I had read in *The Crisis* of its beginning but had not seen a copy before. Eagerly I opened it and read the issue from cover to cover and I must say I really enjoyed it. I noticed that you wished to hear from colored children too so decided to write you a few lines concerning myself.

I am a colored boy, brownskinned and proud of it. I am 14 years old. My home is now in Tampa, but at present I am a second year student at the Florida A. & M. College. My father is a doctor and my mother a music teacher. I play four musical instruments: the violin, piano, clarinet and cello, but I like the violin best of all. I started playing the violin when I was six years old. Long ago I completed the Keyser violin method and have subsequently studied awhile in New York and also under a very strict German professor. I've been appearing in public with my violin ever since I can remember. I play very often now. Among my solos are many works of Fritz Kreisler, Dvorak and I just love *Il Trovatore*. I am also very much enthused over "Scene de Ballet" by DeBeriot and play it often, as well as "Ciaconna" by Tommaso Vitali and the Concertos by Seitz. I agree with anyone who says music is great. I find very much pleasure in my violin.

You might infer that it is my aim to be a violinist from the above statements. Perhaps it'll sound strange to you for me to say that I don't, but that's the fact of the affair. I wish to be a writer and give to the world that intense feeling of altruism that is ever and anon tugging at my heart.

I think the readers of *The Brownies's Book* might like for me to tell them about my little den or "office" at home. In it I have a 5 x 8 hand printing press, a sectional bookcase, a desk, colored light oak, a typewriter and a trunk-like box where I keep my "miscellanies."

I love to read and especially do I love to revel in the writings of my own race and those of Dr. Du Bois more than any others. I think "Dark-water" is grand. My favorite authors are Du Bois, Dunbar, Chestnut, Braithwaite, Johnson, Poe, Tarkington, Stevenson, Mark Twain, Scott, Dickens, Kipling, Doyle, Barbour, Hugo, VanDyke and Roosevelt, as well as quite a few others. My favorite magazine without exception is *The Crisis*. Each month I literally devour every line of its contents. I also subscribe for the *Inland Printer* and *American Boy*. My mother usually gets the *Etude*, a musical magazine. I like the *Literary Digest* and the *American* and am very much interested in the *Competitor*, the new race publication.

My aim is placed clearly before me and already, although I have yet to see my 15th birthday, I'm striving to reach it. I know it'll be a long, hard struggle to the top for men of experience have said so in their books. But if grit and unwavering determination are all that's needed—well, I may be over-confident, but I've really no thoughts of failure.

James Alpheus Butler, Jr., *Tampa, Florida*

THE GROWN-UPS' CORNER

Gentlemen:

I have just read your article in the October *Crisis*, "True Brownies," and I wish to say that of all the great things which you have undertaken during the publication of *The Crisis*, I think this the greatest. The idea is wonderful, and it expresses a thought which I have long wanted some information on.

We have one darling little boy, who is nine years of age today. We spend our summers here, as my husband's work is here during the summer months. My boy was born here, and I am sorry to say that he simply hates the place. The entire population is white—colored people come only in the capacity of servants.

The natives are mostly Irish, and the children call my boy "nigger" and other names which make life for him very unpleasant. He comes to us crying about it, and oh, the resentment I feel is terrible! He will fight the smaller boys, but, of course, the large boys he cannot fight. When we speak to their parents about it, they say that they are very sorry, and promise to stop their children from calling him names.

Now, the difficult problem for us is: What shall we tell him to do, and how best for him to answer them, and instill into him race love and race pride?

He is the first and only colored child in Nahant, and since the Great War and the recent race riots, his color seems to be noticed more and spoken of more by the white children.

One day he said to me: "Mother, the only way to fight these white people is to get an education and fight them with knowledge."

I shall await the TRUE BROWNIES number with great joy, as I believe it will be a great help to all of us. I pass *The Crisis* around among my white neighbors here. I want them to read it.

Enclosed please find $1.00 for one year's subscription to TRUE BROWNIES.

Mrs. C. M. Johnson, *Nahant, Mass.*

THE WISHING GAME

Annette Browne

We gathered 'round the fire last night,
Jim an' Bess an' me,
And said, "Now let us each in turn
Tell who we'd rather be,
Of all the folks that's in our books."
(Of course, we wouldn't want their looks.)

Bess wished that she'd been Betsy Ross,
The first to make the flag.
She said, "I'd like to do some deed
To make the people brag,
And have the papers print my name—
If colored girls could rise to fame."

An' I stood out for Roosevelt;
I wished to be like him.
Then Bess said, "We've both had our say,
Now tell who you'd be, Jim."
Jim never thinks like me or Bess,
He knows more than us both, I guess.

He said, "I'd be a Paul Dunbar
Or Booker Washington.
The folks you named were good, I know.
But you see, Tom, each one
Of these two men I'd wish to be
Were colored boys, like you and me.

Sojourner Truth was colored, Bess,
And Phillis Wheatley, too;
Their names will live like Betsy Ross,
Though they were dark like you."
Jim's read of 'em somewhere, I guess,
He knows heaps more than me or Bess.

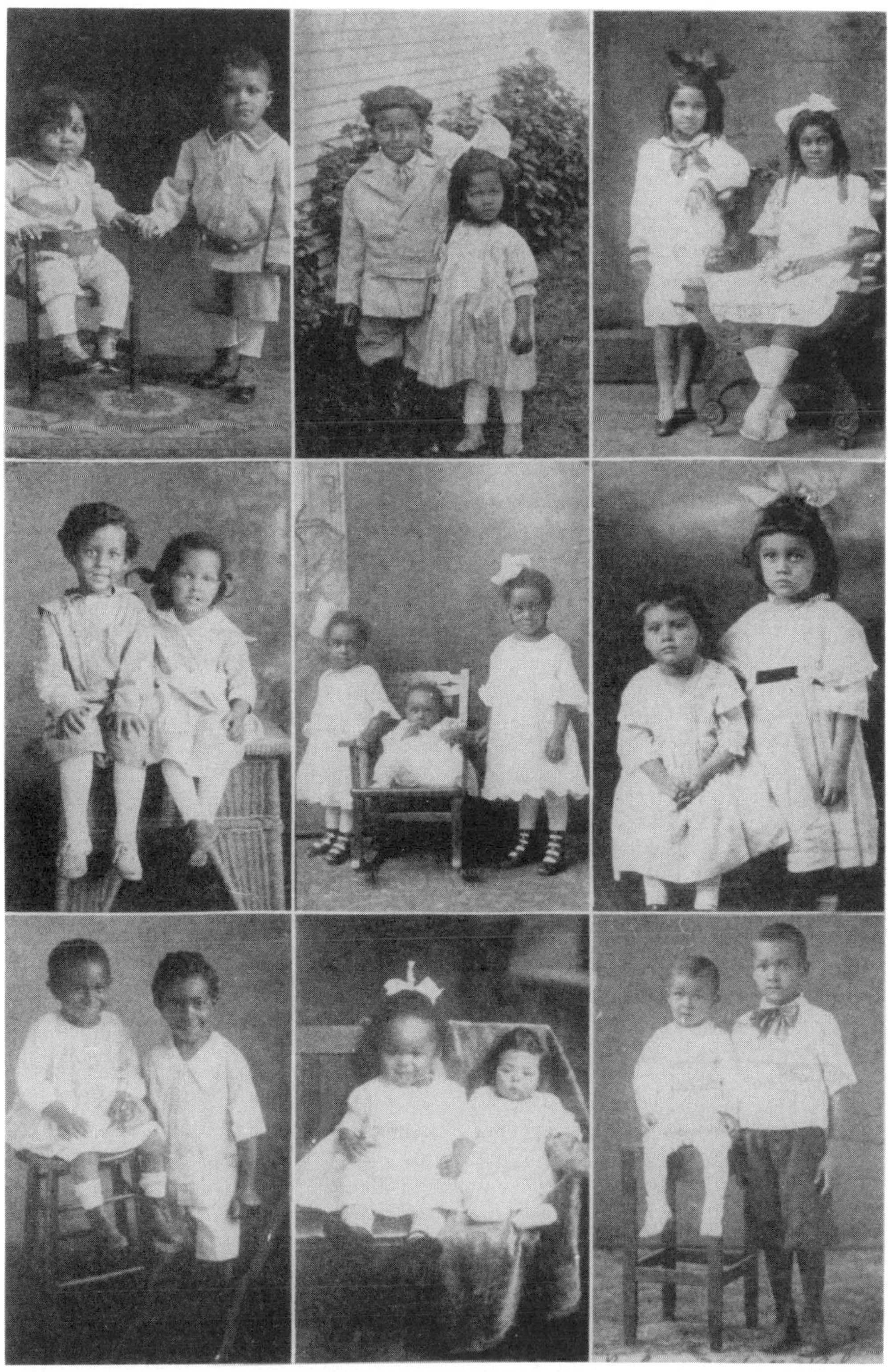

Some Little Friends of Ours

Little People of the Month

There are some folks who take a real interest in their studies—they're obedient, attentive and earnest scholars. Such a person is Ammie Rosealia Lewis. Out in Imperial County, Cal., at the Calexico High School, Ammie ranked highest in educational attainments among 105 students. We Brownies, of course, are very proud of our Ammie; but do you know—there were two girls and three boys—Mary Culver and Gladys Forrest, Edwin Kessling, Laurence Little and Otis de Riemer—who could not bear to realize that a Negro should be an honor student and refused to sit on the same platform with Ammie at graduation time. Professor Vinacke characterized these white children's attitude as "a lack of understanding of Americanization."

It's so wonderful to be an artist, and make pictures of beautiful flowers and trees and oceans and skies, and of the gray cat watching to catch the pretty pigeon for a meal, and of lovely Wilhelmina and dear Billikins. Well, at Boston, Mass., there's a Brownie, 14 years of age, who has won her second scholarship at the Museum of Fine Arts. Her name is Lois M. Jones and she's an honor student of the High School of Practical Arts at Boston.

Mamie E. Davis is the winner of a prize in the War Department's contest on "What are the Benefits of an Enlistment in the United States Army." She is a pupil in the 7th grade of the Slater School at Birmingham, Ala., and the only pupil in the colored public schools of Birmingham and Jefferson Counties to win a prize. Her teacher is Miss Elizabeth C. Towns. On the Board of Judges were Secretary of War Baker, General March and General Pershing. Miss Davis' principal says of her: "During the last six years, in which she has been a pupil at the Slater School, she has shown herself to be a hard worker and one of the most obedient pupils. During the time of the World War, as one of the junior speakers of Slater, she delivered many four-minute speeches in the school and in churches."

Dancing is fun for us, but Lillian Jones has made her dancing bring greater pleasure, for at the annual circus of the West Philadelphia High School, from which Lillian graduated in June, she interpreted Nevin's "Narcissus" and was awarded a prize. This marked her second annual award.

Top: Graduates of I. C. Norcom High School, Portsmouth, Va.
Center, left to right: Hartley G. Williams (Virginia Union), Miss O. G. Miller (Charlton High, Beaumont, Tex.), Ruby Riley (Colored High, Shreveport, La.), Kenneth Meade (Dunbar High, Fairmont, West Va.)
Bottom: High School graduates of Straight College, New Orleans, La.

THE HERITAGE

Blanche Lynn Patterson

The calendar and the glowing March sunshine marked the beginning of spring, but in the heart of the young girl stumbling across a vacant lot, whose brown surface was dotted here and there with tips of venturous green—it was winter, grim and dreary. The playful wind blew back the flimsy brim of her velvet hat, and tried to smooth away some of the unhappiness from her fatigued brown face. Passing through a gateway, she followed a broken-planked walk to the open door of a little unpainted cottage. Dropping an armful of books on the porch, she crumpled down in the doorstep. Throwing the limp piece of head gear to the ground, she sat staring into the back-yard, full of flapping clothes.

At the sound of the falling books, an elderly woman came to the door, a smile of welcome on her dark face.

"Why howdy, Julie. How are you? You ain't been to see me for a long time."

"I'm—I'm—" began the girl, but the remainder of the sentence lost itself in a choking sob.

"Why, chile!" exclaimed Mother Mason. "What on earth is the matter?"

Then as she saw twin streams of tears coursing down the girl's pale brown cheeks, she interrupted her speech, and sat down on a bench near the dejected figure, waiting.

"I'm going home," came the muffled declaration at length. "I'm going to leave school."

"Leave school?" shrilled the older woman, leaning forward in her seat.

"Yes. I'm sick and tired of it all," came the bitter affirmation.

"You tired of school, Julie?" the old woman asked in amazement. "Why you seemed so set on your books."

"I love my books as much as ever, but I'm tired of working myself to death to stay in school. It isn't worth it," came the vehement explanation. She dabbed her wet cheeks fiercely.

"Shorley you ain't going to give up all yo'r plans for gettin' an education, jest because you're a little bit fagged!"

"I'm not a little bit tired," retorted Julia. "I'm worn out; I haven't had a moment's rest for two years. I've been pegging away from half-past six in the morning till half-past twelve at night. I can't keep on working and studying like that. It's killing me."

This bitter outburst left a silence; then Mother Mason said slowly:

"I know how hard you have to work to keep yourself in school, and I've always held you up as an example to other girls. You've gone so far that you ought to keep on now in spite of everything, if you possibly can."

"Well I can't," replied Julia quickly. "I've worked away endlessly about as long as I can stand it. I've never had decent clothes or any good times. It has just been work, work forever. I'm left out of everything." The girl's voice broke and she sat motionless looking out at the wind harassed clothes on the lines.

"I understand, Julie," said Mother Mason comfortingly, "but two years more is such a short time, after all."

"Two years more of slaving is more than I can stand anyway," put in Julia abruptly.

"Two years ain't nothin' in comparison with three hundred years that yo'r fo'parents spent in endless drudg'ry without no hope of reward."

The sober face of the older woman had the effect of making the girl forget her own problems for a few minutes, but at length she said.

"But that is all over and—"

"No, it ain't all over," put in the old woman quickly. "That's jest it. You young folks have ev'ry chance that yo'r parents didn't have. You owe it to them never to quit till you have showed that you can use the opportunities you have."

"Why, I never thought of owing anything to anybody," said the girl.

"I know you never, honey, but you do, jest the same. The only reward that yo'r unhappy fo'fathers ever will get is through you, an' if you fail, you disappoint yo'r whole race."

"Why, Mother Mason!" exclaimed Julia in surprise, and with a look of pride in her dark eyes, "Is it true then that I am not struggling alone, and that I have my whole race to work for?"

"That's jest it, chile; you are the third generation since life for our people really begun an' you have two generations' hopes to fulfill."

Julia sprang to her feet; the March wind, blowing through her crisp black hair, flung little locks of it against her glowing cheek.

"Oh I am so glad you told me. I might have given up and been a failure and disappointment. Now I have something to work for, and *I'll keep on, Mother Mason. I'll keep on!*"

Children in the "Silent Protest" Parade, New York City

KATY FERGUSON

A TRUE STORY

Did you ever hear of Katy Ferguson? I confess I did not until a very short while ago, and yet without my knowing it, Katy Ferguson must have been exerting a great influence over me for at least sixteen years. And unless I am very much mistaken, she has been influencing you, too.

If you are being brought up as I hope you are, you go to school every week-day, except Saturday, and on Sundays you go to Sunday School. There you sit and listen to the really wonderful church music and learn a great many beautiful texts and chat with the other boys and girls and enjoy yourself famously. Then you go home feeling very good and somewhat solemn, not very sorry that Sunday School is over, but on the whole perfectly willing to go back next Sunday.

"But what has Katy Ferguson to do with all this?" I hear you wondering.

Wait a moment.

Long, long ago, in 1774, Katy Ferguson was born to the cruellest fate that ever awaited a child. She was a slave. Stop and think about that a little while, try to picture the horrors of such a condition, and resolve that in no sense of the word will you allow such a fate to overtake you and yours. Evidently Katy thought something like this, for when she was eighteen, due to her own efforts and the fortunate impression she had made on some friends, she became free.

Not long afterwards she married, but neither her husband nor the children who came to her lived very long, and presently she was by herself again, living her life alone in the city of New York.

Now Katy was a very good woman—tender, kind-hearted, and sensible. She did not let her sorrows crush and enfeeble her. On the contrary, she looked about her to see what her hands could find to do, and having found it, she did it. In her neighborhood in New York there were very many neglected children, both white and colored, and to them she gave her attention. Some she sheltered in her own house, and for others she found positions. During her lifetime she helped in this way forty-eight needy children—a tremendous job for a poor woman.

But what interested Katy even more than caring for little children's bodies, was caring for little children's souls. So every Sunday Katy had children to come to her house so she could tell them about "God and the world to come." When her class grew too large and its instruction too much for her limited knowledge, she called in other good Christian folk to help; but of these none, I am sure, worked more willingly or more successfully than Katy.

One wonderful Sunday, Dr. Mason, the kind minister of a church on Murray Street, who had helped Katy in many ways when as a little girl she was beginning to seek "the way, the truth and the light," walked into Katy's house and found her surrounded by a group of interested and happy children.

"What are you about here?" he said. "Keeping school on the Sabbath? We must not leave you to do all this." And off he went and told the officers of his church and some other good people about it, and in a short while the lecture-room was opened to receive Katy's little friends. So the church in Murray Street opened a Sunday School, and it is generally conceded that Katy Ferguson, colored, and once a slave, was the founder of the first Sunday School in New York City.

Of course, Katy did many other things—she toiled hard for her daily bread and she received many opportunities to work, for she was a wonderful laundress and a ravishing cook. She was interested in the cause of missions, too, and let no chance of aiding them pass by. But don't you like best the notion of her getting the little children together and telling them that "of such is the kingdom of heaven"? I do.

And I think that those of you who read this little history will go to Sunday School some Sunday and instead of whispering to the pupil next to you, you will look right into the wonderful glory that comes pouring through the stained-glass windows on Sunday afternoons, and in your heart you will say, "Dear God, I am thankful for Katy Ferguson."

So now you know the story of a noble colored woman. But she is not the only colored woman to do great deeds for her race. There are many splendid colored men, too. Think of all the wonderful folks you have still to hear about!

A Pioneer Suffragette

Now that the right of women to vote is gradually being conceded throughout the United States, few people stop to realize for how many years women have had to work and fight and wait in order to reach this goal. Even our boys and girls remember the disrepute in which suffragettes were held in England prior to, and even at the beginning of, the World War. And some echo of that unpopularity crossed the seas and was heard again in the treatment given not long ago, in this country, to the advocates of Woman Suffrage in Washington.

However, to women who many, many years ago started the movement, and watched its course often with an anxious, though never with a despairing eye, the state of suffrage for women today would seem nothing short of a miracle. History can hardly emphasize too strongly what of shame, ridicule, and disappointment those true heroines were called upon to endure.

To one of those early leaders of women the disfavor arising from being associated with the unpopular cause of Woman Suffrage meant nothing, for she had long since been associated with a cause far more unpopular—that of Abolition.

Sojourner Truth—for that was the remarkable name of this extremely remarkable woman—was born an American slave. The exact date of her birth is not known, but it is generally granted that she must have been born between 1785 and 1798. She belonged to a man named Ardinburgh, who lived in Hurley, Ulster County, New York. Her name in those early days was Isabella, and this she kept for many years. Isabella's life was a sad one. She was a sensitive child and while still very, very young she received impressions of one of the chief horrors of slavery—that of the separation of slave parents from children. This remained with her all her life. She herself shows, unconsciously, how tragic her childhood must have been when she relates this incident.

"I can remember," she says, "when I was a little, young girl, how my old mammy would sit out of doors in the evenings and look up at the stars and groan, and I would say, 'Mammy, what makes you groan so?' And she would reply, 'I am groaning to think of my poor children: they do not know where I be and I don't know where they be. I look up at the stars and they look at the stars!'"

It was among such sad conditions as these that Isabella grew into young womanhood. In the course of time she married and had many children. One of these was a son who, while still a mere youth, was stolen away and sold outside of New York, his native state. Even in those sad times there were laws in New York forbidding the selling of slaves outside the state boundaries, but these were violated in this case. This slave-mother had already seen the suffering caused her own mother by the loss of her children; now she realized that the same anguish had come to her, and might befall her many, many times.

From that time on she began a violent protest against slavery which never ceased until finally that curse was lifted from the land. This was made the more possible by the fact, that in 1827 she received her freedom by a law which granted freedom to all slaves, in the state of New York, at the age of forty.

She had a long and remarkable career, and did many strange and unusual things. Among others she changed her name, about 1837, to Sojourner Truth and that was the name by which she was called ever after.

Sojourner Truth

Many of her striking sayings have come down to us. People tell how Frederick Douglass once showed plainly that he was very much discouraged at a meeting in Boston, and seemed to doubt if slavery ever could be wiped out. Then Sojourner Truth rose slowly from her place in the audience and stretching forth a long arm, exclaimed: "Frederick, is God dead?"

On another occasion a white man asked her at the close of a lecture if she supposed anybody really minded her talks against slavery. "I don't care any more for your talk," said he, "than I do for the bite of a flea."

"That may be," said Sojourner Truth, "but with God's help, I'm going to keep you scratching."

Long before the Civil War, she was lending her influence and eloquence to Woman Suffrage. Her mind was so keen and so broad that she quickly realized that the refusal of the right to vote to women, was only another form of slavery.

The second State Woman Suffrage Convention of Ohio was held in Akron, May 28 and 29, 1851. Sojourner Truth was present both days. On the second day the meeting was very stormy: several ministers who were present spoke very strongly against "votes for women." One said men had superior rights, because men had intellects superior to women's. Another said that the fact that Christ was a man proved that God considered women inferior to men. Things were going very badly for the suffrage cause, when Sojourner Truth arose to speak. Some of the leaders were afraid to have her talk, fearing she would make the cause ridiculous, and they urged the presiding officer, Mrs. Francis Dana Gage, to silence her. But Mrs. Gage was brave and rose and announced in the midst of a great hubbub—"Sojourner Truth!"

Immediately all the confusion died away, for everyone, whether approving of Woman Suffrage or not, wanted to hear this wonderful woman. She must have been an impressive figure as she stood there, for she was very tall and dark, with a keen, unflinching eye. Her full deep tones resounded through the hall. Being uneducated, of course, she spoke in dialect or broken English, which I shall not attempt to reproduce here, though her speech, evidently, lost nothing by its use.

She pointed to one of the disapproving ministers—

"That man over there," she began, "says that women need to be helped into carriages, and lifted over ditches, and to have the best help everywhere. Nobody ever helps me into carriages, or over mud-puddles, or gives me the best place. Well, I'm a woman, ain't I? Look at my arm," she went on, "look at my arm!" And she bared her right arm to the shoulder. "I have ploughed, and planted, and gathered into barns, and no man could head me! And ain't I a woman? I could work as much and eat as much as a man—when I could get it—and bear the lash as well. And ain't I a woman? I have borne thirteen children, and seen them most all sold off to slavery, and when I cried out with my mother's grief, none but Jesus heard me! And ain't I a woman?

"Then they talk about this thing in the head, what do they call it?" Some one nearby told her "Intellect." She nodded her head vigorously. "That's it, honey. What's that got to do with women's rights or niggers' rights? If my cup won't hold but a pint and yours a quart, wouldn't you be mean not to let me have my little half-measure full?

"Then that little man in black over there, says women can't have as much rights as men, because Christ wasn't a woman! Where did your Christ come from? From God and a woman! Man had nothing to do with him!"

Sojourner Truth had won the day as the deafening applause acknowledged.

She was an old, old woman when she died in 1883—very nearly a hundred years old. Her life had been

"full of weary days,
But good things had not kept aloof."

In some respects her life seems more wonderful than any fairy tale that ever was written. She had been a slave: she had lived to see not only herself set free, but to see slaves set free all over the country. And she had helped to bring it to pass. She, who had started out in life as nobody, numbered the greatest man in the country, President Lincoln, among her friends. Absolutely uneducated and untrained, she sat in council with some of the most advanced minds of her day. And the cause of Woman Suffrage is in her debt.

Indeed her interest in this cause is the surest proof that she was a sincere advocate of liberty. For though the needs of her own people were so pressing, she felt that it was also her business to help the cause of all womankind.

No tablet, so far as I know, has been erected to her memory. But her own life is her best memorial. As a great Roman poet said hundreds of years ago, before Sojourner Truth had died, or was born, she

"raised a monument more enduring than
bronze.
Which shall last throughout the years."

SLUMBER SONG

Alpha Angela Bratton

Close those eyes where points of light
Shine like stars through the velvet night,
    Brownie Boy.
Lightly float in a dimpled smile
Out on the sea of "Dream-a-while."
With gold nets, dream-fish to beguile,
    Brownie Boy.

See how the big moon dips and swings,
Shaking the stars from its silver wings,
    Brownie Boy.
Come, let us follow, you and I.
Follow its flight across the sky.
Into the land of "Bye-and-Bye."
    Brownie Boy.

The changing years will come and go—
Summer's rose and winter's snow—
    Brownie Boy.
Stealing my brown boy from my breast;
Bringing him manhood's eager quest,
And splendid strength for every test,
    Brownie Boy.

Teaching you, too, from History's page,
The joy of your noble heritage,
    Brownie Boy.
Ah! You must needs be doubly true,
Doubly strong in the task you do.
Nor fail the Race that speaks in you,
    Brownie Boy.

DOLLY'S DREAM

Nora Waring

Of course Dolly Gray's real name was Dorothy, but from the moment she opened her big, bright eyes, her deep, deep, brown eyes, she had been called Dolly.

She lived with her dear mother and father in a pretty, white cottage with a porch and a small garden in which grew the loveliest flowers in the world, so Dolly thought. Dolly loved to sit on the porch with her dolls and make up stories about these flowers—and such dear, funny stories they were, for you must remember Dolly was just six years old.

"Dolly"

One warm summer afternoon after dear mother had bathed and dressed her, Dolly went out and sat on her big, soft cushion on the porch. She had her dolls with her as usual, the whole family, Louise, Helen, Violet and Baby. She had put all to sleep except Violet, who had long golden curls and was Dolly's favorite.

Now I am going to tell you a secret, not even dear mother knew this—Dolly wished oh so much for long, golden curls just like Violet's. I am sure if she could have known how lovely she was with her soft "cwinkley" (Dolly could not say crinkly) black ringlets around her little, dimpled face of rosy tan, she would not have wished for long golden curls. But she did wish for them and she finally fell asleep still wishing.

Then a most wonderful thing happened. Dolly felt a gentle touch on her shoulder and looking up she saw a tall, beautiful lady, clad in the most wonderful dress Dolly had ever seen.

"Oh," cried Dolly, "are you my Fairy Godmother?"

"Yes, dear," replied this gorgeous one, "I am your Fairy Godmother and you may have anything you wish. Now think! What do you wish for most?"

"Long, golden curls," Dolly almost shouted, she was so delighted.

Her Fairy Godmother smiled and said, "Very well, Dolly," while she gently touched her head with her magic wand, and then disappeared. Immediately long golden curls fell around Dolly's shoulders. But another change had come over Dolly, too, for of course as you know golden curls belong to people with pinky white skin and blue, blue eyes, so with her golden curls came also the pinky white skin and the blue, blue eyes. Dolly would not have known herself had she looked in a mirror. She could see her golden curls, however, and she was so proud of them! She decided to go for a walk.

When she saw her little playmate Gladys Green running towards her, she stopped and meant to ask her how she liked her golden curls, but Gladys looked at her strangely and ran on.

"That's funny," said Dolly to herself, "I just gave her one of my doll's best hats this morning."

The next person she met was Mr. Smith who lived next door.

"How do you do?" said Dolly politely.

"How do you do, little girl, aren't you lost?" asked Mr. Smith, for he had not seen any golden-haired children in that street before.

"Oh, no," Dolly started to say, "I am Dolly Gray, only my hair is gold instead of black."

But with a smile Mr. Smith had passed on. Dolly was very disappointed too, for Mr. Smith always had a stick of candy or a lollipop for her.

"Well," she said quite wisely for such a little lady, "I 'spose I do look diffrunt." Then she thought that while she was walking she would go around the corner to her Aunt Nell's, for Dolly was now very much concerned about her looks and she wanted to see herself in her Aunt's tall mirror. Again she was disappointed for Aunt Nell was not at home. She thought she had better go home now for she had never been so far before without asking dear mother.

As she started back to the corner she saw her Aunt Nell coming towards her. With a glad, little cry she ran to meet her, but her Aunt Nell, her very own, beloved Aunt Nell just smiled at her pretty little face and went hurriedly by before Dolly could say a word. Then the big, big tears came into the blue, blue eyes and splashed down the pink face and upon the golden curls.

She walked on sobbing to herself. At the corner a lady stopped her.

"Why, my dear, what is the matter?" she asked Dolly.

"Oh," wailed Dolly, "I'm not me."

"Why, what do you mean, child?" the lady asked kindly.

"I m—m—mean I—I—'m not m—me."

The lady looked very puzzled and then asked, "Where do you live?"

"Just around the corner, Number 826," Dolly mumbled between her sobs.

"Well now, don't cry any more. I'll take you home."

When they reached Dolly's home dear mother was crying and talking to a neighbor and dear father was frantically telephoning to all the police stations.

When dear mother saw Dolly and the lady coming in she cried, "Oh, no, that's not my Dolly." She thought the lady knew her Dolly was lost and was bringing this little girl to her.

Dolly, when she heard her mother say this, gave such a shriek that she woke up to see dear mother bending over her but she just couldn't stop crying.

"Why, Dolly darling, what is the matter?" asked dear mother.

"Oh, mother," cried Dolly, "take them off, take them off!"

"Take what off?" asked her mother.

"Those golden curls. I want my own black hair so you and Aunt Nell, and Mr. Smith and Gladys Green will always know me."

She was still crying and her mother hugging her real close said, "Why, Dolly, you've just been dreaming. Your pretty black curls are just the same."

Dolly was quieter now and wide awake.

"Dreaming," she repeated after her mother, as if trying to think it all out, and then, "Oh, Mother," she cried flinging her arms around her mother's neck, "I am so glad it was all a dream and I just love my 'cwinkly' black curls."

THE KING'S DILEMMA
A PLAY IN ONE ACT

Willis Richardson

CHARACTERS

The King
The Chamberlain
The Physician
Nyanza, The Prince
Zanzibo, the Prince's black playmate
The Queen
The Queen's attendants, the Prince's playmates, sentinels.
Time—The Future.
Place—The last Kingdom of the World.

When the curtain rises we see a great, high-ceilinged hall. At the right is a dais upon which are three chairs—one large and high-backed, with one smaller chair at each side of it. This room is sometimes used as a reception hall and sometimes the King sits here and judges the affairs of his subjects. In the center of the rear wall is an arched doorway. At each side of this doorway a sentinel marches to and fro. For a while they march to and fro in silence but they soon become weary of this and begin to talk.

FIRST SENTINEL (Stopping)—The place is dreary since the Prince has gone.

SECOND SENTINEL (Stopping)—He has not gone.

FIRST SENTINEL—I mean since he goes out so often.

SECOND SENTINEL—His going out all day has been food for his health.

FIRST SENTINEL—Where does he go?

SECOND SENTINEL—To play.

FIRST SENTINEL—I know he goes to play and playing has made him a robust fellow; but *where* does he play?

SECOND SENTINEL—He plays in the castle gardens out of sight of anyone looking from the castle windows. To see him one must go without the gates and walk as far as the ivy-colored wall and look to the left.

FIRST SENTINEL—Does the King go there?

SECOND SENTINEL—No.

FIRST SENTINEL—You speak as if you are quite sure of it.

SECOND SENTINEL—I know a secret.

FIRST SENTINEL—A secret about whom?

SECOND SENTINEL—About the Prince's playing.

FIRST SENTINEL—What do you know?

SECOND SENTINEL—The Prince plays with boys.

FIRST SENTINEL—Boys!

SECOND SENTINEL—Urchins.

FIRST SENTINEL—But the King has ever forbidden that.

SECOND SENTINEL—I know. I said it was a secret.

FIRST SENTINEL—The Chamberlain has orders from the King.

SECOND SENTINEL—And the King has ordered him to obey the Prince.

FIRST SENTINEL—What if the King's orders and the Prince's orders conflict?

SECOND SENTINEL—Then the Chamberlain must use whatever judgment he has to bring them into harmony.

FIRST SENTINEL—What of these boys? How do they enter the outside gates of the garden?

SECOND SENTINEL—The Chamberlain lets them in at the Prince's orders.

FIRST SENTINEL—But if the King should learn?

SECOND SENTINEL—Then the Chamberlain must justify his act as best he can.

FIRST SENTINEL (Raising a warning hand)—Someone comes.

(They resume their march to and fro, the King enters, followed by the Chamberlain. Although it is in future times, the King is dressed in the royal robes of the ancient Kings.)

THE KING (To the Chamberlain)—I must commend you for your good care of the Prince. His health has improved wonderfully.

THE CHAMBERLAIN—It was my duty, Sire.

THE KING—And you have ever been faithful to your duty. The Physician is on his way here after a year's travel in foreign lands. He will wish to know with what success his plans have been followed concerning the Prince's health. He will commend you. Others advised that the Prince be allowed to go among the common children, but we find that playing alone in the castle grounds was good.

THE CHAMBERLAIN—Yes, Sire.

THE KING—Do not leave my side while he is here, and you shall hear his story of other lands where monarchies have fallen and there are no kings, of wild, unreasonable places where no one rules but a band of serfs.

THE CHAMBERLAIN—How do serfs rule? Their business is but to obey.

THE KING—Well said. Then you shall hear of their misrule. And when this man of medicine has gone I shall reward you for your great part in helping to bring back the Prince's health.

THE CHAMBERLAIN—Sire, a thousand thanks.

THE KING—If this Physician's story of other lands is one of discontent and unhappiness then this, the latest kingdom of the world, should increase in power and increasing last forever.

THE CHAMBERLAIN—I see no reason why it should not last.

THE KING—Send a messenger to learn if the Physician has come; and if he has come have him directed here.

(The Chamberlain goes to the archway, claps his hands for a messenger, and gives the order.)

THE KING (As the Chamberlain returns)—I am most anxious about these other countries. If all their plans succeed our kingdom may be doomed.

THE CHAMBERLAIN—They cannot succeed, Sire. The lower orders will never learn to rule.

THE KING—I know it. I know it well; and still I fear.

(The Physician enters. He is too democratic to kneel. In fact, all classes have lost much of their servility in these days.)

THE KING—Welcome to our kingdom, the last of the world.

THE PHYSICIAN (Bowing)—It is good, Sire, to see you so alive, so strong and healthy.

THE KING—Good health is the blessing of my line.

"He is my friend!"

THE PHYSICIAN—For that reason I knew the Prince would be himself again. He has improved?

THE KING—More than my fondest dreams could picture him.

THE PHYSICIAN—Then I am well rewarded.

THE KING—You must see him.

THE PHYSICIAN—I wish to, Sire.

THE KING (To the Chamberlain)—Have the Prince hailed before me.

THE CHAMBERLAIN—I would go for him, Sire.

THE KING—No, have him hailed. I wish you here.

(The Chamberlain goes to the archway and gives a messenger orders to have the Prince brought before the King.)

THE KING (To the Physician)—How found you the rest of the world?

THE PHYSICIAN—The rest of the world is happy beyond all dreams of happiness.

THE KING—You mean the people rule with some success?

THE PHYSICIAN—With all success, Sire.

THE KING—But wars and discord should keep them unsuccessful.

THE PHYSICIAN—They have no wars.

THE KING (In surprise)—No wars!

THE PHYSICIAN—They know that they must fight the wars themselves, so they have no wars.

THE KING (Sadly)—If what you say is true, my kingdom surely cannot last forever.

THE PHYSICIAN—I fear not, Sire.

THE KING—I notice even here there is some discontent; the people talk of equality and are hearing things from abroad.

THE PHYSICIAN—Your kingdom may last long; it may fall soon.

THE KING—If it but last my reign!

THE PHYSICIAN—And of your son, the Prince?

THE KING—The boy is young. He can remold himself to the ways of the world.

THE PHYSICIAN—Yes, youth can endure the change better than age.

THE KING—I sadden when I think of the state of the world—the people forgetting authority, forgetting the difference between King and slave, not knowing Prince from menial.

THE PHYSICIAN—The Utopia of which they preached has come.

THE KING—And what Utopia do they preach of now?

THE PHYSICIAN—They say they will enjoy these new worlds for a while, then think of the future.

(There is a great noise heard in the hallway.)

THE KING (Turning)—What noise is this?

(As the Chamberlain starts to the doorway, the Prince, a boy of twelve, enters, followed by four or five boys of similar age. They are all ragged and dirty.)

THE KING—What can this mean?

THE PRINCE—You wished me, Sire?

THE KING (In angry tones)—Must I pick out the Prince from all this rabble? What means it, Chamberlain?

THE CHAMBERLAIN—I know not, Sire. I was commanded to remain with you.

THE PRINCE—These are my friends.

THE KING—Friends!

THE PRINCE—Yes, Sire.

THE KING (To the Chamberlain)—Were you commanded that he play alone?

THE CHAMBERLAIN—Yes, Sire.

THE KING—Friendship does not become full grown in an hour. What means it? You ignored my commands?

THE CHAMBERLAIN—Sire, you commanded; and in all things I obey you. But you also commanded that I obey the Prince; and the Prince commanded that I open the garden gates.

THE KING (To the Prince)—Is this true?

THE PRINCE—Yes, Sire.

THE KING—Did I not say it was uncomely to mingle with inferiors?

THE PRINCE—They are my equals.

THE KING—Equals! Have I lived to hear equality preached by a Prince of my own blood?

THE PRINCE—They have proved it, Sire.

THE KING—How proved themselves your equals?

THE PRINCE (Indicating a black boy)—Zanzibo can throw me to the ground, but I can beat him in a race. (Indicating another boy)—This boy can cast a stone farther than I, but I outswim him. (Pointing to another boy)—That boy, the other black one standing there, can climb to the summit of the highest tree, while I climb half the height.

THE KING (Impatiently)—But of your blood. Why speak of these mean things? What of your blood?

THE PRINCE—We tried that, Sire. Each of us pricked himself with a needle's point and gave one drop of blood upon a parchment. Then walking at a distance, turned again to where the parchment lay, but could not tell one drop of blood from the other.

THE KING—How long has this been going on?

THE PRINCE—Since I began to play.

THE KING—Then it must stop at once.

THE PRINCE—I will not play without them.

THE KING—Do you not know that every moment you play with them you lose a certain measure of their respect?

THE PRINCE—I will not play if they are taken from me.

THE PHYSICIAN—Sire, the Prince must play or his health will fall to what it was before.

THE KING—Then he must play alone.

THE PRINCE—I will not!

THE KING—I'll throw you into chains!

THE PRINCE—Humiliate a Prince of your own house?

THE KING (After pondering)—I'll compromise. I still remember that a Prince of the blood is above the punishment we give to menials. Choose one of these as playmate and let the others go.

THE PRINCE—And may this one remain within the castle?

THE KING—Yes.

THE PRINCE (Putting his hand on the shoulder of the black boy who stands beside him)—Then I choose Zanzibo.

THE KING—What! Choose a black!

THE PRINCE—He is my friend!

THE KING—Choose you a white one.

THE PRINCE—You said choose *one*. You said not black or white, and I have chosen.

THE KING—Will you cross me in all things?

THE PRINCE—Zanzibo is my friend. We love each other.

THE KING (After pondering a moment)—Chamberlain, take those two away, clean them and dress them in the finest garments and bring them back as quickly as you can. Send these others out and have it announced to the Queen that the King would see her here.

(The Chamberlain and all the boys go out.)

THE KING—This new idea is flying through the world; the pauper thinks himself the Prince's equal. The black and white have come too close together. It must be stopped.

THE PHYSICIAN—Nothing can stop it, Sire; the world is wild with new ideas.

THE KING—And he even chose a black for his companion!

THE PHYSICIAN—Blacks have been kings of the world in other days.

THE KING—That's where the trouble comes.

They are too numerous, too dangerous; they may usurp the power of the world again.

THE PHYSICIAN—The power of the world belongs to all the people, and no one race shall rule the world again.

THE KING—I have a plan that will subdue the Prince, will make him spurn that black.

THE PHYSICIAN—A new idea—

THE KING—The Queen comes.

(The Queen and two ladies have entered. The King and Physician bow.)

THE QUEEN—Sire, you wished me here?

THE KING—I am in a dilemma.

THE QUEEN—What puzzles the King?

THE KING—The Prince has chosen a black boy for his companion and will not play without him.

THE QUEEN—Why must he have a companion?

THE KING—He will not play without one.

THE PHYSICIAN—And play is necessary to his health.

THE KING—I have a plan that will settle that.

THE QUEEN—What plans the King?

(The King goes up to the large chair and sits.)

THE KING—In all my years of rule one thing I learned and learned as thoroughly as I learned the book, and it is this: Kings and Princes and those of higher blood hate others who rise up from lower classes to be their equals, nor do they love too much equals in their own class.

THE QUEEN—And what of this?

THE KING—On this I'll base my plan to outwit the Prince. He chose that black boy; now I'll promise him to let the boy stay if he will agree to have the boy made an equal unto him, a Prince of these domains.

THE QUEEN (In surprise)—A black Prince!

THE KING—A black Prince if he will, but our Nyanza will tire of this unreal equality when he sees one rising from far below to share his power.

THE QUEEN—I do not like the plan. Suppose Nyanza willingly accepts him? You say a strange idea is in the world, and strange ideas are appealing to the young. If he is once accepted you cannot break your promise. The King's promise cannot be broken.

THE KING—It cannot fail. The law runs through all nature. The Prince looks down on the man, the man on what's lower than he is, on down to the toad that looks upon the snake as his inferior.

THE QUEEN—I do not like the plan.

THE KING—It cannot fail. Watch, when I state it, Nyanza spurn the black.

(Nyanza and Zanzibo return, followed by the Chamberlain. Both are dressed in the finest garments, and the black boy looks equally as princely as the white. They stand before the King.)

THE KING—Chamberlain, you have done well. (To the Prince) When you, Nyanza, chose this boy your friend, a plan occurred to me. The nation is one-fifth black, and I am old. Now if you love the boy as friend and equal I promise to make him a Prince equal to you in power, and at my death ruler of half the kingdom.

THE PRINCE (In surprise)—Sire, is this a promise?

THE KING (Thinking he has gained his point)—I speak it from my heart, and the King's promise cannot be broken.

THE PRINCE (To his friend)—What say you, Zanzibo?

ZANZIBO—I say that if the King so honors me, my whole life shall be given to the task, and all the effort within human power will I extend to fill the place with honor.

THE PRINCE—Well said. (To the King) Now, Sire, I like your terms and I accept!

THE KING (Startled)—You accept.

THE PRINCE—Yes, Sire.

THE KING—You accept as equal that boy standing there?

THE PRINCE—According to the terms of your promise, Sire.

THE KING (Rising)—Have you thought, Nyanza? This makes him a Prince, and equal unto you in all things.

THE PRINCE—Sire, I accept your terms.

THE KING—And you hold me to my promise?

THE PRINCE—The King's promise cannot be broken.

THE KING (Stepping down in anger)—You balk me at every turn. A black shall not rule in this kingdom!

THE PRINCE—The King's promise cannot be broken.

THE QUEEN—I said at first I did not like the plan.

THE KING (Trembling with anger)—Chamberlain, help me out.

(The Chamberlain assists the King to the door where the King stops and turns, pointing his trembling finger at his son.)

THE KING—Undutiful son, you shall have your fill of this equality. I said a black should never rule in this kingdom. The King's promise cannot be broken. At the coming midnight and forever after, there shall be no more kingdom. The power shall go into the hands of the people. Now glory in your equals!

(He goes out.)

THE PRINCE (Pleased)—This last decree is better than the first. At last the people will be happy!

(He and Zanzibo join hands as the others go out.)

Curtain.

CHILDREN OF THE SUN

Madeline G. Allison

Dear little girl of tender years,
Born of a race with haunting fears—
Cry not nor sigh for wrongs done you,
Your cloud has silv'ry lining, too.

Dear little son, be not in gloom,
For fears this world has no more room;
God in his Wisdom gave you hue
Of which He's proud—yes, proud of you!

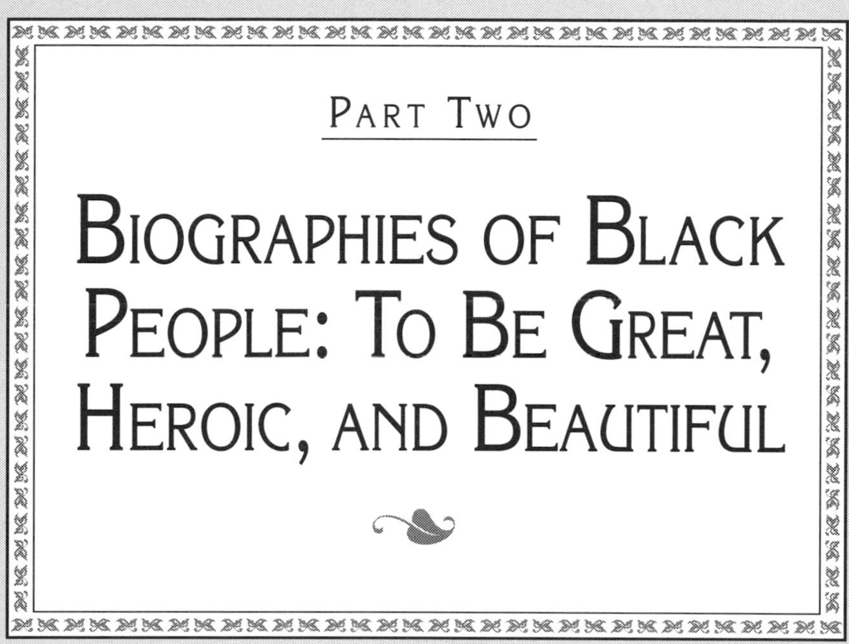

Part Two

Biographies of Black People: To Be Great, Heroic, and Beautiful

In 1919, when W. E. B. Du Bois was thinking about creating The Brownies' Book, he shared these concerns with the readers of The Crisis:

> Heretofore the education of the Negro child has been too much in terms of white people. All through school life his text-books contain much about white people and little or nothing about his own race. All the pictures he sees are of white people. Most of the books he reads are by white authors, and his heroes and heroines are white. If he goes to a moving picture show, the same is true. If a Negro appears on the screen, he is usually a caricature or a clown. The result is that all of the Negro child's idealism, all his sense of the good, the great and the beautiful is associated almost entirely with white people. The effect can be readily imagined. He unconsciously gets the impression that the Negro has little chance to be good, great, heroic or beautiful.

The pieces in this section were chosen to remedy this anti-black bias: many people of African descent were, in fact, great, heroic, and beautiful.

Several of the people whose stories are told here are considered heroes because they were able to find a way to escape from slavery. Some of them began their lives in African countries. It is important to remember that the history of American Negroes did not begin with American slavery. As one of the stories mentions, sometimes Africans sold other Africans into slavery. But you should know that the kind of slavery practiced in some places in Africa was very different from American slavery. One of the differences was that in American slavery it was particularly difficult for slaves to change their station in life. They were usually born as slaves and died as slaves, with little opportunity to be educated or to attain freedom. In the story of Betsy Blakesley, you will read of the Fugitive Slave Laws, which allowed northerners to sell escaped slaves back to traders and to their former owners. So it was miraculous for those who escaped to do that and sometimes return to help rescue others.

People in 1920 talked about boys and girls and men and women differently than we do now. In the story about Paul Cuffee, the storyteller talks about boys who dream of becoming sailors. Today, we know that both boys and girls can become sailors. Another selection recounts the life of Benjamin Banneker, the man largely responsible for surveying the city of Washington, D.C., and helping design its street layout. The writer tells us that Banneker "lived like a man" even though he cooked for himself and did his own laundry. Today, we realize that all people are capable of doing various kinds of tasks, and those abilities have nothing to do with whether they are men or women.

The stories here are about people who were famous, important, or even heroic. One letter is from a parent who encourages the magazine to continue publishing biographies. Another letter is from a reader who has read about one of her neighbors in the pages of The Brownies' Book. Some of those whose stories appeared in the magazine were still alive when the magazine was published, but others were no longer living. Some of them were from America, but others were from Africa or from other parts of the African diaspora—all of the places in the world where people of African descent lived, such as England and the Caribbean islands. Mahatma Gandhi's story is told here, too, because, even though he was from India, the creators of The Brownies' Book thought that it was important for people of color all over the world to know about each others' lives. They wanted the readers to be aware of all of the heroes, because their achievements contributed to African-American communities and to the nation as a whole.

THE JURY

I have never liked history because I always felt that it wasn't much good. Just a lot of dates and things that some men did, men whom I didn't know and nobody else whom I knew, knew anything about. Just something to take up one hour of the three hours left after school.

But since I read the stories of Paul Cuffee, Blanche K. Bruce and Katy Ferguson, real colored people, whom I feel that I do know because they were brown people like me, I believe I do like history, and I think it is something more than dates.

I read these stories to a little friend of mine, Beatrice Turner, who is only eight years old, and she said, "Now that's just the kind of history I like. Won't you ask *The Brownies' Book* to tell some more stories like that? I would like so much to know the story of John Brown. I have heard so many people talk about him and we used to sing a song about him, but nobody seems to know what he really did—I don't."

I do wish that you would tell that story sometime in *The Brownies' Book*, and I am sure that all of the readers of *The Brownies' Book* would enjoy it. I hope that I am not asking you too much.

And I wish too, if you can find them, that you would publish the pictures of Katy Ferguson and Paul Cuffee—especially of Katy Ferguson. Of course both of them were perfectly wonderful, but I just love to think about that nice old lady and all she accomplished, although she began with nothing. When I think how much more happily colored girls start out in life now it seems to me we ought to be able to accomplish almost anything.

Pocahontas Foster, *Orange*, *N.J.*

I get so tired of hearing only of white heroes and celebrating holidays in their honor. I think every year we ought to have parades or some sort of big time on Douglass' birthday and on the anniversary of Crispus Attucks' death. I wish you'd say something about this in *The Brownies' Book*. All the colored girls in my class said they wished so too when I told them I was going to write you.

Claudia Moore, *Pittsburgh*, *Pa.*

I received *The Brownies' Book*. I think it is very nice. I think you learn a lot in those little paragraphs, "As the Crow Flies." I like the Easter number best of all. If I write a story will you publish it in *The Brownies' Book*? There is one paragraph I was interested in about Mr. Matthew Henson. I know about Mr. Henson—his wife sings on our choir at Abyssinia Baptist Church, and I love to read about people I know. I'm anxiously waiting for the May number. I hope it will be as nice as the Easter number.

Edith M. Louis, *New York City*

I wish you would tell me what to do. I am fifteen years old, and I want to study music. My mother and father object to it very much. They say no colored people can succeed entirely as musicians, that they have to do other things to help make their living, and that I might just as well start doing this first as last. Of course, I say that just because things have been this way, that's no sign they'll be like that forever. But they talk me down.

Won't you tell me what you think about this? And tell me, too, about colored musicians who have made their living by sticking to the thing they love best? Of course, I know about Coleridge-Taylor and Mr. Burleigh.

Augustus Hill, *Albany*, N.Y.

This might be "The Jury," but in fact it is a colored teachers' music class at Medford, Mass.

A Great Sailor

Boys who dream of becoming sailors will like the story of Paul Cuffee, who more than a hundred years ago made voyages in his own vessel to the Southern States, the West Indies, England, Russia, and Africa. That was no small adventure in those days, when the Atlantic sea lanes were comparatively uncharted and life-saving devices few and uncertain.

Paul felt the call of the ocean when he was still a little boy, but it seemed unlikely that he would ever be able to fulfill his dearest wish. He was one of the ten children of John Cuffee, a slave who had, through great and unswerving persistence, bought his freedom. That was a happy day when, in addition to the ownership of himself, he became the owner of a farm on one of the Elizabeth Islands, near New Bedford, Massachusetts.

Of course, in the beginning when Paul was a little fellow, sheltered and protected by the love of his brave father and his dauntless Indian mother, all things seemed possible. But in 1773 the father died, and Paul, who was then fourteen, had to enlist with his three brothers, in the business of taking care of his mother and six sisters.

For a while, it seemed as though fishing were the only industry which would keep him in touch with the sea. But no matter what his duties, he never gave up his secret desire to guide a ship over the waves. All his studies—and there were no schools about—tended in this direction. Before long, he was known for some distance around as an expert in navigation. When he was not studying, he was engaged in teaching this useful art, and at night during the rigorous winters many a boy learned of the sea and the stars from Paul Cuffee.

At First He Owned Only An Open Boat

He must have inherited his father's perseverance, for although he started out as owner of only an open boat, by 1806 he was the owner of a ship, two brigs, and several smaller craft. Nor were his possessions only those for the sea, for he had invested to a considerable degree in land and houses.

After Cuffee had thus gratified the wish of his heart—the desire to ride the seas—he bent every effort toward satisfying his other ruling passion—that is, his ambition to help his fellow man. The people in whom he was most deeply interested lived in two widely separated lands—in Massachusetts and in Africa. Captain Cuffee first built a school for his own children on his own estate and gave his neighbors the free use of it. He himself had never gone to school, and it gave him a vast satisfaction to see his boys and girls and others gaining, through his efforts, the thing which he had so much missed.

Having done thus much for American Negroes, he turned his attention toward his people in Africa. He had long yearned to do something serviceable there, and in 1811 he manned his own brig with colored people and set sail for Africa. He went first to Sierra Leone, which is a portion of Africa lying to the north and slightly to the west of what we now know as Liberia.

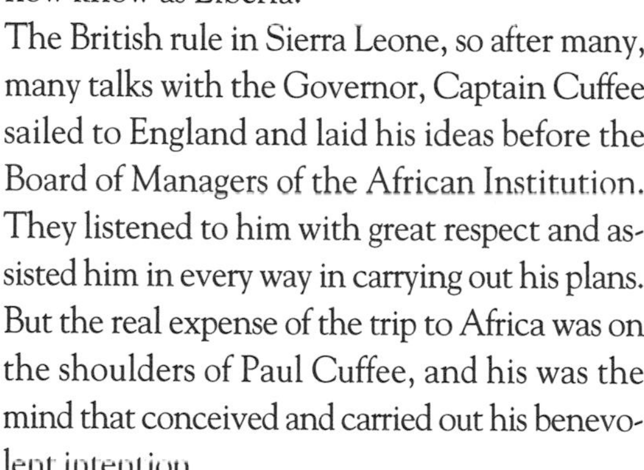

A brig

The British rule in Sierra Leone, so after many, many talks with the Governor, Captain Cuffee sailed to England and laid his ideas before the Board of Managers of the African Institution. They listened to him with great respect and assisted him in every way in carrying out his plans. But the real expense of the trip to Africa was on the shoulders of Paul Cuffee, and his was the mind that conceived and carried out his benevolent intention.

That first visit to Africa was necessarily brief, for the Captain had many business projects awaiting him on this side. But it was long enough to fire him with enthusiasm and with the desire to make another voyage. The War of 1812, between England and the United States, thwarted this desire; but by 1815 it was possible for him to start out again. This time he took with him thirty-eight colored people, who were to instruct the natives of Sierra Leone in agriculture and mechanics. It took them thirty-five days to make that voyage! This in itself shows Captain Cuffee's vast determination. Thirty-five days on board ship even in these days would mean several days of discomfort, but a hundred years ago, it meant a solid month of inconvenience and peril.

After a stay of two months, Captain Cuffee returned to America and presently started making arrangements for a third voyage. But he was taken ill with his final illness and died in 1817, at the age of fifty-nine. He did his life work in less than sixty years. From a poor little boy, the son of an ex-slave, he developed into a Captain and ship-owner and a great doer of good to people of Negro blood, both in America and Africa. The best people both of this country and of England respected him and his opinions. The world is truly better because he lived in it.

A Story of a Former Slave Boy

Arthur Huff Fauset

In slavery days, colored boys and girls could not go to school. Very often they were not even permitted to learn how to read. Nevertheless, many of the young slaves were determined to learn somehow, no matter in what manner. Such a boy was Booker T. Washington; another was Frederick Douglass; still another was Blanche K. Bruce.

When Blanche was a boy, he had to work as a slave on a plantation in Mississippi. Like many a slaveowner, his master needed him too much to allow him any time to get an education. But young Blanche made up his mind he was going to learn his abc's the best way he could, and get all the knowledge that was possible for himself, so that when he became a man he might help his people and his country. Every spare minute he could get away from his slave toil, he would go off to himself and work hard over the few books he was able to get hold of. In this way he learned quite a little bit.

In 1863 Abraham Lincoln freed the slaves throughout the entire United States. Blanche Bruce was a free man. How glad he was that he had studied hard while he was a slave! Now he had a chance to use his learning.

People began to take notice of this earnest, bright, young fellow. They continued to admire him, and encouraged him in his efforts to rise in the world. Each passing year found him a little higher than before, and the time came when the people of Mississippi, both white and colored, called on him to take one of the greatest positions a state has to offer—to be a Senator from the State of Mississippi, in the great Congress at Washington. Here, with one other Senator from Mississippi, and a number of Senators from all the other states of the Union, Bruce was to help make the laws for Mississippi, and the whole United States. Bruce and his friends rejoiced that he had studied so earnestly when a youth, that he was able to take up the big task at Washington.

While he was in Washington, assisting Congress and the President of the United States to make our laws, word came to him of his old slavemaster. He was no longer rich but was heavily in debt, and was so poor and friendless that the State of Mississippi had decided to send him to the poorhouse, a place where no respectable man cares to go. Bruce felt sorry for his former master. He set to work immediately to help him. Through a friend, he learned that at Vicksburg, Mississippi, a man was needed to inspect the ships as they came into port. Bruce saw his chance to assist the aged slaveowner.

He went directly to the President of our country, and asked a favor of him.

"My dear Bruce," said the President, "I'm only too glad to be able to serve you. What can I do for you?"

Bruce replied, "Mr. President, there is a position open at the port of Vicksburg, Mississippi. May I name an old friend of mine to take the place?"

"That's a small favor you ask," said the President. "Of course, your friend may have it. You may name him any time you wish."

Bruce went away happy.

But the thought occurred to him that his proud old master would, doubtless, rather go to the poorhouse than feel that he owed his rescue to a Negro who once had been his slave.

"He must never know I got the job for him," said Bruce to himself.

He straightaway went to the other Senator from Mississippi, a white man, and told him the story.

"And I want you to name him for the position," Bruce said, "for if he knows that I, a colored man and his former slave, named him, he will feel so humiliated, he won't accept the position."

The other Senator agreed, and he himself named the former slaveowner for the position at Vicksburg.

Blanche K. Bruce

You may be sure Bruce's old master was happy when he learned that he did not have to go to the poorhouse, but that he had a fine position, instead.

He never knew to the day he died that it was his former slave, Blanche K. Bruce, who had saved him from disgrace.

Graduates of Dixie Hospital, Hampton, Va.

TOUSSAINT L'OUVERTURE

What sort of story do you like best? I confess my favorite is the one where the poor or unknown boy or girl, man or woman, struggles up, up, up until he becomes rich or famous, or useful, or the leader of his people, the saviour of his fatherland. All other stories of no matter how splendid adventures and achievements fade into nothing for me beside the heroes who mount—as the Romans used to say—*per aspera ad astra*, "through rough ways to the stars"! And when the stories are of real people who have passed through real suffering and have achieved real triumph, my admiration goes beyond all bounds. Even if the hero afterwards meets with misfortune, what of that? Everything that has been done once, may be done again, and some day some man realizing what one before his time has accomplished, will do all that and more. Sometimes a defeat can be more splendid than a victory.

Toussaint L'Ouverture, the hero of this story, came of a royal line. His grandfather was Gaou Guinou, King of the Arradas, a powerful tribe on the West Coast of Africa. The son was captured by a hostile tribe and sold into slavery in one of the West Indian islands, Santo Domingo. Here his son, Pierre Dominic Toussaint, better known as Toussaint L'Ouverture, was born in 1743, a slave but the grandson of a king!

Nothing very much is known of his boyish days, except that he was very intelligent and loyal. Because of his faithfulness he rose rapidly from the occupation of shepherd to coachman and thence to the position of foreman of the large plantation where he lived.

He was always fond of reading, and managed remarkably enough to become acquainted with one or two foreign languages; certainly he knew Latin. His tastes were various but chiefly he read the writings of Epictetus, himself once a slave in Greece, who later became a philosopher. Isn't that a fine picture—this boy on the tropical plantation reading the works of one whose early life had been as his own and who later on arose to fame? Besides Epictetus, Toussaint read Plutarch's "Lives," and several very technical, informing works on warfare and the conduct of battles.

But chiefly he liked the Frenchman Diderot's "History of the East and West Indies," in which Diderot, writing under the name of Abbé Raynal, said:

"Nations of Europe, your slaves need neither your generosity nor your advice to break the sacrilegious yoke which oppresses them. They only need a chief sufficiently courageous to lead them to vengeance and slaughter. Where can this great man be found? Where is this new Spartacus? He will appear, we cannot doubt it; he will show himself to raise the sacred standard of Liberty and gather round him his companions in misfortune! More impetuous than the mountain torrents they will leave behind them on all sides the ineffaceable signs of their great resentment!"

Self-confidence is a part of greatness. Modesty is a good thing, a fine thing, but one does not get very far on that quality alone, no matter how deserving. Toussaint, poring over these words from his youth up, feeling more and more keenly the horror of his condition, finally became convinced that these words applied to him and that he was that promised leader. Yet fifty years elapsed, before even he acted on this. When he was fifty-four he tells us: "Since the blacks are free they need a chief, and it is I who must be that leader predicted by the Abbé Raynal."

The island of Hayti and Santo Domingo—these two provinces form the same island, you must remember—was in a terrible plight in those days. Fighting, misgovernment, slavery and disaster ruled on all sides. Three powerful nations of Europe, England, France and Spain, were warring with each other because of their interests, and rebellions on the part of the slaves were constantly breaking forth against their various masters. French slavery flourished most in Hayti, where conditions were unspeakable for over a century. Finally, after the outbreak of the French revolution, the Haytians sent two delegates to Paris. One of them, Ogé, on his return started a small rebellion which led to much bloodshed.

Now many black Haytians had in various ways achieved their actual freedom, but did not have the rights of freemen. In order to offset the consequences of Ogé's rebellion France granted to these free Negroes all civil privileges, making them free in deed as well as in name. Immediately a new confusion arose, for the free Negroes took up arms against the white owners of slave plantations and four hundred and fifty-two thousand slaves rose up to take sides with them.

This was in August, 1791. Toussaint, still a foreman on his master's plantation, felt his time had come. He first helped Bayou de Libertat, the overseer in general of the plantation, who had been very kind to him, escape with his wife and family. Then he enlisted in the Negro camp. He was a surgeon at first, but in the general confusion he realized that a good drill-master would be of more service and so he began to train and direct. His early reading doubtless helped him out here, but he was a natural leader, and generalship came as easily to him as breathing.

He seems to have been fitted in every way for the position which was finally his. His tastes and needs were extraordinarily simple. As a rule his meals consisted of a few oatmeal cakes, two or three bananas and water. He never touched wine. Nothing was too strenuous or fatiguing for him; he did not know the meaning of fear. He could do without sleep and frequently went with no more than two hours of slumber a night, and he was a magnificent horseman. Then too, he had "good luck." In seven years of campaigning he was wounded nineteen times and never once seriously. He had great personal magnetism and impressiveness and an abundance of self-confidence.

At first Toussaint allied himself with the Spanish who were fighting the French. Under his leadership the Negro troops advanced from victory to victory. It was at this time that Toussaint took on the extra name of *L'Ouverture*, because he believed that he was "the opening" or door to brighter things for his fellowmen. In spite of his many triumphs and his steady advance he never stooped to base actions, never inflicted unnecessary cruelty or imposed punishments purely for revenge. And it was proverbial among French, Spanish and English that he never broke his word.

Now although Toussaint had taken up arms against France, his heart was really with the French. Theirs were the traditions, customs and training that he really admired and with which he would have preferred to ally himself. When, therefore, the French, hard pressed by British and by Toussaint's troops alike, finally proclaimed the abolition of slavery in Hayti, Toussaint immediately left the Spanish and united with the French. From this stand nothing could move him. General Maitland, head of the English forces, offered the supreme control of Hayti to Toussaint. But he refused. He wanted slavery abolished, but he wanted to be free under France.

By 1800, Haytian affairs had begun to calm down. The Spanish and English forces withdrew, and the French, although unwillingly, left the island also, with L'Ouverture as Commander-in-chief of Forces. He showed himself as able a ruler in peace as in war. He drew up a constitution under which Hayti was independent. He was to be governor or president for life and had the power to name his successor. There was to be religious freedom throughout the province and the ports of the island were to be thrown open to the world.

He sent a draft of this constitution to France for official confirmation. But Napoleon, alas! had never forgiven the Haytian warrior for his successful resistance to France. Instead, therefore, of honoring Toussaint's suggestion, the French ruler sent an immense army of 60,000 men to the island, to call on him to surrender. When Toussaint saw the fleet coming into the harbor he knew resistance was useless and rushed to Cape François to tell his people not to take

TOUSSAINT LOUVERTURE
Chef des Noirs Insurgés de Saint Domingue

part in an opposition which could avail them nothing. But he arrived there too late. His general, Christophe, had refused to let the white troops land and the fighting was already on. Toussaint felt that he must for loyalty's sake join in, but the odds were too heavy and he was forced to retreat.

As it happened both Toussaint's own son, Isaac, and his step-son, Placide, had been sent to France to complete their education. These Napoleon had sent back with the fleet to Hayti, and these were now brought to their father by the French General LeClerc to urge him to surrender to France. Toussaint, who was both proud and just, told the boys to choose between him and their foster country, he would love them none the less, no matter what their decision.

Strangely enough, Isaac, his own son, said, "You see in me a faithful servant of France, who could never agree to take up arms against her." But Placide, who was bound to him by no tie of blood, but who owed all his position and training to him, exclaimed, "I am yours, father! I fear the future: I fear slavery. I am ready to fight to oppose it. I know France no more!"

Isaac returned to LeClerc to tell him his father's and brother's decision, but Placide stayed and fought at the head of a Negro battalion.

It is sad to admit that Toussaint finally had to yield. He retreated to his home at Gonaives and even then he might have lived out a peaceful and comparatively happy existence. But, induced by a message, he visited, unarmed and alone, the house of a treacherous General Brunet, where he was seized, put in irons, placed on board the French man-of-war *Héros* and taken with his wife and children to Brest. They never saw Hayti again.

He never lost his superb courage. He said to his captors, "In overthrowing me, you have only cut down the trunk of the tree of Negro Liberty. Its roots will sprout again, for they are many in number and deeply planted!"

At the harbor of Brest in France he bade a final good-bye to his family, and was removed to Fort Joux on the edge of the Jura Mountains. Here he was placed in a damp dungeon which in itself was fatal to a man used as he was to tropical light and sunshine. He was very closely confined here, every indignity heaped upon him, his faithful servant Mars Plaisir was taken from him and finally, lest he should commit suicide, his watch and razor were removed.

But this sort of insult meant nothing to that unvanquished spirit. "I have been much misjudged," he said scornfully, "if I am thought to be lacking in courage to support my sorrow."

For eighteen months he lingered on. Then one day the governor of the prison took a holiday, leaving things in charge of Lieutenant Colomier, and hinting to him that if the venerable Haytian were dead on his return, there would be no inquiries made. It is pleasant to know that Colomier, far from responding to such a dastardly hint, took advantage of the governor's absence to give Toussaint coffee and other comforts which he had so long desired. The governor, finding on his return that his trick had not worked, took, not long after, another holiday. This time he took the keys with him, and left no one in charge, saying that everyone had been attended to.

He stayed away four days. When he came back, Toussaint L'Ouverture lay in his cell cold and dead from starvation.

But does it greatly matter? If he had been asked, which do you think he would have preferred—life and ease or the implanting and fostering of the idea of liberty in the Negroes of Hayti? No need to guess. His name lives on beyond his own fondest dreams. Lamartine, the

French poet, dramatized him; Auguste Comte, the great philosopher, counts him among the fifty finest types of manhood in the world; our own Wendell Phillips, in the oration which all of you know, calls him "soldier, statesman and martyr."

But the best of all his influence lives on. Wordsworth truly wrote to him—

Thou hast left behind
Powers that will work for thee; air, earth, and
skies;
There's not a breathing of the common wind
That will forget thee; thou hast great allies;
Thy friends are exultations, agonies,
And love, and man's unconquerable mind.

It was in April, 1803, that he died. And today Hayti is again struggling against a foreign invasion. But she does not falter. She knows that the spirit of Toussaint lives eternally among her men, urging them ever and always on to freedom. The light of great men lies forever across the pathway of those that follow.

THE BOY'S ANSWER

A. U. Craig

One day, while in a park, I saw a little ten or twelve year old boy sitting on a bench and, on taking a seat by him, he looked at me and I looked at him; he smiled and I smiled.

"Little man, what are you going to do when you get to be a man?"

"Well," said the little boy, "I am going to be a Civil Engineer, like my father."

The little man's answer was a surprise to me, because most little brown boys of whom I ask the question, "What are you going to do when you get to be a man," usually say, "I don't know." This little fellow gave me his answer at once and said he was going to be a Civil Engineer! (All boys who know what a Civil Engineer is and some of the things he does, hold up your hands.)

His next answer to my question surprised me even more, when I put this one to him, "What do you know about Civil Engineering?" Without hesitating, he said: "I can draw a railroad bridge, and its joints; I can draw the sections of the different kinds of sewers; and I can draw a map with the contour lines."

I heard a whistle in the distance and my little friend said, "Mother is calling me." And away he ran, leaving me to think that I had met a little brown boy who would some day become a great Civil Engineer. At the age of ten or twelve this little boy knows more about Civil Engineering than most men do when they enter college to learn Civil Engineering, and so he is sure to be far ahead of his class as he goes through college.

How many boys, who expect to be physicians, can, at the age of—say 15, name one-half of the bones in their bodies, or locate their stomach or liver?

Nearly all great men have shown remarkable interest in their chosen calling when they were still very small boys. Coleridge-Taylor was playing on his violin when he was only five!

Benjamin Banneker

Elizabeth Ross Haynes

One winter evening long ago, everything in Baltimore County, Maryland, was covered with deep snow. Icicles nearly a foot long hung from the roofs of the rough log cabins. And the trees of thick forest which extended for miles around stood like silent ghosts in the stillness, for no one in all that wooded country stirred out on such an evening.

Far away from the other cabins stood the Banneker cabin. Little Benjamin Banneker was busy before a glowing wood fire roasting big, fat chestnuts in the hot embers. His grandmother sat in the corner in a quaint splint-bottom white oak chair. It is true she was sitting there knitting but her thoughts carried her far away to England, her native country. With the eyes of her mind, she saw the River Thames, the Tower of London, and Westminster Abbey.

All was still except for the moving of Benjamin now and then and the sudden bursting of a chestnut. Benjamin's grandfather, a native African, who was sitting on the left, and whom Benjamin thought was asleep, broke the silence. Said he, "Benjamin, what are you going to be when you are a man, a *chestnut* roaster?" "I am going to be—I am going to be—what is it, Grandmother?—You know you told me a story about the man who knew all the stars," said Benjamin. "An astronomer," replied his grandmother. "That's it, I am going to be an astronomer," answered Benjamin. "You have changed in the last day or two then," said his grandfather. "The day your grandmother told you about the man who could figure so with his head, you said you would be that." "That man was a born mathematician," suggested his grandmother. Benjamin began to bat his eyelids rapidly and to twist and turn for an answer. The minute the answer came to him his mouth flew open saying, "Well, I'll be both; I'll be both."

Just then his grandmother interrupted by saying, "I wonder what has become of my little inventor. Benjamin, you remember what you said when I told you the story about that inventor." Benjamin gave that look which always said, "Well, I am caught." But soon he recovered and with this reply, "I can tell you what I am going to do. I am going to school first to learn to figure. And then while I am farming a little for my living I can stay up at night and watch the stars. And in the afternoon I can study and invent things until I am tired, and then I can go out and watch my bees."

"When are you going to sleep, my boy?" asked his grandmother.

"In the morning," said he.

"And you are going to have a farm and bees, too?" she asked.

"Yes, Grandmother," said Benjamin. "We might just as well have something while we are here. Father says that he will never take mother and me to his native country—Africa—to live. Grandmother, did you and grandfather have any children besides mother?"

"Yes, there were three other children," replied his grandmother.

"When father and mother were married," said Benjamin, "mother didn't change her name at all from Mary Banneker, as the ladies do now. But father changed his name to Robert Banneker. I am glad of it, for you see you are Banneker, grandfather is Banneker, I am Banneker and all of us are Bannekers now."

"My boy," interrupted his grandfather, "I am waiting to hear how you are going to buy a farm."

"Oh, Grandfather," said Benjamin as he rose, "you remember that mother and father gave Mr. Gist seven thousand pounds of tobacco, and Mr. Gist gave them one hundred acres of land here in Baltimore County. Grandfather, don't you think father will give me some of this land? He can not use it all."

"Yes, when you are older, Benjamin. But you must go to school and learn to read first," answered his grandfather.

"Yes, but—ouch, that coal is hot!" cried Benjamin as he shook his hand, danced about the floor and buried his fingers in the pillow. That time he had picked up a hot coal instead of a chestnut. And he had a hot time for a while even after his fingers were doctored up and he was apparently snug in bed for the night.

Benjamin Banneker did retire for the night but he did not sleep twenty years like Rip Van Winkle. He rose the next morning. And a long while after breakfast he began again to roast chestnuts. When the snow had all cleared away he entered a pay school and learned to read, write and do some arithmetic. Then he began to borrow books and teach himself.

When he was about twenty-seven years old his father died. And just as he had prophesied when he was a boy, his father's farm, bought with the tobacco, became his. On this farm was Banneker's house—a log cabin about half a mile from the Patapsco River. Along the banks of this river he could see the near and distant beautiful hills. What he said about his bees when he was a boy came true also. These he kept in his orchard. And in the midst of this orchard a spring which never failed, babbled beneath a large, golden, willow tree. His beautiful garden and his well kept grounds were his delight.

Banneker never married, but lived alone in retirement after the death of his mother. He cooked his own food and washed his own clothes. And yet he lived like a man and was well thought of by all who knew him and especially by those who saw that he was a genius. He was glad to have visitors. And he kept a book in which was written the name of every person by whose visit he felt greatly honored.

Some one who knew him well says that he was a brave looking, pleasant man with something very noble in his face. He was large and somewhat fleshy. And in his old age he wore a broad brimmed hat which covered his thick suit of white hair. He always wore a super-fine, drab broadcloth, plain coat with a straight collar and long waistcoat. His manners were those of a perfect gentleman—kind, generous, hospitable, dignified, pleasing, very modest and unassuming.

He had to work on his farm for his living but he found time to study all the books which he could borrow. He studied the Bible, history, biography, travels, romance and other books.

But his greatest interest was in mathematics. And he became familiar with some of the hardest problems of the time. Like many other scholars of his day, he often amused himself during his leisure by solving hard problems. Scholars from many parts of the country often sent him difficult problems to see if he could work them. It is said that he solved every one and often returned with an answer an original question in rhyme. For example, he sent the following question to Mr. George Ellicott, which was solved by a scholar of Alexandria:

"A Cooper and Vintner sat down for a talk,
Both being so groggy that neither could walk;
Says Cooper to Vintner, 'I'm the first of my trade,
There's no kind of vessel, but what I have made
And of any shape, Sir—just what you will,
And of any size, Sir—from a ton to a gill!'
'Then,' says the Vintner, 'you're the man for me—
Make me a vessel, if we can agree,
The top and the bottom diameter define,
To bear that proportion as fifteen to nine;
Thirty-five inches are just what I crave,
No more and no less in the depth will I have,
Just thirty-nine gallons this vessel must hold,
Then I will reward you with silver and gold—
Give me your promise, my honest old friend?'
'I'll make it tomorrow, that you may depend!'
So the next day the Cooper his work to discharge,
Soon made the new vessel, but made it too large;
He took out some staves, which made it too small,
And then cursed the vessel, the Vintner and all.
He beat on his breast, 'By the Powers!' he swore,
He never would work at his trade any more!
Now, my worthy friend, find out, if you can,
The vessel's dimensions, and comfort the man."

When Banneker was about thirty-eight years old he made a clock. It was made with his imperfect tools and without a model except a borrowed watch. He had never seen a clock, for there was not one perhaps within fifty miles of him. An article published in London, England, in 1864, says that Banneker's clock was probably the first clock of which every part was made in America. He had to work very hard to make his clock strike on the hour and to make the hands move smoothly. But he succeeded and felt repaid for his hard work.

Time passed, and after some years Mr. George Ellicott's family began to build flour mills, a store and a post office, in a valley adjoining Banneker's farm. He was now fifty-five years old. And he had won the reputation of knowing more than any other person in that country. Mr. Ellicott opened his library to him. He gave him a book which told of the stars. He gave him tables about the moon. He urged him to work problems in astronomy for almanacs. Early every evening now Banneker wrapped himself in a big cloak. He stretched out upon the ground and lay there all night studying the stars and planets. At sunrise he rose and went to his house. He slept and rested all the morning and worked in the afternoon. Because his neighbors saw him resting during the morning, they began to call him a lazy fellow who would come to no good end.

In spite of this he compiled an almanac. His first almanac was published for the year 1792. It so interested one of the great men of the country that he wrote two almanac publishers of Baltimore about it. These publishers gladly published

He lay there all night, studying the stars and planets.

Banneker's almanac. They said that it was the work of a genius, and that it met the hearty approval of distinguished astronomers.

Banneker wrote Thomas Jefferson, then secretary of the United States, on behalf of his people and sent him one of his almanacs. Mr. Jefferson replied:

"Philadelphia, Pa., August 30, 1791. Sir—I thank you sincerely for your letter of the 19th inst. and for the almanac it contained. Nobody wishes more than I do to see such proofs as you exhibit, that nature has given to your race talents equal to those of the other races of men.

"I am with great esteem, Sir,

"Your most obedient servant,

"Thos. Jefferson."

This strange man, Benjamin Banneker, never went away from home any distance until he was fifty-seven years old. Then he was asked by the commissioner appointed to run the lines of the District of Columbia, to go with him and help in laying off the District of Columbia. He accompanied him and helped to lay off the District of Columbia and he greatly enjoyed the trip.

On his return home he told his friends that during that trip he had not touched strong drink, his one temptation. "For," said he, "I feared to trust myself even with wine, lest it should steal away the little sense I had." In those days wines and liquors were upon the tables of the best families. Therefore wherever he went strong drink was tempting him.

Perhaps no one living knows the exact day of Banneker's death. In the fall probably of 1804, on a beautiful day he walked out on the hills seeking the sunlight as a tonic for his bad feelings. While walking, he met a neighbor to whom he told his condition. He and his neighbor walked along slowly to his house. He lay down at once upon his couch, became speechless and died.

During a previous illness he had asked that all his papers, almanacs, etc., be given at his death to Mr. Ellicott. Just two days after his death and while he was being buried, his house burned to the ground. It burned so rapidly that the clock and all his papers were burned. A feather bed on which he had slept for many years was removed at his death. The sister to whom he gave it opened it some years later and in it was found a purse of money.

Benjamin Banneker was well known on two continents. An article written about him in 1864 by the London Emancipation Society says, "Though no monument marks the spot where he was born and lived a true and high life and was buried, yet history must record that the most original scientific intellect which the South has yet produced was that of the African, Benjamin Banneker."

There are big heroes, but who ever hears of little heroes?

Well, *we* have one this month.

His name is Harold P. Tardy, and he's in his sophomore year at Fifth Avenue High School at Pittsburgh, Pa.

On January 23, Harold was on his way to school. When he passed the home of a white family named Bleckley, 1711 Webster Avenue, he heard screams. Thinking that he might be of some service, he ran into the house and found little Margaret Bleckley, four years old, in flames. With great presence of mind and at considerable personal peril, he seized a blanket and wrapped the child in it. Then he picked her up and rushed to the office of Dr. P. W. Bushong, 1824 Webster Avenue, where first aid was administered. Then, despite the fact that the streets were a glare of ice, he carried the child to the Passavant Hospital, about the distance of nearly a half mile. She was burned so severely that she died a few days later.

Now what *big* hero could do more?

OUR LITTLE FRIENDS

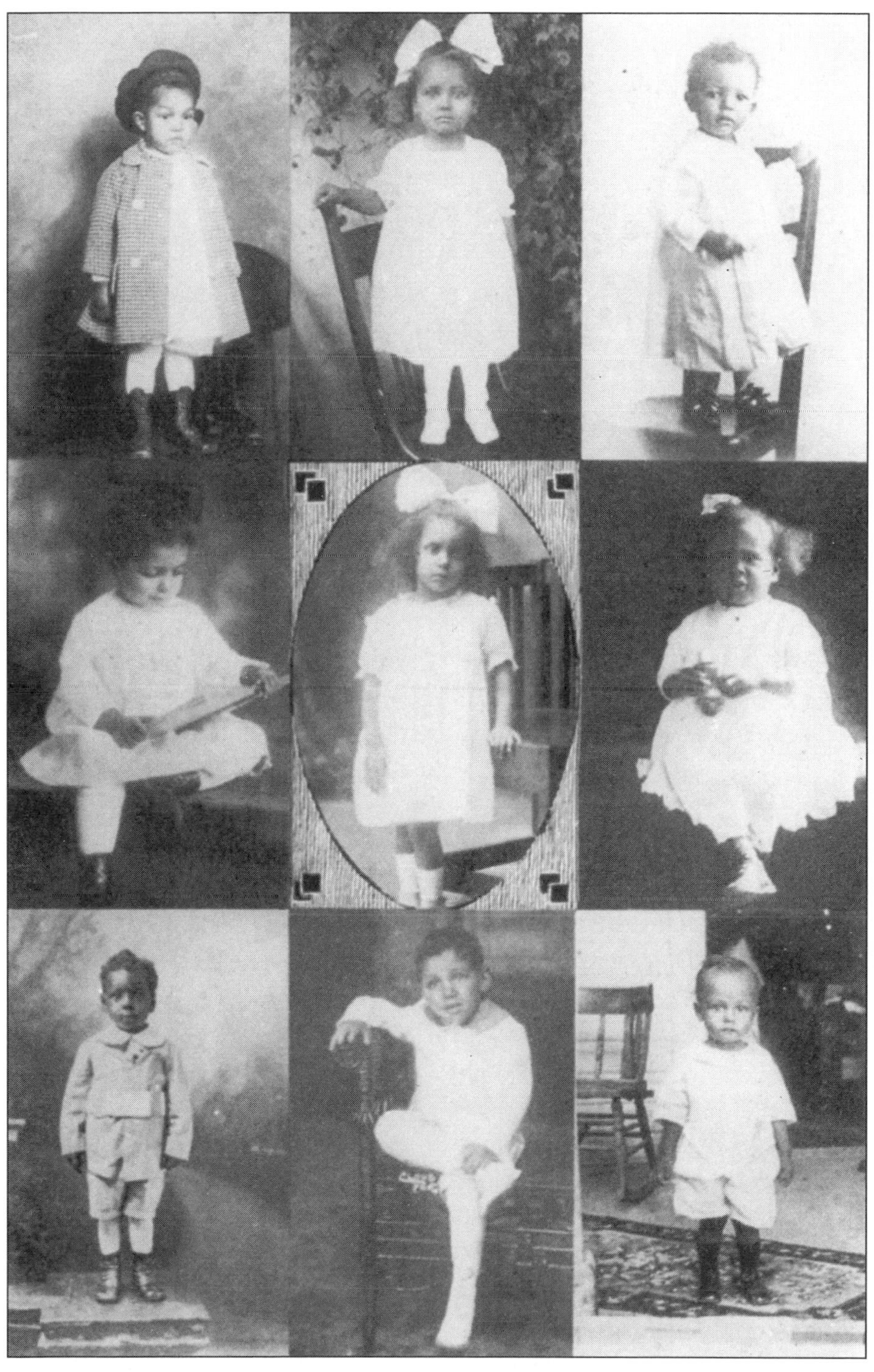

THE STORY OF PHILLIS WHEATLEY

A TRUE STORY

Somewhere in Africa nearly 175 years ago a band of children were playing on the sea-coast. They were youngsters of seven and eight who were so engrossed in their childish games that they did not notice the appearance of a boat with a number of white men in it. When they did become aware of this it was far too late, for the men had stolen up to them and seizing several had rushed off to the boat in which they were carried to a ship anchored not far away.

Only a few of the children escaped but the rest were borne off to America where they were to be sold as slaves. For these white men were slavers and the waiting ship was a slave-vessel.

Among the children who were captured and led off to such a cruel fate was a little girl of six or seven years. She was a slender, delicate little thing who had never gone far from her mother's side. Picture then her fear and anguish when she found herself torn away from everything and everybody whom she had ever known, on her way to a strange land full of queer looking people who were going to subject her to she knew not what experiences and hardships.

After a long and stormy voyage, during which the little girl was very seasick, she arrived, thin and wretched, with only a piece of carpet about her fragile body, in Boston where she was offered in the streets for sale. This was in 1761.

Of course the best thing that could have happened to this little child of misfortune would have been to be left with her mother in Africa. As that could not be, it is pleasant to realize that the next best lot was hers. A well-to-do tailor, John Wheatley by name, happened to be in that neighborhood that day. He had long been looking for a slave girl to be a special servant for his wife and his twin children, Mary and Nathaniel. He spied the wretched little African maiden, and despite her thinness and her miserable appearance, or maybe on account of it, it occurred to him that this was just the kind of child to whom to give a home. So he bought her for a few dollars and took her to his house to live.

The Wheatley family was a kind one. They received the little stranger gladly, named her Phillis Wheatley and proceeded to make her acquainted with the strange new world to which she had come and to the part which she was to play in it. In particular little Mary Wheatley became fond of her slave playfellow and between her and Phillis there seems to have developed a strong attachment. At first Phillis' place in the house was simply that of servant, though partly because of her extreme youth and the considerateness of the Wheatleys it seems likely that her duties were not very arduous. But before long, owing to what was considered a remarkable tendency in a slave child of such tender years, her lot became very tolerable indeed.

This was what happened. One day Mary Wheatley came across Phillis busily engaged in making letters on the wall with a piece of charcoal. Phillis had already shown herself apt at picking up the spoken language but that she should display an interest in writing was a new idea to the Wheatleys and gave them much pleasure. From that day on Mary constituted herself Phillis' teacher. They progressed from letters to words and from words to complete sentences. And behold the keys to the treasure-houses of the world were in little Phillis' hands for she had learned to delve into books. Short of granting her her freedom, the Wheatleys could not have bestowed on her a greater gift.

She seems to have been of an extraordinarily studious disposition. Mostly her mind took a literary bent, for she read all kinds of books in English and even mastered Latin enough to become acquainted with some of its masterpieces. It is not surprising then that a mind so eager to take in should at last become desirous of giving out. And so we have the remarkable phenomenon of Phyllis the little slave girl totally unversed in the ways and manners of western civilization, passing through a period of study and preparation and developing into Phillis the writer.

Her chosen medium of self-expression was through poetry. In 1767, at the age of 13, she had written a poem to Harvard University which was even then in existence. This was passed about among the "intellectuals" of New England, and was the occasion of much genuine astonishment and admiration. And well it might be for it was written in a lofty vein and was full of fine sentiments such as one would hardly expect from the pen of a little girl. In 1768 she wrote a poem to His Majesty King George of England—America was still a colony in those days, we must remember—and in 1770 she wrote an elegiac poem or a lament on the death of George Whitefield, a celebrated divine.

As the years went on the number of her poems grew. Their reputation grew, too, not only at home but abroad. In 1772 her health became impaired and the Wheatley household did a wonderful thing. Nathaniel had to go on a business trip to England and it was arranged that Phillis the prodigy and poet should accompany him, for the sake of the sea-voyage. Imagine her astonishment when on arriving in England, she found that her fame had already preceded her! London society took her up and could not make enough of her. She was courted and petted to an extent which might well have turned a less well-balanced head than hers. In particular she was made a special protégée of a Lady Huntingdon and a Lord Dartmouth who at that time was Lord Mayor of London. Through their persuasion and influence she collected a number of verses which she had been writing for the last six years and actually had them published—to our great good fortune.

The quaint title reads: "*Poems on Various Subjects, Religious and Moral. By Phillis Wheatley, Negro Servant to Mr. Wheatley of Boston. Dedicated to Lady Huntingdon.*" The particularly interesting thing about this book is that as so many people doubted the ability of a girl so young and of slave origin to write such verse, it contains a certificate attesting to the authenticity of the poems, and the signatures of many prominent men.

The certificate says in part:

"We whose Names are under-written, do assure the World that the Poems specified in the following page, were (as we verily believe) written by Phillis, a young Negro Girl, who was but a few Years since, brought an uncultivated Barbarian from Africa, and has ever since been, and now is, under the Disadvantage of serving as a Slave in a family in this Town. She has been examined by some of the best Judges, and is thought qualified to write them."

Those days in London were probably the happiest and brightest of Phillis' brief life. But while yet abroad she received the news of the precarious state of Mrs. Wheatley's health. And so although arrangements had been made for her to meet the king, she hastened back to America, just in time to see her mistress once more before she died.

Poor Phillis! After Mrs. Wheatley's death she seems to have fallen on

"Evil times and hard."

For Mary Wheatley was married and of course lived apart from her. Nathaniel Wheatley had his own affairs and here was Phillis all alone in the world. Naturally enough she turned to marriage and became the wife of John Peters, a Negro, "who kept a shop, wore a wig, carried a cane, and felt himself superior to all kinds of labor." Historians disagree on his real calling. Some say he was a grocer, others a baker, a man of all work, a lawyer and a physician. All agree, however, that he lost his property during the War of the Independence and that he and Phillis became very poor. Sad to relate, all agree also that he did not try very hard to relieve their condition. Finally he allowed himself to be arrested for debt, and poor Phillis was in a sorry plight indeed.

She was a proud woman. She would not seek help of either Mary or Nathaniel Wheatley. Nor at their death would she approach their friends. Fortunately at Mrs. Wheatley's death she had been set free and this gave her a chance to earn an independent livelihood. She dragged out a miserable existence in a colored boarding house doing work for which she was little fitted. Her pride and misery made her very retiring. So that when she died in December, 1784, few would have known of her death had it not been for the notice which appeared next day in the *Independent Chronicle*. It read:

"Last Lord's day, died Mrs. Phillis Peters (formerly Phillis Wheatley), aged thirty-one, known to the literary world by her celebrated miscellaneous poems. Her funeral is to be this afternoon at four o'clock, from the house lately improved by Mr. Todd, nearly opposite Dr. Bulfinch's at West Boston, where her friends and acquaintances are desired to attend."

Phillis Wheatley possessed undoubted poetical ability. It is true that viewed from our modern standards she seems stilted, even affected in style, but we must remember that with few exceptions such was the tendency of those days. Undoubtedly she was the possessor of a fine vocabulary and a really broad grasp of classical and literary allusions and figures. But these are hardly in themselves the reasons why colored Americans should hold Phillis Wheatley in such high esteem. There are others more striking. In the first place, she is the first Negro in America to win prestige for purely intellectual attainments. And she won it, oh so well! Secondly, her writings influenced and strengthened anti-slavery feeling. When the friends of slavery made as a reason for holding human beings in bondage the statement that Negroes were mentally inferior, the foes of slavery pointed with pride to the writings of this girl who was certainly the peer of any American poet of those days. Lately, Phillis Wheatley showed by her writings that she favored the cause of the colonists rather than that of England. Thus she proved that the sympathies of Negroes are always enlisted in the fight for freedom even when, as Roscoe Jamison, not her blood but her poetical descendant, wrote

"their own is yet denied."

In those brief years Phillis made a gallant showing. In all she wrote five volumes of poems and letters and received the recognition of England's peerage, of America's George Washington, and of many other possessors of honored and famous names. We are sensible of a deep gratitude toward this little lonely figure who came from Africa determined to give voice to her precious dower of song, even though she had to express it in a far country and in a stranger's tongue.

THE STORY OF FREDERICK DOUGLASS

A TRUE STORY

Laura E. Wilkes

On or about the 14th of February, 1817, on a large plantation down on the eastern shore of Maryland, there was born a little Negro slave boy. This child, whom we shall henceforth know as Frederick Douglass, lived with his old grandmother, his mother being hired out by her master. The grandmother was a fisherwoman of much note; she was also skilled in the manufacture of fish nets and was famous for her success in the planting of sweet potatoes. She was treated with more than ordinary respect by all who knew her.

Of the early childhood of Douglass there is little to tell. While in his grandmother Betsy's care he lived in a little cabin which was several miles away from those of the other slaves, as the old lady had been excused from labor on account of her great age. The log hut was bare enough; it was neither painted nor whitewashed; it contained two rooms, one above the other—that above with a floor made of fence rails, which did double duty as floor and bed; that below was windowless, with its floor of cold brown clay, and earth-and-straw chimney. The stairway was a ladder. There was little furniture—a table, a stool or two, no stove, but instead a wide chimney place in which sweet potatoes were roasted and corn pone and johnny cake baked.

In such a home as this young Frederick spent the first six years of his life, with none of the diversions considered necessary for the happiness of children. In the summer there were the birds to listen to and the squirrels to watch as they gathered nuts for the long, cold winter; or there was fishing in the Choptank River when his grandmother measured her strong arm with the best of the men in the catching of shad and herring.

Another thing the little fellow found interesting was to draw water from the deep old-fashioned well, so full of mystery to him, and to gaze into its depths at the reflection of the clear blue sky with the woolly white clouds sailing by like great birds. He liked to muse on the hillside and watch the water fall over the wheel of the old mill when the people brought their corn to be ground by Mr. Lee, the miller, and to drop his line, with its hook of bent pin, into the millpond for the fish that he never caught.

All these things came to an end when between the age of six and seven he was carried to the home plantation of his master, Colonel Anthony, a large land owner on the banks of the Wye River. The trip of 12 miles was all made on foot by the grandmother, who carried little Frederick in her arms when he grew too tired to walk. Here he met a brother and two sisters—Perry, Sarah, and Elizabeth—of whom he had heard much, but whose relationship to him he could not appreciate.

Life now took on a great change. There was no grandmother on whose lap he might cry out his childish woes and have them soothed away by her kindly hands. Instead, there was Aunt Kate, who, having been given unusual authority by her master, was very cruel and unkind to the plantation young folks, who were all under her care. She gave them very little to eat, and young Douglass often fought for crumbs and other fragments of food with Nep, the watch dog. To dip his bread into the water in which bacon had been boiled was a luxury, while a bit of rusty bacon rind was the greatest of delicacies. Too young to work in the fields, he had to drive the cows up at sunset, keep the front yard clean, and go small errands for his young mistress. This lady was very kind to him and often gave him bread and even butter from her own table. He learned a trick of singing under her window when very hungry; she soon understood what was expected of her and accordingly remunerated the singer with food, which was often Maryland biscuit, and thus he formed a liking for that delicacy which he never outgrew.

There was no difference between his life and that of the other slave boys and girls. He, like them, had neither shoes nor stockings, jackets nor trousers. Two coarse tow linen shirts were all that were given for the whole year, and if these were worn out before allowance day came, the little one went naked until that time came again. There were no beds; the children slept in the corners, often near the chimney, in order to keep warm, for only adults were given a blanket, and that was a rough one. Douglass slept in a little closet, he shared the children's regular diet, which was a large trough of corn meal mush from which all ate at once, each scooping out his share with an oyster shell or a piece of shingle. Of course the one who could eat most quickly and was the strongest got the lion's share. Before he was twelve years old he went to Baltimore. Great were the preparations made for this most eventful trip. The best part of three days he spent in the creek, for he had been promised a pair of pants—his first—on this condition however, that he made himself exceedingly clean. The warning had the desired result. He received the trousers and became so excited that he could not sleep for fear of being left.

Having reached the city he entered the family of a relative of his master. Here his duty was to attend the wants of a little boy about his own age. This marked an epoch in the life of our hero, for he was given a comfortable room to sleep in and plenty of good food to eat.

His new mistress, Mrs. Auld, unused to slaves, manifested much interest in him, and even allowed him to stand at her knee, and learn his letters with her little son Thomas. She was so pleased with his progress that she told her husband, who became angry and requested her to stop teaching the little "*nigger*" at once, which she did. Young Douglass had, however, become ambitious, and though Mrs. Auld gave him no more lessons, it was out of the question to expect him to give up trying to learn. He earned a few dimes blacking boots, and with these he bought the "Columbia Orator," a book he had heard some white schoolboys mention. These boys had given him, also, much assistance in learning how to spell.

Although at this time he was still very young, he had already begun to feel a growing discontent at being a slave, and two selections contained in the Orator had much to do with increasing his dissatisfaction. These were "A Dialogue between the Master and his Slave," in which the slave argued so well that he was emancipated; and the great English orator Sheridan's speech on "Catholic Emancipation."

For seven years he remained in Baltimore. During this time he became acquainted with a pious old man known as Uncle Lawson. This poor slave was a person of much religious devotion and through his influence Douglass' thoughts were centered on his Creator, and once in this frame of mind he became more cheerful. Little Thomas Auld had meantime become a great schoolboy and no longer needed his care. He was, therefore, given work in the shipyard of Mr. Hugh Auld, and in this work he learned to write in a most novel way by copying the letters "L," "S," "L.A." and "S.A." which meant Larboard, Starboard, Larboard-aft, and Starboard-aft, and were to be found on the sides of vessels. Encouraged by his success he began copying the italics in Webster's spelling book, and ended up by taking possession of some finished copy books of Thomas Auld which had been most carefully put away as treasures by the latter's mother. These Douglass used as tracing books.[1] Night after night when his hard day's work was ended, in a bare little garret bedroom he worked by the light of a tallow candle with an old barrel for a desk.

Through many changes brought about by the death of his old master, Douglass found himself at St. Michael's, Md., in 1833, with a new master and mistress.

Until Christmas Day, 1834, he was hired to a very cruel man named Covey, who starved and beat him unmercifully. Douglass' strong resentment at the indignities put upon him by this man gave him the determination to resist Covey's second attempt to whip him. This he did with so much physical force that the latter was absolutely beaten and badly hurt. The moral effect of this victory upon the slave was that from the hour of his conquest he was in mind a free man. The next man who hired him was very kind. On his farm he did very hard work as a field hand. Here he opened a Sunday School and had about thirty pupils, when it was broken up by the masters of the members. A second school was opened and secretly conducted in the woods.

In the beginning of the year 1836 Douglass made a vow that before its close he would make an effort to free himself. This determination he made known to five of his friends who were likewise inclined, and they began to make arrangements to that end. Passes were written, food prepared, and clothing packed. The plan was to go down the river in an open boat and around up the bay toward Delaware. The plot was betrayed, however, on the very day fixed for departure, by one of the five who had his courage lessened by a Friday night's dream. The young men were carried to jail and a search was made for the passes Douglass had written. These were not found, for Douglass had thrown his into the fire and the others had eaten theirs on the road. They were imprisoned at Easton, but all were set free after a few months, except Douglass, for it was generally understood that he had originated the plan. So he was detained much longer with the threat of being sent South. This did not happen, for he was finally sent again to Baltimore to learn a trade, with a promise that he should be free at the age of twenty-five.

During the spring and summer of 1836 he worked at calking in the shipyard of Mr. Gardiner. Here he was nearly killed by the poor white apprentices, who objected to working with a Negro. These things—contact with free men of his own race and the fact that he was forced to hand over each Saturday night all that he had earned during the week to a white man—served to make him more discontented with slavery. He sought and was at first refused the privileges of hiring his own time. It was afterward given him only to be taken away within a few months. Although disappointed in this venture, which he had intended should be a step nearer freedom, he was not despondent, but determined to make another effort to secure his heart's desire.

Accordingly on the 3rd of September, 1838, dressed in a sailor's outfit borrowed from a sailor friend, with a sailor's passport in his pocket, and a little money furnished by the woman who afterwards became his wife, he boarded a moving train in Baltimore, in order to avoid the showing of free papers, of which he had none, answering the usual questions and measuring—all of which were necessary when a colored person attempted to buy a railroad ticket. While on the train he was several times exposed to the view of those who knew him, but so complete was his disguise, that he reached New York City twenty-four hours after starting, without accident. Fearing to remain in New York where there was every danger of being discovered and returned to slavery, and discouraged by his failure to secure work, he left in a few days for New Bedford, Mass., accompanied by his wife, who, being a free woman had left Baltimore immediately after his departure and had joined him in New York, where they were married.

In New Bedford he was variously employed as charboy, as worker in an oil refinery, and in a brass foundry; in this latter position the work was very hard, but so great was his desire for knowledge that often while at work over a furnace hot enough to keep metals in a liquid state, he would nail a newspaper to the post before him and read as he worked.

The first Anti-Slavery Convention he attended was in Nantucket, in 1841. Here he met William Lloyd Garrison, who was then a young man, and afterward became famous as an abolitionist. Mr. Douglass was introduced to the public in this meeting by W. C. Coffin, another noted abolitionist, and made a speech which was so impressive that he was invited to become an agent of the Massachusetts Anti-Slavery Society. This he did. With other members of the organization it now became his duty to go about in the New England States and protest against slavery. Sometimes he suffered many indignities; again he was treated with deference and respect. In Grafton, N.H., he was refused the use of any hall or church in which to assemble an audience. So great was his determination to speak in the town, in spite of this opposition, that he borrowed a dinner bell from the hotel and went through the streets crying out, "Notice! Frederick Douglass, recently a slave, will lecture on American slavery, on the common, this evening. Those who would like to hear the working of slavery by one of the slaves are respectfully invited to attend." He had a crowd that evening and afterward there was no trouble in the effort to secure an assembly hall in Grafton.

He was made to ride in Jim-Crow cars. On one occasion, when avoiding these cars, he was beaten by the brakeman. On another, when refusing to take second-class fare on a first-class ticket, the conductor and others, in the attempt to move him, brought away also a part of the seat to which he clung most firmly. While lecturing in Indiana he was beset by a mob who threw bad eggs at him and his associates, and used such personal violence that Douglass was left with a broken hand and unconscious.

All of this public speaking was attended with great danger. There was every possibility of his being captured and returned to slavery, and there was also the liability of death at the hands of Southerners or their sympathizers. Consequently about the year 1844 he decided to leave America and become a refugee in England.

While in Great Britain he associated with such kindred spirits as John Bright, Peel, O'Connell, Disraeli, and many other famous statesmen. Affinity with such persons served to imbue him with a larger love for freedom. Unlimited opportunities were given him for addressing the public—one being at the World's Temperance Convention, held in Covent Garden, London. While abroad the sum of one hundred fifty pounds sterling was collected by English friends and sent to Hugh Auld as purchase money and thus Frederick Douglass became literally a free man. After remaining away nearly two years, he returned to America despite the protests of friends on the other side of the water and again took up active work for the liberation of slaves.

Discouraged in the effort to edit an Anti-Slavery paper in Boston, he moved to Rochester, New York, and there in the fall of 1847, issued the *North Star*, afterward known as *Frederick Douglass' Paper*. Mr. Douglass received material aid from such men as Gerritt Smith, Chief Justice Chase, William H. Seward, and Charles Sumner.

He made another visit to England in 1850, due to fear of arrest and implication of complicity in the John Brown raid at Harper's Ferry, W. Va. But he returned to America as soon as the threatened danger was past, to take up his work again with new zeal.

During the Civil War which soon followed this raid, Mr. Douglass was active in the raising of the 54th Massachusetts Regiment of colored troops, whose magnificent work under Colonel Shaw at Fort Wagner, South Carolina, can never be forgotten. He also visited President Lincoln and Secretary of War Stanton, in the hope of securing commissions for colored men, who until then had been enlisted only as privates. In this he was unsuccessful, though the Secretary promised him a position as Adjutant to General Thomas, then in the Mississippi Valley. He waited for it anxiously, but the papers never came.

When the war ended in 1865, and the slaves were emancipated, Mr. Douglass took up a new line of work as a public lecturer. His favorite topic was, "Self Made Men." In this he was very successful. His high sense of honor and right impelled him to decline to follow the advice of many friends to go South and live in a thickly populated Negro district, in order to come to Congress through their vote. In the early 1870's he took up a residence in Washington, and became editor-in-chief of a race paper—*The New National Era.* The promised support not being given, he afterward bought this paper and gave over the management of the same to two of his sons, Lewis and Frederick.

Mr. Douglass became president of the Freedman's Bank, an institution in which the recently emancipated slaves all over the country were encouraged to deposit their earnings, and in vindication of his fair name, let it be understood that he lost no time in ascertaining the true condition of the bank, and this done, he endeavored at once to restore things to their proper condition, and to meet as far as possible, the honest demands of the depositors. In this he was thwarted by the directors and other officers of the bank.

In June, 1871, he made an address at Arlington on the occasion of dedicating the monument to the unknown dead. He also made the address at the unveiling of the Lincoln Monument in Lincoln Park, Washington, D.C.[2]

On the death of Vice-President Wilson, he was one of those appointed to accompany the body to Boston. He was made Marshal of the District of Columbia by President Hayes, in 1877.[3] Before this time he served in the Legislature for the Government of the District, now replaced by a Board of three Commissioners. Mr. Douglass served also on a Commission sent by President Grant to Santo Domingo to consider the annexation of that Island with the United States. Through the appointment of President Garfield he held the position of Recorder of Deeds[4] for nearly five years. Until then no colored man had received this office. Since that time it has until recently always been given to a member of Mr. Douglass' race.[5]

In 1886, Mr. Douglass having previously married a second time, made the third and last trip to Europe, accompanied by his wife, a lady of the Caucasian race. This trip included many old and renowned cities in the southern part of the Continent, and extended even to Egypt.

In 1886 he was appointed to his last public office by President Harrison, as United States Minister to Haiti. As if to show her great confidence and esteem in him, Haiti made him her representative to the World's Fair in Chicago, in 1893. The appreciation of this compliment Mr. Douglass showed by his efforts to place the little Republic on a level with her sister governments at this mammoth exhibition of the world's progress.

On the 20th of February, 1895, the life of this grand man came suddenly to an end at Cedar Hill in Anacostia, D.C., shortly after reaching home from a meeting of the National Council of Women. There was neither pain nor suffering. Funeral services were conducted in the Metropolitan A.M.E. Church in Washington, D.C. It is estimated that upward of ten thousand people of both races viewed the remains as they lay in state in this church he loved so well, while nigh three thousand gained admission to the services. He was buried in Mount Hope Cemetery at Rochester, N.Y.

Long and lasting will be the influence of Frederick Douglass. His life is a sublime inspiration to his race. As an orator he has had no equal—forcible, strong, and true in his utterances, full of quiet and gentle humor—one never tired of hearing him. He always had something to say and was a master hand at saying it. Personally he had a magnetic force which drew all to him. He was of noble bearing, and possessed a physique of handsome proportions, crowned by a glorious head of silvery-white hair. His kindly voice and warm hand grasp dispersed the fears of the most timid at once. He was a believer in the righteousness of woman's suffrage and lifted up his voice many times in a struggle for woman's rights. He was a lover of little children and was passionately fond of animals. He never whipped his horses and his voice was sufficient to calm them, no matter how frightened they were. He loved vocal and instrumental music, had a magnificent voice for singing, and was a great admirer of the violin, which he often played.

A monument to the memory of Mr. Douglass was unveiled in one of the public squares of Rochester, N.Y., on June 6, 1899. The Governor of the State, Hon. Theodore Roosevelt, made the address. Over thirty thousand strangers visited the city on this occasion. A singular incident is, that until this time Rochester had had but one monument, that of the great Emancipator, Lincoln.

---

[1] Until he reached New Bedford, Mr. Douglass had answered to the name Frederick Bailey, in order to be less easily traced after his escape from slavery. He decided to change his name, and acting upon the suggestion of an ex-slave, who had read the story of Douglass of Scotland he chose for himself the same name, which he afterward bore quite as well as the brave Scot.

[2] Much of the money which purchased this monument was contributed by ex-slaves.

[3] The Marshal of the District supervises the execution of all orders of the Supreme Court of the District of Columbia, such as arresting prisoners for grand larceny, felony, murder, and the like, and the extradition of prisoners who are to appear before that court, either in civil or in criminal cases. This official also leads the Inaugural Processions. Mr. Douglass led that of President Garfield.

[4] The Recorder of Deeds is appointed by the President of the United States. This office is located in the United States Court House, better known as the City Hall, in the city of Washington, D.C.

It is his duty to supervise the recording of all deeds, contracts, and other instruments in writing affecting the title or ownership of real or personal property in the District.

[5] President Wilson appointed an Indian to this position.

"The Bravest of the Brave"
A True Story

Lillie Buffum Chace Wyman

Some great dread of what might happen must have come to a nineteen-year-old girl in the winter of 1849–50 so that she had to decide whether or not she should plunge into other horrors to escape the thing she feared.

I do not know exactly what her trouble was, but one can guess at its nature for she was a mulatto girl named Elizabeth or Betsy Blakesley, and she was a slave in North Carolina. No slaves could be legally married, but slave boys and girls, men and women, did love each other, and they formed unions to which they would often have been glad to be true. Their masters, however, could sell them apart, sell their children from them and they also often forced the slave women to live as wives with men with whom they did not want to live. Betsy had a little baby. We can pity her trouble even though we do not know just what it was then, or had been for a long time.

She made up her mind to run away to the North. But she could not take her baby with her. She knew that her own slave mother had never been able to help her in any trouble that grew out of their enslaved condition, and so she knew that she could not make life right for her child if she stayed with it.

Betsy hid herself on a coast vessel which was bound for Boston. Probably some northern sailor helped her to stow herself away, but we have no record of that. Wendell Phillips, the abolitionist orator, did, however, in one of his speeches say that Betsy was hidden "in the narrow passage between the side of the vessel and partition that formed the cabin." Two feet and eight inches of space—into that she cramped her young, sensitive body. No place for a baby there—and it might have cried and betrayed her presence.

Her master missed her soon after she left for the boat and the vessel was held at the dock while it was searched. She was not found. Her master still felt sure that she was on board, so he had the boat smoked three times over with sulphur and tobacco. Betsy did not crawl forth from that closet of horror, but the baby would have died had it been subjected to such torture.

At last the boat swung out and on to the tossing ocean and day and night the cold stiffened her limbs and struck inward like sharp knives, and the rolling waves outside seemed to enter her hiding place and like demons to crush her and bruise her body against the timbers of her prison cell.

Betsy reached Boston in January, 1850. There were many mysterious ways in which the Abolitionists learned whenever a fugitive slave had come into their vicinity. And so Betsy, half frozen and scarcely able to walk,

Betsy hid herself on a coast vessel.

soon found herself among kind friends who ministered unto her.

These friends were so much shocked by her condition that they did a more daring thing than I have ever known any Abolitionist to do at any other time in connection with a fugitive slave. They wanted many Boston people to see Betsy so that a profound feeling of the wickedness of slavery should stir the northern world. As the law then stood they believed that she could be publicly shown for an hour or two, before the legal machinery to arrest her could be brought to bear upon her personally. And Betsy was brave enough to do what her new friends wanted her to—and she trusted them when they told her, as they must have done, that it would help to make people want to free all the slaves if she would do what they said. Her baby was a slave, you see.

The Abolitionists took Betsy to an anti-slavery meeting in Faneuil Hall. She sat on the platform beside Wendell Phillips, who was a handsome, blonde man, then not quite forty years old.

Frederika Bremer, a renowned Swedish novelist, sat very near the platform beside Charles Sumner, with whom she had come as a sight-seer. At a given moment, Lucy Stone, young, fair in the face, and clad in white, led Betsy forward, and holding her hand she told the audience how, driven by unutterable woe, Betsy had come to Boston through brimstone smoke and winter cold. Lucy Stone had one of the sweetest speaking voices that was ever heard in this world. Once, as she spoke, she lifted her hand and placing it on Betsy's head called her "my sister."

Miss Bremer had never before seen an American slave. She was emotionally humane. Wendell Phillips came down from the platform to speak to his very dear friend, Charles Sumner, and to be introduced to Miss Bremer. She gave him a rose to take to Betsy. I wish I knew whether it were a white or a red rose. Then Betsy suddenly and quietly disappeared. She was taken out of the Hall, and started on the so-called Under-Ground Railroad, and she was borne swiftly to Canada and to freedom.

The Fugitive Slave Bill was passed before that year ended. The Abolitionists would not have dared to show Lucy for even two minutes after that.

Lucy Stone remained always the friend of the slave. Frederika Bremer, though never approving of slavery, sentimentalized away much of her objection to it. But Elizabeth Blakesley—was she not like Joan of Arc in her courage? I think every white child and every colored child in this country should be proud because she was an American girl.

SAMUEL COLERIDGE-TAYLOR

A TRUE STORY

Madeline G. Allison

Picture a West African grammar school lad in Sierra Leone, later in England at Taunton College; he is now a short, very neat person whose charming manner wins friends for him among his teachers and fellow students. In less than the usual time he is graduated from University College as a surgeon and is made a member of the Royal College of Surgeons and licensed under the Royal College of Physicians. All this happened before he was 23 years of age.

Think of that!

And it's about Daniel Hughes Taylor. He married Alice Hare, an Englishwoman. On August 15, 1875, a son was born to them and named Samuel Coleridge-Taylor, after a great English poet.

One day a Mr. Joseph Beckwith, conductor of the orchestra at Croyden Theatre, saw Coleridge-Taylor, a well dressed, curly headed, dark, little boy, holding a very small violin in one hand and playing marbles with the other.

I'd like to have seen him, wouldn't you?

Mr. Beckwith succeeded in coaxing little Coleridge-Taylor into his house and placed before him a few simple violin pieces. He was amazed to hear the little boy play some of them in perfect time and tune, and he undertook to teach him about the violin and music in general.

Samuel Coleridge-Taylor

Within a year or two Coleridge-Taylor was able to appear as a violin soloist with the natural skill of a born musician. As to his size at this time, Mr. Beckwith says: "He was so small that I had to stand him on some boxes that he might be seen by the audience above the ferns."

So, you see, we're never too young to do wonders.

Coleridge-Taylor was of a quick, nervous, shy and lovable temperament. He was devoted to his mother and tales have been told of his coming into the kitchen, where she was busy with home duties, to sing over to her a tune that he had written.

He attended the old British School in Croyden, where with his violin he led his class in singing; for he also was a singer with a treble voice that was true and sweet and won for him the place of soloist in St. George's and St. Mary's choirs.

It was the Christmas term in 1890 that he became enrolled at the Royal Academy of Music through Mr. Herbert A. Walters, honorary choirmaster at St. George. Here he studied violin, piano and harmony. In 1891 he had one of his compositions published through Novello & Company, "In Thee, O Lord." He was at this time only 18 years of age.

Coleridge-Taylor, I think, made even more rapid strides than his father.

But this is as it should be and would be with each one of us if we'd keep ambitious and happy—no matter how poor or rich, how homely or pretty we are—through each hard lesson and trying time.

In March, 1893, Coleridge-Taylor won a scholarship in composition and for two successive years, 1895–6, he won the Lesley Alexander prize for composition. His education had been that of an elementary school, but he was such a diligent reader, and so quick was his wit, so great his powers of assimilation, so reten-

"His grave is marked by a headstone of Carrara marble."

tive his memory, that he was able to hold his own among students of far more expansive education.

At the age of 19 he made his first independent public appearance at Small Public Hall, Croyden; on a program of six numbers four were his own compositions. He was graduated from the Royal Academy of Music in 1897 with honors.

Unknown to Coleridge-Taylor then, there was at Royal College an Englishwoman, a Miss Jessie S. Fleetwood Walmisley. She was dark, attractive and vivid and had a beautiful voice both for singing and speaking. Later the two met and married. To this union two children were born, Gwendolen and Hiawatha, who are both musical geniuses.

Among Coleridge-Taylor's compositions are songs, pianoforte and violin pieces with orchestral accompaniment, trios, quintets for strings and the clarinet, incidental music, symphony, orchestral and choral works. He found his greatest inspiration in the Negro folk-song and wrote "Africa and America," "African Romances," "Songs of Slavery," "Three Choral Ballads" and "African Dances." Other works are "Othello," "A Tale of Old Japan" and "The Song of Hiawatha." Among his publishers are Novello, Ditson, Schirmer and Ricordi. He became an associate of the Royal College of Music, a professor in Trinity College and Crystal Palace, conductor of the Handel Choral Society, the Rochester Choral Society, the Choral Choir and of the orchestra and opera at the Guildhall School of Music.

Coleridge-Taylor visited the United States three times; it was in England, however, that all these wonderful things came to him.

And then one morning in August, Coleridge-Taylor said to his wife: "I have had a lovely dream."

Upon her asking what it was, he said: "I dreamed I saw Hurlston in heaven. I was just entering. Of course, we couldn't shake hands, but we embraced each other three times. You know what that means," he added. "I am going to die."

On Sunday, the first of September, 1912, one of the few pleasant days after a miserable summer, Coleridge-Taylor seemed weak; his wife read to him from one of his favorite works. Mr. W. C. Berwick Sayers, who has published through Cassell and Company a book on "Samuel Coleridge-Taylor—Musician—His Life and Letters," says: "Propped up by pillows, he seemed to imagine an orchestra before and an audience behind him. With complete absorption, and perhaps unconsciousness of his surroundings, he conducted the work, beating time with both arms, and smiling his approval here and there. The smile never left his face, and the performance was never completed on earth. Still smiling and conducting, he sank back on his pillows, and in that supreme moment of devotion to his art, his beautiful spirit set out on its voyage to the Land of the Hereafter."

He was only 37 years of age, but think of his accomplishments, his fame and his heritage to the world of mankind and to a race of people whose struggles and sufferings ever echo and re-echo in the hearts of their children.

In his coffin were placed masses of violets, his favorite flower, and his love letters. At Bandon Hill Cemetery, near Croyden, he was laid to rest amidst affection and regret. His grave is marked by a headstone of Carrara marble, erected by his wife and other lovers of the man and his music.

ALEXANDRE DUMAS, A GREAT DRAMATIST

A TRUE STORY

Madeline G. Allison

When Alexandre Dumas was born no one, of course, dreamed that some day the world would proclaim him as one of its greatest writers.

Dumas was the grandson of the Marquis de la Pailleterie of Versailles, Antoine Alexandre Davy, and Marie Cessette Dumas, a Negro woman of San Domino. He was the son of General Thomas Alexandre Dumas, who married Marie Elizabeth Louise Labouret, the daughter of an innkeeper at Villers-Cotterets, France. Some of Dumas' most tender and touching memoirs are those which relate to his boyhood days with his mother.

Villers-Cotterets, France, a little country town 40 miles from Paris, is the birthplace of Dumas. He was born July 24, 1802, at 54 Rue de Lormet. Since 1872 Rue de Lormet has been known as Rue Alexandre Dumas, and the house is still standing, though it has had many changes of owners.

After sufficient service in the Army, General Dumas was pensioned, receiving £160; but at the early age of forty-four years, he died.

Life became a financial struggle for the family. Aimée Alexandrine, the daughter, was put into a boarding school in Paris. The mother hoped that Dumas would become a musician, so she kept him with her and procured Professor Hiraux to give him instruction on the violin; but after three years the professor concluded that Dumas had no sense of music in him and stopped the lessons.

Dumas' mother thought of his becoming a minister; Dumas, however, didn't fancy this profession either, and when he was about to be sent away he said: "I will *not* go to the seminary!" Then he ran away from home, leaving a note to lessen his mother's anxiety, and for three days and nights he lived in a hut in the forest with a native. But he returned to his mother, and began to study Latin under an abbé, and arithmetic and writing under the village schoolmaster.

Dumas was an unsuccessful pupil at figures, but he became a neat and rapid writer. At the age of 16, he began to work as an apprentice in the office of a lawyer.

There now came to Villers-Cotterets, a youth of noble birth, Adolphe De Leuven, who eventually became known as an author and a writer of vaudevilles and comic operas. He met Dumas and the two boys confided their literary ambitions. Dumas began the study of Italian and German and later he and Leuven became collaborators.

Then some students performed Ducis' "Hamlet" at Villers-Cotterets, and among the audience was Dumas! So interested was he in the play that he sent to Paris for a copy of it and learned the part of Hamlet. He says: "The demon of poetry was now awakened in me, and would give me no rest."

But the family was facing poverty, and Dumas, through his mother, was given a position in the office of M. Lefevre, a lawyer at Crepy.

One of M. Lefevre's habits was to make frequent trips to Paris, remaining several days. During one of these vacations, Dumas, with one of his friends, also went to Paris. This time, though, M. Lefevre returned sooner and found Dumas away.

M. Lefevre said when Dumas returned: "May I ask if you have any knowledge of mechanics?"

Dumas answered that he thought he knew something of mechanics in practice, though not in theory.

"Very good," said M. Lefevre—"you will doubtless then be aware that for a machine to work properly, every one of its wheels must contribute to the general movement."

When the parable was applied to Dumas, who had been away three days, he decided to consider himself dismissed.

Dumas had played many games of billiards with his friends, and now through this means he gained fare to Paris, where he sought work. At first he met only with failures, but finally he came upon General Foy, who obtained for him the position of Supernumerary Clerk in the Secretarial Department of the Palais Royal; his salary was 1,200 francs, or about $240.

Dumas told General Foy: "I am going to live by my penmanship now, but some day, I promise you, I shall live by my pen."

Twenty-one years of Dumas' life had now passed. He was 6 feet tall, slim rather than otherwise—with dark, curly hair, small and delicate feet and hands, and bright, quizzical eyes.

Since 18 years of age Dumas had been gaining in his literary ability, and at the age of 27, in 1829, he had a historical play, "Henri III," produced at the Thèâtre Français.

After spending the day beside his sick mother, Dumas hurried to the theatre, at 7:45, and took his seat alone and unobserved in a small stage box, and waited for the curtain that would rise on his play and on his future. Three times during the performance he rushed from the theatre to see how his mother was getting on. As the curtain was falling, there were "thunders of applause"; then Firmin, one of the players, stepped forward and announced the author, and the spectators, among whom was the Duke of Orleans, rose to mark their respect. Dumas received many congratulations and when he returned to his home, his mother was sleeping quietly—and their financial struggles were at an end.

On August 1, 1838, Dumas' mother died. Dumas had been a good son, but because he had at times been a bit thoughtless, he tells us:

"Ah! Think how ready we are, for any light caprice of youth, to leave a mother while she lives, until some day comes the awful and inevitable hour when she must leave us! Then when it is too late, we weep and reproach ourselves for all that neglect and indifference which parted us needlessly from the guardian angel now parted from us forever."

When Dumas was 44 years old, he contracted to furnish two newspapers during the year with an amount of manuscript equal to 60 volumes.

It is said that Dumas' name is attached to 1,200 separate writings; among his best known books are "The Three Musketeers," "Monte Cristo," and "La Reine Margot."

Alexandre Dumas married Ida Ferrier, an actress, of Porte Saint-Martin. On July 28, 1824, they became the parents of Dumas III, who in 1875 was elected a member of the French Academy. He lives in France.

And then on December 5, 1870, keeping a promise to her father that she would not let him be overtaken by death without receiving the last rites of religion, Dumas' daughter, Marie, sent for a priest who administered the communion—and Alexandre Dumas died at the age of 68.

A statue to his memory has been erected in the Place Malesherbes in Paris.

DENMARK VESEY

A MARTYR FOR FREEDOM

M. G. Allison

How fortunate are Brownies of our time!

It was during a voyage, when a little colored boy was fourteen years of age, that Captain Vesey gave him a name, "Telemaque."

Even though he was so young, this little boy was among 390 human beings who were to be owned by whoever would buy them. Telemaque's "beauty, intelligence and alertness" caused him to be separated from the rest of the slaves and made a sort of pet among the officers; but at the end of the voyage, which was between St. Thomas and Cap Français, Telemaque, too, was sold as a slave.

The town physician at Santo Domingo, however, gave Telemaque's owner a certificate which stated that the boy was subject to epileptic fits. The law required that sales of persons of unsound health should be cancelled; so Telemaque and Captain Vesey resumed their life together.

In the speech of the slaves, "Telemaque," with the long *a* pronunciation, was changed to Denmark, and we know of this man as Denmark Vesey.

For over 20 years Denmark Vesey served as a faithful servant to Captain Vesey, who retired at Charleston, South Carolina. Denmark Vesey became interested in lottery games, in which people are given prizes by chance. And in 1800, as a patron of the East Bay Street Lottery, Denmark Vesey won a prize of $1500! With this he bought himself from Captain Vesey, at a price of $600, and began to work as a carpenter.

Denmark Vesey had many children—but the Slave Code made them personal property of other men. This cruel situation embittered Vesey—not only because he was personally involved, but because his great-heartedness made him want to do something to blot out such sorrow from others' hearts.

By this time Denmark Vesey, through his travels with Captain Vesey, had learned to read and write and speak French and English fluently.

Eventually Vesey began to plan an idea for resisting the slave system. He was a cautious man, and in this manner he gained the attention of the slaves, to whom he spoke of their inalienable human rights. For nearly four years he carried on a secret agitation among the slaves. He did the work alone, but the city of Charleston, South Carolina, and 100 miles of adjacent country were covered—and then, in 1821–22, Vesey's effort became an organized movement.

Five men were chosen by Vesey as associate leaders. One, Rolla Bennett, was a bold and ardent person; Ned Bennett was a man of firm nerves and desperate courage; Peter Poyas was cautious and true; Gullah Jack was regarded as a sorcerer—artful, cruel and bloody; Monday Gell was firm, resolute, discreet and intelligent.

With such an aggregation of men and several thousand members enrolled, Vesey started an uprising against slavery. His plans were that the leaders of the movement, at the same time and from six different quarters, would attack the city of Charleston, and seize its strategical points and buildings, taking the arms and ammunition; with horses they would keep the streets clear, cutting down without mercy all persons, white and black, who tried to hinder the uprising.

The time was in 1822, and the insurrection was planned for Sunday at midnight, July 14; but about the last of May, there were indications that the plot had been discovered, so Vesey changed the date of attack to June 16.

After all, though, someone betrayed them! This happened on the morning of May 30, and by sunset the city authorities were ready to guard against the supposed surprise. The week following was one of watchful waiting for all concerned; Vesey, however, carried on his work.

Don't you admire his wonderful courage!

And finally the city officials found one who was so disloyal, so unmanly, as to tell them Vesey's plan.

On June 15, Peter Poyas, Rolla, Ned and Batteau Bennett were arrested; Vesey was not captured until the fourth day following; Jesse Blackwood was taken the next day; Monday Gell was arrested four days later; and on July 5, Gullah Jack was captured. In all there were 131 Negroes arrested, 67 convicted, 35 executed and 37 banished from the United States.

To Denmark Vesey, Peter Poyas, Rolla and Ned Bennett and Gullah Jack is the honor of remaining absolutely loyal and brave, with their vows unbroken.

This cannot be said of Monday Gell, who though he was brave and loyal throughout his trial, betrayed his fellows to save his own life.

And so, on July 2, 1822, Denmark Vesey, Peter Poyas, Rolla, Ned and Batteau Bennett and Jesse Blackwood were hanged; ten days later Gullah Jack was hanged; and on the twenty-second of July, 22 black martyrs were hanged for the cause of freedom.

"When Vesey was tried, he folded his arms and seemed to pay great attention to the testimony, given against him, but with his eyes fixed on the floor. In this situation he remained immovable, until the witnesses had been examined by the court, and cross-examined by his counsel, when he requested to be allowed to examine the witnesses himself. He at first questioned them in the dictatorial, despotic manner, in which he was probably accustomed to address them; but this not producing the desired effect, he questioned them with affected surprise and concern, for bearing false testimony against him; still failing in his purpose, he then examined them strictly as to dates, but could not make them contradict themselves. The evidence being closed, he addressed the court at considerable length. . . . When he received his sentence, the tears trickled down his cheeks."

Denmark Vesey was a black man, and handsome. He was physically strong and had a powerful mentality. He has been referred to as an old man but, though his hair was probably white, he was only 56 years of age when he died on the gallows at Charleston, South Carolina, nearly one hundred years ago—for that Freedom which is ours; that Freedom which we shall ever cherish!

THE STORY OF HARRIET TUBMAN

Augusta E. Bird

On the eastern shore of Maryland, in Dorchester County, about the year 1821, a wee little baby girl was born, who grew and grew and grew in spirit, as well as in stature, until she was known all over the nation as the greatest and noblest of heroines of anti-slavery. Some will think it was very extraordinary for such a wonderful woman to be the grand-daughter of a slave imported from Africa. Her parents were Benjamin Ross and Harriet Greene, both slaves, but married and faithful to each other. They named their little baby Araminta, but later she adopted the name Harriet as a Christian name. As she married a man whose surname was Tubman, she is better known as Harriet Tubman.

She had ten brothers and sisters, not less than three of whom she rescued from slavery among the hundreds of other slaves, and in 1857, at a great risk to herself, she also took away to the North her aged father and mother.

When Harriet was six years old (nothing more than a baby herself), she was sent away from her home to another home to take care of a baby. You can imagine how tiny she was when she had to sit down on the floor and have the baby placed in her lap in order to mind it. One morning after breakfast she was standing by the breakfast table while her mistress and her husband were eating, waiting to take the baby. Just by her was a bowl of lump sugar. Now every little girl who knows how tempting lump sugar is, can easily realize how much more tempting it must have been to little Harriet who never had anything nice like most little girls of six have nowadays. So while the baby's mother, who, possessed of a violent temper, was busily engaged in a quarrel with her husband, Harriet thought she would take a lump of sugar without being seen. But the woman turned just in time to see her fingers go into the sugar bowl, and the next minute the raw hide, a whip used—in those days alas!—to beat slaves with, was down from the wall.

Little Harriet saw her coming and gave one jump out of the door. She ran and ran until she passed many houses. She didn't dare to stop and go into any of these houses for she knew they all knew her mistress, and if she appealed to them for protection she would only be sent back. By and by she came to a large pig-pen, which belonged on one of the farms. She was too small to climb into it, so she just tumbled over the high board and for a long time lay where she had fallen, for she was so tired. There with that old sow and eight or ten little pigs Harriet stayed from Friday until the next Tuesday, fighting with those little pigs for the potato peelings and scraps that would come down in the trough, with the old mother sow not so kindly disposed towards her either for taking her children's food. By Tuesday she was so hungry that she decided she would have to go back to her mistress. You see in those days no one had conceived the idea of the Society for the Prevention of Cruelty to Children and Harriet had no other place to go. Harriet knew what was coming but she went back.

Harriet Tubman

It is impossible to give the many accounts of hardships which this little girl went through, but she thinks she was about twenty-five when she decided to make her escape from slavery, and this was in the last year of James K. Polk's administration. From that time until the beginning of the war, her years were spent in journeying back and forth to rescue her fellow brothers, with intervals between, in which she worked only to spend what her labor availed her in providing for the wants of her next party of fugitives. By night she traveled, many times on foot over mountains, through forests, across rivers, oftentimes sleeping on the cold ground. She traveled amid perils by land, perils by water, perils from enemies, perils among false brethren, but with implicit faith in God she always returned successful.

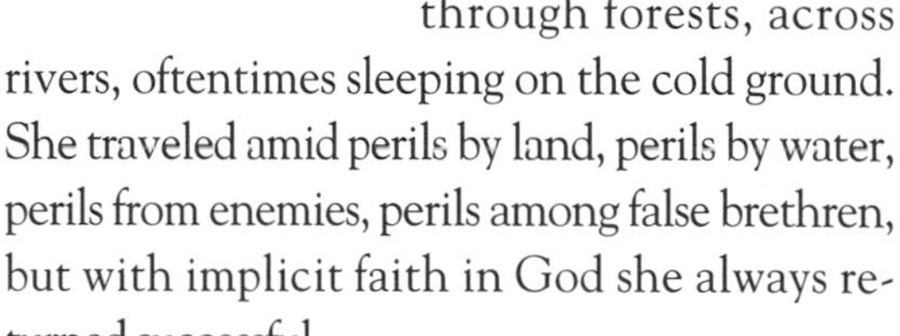

Sometimes members of her party would become exhausted and footsore, and declare they could not go on; they must stay where they dropped down, and die. Others would think a voluntary return to slavery better than being overtaken and carried back, and would insist on returning; then there was no alternative but force. The revolver carried by this bold and daring pioneer would be pointed at their heads.

"Dead niggers tell no tales," said Harriet. "Go on or die." And so she compelled them to drag their weary limbs on their journey north. The babies she managed by drugging them with opium. No wonder a price of $40,000 was put upon her head by the slaveholders. Oftentimes when she and her party were concealed in the woods they saw their pursuers pass, on their horses, down the high road, tacking up the advertisements of the rewards for the capture of her and her fugitives.

"An' den how we laughed," she said. "We was de fools, an' dey was de wise men; but we wasn't fools enough to go down de high road in de broad daylight."

America in particular, as well as humanity, owes Harriet Tubman much. To Colonel Higginson, of Newport, R.I., and Colonel James Montgomery, of Kansas, she was invaluable as a spy and guide during the Civil War. She also rendered great service to our soldiers in the hospitals as well as to the armies in the fields. In this way she worked day after day until late at night. Then she went home to her little cabin and made about fifty pies, a great quantity of gingerbread, and two casks of root beer. These she would hire some contraband to sell for her through the camps, and thus she would provide her support for another day. For this service Harriet never received pay or pension, and never drew for herself but twenty days' rations during the four years of her labors.

At one time she was called away from Hilton Head, by one of our officers, to come to Fernandina, where the men were dying very fast from a certain disease. Harriet had acquired quite a reputation for skill in curing this disease by a medicine which she prepared from roots which grew near the waters which caused the disease. Here she found thousands of sick soldiers and contrabands. She immediately gave up her time and attention to them. At another time, we find her nursing those who were down by hundreds with small-pox and malignant fevers. She had never had these diseases, but she never seemed to fear death in one form more than in another.

"A nobler, higher spirit, or truer, seldom dwells in the human form," was a tribute paid to her by W. H. Seward, one of her many influential friends who tried very hard, although unsuccessfully, to secure for her a pension from her government. So you see how much the government is indebted to Harriet Tubman and her people.

After the war Harriet Tubman made Auburn, N.Y., her home, establishing there a refuge for aged Negroes. She died at a very advanced age on March 10, 1913. On Friday, June 12, 1914, a tablet in her honor was unveiled at the Auditorium in Albany. It was provided by the Cayuga County Historical Association. Dr. Booker T. Washington was the chief speaker of the occasion, and the ceremonies were attended by a great crowd of people.

The tributes to this woman whose charity embraced the whole human race, the slaveholders as well as the fugitives, were remarkable. Wendell Phillips said of her: "In my opinion there are few captains, perhaps few colonels, who have done more for the loyal cause since the war began, and few men who did before that time more for the colored race than our fearless and most sagacious friend, Harriet." Abraham Lincoln gavc her ready audience and lent a willing ear to whatever she had to say. Frederick Douglass wrote to her: "The difference between us is very marked. Most that I have done and suffered in the service of our cause has been in public, and I have received much encouragement at every step of the way. You, on the other hand, have labored in a private way. I have wrought in the day—you in the night. I have had the applause of the crowd and the satisfaction that comes of being approved by the multitude, while the most that you have done has been witnessed by a few trembling, scarred, and footsore bondmen and women, whom you have led out of the house of bondage, and whose heartfelt 'God bless you' has been your only reward."

BERT WILLIAMS

Do you think, BROWNIES, that some day little Ernest will be as great a comedian as our Bert Williams?

Mr. Williams, you know, is a great comedian. He played in a show of his own—the Williams and Walker Company, for a long time. Then he came to be the only colored actor in the Ziegfield "Follies"—one of the most celebrated shows in New York City. He is now starring with George Lemaire in "Broadway Brevities." When the name *Bert Williams* is displayed in big electric lights, it is really an advertisement—and few people fail to see the show.

A Black Russian

A True Story

Catharine Deaver Lealtad

Long years ago, Peter the Great bought a young black lad who, historians say, was an African prince. Abraham Hannibal (for so he was called) was brought to the Russian court. He was quite a favorite with Peter the Great who gave him a splendid education and placed him in a government office where he rose to the position of general. Hannibal's granddaughter was the mother of Alexander Pushkin, who stands as the creator of Russia's national literature.

Pushkin was born in Moscow in 1799. His family was wealthy, lived for pleasure, played havoc with their estates, and troubled themselves little about rearing their children. From his father he inherited his love for frivolity and dissipation.

His early years were spent in Tsarkoye Telo, a village near the capital and the home of the last Czar of Russia and his family. Here he attempted drama, verse and fable in imitation of French classics. He received his early training from foreign tutors who taught him the French language, everything in fact French. Rodionova, his Russian nurse, gave him his store of Russian fairy stories and Russian legends. There was a warm and lasting friendship between Pushkin and this fine woman. At the height of his popularity he often slipped away from the gay capital to spend a few quiet days with the "darling of his youth."

Alexander Pushkin was not a prodigy in learning, not even a good student. He had no special aptitude for learning except for French, but in his teens he suddenly developed a passion for reading. He was left alone in his father's library which was exclusively French. Voltaire, Molière and La Fontaine were his favorites. This sort of reading is not to be recommended for most children, but it gave this one a mastery of French. In fact his school-fellows called him "Frenchman" and made fun of his bad Russian.

Like other boys of rich parentage, he was sent to the Lyceum for six years. Here he began to write poetry, first in French and then in Russian. When he was fifteen years old, some of these poems were printed. During one of the school affairs to which celebrities were invited, Pushkin declaimed one of his own works. Derghávin, one of the foremost literary critics of the day, was so pleased he publicly blessed the boy.

After leaving the Lyceum, he entered a foreign office. At this time he joined a literary club formed for the purpose of freeing the literature of the country from the trammels of artificiality. There was no Russian literature. The nobles were ashamed of their language and their civilization. They imitated and affected things French. But Pushkin's first poem showed nationalism and realism. It was not anything extraordinary and did not call for the extreme praise or condemnation which it received. But official Russia felt that "the hour had struck."

Pushkin's association with a group of young political liberals was reflected in his poetry. When the officials frowned on his writings, dreading that his youthful enthusiasm for the time "when Russia shall arise from her sleep and on the ruins of Autocracy shall inscribe our names" might be dangerous, he retorted with a number of striking epigrams on the vice of the imperial court. This called forth an order for his banishment.

Alexander Pushkin

Only the power of influential friends saved him from a life of imprisonment in a monastery. He was banished to southern Russia when he was twenty. He loved the gay society of the capital but the change was good for him. He became acquainted with General Raevsky while in the South, and came to know and admire Byron, who was ardently talked of by the general's family. Some of his works are quite in the Briton's style. He made use of this exile to make the customs and scenery of the Caucasus better known to the rest of Russia. His descriptions are as real as photographs:

"Eternal thrones of snow
Whose lofty summits gleam to gaze
Like one unbroken, motionless chain of clouds,
And in their midst the urn peaked colossus
Glittering in the glowing crown of ice,
The giant monarch of mountains, Elbruss,
Whitens up into the blue depths of heaven."

He roamed about the Crimea and learned here many a legend, in the palace of the old Khans, from which he afterwards developed poetical gems.

He also wandered about with the gypsies and wrote his "Gypsies" based on direct observation.

After four years of exile he was permitted to return home. During that time, however, the simplicity and sincerity of the peasant life had intensified his patriotism. He studied Russian history and the habits and traditions of the people.

Pushkin was the first Russian to use national types in literature. His characters are truly Muscovite and the dominant note of his work is nationality.

In "Onyegin" we have a definite type of Russian society. The hero has every social advantage, is blasé, weary of life and has nothing to do except amuse himself—absolutely purposeless—a typical Russian aristocrat. On the other hand, there is Lensky, educated away from the turmoil of society. He knows the short-comings of Russia but is unable to make his influence felt and he displays the hopeless attitude toward social conditions, so characteristic of Russians.

In 1831 Pushkin married Natalia Gonscharoff, a young woman of fine family. He received an appointment as Historiographer of Peter the Great. He was favored by the Czar and idolized by the people. Everything seemed to point to a long happy life ahead. But the court nobles were jealous and treated his wife with disdain at state balls and social functions. His means were not sufficient either to meet the strain of court life. Finally, a notorious libertine, Baron Dantés, circulated some scandal about Pushkin's wife. Dantés proved to be the sole author and publisher of the vile stories. Although Pushkin never credited the tales, in accordance with the custom of the time he had to challenge Dantés by an appeal to arms to vindicate his wife's honor. On the banks of the Black River in 1837, he was fatally wounded. For two days, he lingered in agonizing pain, the center of one of the most dramatic scenes in history. The Czar regarded his death as a personal loss and the whole nation was moved. Dantés had to flee the country. Pushkin had to be buried by stealth lest public indignation cause riot and bloodshed. Czar Nicholas took his wife and children under his protection, paid his debts of £15,000 and ordered a complete edition of his works.

His career closed before he reached his height and in his own words:

"Happy the man who early quits
The feast of life, not caring to drain
The sparkling goblet, filled with wine.
Happy the man who dares not wait
To read the final page of life's romance
But suddenly bids the world adieu."

Because of his early association with liberals, his intimacy with the Czar after his return from exile caused some to brand him as a traitor to his previous declarations for freedom. The grace and good will of the emperor and the outward splendor of Russia dazzled him. The last ten years were unhappy ones. Only a few lauded his literary works. The public turned away from the one time supporter of the Revolution, who was now a supporter of Autocracy. In the forties Belinsky pointed out the beauties of his works. But not until 1881 at the unveiling of the Moscow Memorial to the poet was he accepted unanimously, though Dostoievsky had admired the "world genius."

His poetry is the revelation of a soul. His works are unfinished but have a magic rhythm. In translation they lose much of the fine emotional shadings and musical rhythm. They are heard best by "Neva's Frozen Shores."

Pushkin is the national poet of Russia. He put life into the old Russian legends. His ease in verse, richness of language, pictures and fancies stand out against the old, arid Russian style. He is no dramatist or historian. He is a lyric poet, the echo of Russia, a genuine artist.

AN INTERVIEW WITH CHARLES S. GILPIN

Ruth Marie Thomas

Having planned for an interview with Mr. Charles S. Gilpin, who is starring in "The Emperor Jones," I had wondered how the interview would be. Finding the stage entrance, my sister and I climbed up to his dressing room, after informing the maid that we had an appointment with him. Reaching his dressing room we were met at the door by Mr. Gilpin's valet, who, after seeing our credentials allowed us to enter. Indeed, we were greatly honored at not having to await him in the reception room but having the special privilege of going to his private room.

Charles S. Gilpin, in "The Emperor Jones"

How did Mr. Gilpin look? What was he doing when we entered? Now for the grand surprise. Mr. Gilpin was washing his feet! ! ! I know this is funny but his part requires that he be barefooted and of necessity after each performance he has to bathe. Mr. Gilpin is an American Negro of striking appearance. He is tall, well-built, of nut brown complexion and clean-cut features. His appearance was very neat. I was surprised to see that he looked to be about thirty-five years old, since I know that he is older.

We made ourselves at home and then Mr. Gilpin told me to fire away. Though I was somewhat taken by surprise because he was conversing with his valet, continuing to dry his feet, and answering my sister I managed to ask him my questions. Mr. Gilpin answered them in an easy drawl.

Mr. Gilpin was born in Richmond, Virginia, and attended St. Francis, a Roman Catholic School. As a boy he was much interested in acting and took part in many of the school theatricals. He entered the profession when he was offered a part during an unemployed time. Mr. Gilpin has been in the profession for twice as many years as I am old. When asked how old I was he said seventeen which is perfectly correct.

A good common education at least is needed for acting, Mr. Gilpin thinks, because it gives an understanding of the setting and also enables one to understand the character of the person portrayed.

The characteristics that are necessary for success in this line of work are an optimistic disposition, ability to stand many hardships and much discouragement. A person must have a vivid imagination, that is one that will enable him to put himself in another one's position. Perseverance in studying is an essential thing. There must be an affection for the work, not for the dollar side of it.

There are great opportunities for the colored women in the profession, Mr. Gilpin stated, if they enter with the right idea. Only the majority of women who enter this field are not willing to study but go in with the desire for the flash and excitement of the stage. Success can not be reached if there is a lack of ambition for the things that require hard labor.

His ambition for the future is to establish a small business, because the theatrical life is so strenuous, but he thinks he will undoubtedly return to the stage as there seems to be an irresistible longing to go back to the stage in most cases.

Mr. Gilpin was asked if he wasn't deadly in love with his profession. He answered that he could not say that, but he did have an affection for it but it was also a business to him.

Mr. Gilpin laughed when I had finished my questions and told me that I, of course, would have to write about how he impressed me. I said that I would surely write that he had a wonderful, kind disposition. Mr. Gilpin wished that I also say that he is an extremely moody man and that I had caught him in one of his bright humors. He is very sympathetic and entered into my interview with complete sincerity. He is known to be especially interested in school children, as he has a son, who is eighteen years old attending school. He has a very straightforward and frank way of speaking when addressing one. When we left he stood and shook hands with us in a very cordial manner. My own opinion is that Mr. Gilpin is a wonderful man, a thorough gentleman and above all he is not egotistical.

"Saint" Gandhi

The Greatest Man in the World

Blanche Watson

About two thousand years ago there lived a man who said, "He that taketh the sword shall perish by the sword"—that is, He tried to make people see that war was wrong—that all killing was wrong—because *all* human life was sacred. The world, since that time, has listened to that message, but it has not understood it—all of which means that this man came before the world was ready for Him, and (not being ready) it crucified Him!

When I say the world, I do not mean everybody in it. There were some few people who did understand what Jesus, the Christ, taught, and who tried to live by those teachings.

Now, today, on the other side of the world, in far away India, a man is preaching as did Jesus of Nazareth, "Love your enemies"; "Do good to them that hate you"; "Do unto others as you would that they do unto you." Like Jesus, he goes out under the blue sky and gathers the people around him. Like Jesus, he says "Follow me!" And the people follow him—not by the hundreds—but by the millions—for India is a nation numbering more than 300 million souls!

The people of India want the right to govern themselves as we govern ourselves in this country—as they governed themselves a great many years ago! Usually when a people decide that they want to be independent (as we call it) they "go to war"—that is, they gather together armies and go out and kill one another—forgetting what Jesus said—forgetting that we are all brothers and that God is our Father.

Now this man, who is leading the Indian people—"Saint" Gandhi as he is called—is giving to his people, after all these years, the message of the Man that we Christians call our leader. He, too, says: "He that taketh the sword shall perish by the sword," and—if you will believe it—the British Empire, that has held India against its will for a hundred and sixty years, is more afraid of this man than any "general," that is, any fighting man—that has ever arisen during that time.

You ask me, "Why?"

Let me tell you. Gandhi, this saint, says, "Don't have anything to do with this government and the people it sends here to rule us; but do not hurt them—do not lift a finger against them: just love them!" That is why the British government is so afraid of this great leader. When a man persists in loving you—in spite of all you do to him—you can't keep on hating and misusing that man forever! More than that—any group of people that is held together by hate and bitterness *must* fall to pieces sooner or later. Hate is destructive—it kills! But a group of people held together by good-will, by love, is mighty—for love is constructive—that is, it builds.

Gandhi says to his people, "If you follow my way, you will be a free people"; and when he speaks thus—this little brown man who has to sit in a chair on a table when he speaks—no one can disagree with him. No one can look in his wonderful eyes and even *think* that he is wrong. Do you know why this is? Because of the strength of his spirit. It is the spirit—the spirit of God himself that blazes there, and his word is the word of God.

The English government (and I do not mean the English *people*—that is a different thing) the English government may not know it, but they are afraid of Saint Gandhi simply because he is speaking with the voice of God, even as did Jesus, the Christ—by the Sea of Galilee hundreds of years ago.

Will the people of India hold out? Will Gandhi succeed? Is the world to learn the lesson that war is murder—that Christ's way is the better way—that love is the "greatest thing in the world"?

Let us all watch India, and Gandhi!

Brave Brown Joe and Good White Men

Lillie Buffum Chace Wyman

The brig, *Ottoman*, sailed from New Orleans for Boston in the summer of 1846. She was the property of a Massachusetts firm, John H. Pearson and Company. Mr. Pearson is credited, in most of the records, which I have seen, with taking the aggressive and responsible position in certain affairs, which have given the ships and the company a shameful place in history.

When the *Ottoman* had been away from port a week, and is supposed to have been outside of the territorial waters of the United States, a fugitive slave, a mulatto lad, named Joe, was found secreted on board. The sailors and the captain all knew him, and had liked him very much. He had been often sent by his master, in New Orleans, on errands to the brig.

He begged these men, who knew him, to do—what? Just nothing at all, but to sail on to Boston whither they were bound. He had heard of Boston, and, once were he there, if only they again would do nothing, he was sure that he could slip away and become free, and nobody need ever know that he had been found at sea on John H. Pearson's boat. It was a fair legal question, whether, at that moment, out there on the ocean, and not having been helped to get there by anyone, Joe was not actually a free man by both human and divine law.

Captain Hannon, of the brig, watched for a vessel which should be on her way back to New Orleans. He intended, if one were encountered, to pass Joe, like a bale of goods, over to her to be returned to New Orleans. No such vessel was met, however, and the *Ottoman* sailed on its course and reached Boston in due time.

Captain Hannon did not let Joe land. He communicated with John H. Pearson and Company who decided that Joe must be sent back to Louisiana on the *Niagara,* another vessel which they owned. They had no legal right to detain him, to put him on another boat, or to send him anywhere. They managed to get him onto a small island in the harbor, intending him to stay there until the Niagara was ready to sail.

He was a brave and resourceful fellow, and he escaped from the island and made his way into the city. No warrant had been issued for his arrest. He had committed no crime against the laws of Massachusetts. No claim had been made upon the authorities for his detention, even as a suspected fugitive from "service or labor." He stood on the Boston pavements an absolutely free man in the eye of the law.

Men were set on Joe's track, either by Captain Hannon or the shipowners—probably because of instructions from the shipowners to the captain. They found Joe in one of the city streets and there they literally grabbed him.

A few puzzled bystanders saw that something peculiar was going on, and they asked what the fuss was all about. They were told that Joe was a thief, and being so assured, it is likely that they took it for granted that he was being taken legally, and certainly righteously into custody.

Joe was put on the *Niagara* and taken back to slavery.

But what had been done in Boston was clearly an act of kidnapping, and that was a crime against the law of the State. Still, I do not know that anybody was arrested for having committed that crime. Perhaps the actual kidnappers were unknown persons, or were men who had already sailed away from the city, and the connection of John H. Pearson with their deed might have been difficult, if not impossible, to establish in a court room. Joe, poor fellow, was beyond the reach of either justice or sympathy. Nothing could be done for him personally. But the story became known in Boston, and public indignation rose up like a giant in wrath. Then good white men showed themselves on the moral scene of action.

Dr. Samuel G. Howe, the famous teacher of the blind, called a meeting in Faneuil Hall to protest against the outrage, the injury to Joe and the defiance of law in the Commonwealth. It was the custom for Boston people to meet in the old Faneuil Hall to express approval or disapproval of great public events.

John Quincy Adams was asked to preside at the meeting. He was then nearly eighty years old, and indeed he died not very long afterwards. He had been President of the United States, and later during many successive years, a member of Congress. It was he who, in a time of unsettled law and custom, had secured for all Americans, white or black, bond or free, the right to send petitions to Congress. It was he, also, who had announced the famous legal opinion, that, should a war occur, the President of the United States or any Commanding General in the field might abolish slavery, in any part of the country under his immediate control.

When the audience assembled in Faneuil Hall, to protest against the kidnapping of Joe, a tremendous sensation went through it, as old John Quincy Adams was seen walking up to his appointed place on the platform.

He told the crowd that, once Elbridge Gerry, a signer of the Declaration of Independence, had been asked to attend a meeting, which had been called to protest because British sailors had forcibly taken a seaman from an American frigate. Gerry had said then, that if he had only one more day to live on earth, he would use it to go to the meeting; and, after repeating what the signer had said of himself, Adams added, "On that same principle I now appear before you."

Charles Sumner, who was to be the greatest and most persistent advocate of Negro rights, in the United States Senate, made a speech, and said of Joe, "That poor unfortunate, . . . when he touched the soil of Massachusetts, was as much entitled to the protection of its laws" (turning towards Adams), "as much as you, Mr. President, covered with honors as you are."

Wendell Phillips declared that the social and religious institutions of the country were morally feeble. Had they, he said, been strong, such a thing as the kidnapping of a defenceless man could never have occurred.

Dr. Howe told Joe's story in detail, while the audience shouted and groaned in sympathetic response. He described, imaginatively, how the young fugitive must have felt, how he had hoped and had believed that in Massachusetts he would be safe—he would be free—if he could only get there. And the fear . . . the horror . . . the desperate effort . . . and he got to Boston! . . . And then—the capture, the agony, and the utter loss of every earthly hope!

Of the owners of the *Ottoman*, Dr. Howe said, "I would rather be in the place of the victim, than in theirs; aye! through the rest of my life, I would rather be a driven slave on a Louisiana plantation than roll in their wealth, and bear the burden of their guilt."

Dr. Howe had, before this day, served in Greece on behalf of her freedom. He had been in a European prison, because he was known to be in favor of liberty. And, in Paris, he had once become a volunteer guard to Lafayette, when the life of that hero of two continents was in peril.

Every man who spoke at this meeting in Faneuil Hall either had already done or was yet to do signal work for American Negroes. All of them were in deadly earnest.

They could not rescue poor Joe from the awful doom to which he had been consigned. But, to quote from Frank B. Sanborn's account: "The upshot of the meeting was the appointment of a Vigilance Committee of forty members, of which Dr. Howe was chairman. This Vigilance Committee looked after the welfare of fugitive slaves and 'in various forms continued to exist' and to work in Massachusetts, until its watchful service was no longer needed, because slavery had been abolished. For several years it kept a yacht in Boston Harbor, ready to sail at a moment's notice, and in some way or other rescue and save from return to the South any other stowaway fugitive who got as far towards freedom as into the harbor."

OLIVE PLAATJE

Sarah Talbert Keelan

It is a far throw from New York to South Africa. A sad bereavement suffered by a well known native family in that far off country has reduced the circulation of *The Brownies' Book* by one interested little subscriber, from Kimberly, South Africa—the diamond city of the world.

Olive Schreiner Plaatje, more intimately known as "Ngoetsi," died on the fourteenth of July, in Bloemfontein, South Africa, at the age of sixteen.

Ngoetsi did her life work at the age of thirteen, during the Fall of 1918—which, by the way, is the South African Spring—when the influenza epidemic swept over Kimberley, and killed in one month, 6,000 people, out of a population of about 30,000. October, 1918, has since been known as the "Black October." All the shops, churches, schools, theatres and market places were closed up and deserted. Drug stores alone were packed with customers, day and night. Nearly all the doctors were ill in bed, and pharmacists had to depend upon one general prescription for all sufferers. Throughout October, when the epidemic raged, the city looked like a huge hospital, for, according to official reports, all but five percent of the entire population of the city of Kimberley had the disease.

Only two Kimberley streets, I learn, were alive with traffic—the road from the City Hall to the hospital, and from the hospital to the cemetery.

The Plaatje household was among those stricken with the "flu" with the exception of Ngoetsi and her father, Mr. Solomon Plaatje, the Brotherhood lecturer, who is well known to many of us Americans. He himself at the time was looking after many of the other sufferers, often leaving his sick family alone with Olive, who, single-handed, was kept busy nursing a household of helpless patients, from her mother and cousins down—to be accurate, eight in all.

Nearly every house in the neighborhood had its funerals, but little Olive, like Mrs. Van Rooyen, over the road, saved every one of her patients.

Three months after the epidemic had passed away, when shops, schools, diamond mines and everything had reopened, and the people were glad it was all over, Olive was seized with an attack of rheumatic fever, which the doctors said was the after-effect of her nursing. She had to give up school and her piano lessons, and on the doctor's advice, her parents sent her to the Hot Springs of Aliwal, North Cape. Upon her arrival there, Olive was not allowed to use the waters, because her skin was not white. However, she eventually got better and resumed her studies at the Wesleyan Methodist High School for colored girls in Natal.

It was there that the rheumatic affection went through little Olive's heart and leakage developed. The teachers sent her home, but she got no further than Bloemfontein, where she died, about one hundred miles from home. Her mother hastened to her side; but her father, being in far off America, did not hear of the end until six weeks afterwards.

It is painful to learn that Ngoetsi most probably would have reached her mother's house but for the shocking "Jim Crow" system, which in British South Africa is even more rigorous than in the United States. It is charged that the sickness was aggravated by the harsh treatment accorded her by the white train men of the South African railways. At a railroad junction, where she waited hours for the Kimberley connection, her escort was not allowed to rest the sick girl in the waiting room or on the platform seats, which are at the disposal of white passengers only. The patient had to wait outside of the depot, without shelter or comfort of any kind.

It will thus be seen that while Brownies are a "problem" everywhere, in their own homeland—Africa—their troubles start rather early in life.

While we are enjoying the benefits of instruction in high schools, conservatories and colleges in New York, Massachusetts, etc., we should remember that in South Africa there are no public schools for colored children. The natives can only get elementary training in the rural and village mission schools. Native children who take advantage of these have to pay their "tickeys" and "tanners" (English nickels and dimes), every week in the primary section, while the fourth and fifth grade pupils pay a quarter or more every Monday morning. In addition to these weekly school fees, the African Brownies have to buy their own books, pencils and slates, which in the South African public schools are supplied to white children free of cost. Therefore, we should appreciate the sacrifices made by Mrs. Plaatje and other African mothers to supply their children with training and strive to make the best use of our superior privileges.

Yet with all these difficulties, our late little Brownie friend had advantages which few of us on this side of the Atlantic will ever be privileged to have. Coming probably from the most polyglot family, of a polyglot country, Olive could write and converse in Sechuana, her father's language, as well as Sixosa, her mother tongue. Her parents, being of two different tribes, have separate languages. Besides these, Ngoetsi could read and write English and Dutch.

Her uncle is chief translater in native languages for the Union Government. One of her cousins is interpreter to the South African Native Affairs Commission; another was until lately examiner for the Cape Education (Graduating) Department. To hold any of these posts, one has to be proficient in at least six different languages, and have a working knowledge of a few more dialects. One girl cousin is in training as a nurse at the Scottish Missionary Hospital, of Lovedale—the Hampton of South Africa.

The late Brownie was named after Olive Schreiner, a great South African authoress; "Ngoetsi" is after a native chieftainess in Africa.

I first met Olive's father at London, England, during October of last year. This summer I went to spend my vacation with my friends, Mr. and Mrs. Burton of Ridgefield Park, N.J. Knowing that Mr. Plaatje was in New York, we invited him to spend a day with us, and on calling him over the telephone, to make the engagement, I learned of his sad bereavement, and of how

Mrs. Plaatje faced the sorrow of laying to rest away from home, the dear little girl who, three years before, had saved her own mother from the "flu."

I feel certain that readers of *The Brownies' Book* will sympathise with Mr. and Mrs. Plaatje, and especially with Violet "Teto" Plaatje, the surviving subscriber to *The Brownies' Book*, for by the death of Olive, a promising young career has been brought to an end; family hopes have been dashed to pieces, and the Kimberley Women's Sisterhood has been deprived of one of their most useful junior members. Peace be to her ashes!

AMERICA'S FIRST MARTYR-PATRIOT

A TRUE STORY

Almost every land boasts of some man who has particularly distinguished himself in the service of his country. Sweden has its Gustavus Adolphus, Italy its Garibaldi, Poland its Kosciusko and America its Crispus Attucks.

Long ago when these United States were still a part of the British Empire and were known as "colonial possessions," a revolt broke out on the part of the colonists against the mother country. English soldiers who were guarding the province of New England—as it was then known—conducted themselves with such arrogance and swagger that finally the "colonials" could stand it no longer. So one never-to-be-forgotten day, the 5th of March, 1770, a small band of citizens made an attack on some British soldiers who were marching through State Street, Boston, and the affray which has come down to us under the name of the "Boston Massacre" took place.

The leader of this band was Crispus Attucks. He was a tall, splendidly-built fellow, and must have been very impressive as he rushed with his handful of men pell-mell into the armed opposition. He knew only too well how precious a thing is freedom and how no sacrifice is too much for its purchase. For Attucks had been a slave and perhaps still was at this date, though a runaway one. Of this we cannot be sure, for history goes blank at this point, but in any event twenty years earlier in 1750 this advertisement had occurred in *The Boston Gazette* or *Weekly Journal:*

"Ran away from his master, William Brown of Framingham, on the 30th of September last, a Molatto Fellow, about 27 Years of Age, named

The Crispus Attucks Monument, Boston, Mass.

Crispas, 6 Feet 2 Inches high, short curl'd Hair, his Knees nearer together than common; had on a light colour'd Bear-skin Coat, plain brown Fustain Jacket, or brown all-Wool one, new Buck-skin Breeches, blue Yarn Stockings, and a checked woolen Shirt.

"Whoever shall take up said Run-away, and convey him to his above-said Master, shall have ten Pounds, old Tenor Reward, and all necessary Charges paid. And all Masters of Vessels and others, are hereby cautioned against concealing or carrying off said Servant on Penalty of the Law. Boston, October 2, 1750."

What had Attucks done in those twenty long years? Certainly whatever else his interests he must have spent some time dwelling on the relationship existing between England and the American colonies. Perhaps he was imaginative enough to feel that if England were so despotic in her treatment now of her colonies, she would be a worse task-mistress than ever as the years rolled by and her authority became more secure. If he had spent his time near Boston, which seems likely, he may have heard the eloquent and fearless assertions of James Otis on the rights of the colonists.

That he was deeply interested in political affairs is shown by this letter which he wrote long before the date of the Boston Massacre to Thomas Hutchinson, Governor of the Province:

> Sir:
>
> You will hear from us with astonishment. You ought to hear from us with horror. You are chargeable before God and man, with our blood. The soldiers were but passive instruments, mere machines; neither moral nor voluntary agents in our destruction, more than the leaden pellets with which we were wounded. You were a free agent. You acted, coolly, deliberately, with all that premeditated malice, not against us in particular, but against the people in general, which, in the sight of the law, is an ingredient in the composition of murder. You will hear further from us hereafter.
>
> Crispus Attucks

Whatever his preparation he was ready on that fateful fifth of March to offer himself up to the holy cause of liberty. At the head of his little host he flung himself on the soldiers of the oppressors shouting: "The way to get rid of these soldiers is to attack the main-guard; strike at the root; this is the nest!"

We are used to terrible descriptions of warfare on a huge plane in these days, but the scene that followed in that quiet street still brings a thrill of horror. For the enraged British soldiers answered the blows and missiles of the American patriots with a deadly shower of bullets. Down fell Crispus Attucks mortally wounded, the first American to die for his Fatherland. And with him fell Samuel Gray and Jonas Caldwell. Afterwards Patrick Carr and Samuel Maverick died also as a result of their wounds received in the fray.

The cost of patriotism had come high.

All down the street, doors and windows flew open. The alarm bells rang and people rushed to the scene from all directions. The bodies of Attucks and Caldwell were carried to Faneuil Hall and laid in state. The other dead and dying were carried to their homes and buried thence. But Attucks and Caldwell, being strangers in the city, were buried from the hall where they had lain. A long procession attended them as a token of respect and appreciation. These two and Gray and Maverick were buried in the same grave and over them was reared a stone on which the inscription read:

"Long as in Freedom's cause the wise contend,
Dear to your country shall your fame extend;
While to the world the lettered stone shall tell
Where Caldwell, Attucks, Gray and Maverick fell."

Many years later Boston showed afresh her appreciation of Attucks in the shape of a new monument which she raised to his memory on Boston Common.

What patriot of any time has done a nobler deed than that of Attucks? *Dulce et decorum est pro patria mori*, says the Roman proverb. "It is a sweet and fitting thing to die for one's country." That is true and many have done it.

But to die as Attucks did for a country which while seeking its own freedom, yet denied his—such an act calls for the highest type of patriotism. I like to think that as his courage was high, so was his faith so abounding that he needs must have believed that America one day would come to realize and put into practice what one of her great statesmen said one famous fourth of July:

"All men are born free and equal."

THE JURY

The Brownies' Book has just come and I'm sitting down to tell you about it. I like the second one better than the first—the drawings of the insects in the story about fairyland are so funny.

If I should write a good piece, would you put it in? I am twelve years old, but most folks think I am younger because I am so short. But you don't have to be tall to write, do you? My mother says I've been scribbling ever since I was very tiny. I'm going to send you one of my pieces.

Elizabeth Harris, *Atlanta, Ga.*

I am a constant reader of *The Crisis* and it takes me from six o'clock until nine to read it from cover to cover, and then there remains an endless year of waiting for the next number. Sometimes I just wish *The Crisis* had a thousand pages; it is really a book that never tires one. I read something in *The Crisis* about a mother sitting alone in despair, thinking about her children long ago lost to her. And it reminds me of another mother, our mother country, Africa, and it was that thought which forced me to write the enclosed poem, "Africa."

I will tell you just a little about myself. I live in a stuffy little town, where things go on year after year the same. I was not born here. The place is too small, it's killing me; my soul calls for larger things, so I appeal to you. I have been called odd—in fact, I know that I am odd and I don't like to do things like other people, that's why I am sending my work on plain paper, and if you don't publish it, burn it up. . . .

I hope I haven't bored you. I hope you will excuse this horrid letter and all the errors.

Pearl Staple, *Charlottesville, Va.*

P.S. I am only fifteen years old, so please have a little pity.

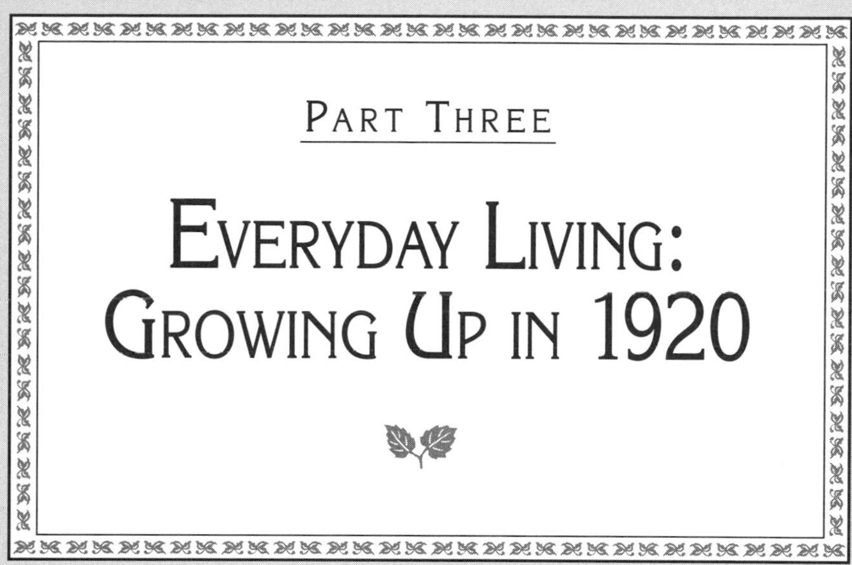

Part Three

Everyday Living: Growing Up in 1920

This section is all about what it was like to be a boy or girl in 1920 and 1921, a boy or girl like the ones who read The Brownies' Book. You will learn what their lives were like by reading some of the stories that they read, written both by the readers themselves and by professional writers like Jessie Fauset. Some of the letters that children wrote to the magazine talk about their dreams for the future. Other pieces talk about the things they do every day—play, go to school, celebrate holidays, visit their grandparents, and learn their manners. You will notice sometimes that some of these ideas—like what are good manners—are different from the ideas that you and your friends have today. On a deeper level, you might be surprised when you read "St. Patrick's Day" that slavery was, during one period of time, a fact of everyday life in Ireland. Perhaps when you have children and grandchildren, their ideas and codes of behavior will be different from yours. The column called "The Jury" is where the different generations discussed the ways in which they lived together no matter what their ideas.

Some of the stories included here should make us think about how people from various segments of a society live together—people whose lives are sometimes very different. For example, some people are rich, some people have just enough to buy the things they need, and some people are poor. We should not judge others on the basis of how much money they have. In the story called "How Johnny Got to Boarding School," the character named Joe is described as "an evil-minded little urchin from one of the poorer sections of town." But the fact that Joe is poor has nothing to do with his being a mischievous boy, as the writer suggests in this description.

In one story the writer uses the phrase "Indian-giving." Unfortunately, this is a phrase that you may hear even now. It means wanting something back after you've given it away—which is what white Americans have accused Native American Indians of doing. In fact, some untrustworthy white people, and the American government, tricked Native Americans out of their land, stole the land from them, or forced them off it. When we say "Indian-giver" we are suggesting something based on lies and disrespect for Native Americans. And as you read this section, remember that the things we say and do every day, often without thinking, are very serious. Most of the time, The Brownies' Book encouraged young people to think more about their words, thoughts, and actions.

You will notice that in some of these stories, the characters speak differently from how we talk today. Sometimes their speech sounds formal. Sometimes it is in what is called dialect, a particular version of a standard language that has unique pronunciations and rules of grammar. Sometimes the way the language looks on the page is not at all how it sounds. Language is very complicated. And variation within one language is natural, because language changes as time passes. We spell words in new ways sometimes, pronounce them in new ways, and sometimes stop using them completely and invent new ones. So have fun with the language. You might even want to read some of the stories and poems out loud and experience them that way. After you've read them all, the lives of the readers of The Brownies' Book might seem more real to you.

THE JUDGE

"I wish," says Billy looking disconsolately at a long line of fractions, "that a fairy would come along and give me three wishes."

"What would you do with them?" Wilhelmina wants to know.

"I'd wish first, that children didn't have to go to school, and second, that children didn't have to go to school, and third, that children didn't have to go—"

"My goodness!" William interrupts, "you'd certainly mean to get your wish."

"As a matter of fact, some children don't have to go to school," says the Judge, "but if they haven't a certain amount of training and knowledge when they get to be men and women, they're mighty sorry for it just the same."

"Well how can they get the training if they don't go to school?" asks William.

Wilhelmina looks thoughtful. "There must be some way though. Don't you remember Maude and Jimmie Keating? They'd never been in a school in their lives, until they came here. And they were smart, they knew all sorts of things. I never saw anybody know so much geography and history as Maude—all about such funny places, too, South America, and—and Guadaloupe—or something."

"Well she ought to," William reminds her, "she'd lived in those places for a long time. Don't *you* know a lot about this town? You've lived here forever."

"You see," says the Judge, "all education is for, is to produce knowledge. Your friend Maude, although she had never been to school, happens to be the child of parents who for one reason or another have travelled a great deal and have done it in all sorts of odd places—that is odd to our notion. Consequently, Maude knows about those foreign countries and that means geography to you. She also may have learned just what combination of former events has made those people decide to live according to certain laws and to adopt certain customs—and that is your idea of history."

"Oh," says Billy in surprise, "is that the way history and geography are made? I never thought they had anything to do with people that you know about."

"Of course that's the way. Some child in France is reading about New York State this minute and thinking how wise he is because he has collected facts which are part of your every day life. But to go back to the business of getting an education. All children can't get their training like the Keating boy and girl by visiting new people and places, so that is the reason why they must learn them from books, which are short cuts to the knowledge gained by actual experience. If Billy were a clerk in a grocery now, he'd learn all about fractions in a short while, because he'd be selling people a fraction of a pound, or of a peck, or of a quart of something, and would be making change for a fraction of a dollar."

"And because he isn't in a position like that," says Wilhelmina with sudden understanding, "he has to learn how to do it in school out of a book—"

"So that if he should ever be in such a position he'd know how to act. Precisely," nods the Judge. "We go to school to fit ourselves as far as we may for all the possibilities of life. Learning things by actual experience is often pleasanter, but it takes a great deal more time."

"Books *are* wonderful things," says William almost reverently. "Why we'd never get anywhere without them, would we?"

"They are probably the greatest *single* blessing in the world," the Judge tells him. "If we didn't have them, and schools, and teachers, it would take a whole lifetime to learn geography, and another one to learn history, and still another to understand arithmetic—"

"Just the same," pipes Billikins, who has been an attentive listener, "I'd like to learn how to do sums in a candy shop."

"Don't think I'se skeered o' you, Jim Dukes."

AFTER SCHOOL

Jessie Fauset

At nine o'clock I always say,
"I wish there'd be no school today."
And while the rest are at their books,
I give the teacher horrid looks—
And think, "The minute school is over,
I'll race and romp with Ted Moore's Rover."
No matter what the teacher's saying,
My mind is off somewhere else playing.
But don't you know when Home-time comes,
I think, "I'll stay and work my sums.
I'll do 'four times four' on the board,
Or write how much wood makes a cord."

And Billy Hughes is just like me,
He stays back just as regularly!
He's always hunting out strange places
Upon the globe, and then he traces
A map with towns and states and mountains,
And public parks with trees and fountains!
And this is what's so queer to me—
Bill just *can't get* geography
In school-time, and I'm awful dumb,
I cannot do one single sum.
But just let that old teacher go—
There's nothing Bill and me don't know!

THE JUDGE

OF PAIN, THE DEVIL

I am afraid Wilhelmina is sulking. She has not been allowed to go to the basketball game. It would have been much more satisfactory in certain ways to have been whipped, but she was not whipped. Father simply said, "No!" He said it with that absence of a smile and click of his lips, which was notice to Wilhelmina that the subject was not to be further discussed.

Now, says Wilhelmina, to herself—"What earthly reason is there for acting in that way?"

The real reason, of course, Father did not state. Possibly he was wrong there. Possibly he should have sat down and taken fifteen or twenty minutes and explained to Wilhelmina. But the difficulty was, she would not have understood his explanation.

And that explanation was something like this: The basketball game was a public game. Everybody who wanted to, could go there. The teams that were to play were composed of young fellows—good-hearted, but poorly disciplined, who had been brought up without whippings and admonitions, etc. The result had been that these basketball games were places where rude and undesirable people were thrown in the company of good folk, and where the teams instead of playing basketball, spent their time in quarreling and even in fighting. Now out of a circumstance like that, could come the most unpleasant consequences. This world has long been unfair to women and girls. It is doing a little better now, but it is not yet doing well. One of the worst things that could happen, is for a half-grown girl to be found, quite innocently, in some assembly of this kind, and then be blamed for the actions of other people—if a fight takes place, or if the police have to arrest folks, or something of that sort. Often, explanations and excuses do not avail, and people have to suffer from this wholesale injustice—but this is the kind of Devil which we have to meet in life. It is an unpleasant thing, and a thing that must be driven out; but until it is driven out, Mothers and Fathers have to guard their young daughters, and sometimes to say simply, "No," without much explanation—when the "No" seems to Wilhelmina unusually hard and unfeeling.

Thomas at breakfast

FOOD FOR "LAZY BETTY"

Children in Philadelphia used to play a game called "Lazy Betty," in which the mother asked plaintively, "Lazy Betty, will you get up today?" Betty, who seems to have deserved her description, used to answer her mother's question with another—

"What will you give me for breakfast, breakfast, breakfast?

What will you give me for breakfast if I get up today?"

Her mother's answer was none too satisfying, for it consisted merely of "a cup of tea and a piece of bread," a repast which is not very attractive. The dinner which the mother promised to Betty's inquiries about that, was even worse, for it was to be,

"A roasted cat
And a piece of fat!"

Imagine Betty's gesture of disgust and refusal!

The promise of "a nice young man with rosy cheeks" for supper, usually brought Betty to her feet. But even that was hardly the right nourishment for a lazy Betty of such tender years. On the whole, I'm inclined to suspect that the reason Betty was so lazy was because she never at any of her three meals had the right kind of food set before her.

Betty would fare better in these days, for wise mothers offer their sons and daughters more sensible food. Most mothers and all teachers know that if Betty seems lazy or Jerry is delicate, or Thomas sits around at recess looking "droopy," it is because these children have not really had enough to eat. Of course, they think they have, and so do their mothers until they stop to think; but presently Betty's mother comes to realize that not quantity, but quality of food is the thing to be considered. A child may eat three large meals a day and yet be as unnourished as the poor youngster who barely receives one.

Betty's dinner

The danger in lack of nourishment for the child lies in the fact that, not so much that he remains a sickly and nervous youngster, but that he produces the listless, inefficient grown-up. Many an adult who is without power of endurance owes it to the fact that in childhood he was really undernourished.

Parents cannot begin too early to select a diet which will strengthen and foster children. Of all food for little folks, milk is the perfect one, because it contains all the elements which the body needs for growth—carbohydrates, to give the body energy; minerals, such as iron, to make "red" blood; and calcium, to make the little bones grow strong and straight; water, to purify the body; fats, to keep it warm, and proteids, to furnish tissue and muscle.

For children, iron and calcium are always required. Iron is to be found in the yolk of eggs, in meat, and in green vegetables. When milk and eggs are scarce, fresh green vegetables afford an excellent substitute. There is never any excuse for lack of this element, for it is to be found in the commonest of green growing things—lettuce, spinach, dandelion greens. And how lovely to eat flowers!

Fruit should be eaten every day—fresh fruit if possible, but if that cannot be had, dried fruit does very well. And a child should eat plenty of bread; the gluten or starch in it belongs to the group of carbohydrates which form one of the chief elements needed to nourish the body.

Wholewheat bread and graham bread are fine for Betty, Thomas, and Jerry, because by preventing constipation, they aid greatly in assisting the process of digestion. Fruit and vegetables lend the same sort of assistance. If it is not easy to provide these two last, coarse bread should be used now and then. But more attractive and more palatable than such bread is the mush made from various cereals. Oatmeal mush is good and so is that made from cracked wheat, but best of all is corn-meal mush. And what can be nicer than coming from school or from skating in the cold winter twilight and sitting down to a steaming plate of corn-meal mush, all gold and glowing, with an island of snowy milk in the middle and silver grains of sugar glittering here and there! You take your spoon and begin at the outside edge, where it has cooled off a little, and soon, "Oh, mother, PLEASE may I have some more!"

Pleasant dreams follow Jerry's supper.

Betty and her brothers do not begin to need all the sweets they beg for and often get. Of course, children do need sugar, for it is a carbohydrate; but the best way to serve sweets is for a dessert. Plain cup-cake is good and cookies, cut in shapes like Betty and Jerry, with currants for eyes. And goodness gracious! Who ever tasted anything better than plain bread spread with butter and brown sugar? Not to mention raisin bread, just the least bit sweet, with butter. Thomas always imagines himself little Jack Horner when he eats this, and puts "in his thumb And pulls out a plum!"

The United States Department of Agriculture has sent out pictures of Betty, Thomas, and Jerry, each eating a meal. Thomas, who is feeling anything but "droopy" today, is enjoying a breakfast of milk, stewed fruit, toast and butter, and oatmeal mush. Betty is having a dinner of baked potatoes, milk gravy, made with bacon or salt pork fat, greens, bread and butter, with sugar on the final slice.

See Jerry at supper. It is simple, but good, and there is plenty of it. He has bread and milk and plain cookies. And he likes it so much that, like Tommy Tucker, he falls to singing, only he does it *after* supper.

All these children are healthy and happy. Look at Betty now. She no longer seems "lazy," does she? She has had the *nicest* breakfast and a "scrumptious dinner." And—

"I eat only bread and milk for supper now," she says confidentially, as the red blood shows up under the brown of her pretty skin. "I'm sure I like it ever so much better than I shall ever like—

'A nice young man
With rosy cheeks.'"

The Adoption of Ophelia

Willie Mae King

One crisp, frosty morning, Mrs. Fannie Graham, matron of the Colored Vine Street Orphanage, mechanically placed her glasses and settled herself in the chair before her desk to look over the morning's mail which had been brought by the postman.

Mrs. Graham was a tall matronly woman of forty-two years. Her dark brown hair, showing here and there a silver strand, was usually combed low over her brown forehead. Her well poised head, firmly set chin and mouth revealed her disciplinary ability. To the children of the orphanage she was simply "mother" not only in name, but in maternal care and devotion.

First, three business letters claimed her attention, then a letter from her sister in California, next her dark brown eyes searched out a narrow light-blue envelope addressed in a small, neat, vertical hand. On opening it the letter read as follows:

October 24, 1919.
DEAR MRS. GRAHAM:

I read in our local paper that a home was wanted for the little orphan Ophelia. We should be very glad to get her and also educate her to the highest. The only thing lacking around this home of ours is a darling sweet baby and I think Ophelia would be satisfied with her new home for we would do everything to make her a happy, healthy baby. We have a six room house and a seven passenger car awaiting her arrival. We both are Christians and belong to the Catholic church. Trusting that we may be thus favored, we are

Sincerely,
MR. AND MRS. B. H. JOHNSON.

Mrs. Graham, half smiling, folded the letter into the envelope and yet a slight shadow seemed to flit over her sunny face. Of course she was glad that the little orphan had been offered such a home and yet her mother-love made her unwilling to part with this lovable brown baby. From the first day the matron had brought Ophelia to the orphanage she had been loved and adored by many other little orphans much older than she. Mrs. Graham stepped to the telephone and called up Mr. G. R. Foster, Superintendent of the Child Placing Agency of the same city.

As Mrs. Graham passed from her office into the hall, her attention was directed to Ward Number One where the cooing baby lay in its bed playing in baby fashion. Ophelia was a plump, brown baby with a tiny brown nose between two sparkling black eyes. The fine silky black hair twisted itself into soft little curls. She was a good-natured, winsome baby and everybody loved her at first sight. In the evening mail Mrs. Graham had received almost a half-dozen letters asking for the adoption of Ophelia.

That same evening after supper was over at the orphanage, Mr. Foster rang the door bell and was ushered into the parlor by Mrs. Graham. They discussed the different homes offered in the many letters and after much deliberation they decided upon the home of Mr. and Mrs. B. H. Johnson who lived only two and a half miles from the city.

Superintendent Foster visited the home next day and arrangements were now completed for the little orphan's adoption. That Sunday afternoon a handsome seven passenger Cadillac suddenly stopped in front of the Vine Street orphanage. A smartly dressed colored man and woman were the only occupants. When the car stopped the woman quickly stepped out and almost ran up the stone steps. Mrs. Johnson was very anxious to get a glimpse of the darling baby which she was to mother. She was shown into the parlor by one of the older girls of the orphanage. In a few minutes Mrs. Graham, her face beaming with a motherly smile, entered the door with a light blue bundle. When Mrs. Johnson stepped forward and looked down upon the plump brown face nestled among the warm blankets, the shining black eyes, which seemed to hunger for mother-love, and the small rose-bud mouth, she gave forth an exclamation of delight and couldn't resist the temptation to kiss the dimpled brown hands.

"A lovable brown baby"

As Mrs. Graham watched the big car swiftly disappear she breathed a prayer of thankfulness for the mother-love in this oft too cruel and harsh world. Few orphans are fortunate enough to get such a home as was Ophelia. With her sunny disposition and cunning ways she won over every bit of the love in the hearts of Mr. and Mrs. Johnson. They were prosperous, industrious colored people and well known in social activities of their city. No energy or money was spared to make Ophelia "a happy, healthy baby" and these two were more than happy as they planned together for the future education and happiness of that small bit of humanity. Under such watchful and loving care Ophelia grew (as do all children under such care) into an attractive, healthy, beautiful child.

Almost seven years had swiftly passed since Ophelia found a mother and "dad." She was a bright, happy, playful child and into her little life of sunshine no dark shadows had dared to come.

Every morning she greeted her "dad" at the door and she loved her foster-parents with such love as only the innocent can give, for she had known no other parental care or protection.

Mrs. Johnson was in the kitchen preparing supper on one of those balmy days in early spring. Ophelia was busy with her paper dolls and books in the living room. Before long she heard what she thought to be the usual footsteps on the porch. Running to the door she opened it but it was not her daddy this time. Before her stood a tall man, light in complexion, of about thirty-two years. His thick, black hair was closely cut and the well-fitted dark gray suit, black shoes and hat gave him a gentlemanly appearance. However, as he held his black hat in his hand his dark eyes seemed weary and uncertain. By this time Ophelia's mother, not having heard the usual greeting from Mr. Johnson, appeared.

"Good evening, madam," said the stranger uneasily. "Can you tell me if there is a man by the name of B. H. Johnson living anywhere in this block?"

"Well, yes, one Benjamin Johnson lives here. The only one I know of on this street. I suppose he is the one for whom you are looking? Is there any word you wish to leave for him, or your name?" inquired Mrs. Johnson.

"I would rather see him personally if possible. May I?"

"Yes, you may come in and wait. It is time he was here now."

"—with wondering eyes"

The stranger was hardly seated five minutes in the pleasant parlor before he heard a laughing child greet a devoted father at the front door. The child had attracted his attention from the first. How beautiful and attractive she was, he thought.

"Someone to see you, daddy," volunteered Ophelia as she led her father to the parlor, where sat the tall figure with troubled brown eyes. As the eyes of the two men met—emotions of love, remorse, and submission almost uncontrollable, struggled in the stranger's heart for freedom.

"Good evening, sir," said Mr. Johnson—"your name?" as he drew up a chair beside him. Mr. B. H. Johnson anticipated some business discussion and was anxious to begin.

"My—name—is Howard Johnson. Don't you know me—your only brother?" He could go no farther.

"Great Heavens!" exclaimed Ben Johnson, jumping to his feet. "Howard, we gave you up for dead twenty years ago."

As these two brothers who had been separated from youth stood with clasped hands they were too happy to speak. Mrs. Johnson kindly received her long lost brother-in-law and even little Ophelia with wondering eyes felt glad too.

After supper that night, Howard Johnson told the sad story of the prodigal son to his brother and his wife. He began with when he ran away from home a mere lad, how he went West to seek his fortune. He told of his adventures, failures and successes; how he came back from the West, met, wooed and married a pretty girl and deserted her very soon after their baby was born. He went back to seek her forgiveness, but no one knew anything of her whereabouts. He had drifted lower each day into the slums of wretchedness and despair; a minister rescued him from the gambling hells of vice and crime and showed him the way to a clean life.

Howard had now found himself. He resolved to prove himself a man in every sense of the word but a dark mist seemed to dim his star of hope. Somewhere in the world he had a little girl and a wife who needed him. Whenever he saw the sweet, smiling face of the happy little girl whom his brother had adopted he felt he must begin the search at once.

Howard dined in silence that night. After reflecting over his dark past thoughtfully, he uneasily inquired of his brother. "Ben, have you the record of this baby you adopted?"

"No, we have only her registration card bearing the name Ophelia Olive Johnson, her weight, description, date of entrance into the orphanage, and the date of her adoption. We were so glad to get her that we didn't take time to inquire into her parentage. She was such an attractive, lovable baby that everybody wanted her. As it happened her last name was Johnson, too, so we didn't have to change her name. Some race it was for this kid!"

"Her last name *was Johnson* before you adopted her?" Howard exploded.

"Y-e-s," replied Ben, astonished as he looked into the flushed face of his brother, who was pushing his chair back from the table.

"My God! *this is my child*, I know it! I feel it. She is just her mother's image all over again! He hastily drew from his pocket a small photograph of the young woman whom he had promised to protect through life. Mr. and Mrs. Johnson glanced from the little worn photo to the sweet face of little Ophelia and they too saw the resemblance of mother and child and understood.

Ben and Howard Johnson went to the Vine Street Orphanage that evening to look up Ophelia's record. Mrs. Graham again told the too often repeated story of the young deserted mother who had come to the big city to support herself and child, how she had struggled with wretchedness and poverty and finally succumbed with a prayer on her dying lips for her orphan child and the wayward father. Mrs. Graham, with sympathetic heart, listened to a solemn vow of a young father to atone for his past life of dissipation. Mrs. Johnson, the only mother Ophelia had ever known, wept as her husband Ben retold her Mrs. Graham's account of the little orphan's mother.

"I don't deserve this happiness," solemnly declared Howard, looking gratefully from his brother to his sister-in-law as they were gathered in the living-room.

Mrs. Johnson told Ophelia that evening the story of her life omitting as much of the sadness as possible.

"Will I have to be adopted all over again?" Ophelia asked, her sparkling black eyes filling with tears. To her childish mind adoption meant to leave the only home and loving parental care she had ever known.

"No, dear," lovingly replied her adopted mother. "You are my own little girl for *all* the time."

"And may I adopt my lost daddy always and forever?" she asked pleadingly.

"*Always* and *forever!*" exclaimed Howard Johnson fondly pressing his little daughter to his happy heart.

Turkey Drumsticks

Jessie Fauset

Four of Mother's school-chums and three of Father's wrote that they were coming to take Thanksgiving Dinner. And all of them, *all* of them were bringing their families!

"Who ever heard tell of such a thing?" said Mother aghast. "Why we've been asking them for years and they've never accepted before—not one—there'll be hundreds of them."

"Millions more likely," muttered Father gloomily, "some of them have lots of children. The Atwells have seven—"

"And they'll never get along with ours! Well you children will have to go over to Grandma Kingsley's this Thanksgiving. I'm not going to have those Atwell terrors putting wrong ideas into your heads. Heavens, suppose Grandma has invited company, too!"

But she hadn't, and when Mother had told her of the difficulty, she laughed right out, in that nice loud way she has and said, "Yes, indeed, I'll be only too glad to take them off your hands." So that was how we came to go to Grandma Kingsley's for Thanksgiving.

Her house is well over on the other side of town. There are seven of us (like the Atwells) and each of us likes to choose his own path, Billy always going up short side streets, while Oliver rides straight up and then across town instead of taking the car on the avenue which runs diagonally. So Grandfather to save trouble drove down in his big seven passenger and we all piled in with such shrieks of joy that we forgot to bid good-bye to poor Mother standing worried at the door, trying at the same time to wave to us and read a telegram. It was from Mrs. Atwell who wanted to know if she might bring Peter and Paul along, too.

"Heavens!" Mother was saying as we drove away, "I don't know whether those are grown-up men or canaries." They turned out to be puppies, but Mother never found that out till she had set up two extra cots in the living-room.

Such fun as we had in that auto! Billy sat up in front, occasionally pulling a lever or pushing things or signalling to passing cars—Grandfather always lets Billy do just as he pleases and so does Grandmother. None of us can see why. Grandpa says it's because Billy looks like him but how can that be, for Grandfather is tall and very wide, with funny short whiskers, trimmed perfectly square at the corners, and white hair and a seal ring. While Bill, though tall for his age I guess, is very thin, just bones, with black, thick, curling hair and with no whiskers or jewelry whatever.

"I don't know where Granddad gets this stuff of me lookin' like him," Billy tells me confidentially, "for I can't see it myself, nor don't want to. But he can believe it as long as he keeps on treating me right."

Well we got to Grandma's without any accident except that our Cordelia nearly made Grandpa lose control of the car by letting out an awful yell.

"I'm sure I felt a mouse," she screamed. "There, there it is under Becky's rug! See it move!" Sure enough something was moving under the rug which was spread loosely across Becky the Baby's lap. Jarvis snatched away the rug and there was our new grey kitten which Becky, unable to endure a night's separation from, had brought along with her.

Billy and Rosemary

That was the night before Thanksgiving and Grandmother sent us right up to bed. She isn't a bit like Mother; you'd never think they were mother and daughter—Grandma's so trusting like. So she never came up to investigate. We had the most wonderful time! The seven of us were in three communicating rooms. Billie and Oliver in the far room, Steve and Jarvis in the middle and we three girls in the big four poster in the next.

Becky went to sleep as soon as her head touched the pillow. But the rest of us had a pillow fight. Each couple did very well and then suddenly Billy, after whispering to Oliver, gave me a wink, and the two of them and Cordelia and I rushed on Steve and Jarvis and nearly smothered them. They're twins and are always bragging about "United we fear nobody!"

The pillow cases were awful next morning. "Gracious!" cried Grandma. "Don't you children ever wash your heads? I ought to speak to your Mother about it!"

"But you won't, you darling brick," said Billy boldly and reached up and kissed her. So, of course, she didn't.

Grandpa did the queerest things before dinner. He beckoned to Billy and the two of them went off and whispered and finally Billy disappeared. When he came back he looked too funny. He was wearing a pair of tight, long trousers—Billy who is only 10!—and a dark shirt of some funny stuff, and a little jacket, cut high, like the boys wear at Eton College in England. He winked at us brazenly and showed us a brand new silver dollar. We rushed on him at that, but he broke away from us and disappeared. We didn't follow because just then Grandfather said something in a low tone to Oliver and we crowded around him trying to make out what had been said. But he kept his secret.

In the midst of all the clamor Grandmother came and ushered us into the dining-room. How we failed to notice Billy's absence I don't know. Perhaps the sight of the table made us forget, for oh, how good it looked! In front of Grandfather's place was a platter bearing a young roast pig. He looked so pathetically lovely, if you understand what I mean. It must be sad to die so young! And at Grandma's place was a huge, brown turkey, already carved and yet with the pieces so well fitted together that he looked absolutely whole. And down the sides of the table were all sort of vegetables, and jellies, cranberry and quince, an oyster pie and a baked Virginia ham.

How glad we all were that Father's and Mother's company had come!

"Too many places here," said Grandfather, and hastily moved away a chair—Billy's—but we were too excited to notice. "Now then," when we had all clattered into our seats, "which will you have first, Oliver"—he is the oldest—"roast turkey or roast pig?"

"Turkey," said Oliver promptly, "and I'd like the drumstick, Grandma—both of 'em would suit me."

"Well," said Grandma gaily, "we'll start you off with one and see how you manage that. Why—where ever are this turkey's drumsticks? They *were* here; I arranged them on the plate myself just a moment ago!"

We all stared bewildered, but Stephen and Jarvis were a little glad, too, for all of us like drumsticks and they knew that Oliver and I being the two oldest would get first choice. Those two boys are so mean they'd rather a turkey should have no legs at all than see me and Oliver get them.

Then I got the surprise of my life.

"Rosemary," said Grandfather looking at me sternly, "Rosemary, are you sure you don't know where those drumsticks are?"

"Why, Grandpa," I stammered ready to burst into tears, but I held them back for I wouldn't have Cordelia see me cry for anything. "Why, Grandpa, you *know* I—"

Just then the door of the closet, which is in the dining-room, burst open and out walked—our Billy—in that same awful get-up and with the two drumsticks, one in each hand. He walked right up to Grandpa. "Sir," he said in a funny grown-up way, "I cannot have you blame this little girl; she did take the drumsticks, it is true, but she took them to give to me, because I was starving." He pointed one drumstick at me and the other at the bosom of his shirt.

Grandma sat as though turned to stone for a moment, then she blushed real red and jumped up and threw her arms about Grandpa. "Oh, Jarvis!" she kept saying over and over. "Oh, Billy!" and kissed and hugged them both.

That might seem a very strange way indeed for grandparents to act, but my Grandmother is not at all old. She is only fifteen years older than my Mother and my Mother is only nineteen years older than Oliver, and Oliver is fourteen.

But even though Grandma was young enough to act that way, we were all amazed that she should do it—all but me, that is. I was so furious at Billy's charge that I couldn't see straight.

"You mean pig!" I said to him. "You wait till we get home. I'll tell Mother. And you give me back my roller-skates right this minute. I'll never, never let you have them again!"

But Billy only smiled sweetly. "Oh, come," said Grandpa, "it's all a joke. Grandma will explain it to you. Let's get on with dinner. Look, the baby has eaten nearly all the cranberry sauce."

And so she had, at least nearly all that was near her. She was trying to feed the rest to the grey kitten which she had managed to sneak to the table, but the kitten, I am glad to say, had the sense to refuse it.

"Tell us what it's all about Grandma," urged Steve and Jarvis.

"Not till after dinner's through," urged Billy, "because I want to eat. And if I do that I can't listen to the story. You see I like to pay a lot of attention to eating."

Of course Grandma did what he asked; she certainly does spoil him. You should have seen her beam on him as she said, "That's right, dear. All that you do, do with your might." So he sat there and ate one drumstick and Jarvis and Steve the other, for neither Oliver nor I would have them after he had carried them around and wiped them against that shirt.

We had a lovely dinner and lots of fun. Billy tried to tease me about the drumsticks, but I managed to keep cool for I was sorry Cordelia had seen me as excited as I was. Grandpa and Grandma let us have everything positively that we wanted, but there wasn't one of us that wasn't glad when dinner was over and the story was about to begin.

It is very nice in Grandma Kingsley's sitting-room. It is a long room with lots of windows and a fire-place. The floor is slippery and the rugs are dark and soft. There are lots of books with red and blue and green covers, and the firelight shines on them and makes them look beautiful. It is a room to make you feel heavenly. Outside a few, slow snow-flakes were falling in a bitter wind. It seemed wonderful that only glass and bricks separated us from the grey, sharp November weather.

Grandma looked at Grandpa. "Doesn't it take you back?" she asked him.

"It was in just such weather as this," she began then, "when I was a little younger than Rosemary. I was sitting in my little bed-room in the back of my Father's house in Germantown, Philadelphia. I hadn't darned my stockings that week, and my Mother, to punish me, had sent me to my room for the afternoon to darn them. I'm afraid I was a stubborn little girl and stood looking sullenly out the window when I saw a boy crossing our backyard. Something seemed strange about him; he looked as though he were trying to avoid attention. I thought he was going to rob the hen-coop and I threw up my window noisily so as to attract his notice, thinking that would scare him away.

"Imagine my surprise then when he looked up at me and met my gaze with a straight, long stare. In another moment he had clambered up on the top of the back porch which ran across the rear wall of my room, but stopped just at my window.

"I don't know why I didn't go away or scream, for he could easily have jumped into the room. We stared at each other a while—I can see him now with his thin, keen face. 'What do you want?' I whispered.

" 'Something to eat, anything,' he told me. 'Oh, little girl, can't you get me something? I've run away.'

"My mother had sent me a tray with some bread and butter on it, a glass of milk and some stewed prunes, which I hated. I hadn't touched any of the things, I was so angry. Now I was glad I hadn't. Silently I handed the various articles to the boy. I hope I'll never see anybody as hungry as that again.

"When he had finished he told me his story. His Mother had died when he was a little fellow and he had gone to live with her sister. She had been very kind to him but her husband had always disliked him. His aunt had died, too, about a year before and he had kept on living with the uncle who had grown steadily more cruel. 'Day before yesterday he beat me with a strap with a buckle on it; my back and arms are all cut; I could hardly move when he got through with me. But that night I crept out and ran away. I'll die before I'll go back to him,' he ended fiercely.

"And then all of a sudden, without any warning, he burst out crying. It seemed to me my heart would break. I was only a little girl and there was not much I could do. He was hungry and cold and sore. I don't know why I didn't tell my mother. 'Don't cry,' I begged him, then I tiptoed to my door. No, everyone was busy down stairs. I crept into the bathroom and brought him arnica for his poor body. I went in the chest in my mother's room and got out a great fleecy blanket.

"'Take these.' I thrust the bottle and the blanket into his hands. 'Now go all the way down the yard. There's an old woodshed down there where I play in the summer time. Wrap yourself up in this and get a good sleep and just as soon as morning comes, climb up here again, and you'll find a package for you.'

"He scurried off and I sat down and darned my stockings, trying to imagine what it would mean to live with a person who hit you with a buckled strap. I had never known anything worse than being shut up in my room for a few hours and being made to eat stewed prunes. That night when everybody was asleep I stole down stairs and got a loaf of bread, a large piece of butter and a half jar of brandied peaches. I wrapped them all in my red petticoat and put them on the roof.

"Very early in the morning I heard a noise and knew that my boy had found his breakfast.

"We kept this up for five days. On the third day my Mother became suspicious. 'I can't think who has been taking my bread,' she complained. 'I've missed two loaves in three days and this morning two herrings had vanished from the ice-chest. I know it's not Rosemary, yet I don't think it can be rats. Isn't it strange?'

"My Father had looked up when Mother mentioned my name, and I'm sure I turned red. But he said nothing and neither did I.

"Things kept disappearing and my Mother became nearly frantic. After that first time I must have looked fairly innocent, and evidently my Father forgot his suspicion, for he neither looked at me or questioned me.

"The day before Thanksgiving I managed to run down into the yard and visit 'my boy,' as I had begun to call him. He did not look very well, even I could see that. Evidently the extremely varied diet I had been bringing him did not suit him. Small wonder, for sometimes his meal would consist entirely of brandied peaches and another time of salt herring. I had to take what I hoped—though always vainly—would not be missed. But what he complained of chiefly was the cold.

"'If I could only get warm once,' he chattered.

"Right then and there I hit upon a plan. If I could only contrive to stay home from church Thanksgiving morning! My Mother knew I loved it. If I could just be naughty enough! Going back to the house I plotted and after dinner I did the unpardonable thing, I set fire to the fringe of the cover on the table in the 'front room,' as we used to call the parlor. My Mother came running. She was a tall woman, very brown with red showing on her high cheekbones.

"'Rosemary! Rosemary!' she screamed. And after she had put the fire out, 'I can't think what's got into you. Now just for that you'll stay in this house by yourself tomorrow, Miss, while the rest of us go to church.'

"But I didn't stay in the house by myself. I don't suppose my Father and Mother and Miss Emmeline Grant—'Aunt Em,' we used to call her—had hardly turned the corner before I had 'my boy' in the house. I sat him down in a wooden arm-chair before the big Franklin stove in the dining-room, and brought him hot water and soap and a brush and comb.

"'Oh,' he sighed finally, 'I feel good. I could hug this stove. Your folks be gone long?'

"'For hours and hours,' I assured him.

"As a matter of fact they were gone only two. Before we dreamed of it, I heard my Father's step in the hall. 'Quick, quick!' I cried, and pushed the boy into an old wardrobe which stood in the dining-room. 'I'll let you out as soon as I can. Don't make a sound!'

"In a jiffy I had the basin and things in the kitchen, and was poring over a 'Chatterbox' before my Mother came in.

"'Gracious!' she said, 'it's hot in here! Your face is red as fire. Come now and we'll get the dinner on the table.'

"Everything had been prepared the day before and it was merely a question of warming things up and getting them to the dining-room. I trotted back and forth, my heart aching for my poor friend. I hated to eat without being able to include him.

"'I guess I'll carve the turkey out here,' mused my Mother. 'There! Do you think you can carry it in?'

"'Yessum,' I said. That was just the thing! He should eat, too, while we were. In a final panic of recklessness, I snatched up both drumsticks, rushed over to the wardrobe and thrust them in on the half-suffocated boy.

"'Here's something for you, too,' I whispered.

"We sat down at the table, my Father and Mother, Aunt Em and I.

"'No need asking you two what you want,' said my Father jovially. 'Mother, you want a drumstick and Miss Emmeline you want a wing and the gizzard.' I felt my head reel.

"'Why, hullo!' said my Father, 'hasn't this bird any legs?'

"'Of course it has,' said my Mother. 'I just fixed them on the platter a minute ago. You saw them, didn't you, Rosemary?'

"'Yessum,' I muttered.

"'Well, they're not here now,' said my Father and then looking at me sternly he asked, 'Rosemary, are you sure you know nothing about those drumsticks?'

"'Why, Father,' I stammered, wondering what on earth I should say for I had never told my parents a falsehood and I was afraid to tell the truth. 'Father, you know—'

"And just then the wardrobe opened and out walked my blessed boy. He pointed to me with one drumstick and with the other he pointed to the bosom of his wretched shirt.

"'You must not blame this little girl,' he said to my Father, speaking up like a man. 'She did take these drumsticks, it is true, but she took them to give to me because I was starving.'

"My Father stared down at him. He was a tall man, very dark, almost black, with thin fine features, and when he got excited he used to pant and spread his nostrils like a race-horse.

"'Where in the name of heaven did you come from?' he cried.

"'Oh, Father, don't scold him,' I begged. 'The man beat him and he was cold and hungry so I brought him in.'"

Grandmother stopped and looked at Grandfather who sat silent, smiling.

"What became of him?" asked Stephen.

"My Father hunted up his uncle and told him he didn't know how to treat a brave boy, and that he was going to adopt him. My Father was a caterer and he took his new charge right into the business."

"Is it a true story?" asked Jarvis, suspiciously. "What was the boy's name?"

Grandfather broke in just then. "Don't you want to see his picture? Here it is," and he held out a photograph. All of us except Billy crowded around it with an interest which changed to amazement.

"Why it's Billy!" said Oliver astounded.

"Yes," Jarvis chimed in. "How'd he get his picture taken so soon with those clothes on?"

"It *is* Billy!" said Stephen.

"No," laughed Grandpa, "it's me."

"But you've got whiskers," Cordelia said stupidly.

But it *was* he, our fine, handsome Grandfather.

"Billy looks exactly as I looked then and now you can see why your Grandmother and I are so fond of him."

"Come and look at it, Bill," urged Oliver, "it certainly does look like you."

But Billy gave a lordly wave of his hand. "Oh it's all old stuff to me," he said loftily. "I saw it and knew all about it ages ago."

It made me so provoked to think he had kept it a secret all this time, when we might have made a game of it and played it rainy afternoons in the garret.

I walked right up to Grandpa.

"Grandfather Kingsley," I said, "what's my name?"

"Why, Rosemary Forest," he replied in some surprise.

"And who is it I'm named for?"

"Your blessed Grandmother," he said, promptly.

"And whom do I look like?"

He hesitated, "Like, like—why God bless my soul—you *do* look like your Grandmother! Why you are the very image of her that Thanksgiving day, with your red cheeks and your black eyes and hair."

"Well," said I, "I should think you would stop admiring Billy just because he looks like you, and leave him to Grandma; *I* should think you'd admire the person who looks like the little girl who helped you long years ago."

"Well," said Grandfather, "I don't know but what you're right." And he took me up in his arms. I was sorry for that, for I don't like Cordelia to see me treated like a baby.

But anyway he gave me a new silver dollar.

A Musician

Most boys and girls are frightened when they get up to "speak a piece" at the Sunday School concert. But Eugene Mars Martin would not be, because he has been used to facing audiences ever since he was very tiny. When he was not quite four years old, he played on his little violin in the auditorium of Grand Central Palace, in New York. Since then he has studied at the In-

Eugene Mars Martin   Lucile Spence   Roderic Smith

stitute of Musical Art, in New York, and also under Edwin Coates for piano and Conrad C. Held for the violin. Last year he appeared in Aeolian Hall, one of the finest musical auditoriums in the country. That was his coming-out concert.

Hasn't he had an interesting life in his fifteen years? And best of all, he is the champion pitcher on the Neighborhood Baseball Team!

A Shining Example

Wouldn't it be wonderful if every child who reads *The Brownies' Book* should have a record like that of Lucile Spence? She came from South Carolina to New York City, and has lived there eight years. When she graduated from the grammar school, out of a class of 150, she received the gold medal for the highest average in general excellence. But this was only the beginning of Lucile's career. She went to the Wadleigh High School and there in her second year, as a result of a fine composition, she became a member of the "Scribes," a literary club which usually receives only third and fourth year pupils. Later she became a member of the Arista, a club whose members excel in scholarship and character, and also of a classical club, the Hellenes. Lucile wrote a number of short stories which were published in the *Owl*, the school magazine; then she wrote and helped produce the first play ever given in Wadleigh, which had a colored theme and was produced by colored students.

Throughout her whole high school life she held some class office and in her senior year was an officer of the General Organization, which governs Wadleigh. It is no wonder, then, that this girl on graduating last year received not only the John G. Wight Scholarship, for excellence in scholarship, character, and service to the school, but also the State Scholarship, which is awarded for highest standing in the Regent's examination.

Lucile is now in Hunter College, getting ready to teach little readers of *The Brownies' Book*.

A MEDALIST

Imagine going to school for thirteen years and never missing a single day! That is the record of Lucy Beatrice Miller when she graduated in 1918 from the Daytona, Fla., Normal and Industrial Institute for Negro Youth. Besides, she has been such a good girl that she helped keep the other pupils good and for this she received the O'Neil Medal in 1916. Then, because she has always stood so well in her studies and has behaved herself so nicely, she received the Bethune Medal in 1918.

How many of you will have a similar record when you graduate?

A LITTLE BUSINESS MAN

Of course, Roderic is proud of his pony. But if the pony only knew, he would be proud of Roderic. For Roderic, think of it—is only eleven years old; yet he has been selling newspapers for four years! Every week he sells fifty copies of the *New York News*, fifty of the *Amsterdam News* and twenty-five or thirty copies of the *Chicago Defender*. Sometimes he sells monthly magazines and in the summer he peddles refreshments.

He lived with his grandmother for a while and then he helped her with his earnings. Now he lives with his mother again, and this year he has bought his shoes and suit for school—for of course he goes to school—he is in Grade 6 B-1. During the month of September, this past year, he was one of nine boys whose names appeared on the Honor Roll. Every Thursday morning he is an early bird, reporting to the office of the *New York News* at *five o'clock*, where he puts inserts in the papers until eight. Then he goes home, gets his breakfast, cleans up, and gets to school on time.

Don't you think that the pony and New York City, where Roderic lives, and all of us ought to be proud of him?

The late Vivian Juanita Long

VIVIAN JUANITA LONG

This little girl, the only child of Abe M. and Amelia Long, left her parents forever August 15, 1919. She is not really dead, though—she is still living.

"In that great cloister's quiet and seclusion,
By guardian angels led."

A GIRL'S WILL

Ella T. Madden

Along the edge of a southern forest, flows a stream called the Isle of Hope River. Void of the rush and hurry of youth, slowly, silently it flows, with an air of quiet serenity and infinite calm; along the edge of the wood, past the villages of Isle of Hope and Thunderbolt, it flows, until it is lost in the waters of the Atlantic, eighteen miles away.

In one of the weatherbeaten fisherman's huts, which nestle under the branches of the great, gnarled, twisted, live oaks which grow along the river's bank, lived Helen La Rose. As the keynote of the stream's personality was repose, the most striking thing about Helen's character was its deep unrest and consuming ambition, coupled with a high-minded, lofty idea of the infinite power of the human will.

It was the week of our graduation from Beach Institute. Helen and I were walking along the water's edge, discussing our future with all the enthusiasm of sixteen. I could talk of nothing but the wonderful career I expected to have in college the next year, for my parents were "well-to-do," and I was the only child. Suddenly, in the midst of my gay chatter, I stopped and looked at Helen.

"Oh, I'm so sorry you can't go, too, Helen; what fun we would have together," I burst out sorrowfully, for pretty, ambitious, Helen La Rose was very poor. Her father had all he could do to support his wife and seven children. Helen had paid her tuition at Beach by helping Mrs. Randolph before and after school and on Saturdays.

"But I am going to college," said Helen, in her quiet voice. "I am going to college and I am going to become the greatest teacher that ever was, if I live long enough. Booker T. Washington worked his way through Hampton and Robert Dent is working his way and so did Mr. Ross. He told me so himself."

"Yes, but they were all boys," I said with emphasis.

"And I'm a girl," replied Helen, "and as smart as any boy. Dad said so. Besides," and her eyes grew large and deep and her voice tense, "I can do anything I want to, if I want to hard enough."

The next week was commencement. Helen was "val," and looked sweet and girlish in her cotton voile dress, fashioned by her own little brown, work-roughened fingers. For her eager face, lit up by the great eyes and a happy—though rather tremulous—smile, did not require a fine toilette to make it attractive.

The weeks passed and I did not see Helen again until the middle of July. We were sitting in my room and I had been showing some dresses I had bought.

"I am going to begin making my things next week," said Helen, happily. "Daddy has let me

"Helen and I were walking along the water's edge."

keep all the money I have earned this summer and I have put it all in the savings bank. Just think, I have been working only nine weeks and I've saved forty dollars. I'll make forty more between now and October and that will be enough for railroad fare and my first quarter's tuition. Mrs. Randolph is going to give me a letter of recommendation to a friend of hers in Chicago and I know I'll get work. Oh, I am so happy! And everybody is so good to me!" Helen danced around the room, hugging herself for very joy.

Early in August, Mrs. La Rose contracted malaria and died after a short illness. Mr. La Rose was heartbroken. There were six small children, ranging in age from three and a half to thirteen years. Quietly, unobtrusively, Helen took her mother's place in the household. She did not allow even her father to realize what the sacrifice of her plans meant to her. She cooked and scrubbed and washed and ironed and cared for her swiftly aging father and little brother and sisters with loving devotion. The little house was spick and span, the children happy and contented; and Mr. La Rose, grown suddenly old, became as calm and placid as the river that flowed past his door.

Four years passed and I received the degree of A.B. and soon after was appointed teacher of English in the high school. I lost no time in looking up my old school chum and telling her of my good fortune. She met me with a glad cry of welcome and rejoiced in her old, frank, exuberant way over my success. But after the first few moments of greeting, I could not help noticing the change in her appearance.

Her figure had grown thin and old-maidish; and the brown cheeks had lost their soft roundness. The eyes, that had held such a marvelous vision of achievement and such undaunted hope in the future, were as deep and dark as ever; but in their depth brooded a wistfulness and a poignant unrest that made me catch my breath, for there came to me a vague realization of the story those eyes told. Bitter must have been the battles waged between ambition and duty. Not a hint of this, however, was in her demeanor. There was not a trace of self-pity or jealousy in her manner as we talked of the past and the present and drew bright pictures of the future.

Then Mary, Helen's eighteen-year-old sister, finished high school. Mary was not studious and had no desire to go to college.

"Now," I said to myself, "Mary will take charge of the house and the younger children and Helen can have her chance. It is no more than right." But I reckoned without my host. Six months after Mary's graduation, she was engaged to be married.

The years flew by, swift as a bird on the wing, and Helen's young charges grew to young manhood and womanhood. Mr. La Rose was dead. The baby was in his senior year at Howard University. Tom was in the mail service and Rose was the happy mistress of her own home. Helen, at thirty-five, was free to live her own life. I went to see her one bright sunny morning in June and found her sitting under her favorite oak tree, her hands lying idly in her lap, her eyes looking off across the water. She greeted me with a happy smile and a humorous glance of her fine eyes.

"Elise, do you remember our old saying, 'You can do anything you want to, if you want to hard enough?' I am going to college in the autumn!"

JIM'S THEORY OF SANTA CLAUS

Pocahontas Foster

"No, there ain't no Santa Claus at all," Jim assured himself and then went to his mother's room to tell her about it.

"Well, Jim," his mother said, "some news for mother?"

"Ma, there ain't no real Santa Claus at all. I know there ain't and I don't believe in him."

"Why, Jim!" his mother gasped. "Don't you know you must not say that? Why, if Santa Claus should hear you he wouldn't even come near this house Christmas, and there you'd be without a single toy on Christmas day."

"But there ain't none," Jim assured her. "So he can't bring no toys. I know all about it. Pa just buys those toys and things from the store, 'cause I heard him say how much my wagon cost. I know, I know; you can't fool me."

"It's not a matter of fooling, but you must not talk so fast. Wait until you really know. Why—"

"But why are there so many?" Jim interrupted. "I know when I was down in Newark yesterday I saw about fifty Santa Clauses, and there's only supposed to be one. In every store and on every corner there was a different Santa Claus. Now how can that be? I know, there ain't none."

"Oh, Jim, you should never talk like that. Why you don't know what you're saying. Come here and let me tell you all about it. You don't know quite as much as you think you do."

Jim went over to his mother and settled himself in the big chair ready to listen, not because he wanted to but because he had to obey.

"Of course there is but one real Santa Claus," his mother explained, "and you see a good many more."

"Yes and—"

"Just a minute, please. Now do you think that Santa Claus himself could make toys enough for all the children in the world? And how could he, without any helpers, visit all the homes in one night? At one time there was but the one Santa Claus, the real one, and he did all the work all alone, but the world got so large and there were so many children that he had to have helpers. All these men you see are Santa Claus' helpers."

"Well, why do they dress like Santa Claus and call themselves Santa Claus? They ain't."

"Those suits are the uniforms that all of Santa Claus' helpers have to wear in order that we may know them when we see them. Do you understand?"

"Yes," said Jim slowly. He really hated to think he didn't know everything, and he had never thought about Santa Claus having helpers.

"And as for the names," his mother continued, "it's much easier for the children to remember the one name than it would be to remember all their different names."

"Well that might be true, but Santa Claus does not bring toys to all the children; he couldn't," protested Jim. "Folks just go and buy them from the stores."

"Now there's where you're wrong again. Santa Claus has a great big factory up at the North Pole where he and his helpers live. They make toys in that factory. Then he sends a sample of each toy to every factory in the country and the different factories make the toys just as Santa Claus directs. Near Christmas, Santa Claus has all the toys shipped to the different stores. You know he has to have some place to put the toys and the stores are the place for them. Then the children go to the stores, pick out what they want, then write Santa Claus so he'll know what to bring."

"But he doesn't bring what you write for," argued Jim. "He didn't bring that base-ball suit I asked for."

"Well wouldn't you expect him to use some judgment? Do you suppose if you should ask for a carving knife that he would bring it to a little boy like you? What on earth would you do with it?"

"No, but a base-ball suit, what was wrong with that?"

"You were too small and Santa Claus knew you'd soon outgrow it and a suit like that costs too much."

"There, I told you so!" Jim exclaimed. "I knew you bought those things. Uh-huh! I know all about it."

"Why of course papa has to pay for them. Did you think Santa Claus could afford to give all those toys away? How could he ever pay his helpers? What kind of a millionaire did you think he was? Why I never heard of such a thing.

"Let me tell you how it is," his mother explained. "You write Santa Claus a letter. He looks it over and decides on the things he thinks you should have. Then he asks your papa if he can pay for all those things. If papa agrees, then Santa Claus puts them on his order and sends them to you. But papa has to pay for them."

"Well, then, what good is Santa Claus, anyway?"

"If there were no Santa Claus, there'd be no toys and nobody to fill children's stockings."

Jim was so disappointed to find that he didn't know as much as he thought, that he just made believe he didn't believe in Santa Claus, although he really did, and he just shouted, "I don't believe in Santa Claus! There ain't none, and if there is he don't need to bring me no toys, 'cause papa has bought them and the store will send them."

Just then Jim heard a voice in the chimney say, "All right, Jimmy; you don't have to believe, and I won't even stop here tonight. We'll see if the store sends any toys!"

"Oh," cried Jim. "I believe, I believe! I was only fooling; I believe!"

And he shouted so loud that he scared himself. He jumped up with a start and rubbed his eyes. "Gee," he said, "I'm glad that was only a dream! I'll run downstairs and see if it's real or not."

There in the living-room was a great big Christmas tree and all the toys Jim had written for. And let me tell you, if there had ever been any doubt in Jim's mind as to whether there was a real Santa Claus or not, it was all cleared away that day.

WHY BENNIE WAS FIRED

Willie Mae King

Bennie Parker was a little colored girl eleven years old but small for her age. Perhaps my little readers will smile to hear of a girl's being named Bennie but many little girls in the South have boys' names. Bennie was the oldest of four children and besides her father was dead. She was quite an attractive child and much petted at school because of her precociousness and industrial activities but at home she was the little mother of the family.

Bennie did chores every day for Mrs. Blair, a white lady who lived on Vine Street about three blocks from where Bennie lived. She helped with the meals, washed the dishes, and swept the porches and walks every morning before school. Bennie was proud of her job for she got three dollars and a half a week. Every morning she rose at 5:30 o'clock and was at her work by 6:00. She had finished her breakfast dishes, sweeping and dusting by 7:45 and was off to school on time. She always had her lessons and seemed no less happy than her more fortunate playmates at school.

Bennie's one great pride was her small bank into which she put one-half of her weekly earnings; the other half she cheerfully gave to her widowed mother towards the general upkeep of her smaller brothers and sisters. A broad smile always revealed two pearly white rows of teeth and lit up the little brown face when Bennie thought of the fat roll of twenty-five dollars tucked away in her little iron bank. This she had saved from her weekly earnings and also she had placed in her bank the extra nickels she made by going to the store for lunch for some of her teachers. Then too Miss Howard, her teacher, often gave her extra nickels for candy, but Bennie kept them tightly tied up in her handkerchief until she got home and then she would carefully deposit the shining coins among her other precious hoard. As soon as she had saved up thirty dollars she planned to put it in the big bank downtown where it would draw interest.

It was near time for school to close and Bennie had almost thirty-five dollars now. She always finished her work earlier on Saturdays. One bright sunshiny Saturday in May she carried her sum of $35.50 to the National Bank in town and as she received a bank book with her name plainly written across the top and the amount stamped to her credit she was very happy. Several people smiled at the independent carriage of that little smiling colored girl as she left the bank.

School would close on the twenty-sixth of May and Bennie would finish from the Eighth Grade and she was the youngest in her class! The school board had offered three prizes for the winners in an oratorical contest for the colored pupils in all the grade schools of the city and there were three. The first prize was twenty-five dollars; the second, ten dollars; and the third, five dollars. Bennie wanted to try for one of the prizes and how she wished she could win the first! Then she would have almost one hundred dollars saved. Oh! if she could only win!

Bennie had never written anything herself—the speaking part wasn't so bad for she had often recited, but to write an essay seemed doubtful. Then, too, there was Evelyn Hill who could write much better than she and Helen Jones who spoke so well, too. She decided that she would not try but that night she dreamed that she won in the contest. Bennie didn't believe in dreams because none of hers ever came true but somehow the next morning on her way to work she resolved to try. The next morning she gave her name to her teacher as one of the contestants.

"I am glad you are going to try, Bennie," pleasantly remarked Miss Howard after hastily writing her name.

Bennie gave as her reply her broad, cheerful smile. She hurried to finish her work that evening and when Mrs. Blair came into the kitchen to tell Bennie she could take home the cake which was left from luncheon she found the work done and Bennie gone.

The thought foremost in her mind was the preparation of her essay. She had now only three weeks to write and memorize it. She could hardly see how she could do it but she must. She made visits to the library during her recess hours and found some material which helped her in writing the composition. Then for over a week she practiced memorizing it.

She rose earlier than the rest of the family and would go over the essay aloud in the kitchen or the woodshed. Bennie found herself running breathlessly in order to get to work on time every morning. She had practiced in the woodshed every morning now because she was afraid her loud talking in the kitchen would cause some member of the household to investigate and no one must find it out.

Friday morning Bennie stayed over fifteen minutes of her time and by the time she ran up the street to the big stone steps of the brick house it was six-thirty. She had been late nearly every day of the week. What would Mrs. Blair say? Bennie wondered if she had yet come into the kitchen as she ran up on the porch. She caught sight of Mrs. Blair's tall but stout form through the glass of the kitchen door.

Bennie quietly walked in with her usual "Good morning, Mrs. Blair." Mrs. Blair was irritated this morning because she had planned to accompany her husband in the car to town that morning and here Bennie had spoiled her arrangement by being late again.

"Bennie, you are late again. You needn't come back tomorrow, you are fired!" was Mrs. Blair's stern verdict. Her piercing blue eyes looked straight into Bennie's wide open deep brown ones. She hastily left the kitchen and the rest of the work for Bennie.

The blow to Bennie was a crushing one. She was almost late for school that morning and she felt that everybody knew she was "fired." She never had been before and she couldn't feel just right again unless she had "a job." What would her mother say? She couldn't tell why she was late. That would give her secret away. After school she slowly turned her steps homeward to tell her mother she was "fired."

"Mother, I got fired this morning," said Bennie slowly, expecting a sound scolding as she placed her school books under the table.

"'Fired'! and all on account of that little un-

"She had practiced in the woodshed every morning."

ruly tongue of yours I suspect," said her mother. "Well school is out next week and I guess another job will turn up soon," she consolingly concluded.

Bennie dared not to attempt an explanation for she was glad to escape. She was thankful for the extra days she had to put in practice and made several extra trips to the woodshed that week for wood.

Commencement quickly arrived and the contest was to be in the city auditorium at eight o'clock Wednesday night. Bennie looked very nice in her white dress, white shoes and stockings which she had earned herself. Six contestants were seated on the platform including one boy, Herbert Brown. The speakers were not to talk over fifteen minutes. Herbert brought forth storms of applause from the interested audience. Bennie was the next and last speaker and her little heart beat double quick time when the master of ceremonies called her name.

Instantly upon rising she gained poise and self control. She delivered her oration with ease, conviction and fluency. When she sat down her ears were tingling with applause, and other demonstrations of her victory were given by various animated ones in the audience. In less than twenty minutes the judges returned and announced the winner. Bennie had won the twenty-five dollars in gold!

Bennie could hardly close her eyes that night for she was so happy. She didn't mind being fired at all now because she had earned as much in one night as she would have earned in one month by being hired out.

She arose early the next morning and ran all the way to Mrs. Blair's, holding tightly to the gold coin in her little brown hand. Mrs. Blair not being able to find any domestic help had resorted to washing her breakfast dishes every morning.

"Good morning, Mrs. Blair," said Bennie in her usual cheerful way as she walked into the open kitchen door.

"Why—er—good morning," stammered Mrs. Blair, as her eyes turned upon the round dimpled brown face just full of smiles. "Did you come back to work?"

"No ma'am, I only came to show you what I got for being fired," and she held out the precious gold coin in her hand. Mrs. Blair's eyes grew larger with surprise and admiration as Bennie proudly related the incidents which led to her victory.

"Why didn't you tell me before, Bennie, that you were in a contest and needed time to practice? You may come back to work if you wish," she replied sympathetically.

"I can't come back now any way, for Miss Howard, my teacher, has promised me a delightful vacation for winning the first prize. You know I've never had a vacation and I am so anxious to find out how one feels," replied Bennie seriously yet with delightful humor.

Mrs. Blair could not but help rejoice with Bennie as she almost danced out of the kitchen door and happily hummed one of her school songs all the way home.

THE JUDGE

"I am making some New Year's resolutions," cries Billikins in triumph. "I'm gonna get up at six every morning and feed my rabbits, and I'm gonna get my arithmetic lessons and—"

"Humph!" says William.

"Well, what are *you* going to do?" asks Billie doubtfully.

"I don't believe in New Year's resolutions," says William.

"Neither do I," says Wilhelmina—"awfully silly, I think—nobody ever keeps them."

"Humph!" says the Judge.

"But *you* don't make New Year's resolutions, do you?" asks Wilhelmina in astonishment.

"Certainly," answers the Judge.

"And keep them all?" asks William.

"No," says the Judge.

"There you are!" says William. "It's just what I say. There's no use in the thing. It can't be done."

"Hitch your wagon to a star!" hums the Judge, "and if it can't be done, hitch it to a mud-turtle, or don't hitch it at all—just let it stand and rot."

"Oh no, not that," answers Wilhelmina. "Of course one ought to make good resolutions even if one doesn't carry them all out, or carry any of them out in the best way—but why make them New Year's?"

"Why not?"

"Oh well, I don't know—but then why not make them Christmas or Labor Day or Fourth of July?"

"Good!" cries the Judge, "and Hallowe'en and Easter and Douglass' birthday or—"

"Good gracious," says William, "we don't want to spend *all* the time *'resoluting'*—it ain't that amount of fun."

"So say we all of us," agrees the Judge, "and therefore let's get rid of the disagreeable duty all at once at the beginning of the year."

"Of course," says Billie, "a year is awful long and p'haps it 'ud be better to sorter divide up and make 'em twice a year."

"Well, Billie, your years will get shorter as you grow. When you're as big as William they'll not be half so long as now—"

"Whoop-ee!" cries Billie. "Christmas every six months!"

"And when you're my age—" but Billie loses interest and runs after Billikins who is trying to hammer a tack with the brand new Christmas poker. Billie could not conceive *ever* being as old as *that*.

"I suppose then," says Wilhelmina resentfully, "that you expect a whole manuscript of goody-goody promises from each of us."

"*One* would be enough—and that not 'goody-goody' either. My idea is that one good, practical promise to one's self at the beginning of a New Year is worth while."

"Even if broken," sneers William.

"Even if broken," repeats the Judge, "and particularly if kept."

"Of course, if kept; but most resolutions are broken."

"True. But some are kept and with these God creates the Heaven and the Earth, the Sea and all that in them is!"

"Don't understand," says Billie, depositing the rescued poker in the ink well.

"I mean that out of all the wishes and Hopes and Promises of each New Year, after subtracting all the Lies and Deceptions and Weakenings and Failures, the Good Spirit of the Universe has enough left to build the Good and the True and the Beautiful things of the Earth."

"Which accounts for the Earth's ugliness," says Wilhelmina.

"And also for its Beauty," says the Judge.

"I'm going to give up cigarettes until I'm 21," answers William.

"I'm going to *try* to understand algebra," says Wilhelmina, "but I make no promises."

CHARLES GETS AN ANSWER

Lucile Stokes

"Aunt Bettee," called little Charles to his pretty young aunt. "What does ap-pre-she-ate mean?"

"Appreciate? Oh, I don't know, sonny."

"But, Aunt Bettee," he cried, clutching her skirt with his little chubby fingers, "I want-a know."

"Sweetheart, I'm so awful busy now, can't you ask Uncle Bob?"

"Uncle Bob, what does ap-pre-she-ate mean?"

"Appreciate? Well, now what do you want to know that for?" And Uncle Bob tossed him up in the air.

"But, Uncle Bob, I want-a know."

"Old man, if you'll wait just a minute, we'll hunt up old Webster and find a good definition."

"What's a def-nition?" But Uncle Bob had gone.

"Grandma, what does ap-pre-she-ate mean?"

"Precious Boy, Grandma's busy. Can't you find Aunt Betty?"

"Aunt Bettee's tryin' to telephone. She won't pay no 'tention to me nohow. I'll just go ask my Mother—that's what I'll do."

"Charles! Come back this instant!" called Aunt Betty.

"But, Aunt Bettee, I want-a know what ap-pre-she-ate means."

"You're as bad as the Elephant's Child."

"What Elephant's Child?" he demanded breathlessly.

"Now I've started him again," thought Betty. "You can ask more questions than any child I ever saw." Then coaxingly, "Listen, Sugar Boy—"

"I'm no sugar boy."

"Listen, anyway, and I'll tell you what appreciate means. If someone gives you something that you like, you say you appreciate it."

"The egg I had for breakfast—I ap-pre-she-ate it."

"No—if you get a present you say you appreciate it—that is, if you do appreciate it—that is—I mean, if you like it."

"*You* say so anyway," remarked Uncle Bob.

"Explain it yourself," retorted his sister. But before Bob could open his mouth, Betty turned from the telephone in dismay. "The telephone's out of order. What in the world will we do?"

Betty's consternation seemed contagious, for in a few minutes the house was in such a confusion that Charles gave up trying to attract anyone's attention and grumbled in his teddy's ear until a new thought struck him. "Say, Aunt Bettee! What do you mean by an Elephant's Child?"

"Charles, if you don't stop asking so everlastingly many questions—"

"Never mind, Aunt Bettee. There's Dad! Dad, what do you mean by an Elephant's Child? Please tell me."

"Not now, Charles." Dad's voice was so stern that Charles looked up in injured surprise which changed to childish bewilderment, for his father's face was so haggard and Uncle Bob was so suddenly serious that he felt something dreadful must have happened. "I'll just go ask my Mother what's the matter," he said to Teddy, but Betty overheard him.

"Charles, if you don't go and play with your blocks, I'll—I don't know what I'll do," she said sharply.

Charles crept away puzzled. "I'll just go hide, Teddy. When they can't find me they'll think I'm dead and then they'll be awful sorry they hasn't any little boy." So he slipped upstairs and crept way back in under his little bed, and before he knew it he was sound asleep.

When he awoke several hours later, the house was very still and nobody seemed to be hunting for a nice little boy. Then he heard Dad's voice, "Charles ! Charles! Where are you, sonny?"

His grievance forgotten, he went clattering down the stairs. Dad was at the foot, his face beaming with joy. "Look here, Partner," he said. "We've got something for you." And a strange creature, a nurse, pulled back a blanket and he saw a tiny, wrinkled face.

"Mother, what is it?"

"It's a brother, dear. A little brother for you to play with."

Slowly he surveyed their happy faces—Mother's, Father's, Grandma's, Aunt Betty's, Uncle Bob's, and a new face—the doctor's.

"Did you bring him?" he asked solemnly. "'Cause if you did—he's a mighty little feller—but I *ap-pre-she-ate* him."

One day while hunting for my cap,
I woke my grandma from a nap.
That's one thing grandma hates—I say—
To be caught napping in the day.
The reason is—so I've been told—
It makes folks think she's getting old.
She eyed me sternly for a bit.
Then slowly she began to knit.
But soon she laid her sweater down
And for her glasses looked around.
I stood there and began to grin,
And right then trouble started in.
She sets great store by those old specs,
And when they're lost she's surely vexed.
"You needn't stand there, sir, and cough,
For I just took those glasses off;
And just now when I turned my head,
They went—and you know where," she said.
"I didn't," I began to say;
"Now hush! they didn't fly away!
You just come here and let me see."
I went and stood till she searched me.
But all the while I thought I'd burst,
And grandma said, "You are the worst!
I know, I'll go and call your Ma,
She'll soon find where those glasses are."
Right then was when I up and spoke,
'Cause mother might not see the joke.
I know I shouldn't have been so horrid,
But grandma's specs were on her forehead!

ST. VALENTINE'S DAY

All historians agree that the fourteenth of February was named after an early Christian priest of Rome who was cruelly murdered way back in the third century. The story goes that his remains still rest in the Church of St. Praxedes at Rome where a gate was named after him—*Porta Valentini* (Valentine's gate).

That is a sad memory to preserve and perhaps no one would rejoice more than poor St. Valentine that very few people connect this memory with the day which bears his name. On the other hand, very few people are able to tell just why it is that the ideas which all of us connect with the fourteenth of February should have sprung up.

It is probable that the name of the day and the customs rose from different sources. The day, as I have said above, was named to do honor to this martyred priest, but the custom of men and women exchanging love tokens was connected with certain feast days which used to occur in ancient Rome and which used to take place around the fourteenth and fifteenth of February.

On the eve of these feast days the names of Roman girls were put in a box and drawn out by chance by young Roman men. This was called a lottery and it was in this way that the custom was first transferred to England many, many centuries ago.

An old historian—Misson by name—tells how in England and Scotland lads and lassies used to gather in equal numbers on the day before St. Valentine's Day. Each one would write his name—real or pretended—on a separate slip of paper which would be rolled up and placed, the men's names by themselves in one box, and the girls' names in another. Then each girl would draw by chance or by lot a name from the men's box, and the men would draw a name from the girls' box.

Each girl would then have a man for her partner whom she called *her* valentine and each man would have a girl for partner whom he called *his* valentine. Of course since the girl would not always draw from the men's box, the name of the man who would draw hers from the girls' box, it happened that each girl and each man had two valentines. The way this problem was solved was for the man to choose the girl whose name he drew, rather than the girl by whom his name was drawn.

The girls must have liked this arrangement very much, for usually the man not only wore the name of the lady in his button-hole or on his cuff for several days, but he was supposed to give one or several parties for her and to send her gifts and various favors. Naturally these attentions often ended in love.

Usually this game was played only by single people, but at one time, especially during the reign of King Charles II, both married and single might be chosen as valentines. Then the person who was chosen was supposed to give a present to the person who chose him. This was pretty hard if you were chosen by someone whom you did not like.

There were some quaint and interesting beliefs connected with St. Valentine's Day. A great many people believed that this was the day when birds chose their mates and that the chance meeting of a single man and woman on this date was of great importance, because it meant that the two were to become sweethearts. The first unmarried man that a girl met, or the first unmarried woman that a single man met on St. Valentine's Day, was destined to become the other's husband or wife, respectively.

As far back as 1755 a girl writes in a celebrated newspaper of the times:

Last Friday was Valentine's Day and the night before I got five bay-leaves and pinned four of them to the four corners of my pillow and the fifth in the middle; and then if I dreamed of my sweetheart, Betty said we should be married before the year was out. But to make it more sure, I boiled an egg hard, and took out the yolk, and filled it with salt; and when I went to bed, ate it, shell and all, without speaking or drinking after it. We also wrote our lovers' names on bits of paper and rolled them up in clay and the first that rose up was to be our valentine. Would you think it?—Mr. Blossom was my man. I lay abed and shut my eyes all the morning, till he came to our house; for I would not have seen another man before him for all the world.

If she liked Mr. Blossom, that was a wise thing for her to do especially if she believed with Gay, the poet:

On Valentine Day . . . the first swain we see,
In spite of Fortune shall our true love be.

In olden times no comic valentines were sent, only courteous messages of affection and love. Thus no one's feelings were ever wounded and the valentine really was what it ought to be according to the Latin word from which it is taken, a message of "well-being."

Little People of the Month

Five years ago a little "Brownie" boy was needed in a moving picture with Baby Marie Osborne, known as "Little Mary Sunshine." Somehow, Frederick Ernest Morrison's father heard about it and he and little Ernie went to the movie studio. Ernie started right in to romp and play and fight to the delight of everybody, and then and there he was engaged to act in the picture—and he's been acting in the movies ever since.

Ernie is said to receive enough salary to own a fine home, several automobiles, and dogs and other pets, just like other movie stars; but for the present he and his father are investing their money in a grocery store and refreshment parlor at 5420 Long Beach Avenue, Los Angeles, Cal., where hangs the sign, "Joseph Morrison & Son. Grocers."

Every morning Ernie is up and dressed at 8 o' clock, and for four hours each day he is taught the mysteries of reading, writing and arithmetic.

Critics say that little Ernie is blessed with a rare gift—that of a natural comedian.

At a moving-picture show recently a little girl remarked, "Oh, there's that funny little colored boy again. I wonder who he is!"

Professionally Frederick Ernest Morrison is known as "Sunshine Sammy," and he co-stars with Harold Lloyd, producer of Lloyd's comedies which are produced at the Hal E. Roach studios in Culver City, near Los Angeles. Little "Sunshine Sammy" also assists Harry "Snub" Pollard, movie comedian, in his laugh producing antics that amuse men, women and children all over

Florence Louise Morrison, Harry "Snub" Pollard, "Sunshine Sammy"

Frederick Ernest Morrison

Helen Dett

the world. Did you see him as the frightened little boy in Harold Lloyd's comedy, "Haunted Spooks"? They recently finished a comedy of telephone strife, called "Number, Please."

Frederick Ernest Morrison has three little sisters and many playmates to whom he's just plain "Ernie"—always ready to romp and play and fight, just like any other seven-year-old boy.

One of Ernie's sisters, Florence Louise Morrison, also acts in the movies, and she's often seen on the stage with Ann Thompson, soprano soloist, and her company of entertainers. Florence says, "Play acting is all right for a little change now and then, but I prefer to go to school and study and learn to be a kindergarten teacher." And she's just five years old!

In Los Angeles, little Ernie is spoken of as a "race benefactor," since each day he makes thousands of people laugh and forget their troubles.

Helen Dett is the daughter of Mr. and Mrs. R. Nathaniel Dett of Hampton Institute in Virginia. Both of Helen's parents are talented musicians—her father is a pianist and composer, and her mother is a pianist. And what shall I tell you about Helen? Simply that she is a wonderful child—she plays her scales on the piano, asks her mother and father for some of the most difficult piano numbers, including *Rondo Capriccioso*, and then tries to imitate them. Indeed, she has succeeded in imitating her mother in a simple part of *Rondo Capriccioso*. And she's only 3 years old.

Helen enjoys a fairy tale immensely, and she fairly bubbles over with delight when *The Brownies' Book* comes.

JERRY'S FAVORITE

Rebecca yearns for May and June,
And Tim likes April and November,
While Alice sings the harvest moon
Of August or of gold September.
"The month I like the most," says Jerry,
"Is little sawed-off February.

"Why think of all its holidays!
Although it seems so short and fleeting,
There's room for mirthful games and plays
And valentines and birthday greeting.
You don't have long to stay in school
When February starts to rule.

"George Washington picked out a day
In February to be born in.
He chose a chilly time, I'll say.
This funny universe to be born in.
He was the Father of the Nation.
And left each boy a day's vacation.

"And Mr. Lincoln came here too
In February's short duration;
He was an honest soul and true.
A man of humble birth and station.
He was the president and martyr
Who put an end to human barter.

"Great Frederick Douglass—grand old man—
Belongs in this month's category,
He freed himself from slavery's ban
And lived to know great fame and glory.
My father says we boys should never
Cease copying his high endeavor.

"Old Valentine—the dear, kind saint.
Had his day too in February.
He left to us a custom quaint,
Which causes fun and makes us merry.
I gave Bill Higgins' little sister
A candy heart and—well I kissed her!

"But there's another reason why
I think this month deserves attention.
Since you don't know, it seems that I
Will have to give the matter mention.
The fact is I, your young friend Jerry,
First saw the light in February.

"My mother's just as proud of me!
She said she thought George Washington
And Douglass, Lincoln too—all three
Were boys no better than her son.
She hugged me then real close and hearty.
And gee! She gave me some swell party!"

THE JUDGE

"If you think," says Wilhelmina with much firmness, "that you are going to the matinee with me in that get-up you are very much mistaken."

"What's the matter?" asks William. "I'm clean, ain't I?"

"I don't know whether you are or not, but I know you are not fresh and smart looking, and I won't be seen on the street with you."

William is disgusted. "Aw, Judge, tell her a boy can't go about all dolled up like a girl; all the fellows would make fun of him and besides it's too great a nuisance."

"Well, I'm not so sure of that," says the Judge gravely, looking over the top of his newspaper. "Didn't I hear you say the other day that the reason you wouldn't take Billikins to the circus was because his blouse was soiled and you didn't have time to wait for him to change? Evidently you didn't want to be seen with him 'looking that way.'"

"Oh, but that's different. Billikins wasn't even clean. Now I'm clean—"

"You don't look it." says Wilhelmina shortly. "Your collar's got a smudge on it, and your tie is bulging—and you've got on a sweater vest—no boy can look clean with a sweater vest on, unless it's a pure white one and not that clay colored thing."

"Why you gave it to him for Christmas," Billy reminds her.

"I know I did, because I knew he'd never keep a white one clean. But I gave it to him for skating and not to—to live in. Mother makes me go about with William all the time—wish I had a brother that would ever look spick and span like Harvey Wilson."

"Dressed up like a dude!" jeers William. "You girls look too much at a fellow's appearance. Now *I* know I'm clean. I had my bath this morning and that's just a little teeny mark on my collar and this sweater keeps me warm. Here I'll tuck my tie in. But what difference does it make?

"'A Man's a man for a'that!'"

Wilhelmina chooses to be stubborn. "He may be a man but he's not the finest kind of a man. I'm sure of that. I think a really first class man will aim not only to please himself but to please others too."

"Wilhelmina's got the idea," says the Judge before William can get his thoughts together. "It is true we do dress for warmth and protection and for the sake of the conventions but we also dress—as we do many other things—to make an impression on others."

"I don't see how," says Billie.

"Well now suppose William and Harvey Wilson—they are both the same age, aren't they?—came to my office for a job. They are in the same grade at school; they bring equally good recommendations. I look them over and I say to myself, 'This boy is untidy and wrinkled; he'd probably keep my papers in an awful mess and any way he doesn't care whether I like his appearance or not. Now this other fellow is clean and smart looking. He wants me to be pleased with him, and I'm sure he'll keep things in order. Harvey,' I say out loud, 'you can have the job.'"

"I thought ability was the only thing that counted," says William.

"In the last ditch, yes; but not anywhere else and not always there. Then another thing, the boys and girls who take care of their personal appearance usually have a good deal of respect for themselves and that causes other people to have it too. I'm not talking about simply being in style, but about being clean and smart and trim."

"I see what you're driving at, sir, but if I don't mind, why should Wilhelmina worry?"

"Because neatness and trimness on the part of an individual mark his attitude toward society at large. Besides a boy can't begin too early to manifest his respect and deference for girls, from his sister on. Furthermore, you never have occasion to be ashamed of Wilhelmina's appearance."

"You bet I don't." William owns up admiringly. "All right, sis. I'll fix up right away. Everybody's got to know that I respect both my sister and myself."

Most of us know that the 17th of March is connected with St. Patrick and the shamrock, but how or why it is not so easy to tell.

St. Patrick was born many, many years ago, probably in 372. If the date of his birth is uncertain the place of it is still more so, for he has been variously claimed by Scotland, England, France and Wales. Of late he has been assigned to Scotland and people who have made a study of the few facts relating to his life say that he was born in Scotland at Kilpatrick, between Dumbarton and Glasgow.

Of course he was not a celebrity when he was born nor even when a boy. On the contrary, he was carried off into slavery by robbers or pirates when only sixteen and sold as a swineherd in the mountains of Ireland. Fortunately he was rescued by some kindly sailors who bore him off in their ship on the first of those long journeys of which he seems to have taken so many.

He was evidently a great traveller and it is commonly believed that the course of his wanderings may easily be determined since he invariably left behind him some spot or building which bears his name. Thus his own birthplace, Kilpatrick (the cell of Patrick) is supposed to have been named for him. Then he lived for a time in Dalpatrick (the district of Patrick) and later visited Crag-phadrig (the rock of Patrick) near Inverness. He founded two churches, Kirkpatrick (the church of Patrick) in Kircudbright and Dumfries. All this was in Scotland. In England he preached in Patterdale (Patrick's dale) and in Wales he founded Llan-badrig (the church of Patrick). Last of all, when he came to Ireland he landed at Innis-patrick which means Patrick's island.

In the course of his wanderings he came to Italy where he was appointed by Pope Celestine to convert the Irish to Christianity. And this marks the beginning of Patrick's career as the patron saint of Ireland.

All sorts of legends have sprung up about the saint and his wonderful powers. Of course we know that practically none of these stories can be true and that what really happened was that Patrick, evidently being a man of strong will and determination, refused to let anything daunt him and so overcame obstacles which seemed insuperable. In this way the legends, which even attribute to him the power of magic, have come into being.

No matter what their origin the stories are interesting and often amusing. Patrick seems to have possessed these strange powers even as a little child. For "they say" that once as a youngster he brought home some snow and ice and his nurse told him that he would have done much better to bring some wood for a fire. Whereupon the little boy heaped the ice and snow together, blew on them and there was a bonfire! His nurse's husband died and she was stricken with grief. So Patrick prayed over the dead man, signed him with the cross and restored him to life. It was a good thing for the nurse that she had such a charge as Patrick, for she seems to have had an unusual run of bad luck. One of her cows was possessed of an evil spirit which also had wounded five other cows. Patrick healed the cattle and drove out the evil spirit.

At another time the nurse fell ill and greatly desired some honey. As there was none handy, Patrick simply took some water and changed it into honey. There were some filthy stables to be cleaned out and, of course, nobody wanted to do it. So Patrick got on his knees and prayed, and the stables were cleaned without hands.

During the brief time he was enslaved, he was sold by one master to another for a kettle. But the man who received the kettle certainly got the worst of that bargain, for no matter how hot the fire, nothing placed in that kettle would ever become warm. Indeed the hotter the blaze the colder became the kettle. So the seller returned the kettle and took Patrick back. Thereupon the kettle behaved as all kettles should.

Patrick's strange powers stood him in good stead when he undertook to convert the Irish to Christianity. The former priests of Ireland had been the Druids and naturally enough they were greatly opposed to the introduction of a new religion which would take away their power. They were great magicians, too, but you may be sure they were no match for Patrick. He tried at first to persuade them to his way of thinking, but, when he found this would not work he was obliged to resort to his magic. He cursed their fertile fields and they became dreary bogs; he cursed their rivers and there were no more fish; he cursed their kettles and they would no longer boil. Finally—a most unchristian thing to do—he cursed the Druids themselves and the earth opened and swallowed them up!

Once on a trip to Britain he spied a leper whom the sailors would not carry in their ship. Touched by the poor creature's distress, Patrick said he, too, should go on the journey if that was his desire. So the saint took a stone altar which had been consecrated by the pope, threw it into the sea and bade the leper sit on it. When the ship set sail, the stone did too. Moreover it kept company with the ship all the voyage and got into port with her at the same time. Of course, this was very wonderful of Patrick, but *I* think that that was a brave leper. At another time a thief stole a goat from Patrick and killed and ate it. The saint accused the thief who stoutly denied knowing anything about the missing animal. Imagine his consternation then when the goat bleated from his stomach. To punish him, all his descendants were thereafter marked with the beard of a goat.

No doubt St. Patrick was a great and good man. Certainly people thought so, for after he died at a ripe old age on March 17 the anniversary of his death became a high festival in the Catholic church. In Ireland the flags fly on the steeples, bells peal until midnight, the rich bestow gifts on the poor and the poor bless the rich, each other and St. Patrick. Boys take part in wrestling games, lads and lassies dance, while women tuck their babies in the hoods of their coats and run about to each other's house to drink a glass of poteen.

And everybody wears the shamrock. The story goes that when St. Patrick landed in Ireland in 433 on his first attempt to convert the Irish, the people tried to stone him. He begged to be heard and tried to explain to them about the Trinity of the Father, the Son and the Holy Ghost. But the people could not understand how this could be. St. Patrick looked about him and picked a shamrock. "See," he cried, "is it not as possible for Father, Son and Holy Ghost to be one as for these leaves to grow upon a single stalk?"

This convinced the Irish. The shamrock had long since been used by the Druids to heal diseases, now here it was introducing a new and beneficent cause. Small wonder then that they adopted it for their national emblem. Nowadays if you should walk through an Irish village on the 17th of March you would find people wearing the little green trefoil and standing in groups singing:

Saint Patrick's the holy and tutelar man,
His beard down his bosom like Aaron's ran:
Some from Scotland, from Wales, will declare
that he came,
But I care not from whence now he's risen to
fame:—
The pride of the world and his enemies scorning.
I will drink to St. Patrick, today in the morning!

He's a desperate, big, little *Erin go bragh;*
He will pardon our follies and promise us joy,
By the mass, by the Pope, by St. Patrick, so long
As I live, I will give him a beautiful song!
No saint is so good, Ireland's country adorning;
Then hail to St. Patrick, today in the morning!

How Johnny Got to Boarding School

Claudia Davis

Johnny Blair was eleven years old and possessed the usual small boy's aversion to the feminine sex. He had absolutely no use for girls, and nursed a grievance against them all, due to a rather forceful and very humiliating boxing of his ears by one young lady to whose luxuriant pigtail he had valiantly tied a dead mouse. From the time of this episode on, he had maintained an attitude of masculine dignity and indifference to all girls in general and to Betty Clark in particular.

Wrightsville Boarding School was the seat of learning for many boys and girls up to fourteen years of age, and it was Johnny's ambition to be there with three or four of his friends who had gone. He lived in Greenville, a town about ten or twelve miles from Wrightsville, and had plenty of opportunity of hearing about its merits and opportunities. He knew the boys made raids on the pantry at night when everyone was asleep and lights were out. He also knew that many boys were sent there because they were considered unruly at home, and their parents had sent them there for the discipline. He knew too that Robert Henson had been sent home after being caught one night climbing down the fire-escape on his way to a neighboring orchard to steal green apples. Nevertheless, Johnny's fondest hopes centered around Wrightsville Boarding School, and he was determined to go there, even if he had to be so naughty at home that his parents would send him.

Johnny's other ambition was to become a public speaker. Once, on a visit to his grandmother's farm, his father had taken him to a Baptist Revival, and the impression of waving arms and thumped tables, and talking through one's nose to a chorus of "Amens" of the congregation, had made a deep impression on his mind, and he was determined to move audiences to do likewise by his eloquence. He didn't remember very much about that revival, but he did remember the long, lank man in the shabby Prince Albert coat talking and gesticulating and drinking water every now and then, while the congregation voiced its approval of his words by loud moans and shrieks and weeping. Johnny didn't know what the preacher was talking about, being too busily engaged in watching his gestures and listening to the continuous undercurrent of the voices of the congregation. However, he didn't want to be a minister; all he had ever seen seemed to be very popular with the girls; he almost hated them all. No, he wouldn't be a clergyman; a public speaker would just about fill the bill and still bring him his deserved popularity (among men).

Betty was Johnny's rival in almost everything in the school they attended. She recited very well, even to Johnny's way of thinking (and he considered himself an excellent judge)—although he wouldn't admit it. She was a bright-eyed little youngster with rosy cheeks and a long braid of curly black hair. Her seat being next to Johnny's, he took delight in worrying her by pulling this braid and tying things to it.

One day the teacher announced that on the following Friday the superintendent of the schools in that district would award a prize of $5.00 to the pupil who, in his estimation, could entertain the best. The pupils were to choose their own form of entertainment, but it was understood they would most likely be limited to recitations and singing and instrumental selections.

It occurred to Betty that if she should win the $5.00, the boys would simply *have* to respect the girls. Each girl nursed a secret desire that if she, herself, did not win the award, some other girl would, in order to pay the boys back for snubbings rendered the fairer sex on various occasions.

The boys, on the other hand, were so sure of Johnny's ability at reciting, that it never crossed their minds that there was a possibility of the girls' winning.

Naturally, on account of the friction existing between the sexes, each faction tried to keep its plans secret. Betty conceived the wonderful idea of having a "bubble dance"; she would have a pretty dress on and would dance to some pretty music which the teacher would play; and then, last of all, she would surprise them all by having real bubbles.

Betty's uncle in the neighboring city kept a toy shop and Betty had $3.50 in her bank. She would spend $.50 for balloons, fifty of them and such pretty ones they would be too, red and yellow and green and purple. Of course, her performance would be the most unique and she would undoubtedly be the winner, and everyone would be so glad the boys didn't walk away with the honors. She had it all arranged; she would have her father fill the little parti-colored bags with hydrogen and then she would have them attached to a string, and at the end of her dance, by pulling the string, she would break it, releasing the "bubbles" which would then float out into the room. She had done a "Butterfly Dance" at the gymnastic exercises the year before, and she would just repeat that dance, adding to it. The boys would be *so* surprised. Betty could just imagine herself claiming the $5.00 afterward, the audience applauding and the boys very much chagrined. She would have her little head high in the air, with her little snub nose pointing straight to Heaven, and she wouldn't notice a thing in the room with trousers on. Yes, she would show them that girls were some use after all.

Betty had a chum to whom she confided all her secrets. That afternoon during recess period, she got Jeanette, or Janey as she was called, in the closet and unfolded to her the plan. One of the boys had once tried to walk up the edge of that door, so in consequence, it was warped, leaving a crack when it was closed. At that time, Johnny, who had been playing ball in the yard, came inside to get a drink of water. While in there, he heard the two girls talking. At first he didn't pay much attention, but "Friday" came to his ears and immediately he was all attention. A little voice told him he shouldn't listen to confidential talks, but his curiosity and his dislike of girls got the better of him. He also tried to gloss over his feelings by saying he was being loyal to the "boys," and it was his duty to warn them of the girls' plans. Therefore, he stayed in the room and listened. He was rather non-plused by the plan at first, but then he remembered that when he began to speak and made such beautiful gestures, the prize would just *have* to go to him; but in the meanwhile, he was going to fix Betty. She was trying to be too smart.

When Friday came, Betty had Janey help her bring the balloons to school while her father would come later to blow them up; this process was to be done while school was in session so that no one but the teacher should know about it. Johnny knew that the balloons burned easily, so he came armed with a box of matches. He was going to burn the string away, before hand, and spoil Betty's scene by releasing the balloons too soon. Of course, he would put out the fire before the flame reached the balloons, but even if he didn't, no harm would result as the woodwork and flooring, etc., were fireproof, due to their having been treated with some chemical.

The younger pupils were called upon first, and they rendered their parts excellently. Then Johnny was called. He mounted the platform from the closet-like room on the side with a great show of importance and began his selection. In a voice as far down in his throat as he could make it, in order to imitate the nasal tones of the country preacher, he recited. His arms were waving, he walked from one side of the platform to the other. He put one hand in his pocket, the other behind his back and strutted, and talked, and thumped the table in true, realistic style. He had had the table put there, with a pitcher of water on it, as the preacher had done, to the great delight of the other fellows.

"Hum-m-m, he thinks he is so much," sniffed Janey.

"Well, he *is* real good," answered Dorothy, who secretly, was a great admirer of Johnny, although he treated her almost as coolly as the others.

"Well, even if he is, Betty will be much better."

"I doubt it; how do you know?"

"Oh, I know, all right."

"You think you know it all," was the retort.

Just then Johnny made an exceptionally broad flourish with his arm and knocked over the pitcher of water, which of course materially detracted from the dignity (?) of the performance. Everyone giggled, and, very red in the face, Johnny tried to continue but finally gave it up and returned to his seat.

"Now, you see," declared Janey to Dorothy.

Dorothy remembered certain snubs Johnny had bestowed upon her, and answered, "Well, I always wanted a girl to win anyway."

When Betty was announced, she was the last

She was graceful and lovely.

on the program. She had on the little chiffon frock teacher had made for her when she danced at the gymnastic exercises the year before. When the first chords of the selection sounded, she poised on one foot, and then began. Round and round she pirouetted, her tiny feet twinkling in and out of the intricate steps. She was graceful and lovely, and even Johnny couldn't help but admire the dance.

"She'll do, for a girl," he muttered.

Then his conscience pricked him and he decided he wouldn't try to spoil it. He admitted to himself she was *nearly* as good an entertainer as he. Then Joe, an evil-minded little urchin from one of the poorer sections of town, whispered, "Are you goin' to do it?"

"No," said Johnny.

"She *is* better'n you, you know."

"Well, if she wins it, she can have it," magnanimously. Then, with a great show of bravado, "She would need it more than I anyway."

"You're scared to," was the retort.

"I'm not."

"You are; you wouldn't dare."

"I do dare."

"You don't. I double dare you."

Now, of course, no boy can let a dare go by, so to redeem himself in the eyes of Joe (and all the other boys as Johnny thought), Johnny crept out of his seat into the little room opening from the platform. Striking a match, he applied it to the string confining the little brightly colored spheres. Just then, Betty, glancing through the door, saw him. Dancing over to his direction, she whispered "Don't do that!" But it was too late. The little flame, creeping up the string faster than Johnny had imagined, reached the "bubbles" and, BANG! the hydrogen exploded.

Johnny was scared nearly to death. He hadn't figured on the balloons being blown up with anything but air, and anyway, never having studied chemistry, he wasn't prepared for the effects of fire applied to hydrogen. There was nearly a panic in the class room, and Betty, so disappointed at missing the thrilling climax to her scene, lay down on the platform and nearly cried.

Johnny got a glimpse of the little white form on the floor, thought he had injured her, and in he rushed. Betty didn't move; she was determined Johnny shouldn't see her cry. By that time, everyone had rushed to the platform to see what was the matter with Betty. When they surrounded her, Johnny was pushed aside. Seeing Janey emerging from the crowd around Betty, he asked her whether Betty was hurt or not. Janey had an idea that Johnny was somewhere at the bottom of the trouble, so she determined to punish him.

"You have put out both of her eyes," she said. Then he almost collapsed.

Just then, two or three balloons that had escaped before the flames had reached them, sailed majestically across the room, one of them directly above the superintendent's head. Said official took it and asked what it was for. The teacher explained.

"Well," said he, "she deserves the prize just for the idea."

By this time, Janey had once more regained Betty's side.

"Close your eyes and make b'lieve you're blind; I'm fooling Johnny," she rapidly whispered. Betty caught the idea at once, and her sense of humor asserting itself, she resolved to get a little amusement out of the situation, even if it had to be at Johnny's expense.

To her father she whispered "Take me home

Dad, before Johnny sees me." Her father complied and before Johnny had got a glimpse of her, she had left.

Johnny suffered all night, believing he had been the cause of Betty's losing her sight. No self-condemnation was too great for him. He was the meanest boy on earth to hurt Betty. Betty had always been a little trump, and even if she had slapped him, it was no more than he had deserved. Johnny could picture himself locked up in jail for the rest of his life, while poor little Betty would have to be led around by some other person, the same as old man Jameson, a War Veteran. She would never be able to dance any more, nor walk without aid. If ever there was a miserable boy in Greenville, Johnny was that lad. He tossed from one side of his bed to the other, but could find no relief from his terrifying thoughts. Betty's little dancing figure seemed to sway before him all night. Toward morning he finally fell asleep, only to be awakened by his mother, as it was time to get ready for school.

Johnny didn't want to go to school; he fairly hated the sight of the building; besides, if he left the house, the Law would have him in its clutches for a murderer. He was forced to go, however, as no one knew he had been in any way responsible for yesterday's accident. Therefore, he bolstered up what little courage he had left, and out he trudged. What was his surprise upon arriving at school, but to see Betty serenely there as large as Life itself.

"Betty," he cried, "I thought you were blind."

Betty laughed. "I wanted to teach you a lesson," she answered. He was so relieved he could have hugged her right there, even if the boys should ostracize him forever afterward.

It was some time before anyone found out how it really happened. Betty wouldn't tell on Johnny, and no one but Joe knew that Johnny had anything at all to do with it. Betty had received the prize, anyway, so she didn't much mind since Johnny seemed to be so sorry. A short while afterwards, Johnny and Joe had an argument over a game of marbles and Joe tattled on Johnny. Of course, no one liked Joe any more, but then, he had never been too popular with either the boys or the girls.

When the truth was found out, everyone rallied around Betty. "Gee, you *are* a brick, not to tell!" many of them told her. Johnny was her staunch champion. He had come to believe that it was the person and not the sex that mattered.

When Johnny's parents heard of it, they were very angry. "I shall send you to Wrightsville Boarding School the very beginning of next term," Mrs. Blair declared. Whereupon Johnny's soul rejoiced.

Then he realized that when he went, he would have to leave Betty. They had grown to be such good chums that the thought of separation was anything but pleasant. But twelve miles wasn't so much; he could return every weekend and holidays. One afternoon, after thinking about the prospect, he took a piece of soft rubber eraser which leaves a mark on wood, and wrote on the high polish of Betty's desk:

"Girls are all right."

"I knew it all the time," wrote back she.

THE JURY

I am a little girl nine years old, residing here now, having recently moved from Columbus, Ga. I am a dear lover of books, and every spare moment I am at the Dryades Street Library, reading.

Seeing *The Brownies' Book* there, I was delighted to read it. For the past six months I've been trying to write little poems. One of them I was asked to send you for publication.

Should you think it not worth publishing in your next edition, please send it to me.

Let me hear from you.

I am in the fourth grade.

Beulah Martha Howard, *New Orleans, La.*

[This is Beulah's "poem."]

Spring

Spring is here, Spring is here,
The time we children think so dear.
When the birds begin to sing,
And the flowers begin to grow.
Then you know that Spring is here.

Spring is here, Spring is here,
When all the children come so near,
When I can see
The little bee,
Then you know that Spring is here.

POLLY SITS TIGHT

Ethel M. Caution

Polly held her breath and sat rigid. For the third time the teacher had asked the question and the last time he had looked directly at her. She knew the answer too! It was an undisputed fact in Room 11, that anytime there came a question no one else could answer, a little black girl with stubborn hair and a voice like a lilting melody would be sure to know. Polly was the star scholar in the class and although she seemed unconscious of her brilliancy, her teacher and her classmates were not.

So now that the question had been asked for the third time and Polly's hand had not been raised, all the boys and girls turned to look at her in genuine surprise.

And Polly's heart was beating a rapid tatoo within her because she *did* know the answer. She had worked until late and had gone to bed determined to rise early in the morning and tackle the problem again. But about two o'clock she found herself sitting bolt upright in bed saying to the darkness, "Of course that is the way it goes," and she lay back into untroubled sleep.

Now it happened that Polly's mother was painfully poor and also that shoes had an annoying habit of wearing out beyond repair. Today Polly had worn her mother's shoes and would probably have to wear them several days, perhaps weeks, until someone gave her a pair or until she could save up enough to buy her own. The latter way meant a long wait for there was food, rent, fuel, and insurance, and her mother's health was breaking so that Polly herself worked afternoons to help out.

Polly thought of her card and the row of 1's; not that she had been a grind to make it so, but she had come to be proud of her record and of the pride her class had in her. She knew the solution but it meant going to the board to demonstrate. That would expose her shoes.

The teacher was still looking at her expectantly. She dropped her eyes to her desk and her glance fell on her paper covered books much marked after the manner of school girls and boys. These words met her gaze: "Sit tight, little girl, sit tight." That was her motto. Her dad had given it to her unconsciously and it had always come to her rescue.

When she was a very little girl, she had been playing with some children in the barn. Tiring of the usual games, one boy had suggested riding horseback. As fate would have it the most restive horse appealed to them and Polly was victim. From frequent pulling against his strap it had weakened, and, frightened by the children boosting Polly to his back, the horse gave two or three vicious tugs and the strap broke.

Before anyone realized what was happening he backed out of the stall and out of the barn and started away on a brisk gallop. Polly's father was working in a field near by and sensing what had happened, cupped his hands and called through them:

"Sit tight, little girl, sit tight!"

And Polly sat tight until her father on a swift horse overtook her and brought her back to safety. Polly remembered little else of her father. He died soon after. But that command hurled at her in time of danger had always stayed with her. It didn't take the tiniest fraction of a second for all these things to flash through her mind. False pride was galloping away with her. What was a pair of over-large shoes against the faith the twenty-odd persons in that room had in her? And what of her mother's faith in her and her own? Would they laugh at her feet? Then let them!

Like an electric flash her hand went up. The tension in the room was broken.

"All right, Polly. I knew you could. Come to the board, please."

And not one person saw her shoes! They just saw a black girl with beaming face, mouth tightly shut, head held high, go to the board and quietly, but quickly and thoroughly demonstrate the solution of the problem that had baffled them all.

But Polly saw her father trumpeting through his hands:

"Sit tight, little girl, sit tight."

Baseball team of Dupont plant, Hopewell, Va.

THANKSGIVING TIME

Langston Hughes

When the night winds whistle through the
 trees and blow the crisp brown leaves
 a-crackling down,
When the autumn moon is big and yellow-
 orange and round,
When old Jack Frost is sparkling on the ground,
It's Thanksgiving time!

When the pantry jars are full of mince-meat
 and the shelves are laden with sweet spices
 for a cake,
When the butcher man sends up a turkey nice
 and fat to bake,
When the stores are crammed with everything
 ingenious cooks can make,
It's Thanksgiving time!

When the gales of coming winter outside your
 window howl,
When the air is sharp and cheery so it drives away your scowl,
When one's appetite craves turkey and will have no other fowl,
It's Thanksgiving time!

AUTUMN THOUGHT

Langston Hughes

Flowers are happy in summer;
In autumn they die and are blown away.
Dry and withered,
Their petals dance on the wind.
Like little brown butterflies.

WINTER SWEETNESS

Langston Hughes

The little house is sugar,
Its roof with snow is piled.
And from its tiny window,
Peeps a maple-sugar child.

THE STORY-TELLING CONTEST

Julian Elihu Bagley

Little Cless' teacher just loved her pupils and she was always doing something to make them happy. "Now of course, children," she explained that Tuesday morning, "you know Thursday is Thanksgiving Day, the time when every one should give thanks to the Creator for the blessings of the year. All of you are going to give thanks, aren't you? I thought so," she said smilingly, after the whole class shouted "yes'm" in one big chorus. "Of course there will be no school Thursday," she continued, "and we shall not have an opportunity to meet together that day, but I've planned a little party—a sort of Thanksgiving dinner for us here tomorrow. We are going to have all the turkey we want. In fact, we are going to have almost a whole turkey. Only one drumstick will be cut from him before he is brought before you, and that drumstick is going to be cut off for a reason. This is the reason. We are going to have a story-telling contest tomorrow, and the little boy or girl who tells the best story will be given a nice, big, brown turkey drumstick. Of course, as I said in the beginning, there will be turkey enough for everybody, but the one who wins the drumstick will have the highest honor of the day. Now who is going to win the drumstick?"

There was no response to the question, but a twinkle of delight and determination in the eyes of every little boy and girl indicated that there would be many story-tellers in the contest the next day. Of course little Cless was going to try, for Granny had told him many tales, and he was sure he could give the class a new one, whether it was a good one or not. He could hardly wait for his teacher to dismiss him that afternoon, he was so anxious to get home and tell Granny about the story-telling contest.

"Granny," he explained when he reached home that afternoon, "we're going to have a story-telling contest tomorrow at school, and the one who tells the best story, teacher says he'll get a nice, big brown turkey drumstick. Which is the best one of the stories you've told me, Granny?"

"The best one for Thanksgiving Day, you mean, don't you, honey?"

"No'm; just the best one," answered Cless, "the best for any day."

"But any day in this case," argued Granny, "is Thanksgiving Day, and none of the stories I've told you will do for Thanksgiving."

Cless frowned desperately.

"Now don't pucker up your face like that, little lamb," begged Granny, "for I think I know a story that will just fit in for the contest." The usual flush of delight danced over the little boy's face. And that same night Granny told him a story which she declared was just the story for Thanksgiving. Little Cless could hardly sleep after he heard it. At regular intervals during the night Granny heard him roll over and over in his bed and sigh wearily: "My goodness! I wish morning would hurry up and come on."

Morning came. The little brown boy sprang from the bed and dressed himself for school. And while Granny prepared the breakfast he followed her around foot by foot, rehearsing the little story which he was going to tell in the story-telling contest. Came the time to go to school. Granny gave him her blessing and he started out. That morning when Cless reached school his room was literally buzzing with delight. The teacher had come early and so had the pupils. There were three grown-ups in the room—total strangers—whom the children had already guessed to be the judges for the contest. But most interesting of all was the platform where the teacher usually sat. On it stood a large table covered with a spotlessly clean tablecloth which was elevated at various heights, according to what it concealed. Of course everybody knew that the really high place in the center was Mister Turkey.

The program began. "My Country, 'Tis of Thee," "Come, Ye Thankful People, Come," and a short prayer by the teacher ended the devotionals. Now the tablecloth was rolled back and the children saw a delicious brown turkey with only one drumstick. And every little eye, and every little heart, and every little mind, was riveted on that one turkey drumstick. The story-telling contest began. Tommy McLaughlin started off with "The Three Bears," but as soon as he announced his title there were a dozen sighs and not a few groans of "Oh pshaw! I've heard that thing a thousand times." Tommy finished. Next a shy little girl got up without giving her title and pitched into "Little Red Riding Hood."

He sliced off a piece of meat from the turkey's breast and gave it to Br'er Rabbit.

"Ump!" grunted a rude boy, "that thing's old as the hills."

The shy little girl heard this grumble and she lost her courage, never to find it again during the course of her story. Well, the contest went on this way for half an hour or more, but the interest was beginning to lag, for the children had already realized that unless someone told a really new story, nobody would get the turkey drumstick. The teacher knew this too. So she asked: "Is there anyone here who has a really *new* story?"

A little brown boy away in the back of the room held up his hand and began popping his fingers to attract the attention of the teacher. This was Cless. "All right, Cless, come to the front and tell us your story."

The little boy sprang to his feet, marched to the front and jumped into his story without saying a word about the title. But the first one or two lines indicated that it was something entirely new. He began:

"Once a long, long time ago, the day before Thanksgiving, Br'er Bear, Br'er Fox, Br'er Rabbit and Br'er Wolf met together to lay plans for their Thanksgiving dinner. Now every one of these creatures wanted some fresh meat for his dinner but nobody wanted to run the risk of catching it.

"'What we going to have?' asked Br'er Wolf.

"'Why, I suggest that *you* go out and fetch in a young lamb,' said Br'er Bear.

"'All right,' said Br'er Wolf, 'now what are you going to bring, Br'er Bear?'

"'Why, I'll just go out and bring in a whole heap o' corn, and we'll have some roasting ears. They're always good for Thanksgiving Day, aren't they?'

"'Oh, yes indeed,' said Br'er Wolf. 'I just love

roasting ears, and especially with young lamb. Now what are you going to bring, Br'er Fox?"

"'Oh, I'll just get a nice big fat turkey,' said Br'er Fox, 'because Thanksgiving is never complete without a turkey. And besides, you know the old saying that the one who gets the right drumstick of a turkey on Thanksgiving Day will have good luck all the year and can call the figures at the Corn Dance, Thanksgiving night. Now one of us is bound to get the right drumstick.'

"Old Br'er Rabbit kept perfectly quiet until Br'er Fox spoke: 'Look here, Br'er Rabbit, what you going to catch?'

"Br'er Rabbit commenced to blink his eyes and work his ears. And by and by he said: 'Well, now, somebody's got to cook this stuff. Who'll cook if I go out hunting?'

"'By the way, we never thought of that,' said Br'er Fox. 'Well, me and Br'er Wolf and Br'er Bear will just go out and fetch in the turkey and the lamb and the corn, and you'll stay home and cook.'

"Of course Br'er Rabbit agreed. And that same morning Br'er Fox and Br'er Wolf and Br'er Bear went out hunting. All came back before sunset. Br'er Fox had his turkey, Br'er Wolf had his lamb, and Br'er Bear had his arms full of corn. Old Br'er Rabbit was so very happy that Br'er Bear and Br'er Fox had to hold him to keep him from dancing himself tired. Everything was ready for the dinner now and Br'er Rabbit knew exactly how to handle it.

"'Br'er Fox,' said he, 'I think you and Br'er Bear and Br'er Wolf better go off and rest yourselves until morning. I'll have everything ready in time for dinner tomorrow.'

"Well, Br'er Fox and Br'er Wolf and Br'er

"You didn't say shoo to the one on the table today."

Bear took Br'er Rabbit's advice and went to bed and slept the next morning until the sun was 'way up in the sky. When they got up they found the dinner all prepared. Noon came. Br'er Rabbit set the table and called the other three animals in. 'Now,' said he, 'I'll ask Br'er Wolf to carve the meat and help the plates.' This just suited Br'er Wolf. He was sure he was going to get that right turkey drumstick, 'cause it was on the under side and he meant to carve off meat for everybody before himself. Then he would give Br'er Fox the left drumstick and save the right one for himself.

"When Br'er Wolf had helped everybody to lamb and corn he asked: 'What part of the turkey do you like, Br'er Rabbit?'

"'Any part 'cept the drumstick,' said Br'er Rabbit. Br'er Wolf didn't say anything, but he sliced off a piece of meat from the turkey's breast and gave it to Br'er Rabbit.

"'And what part will you have, Br'er Fox?'

"'I'll take drumstick—but the right one, please.'

"'Oh, it doesn't make any difference 'bout the *right* drumstick,' said Br'er Wolf, 'one's just as good as the other.'

"'Why, of course,' said Br'er Rabbit. And so Br'er Wolf carved off the left drumstick and shoved it on Br'er Fox's plate.

"'Now, Br'er Bear,' said Br'er Wolf. 'I 'spose you're just like Br'er Rabbit—any part'll do you, so I'm slicing off a nice piece of this white meat for you, too.' Br'er Bear didn't say anything and Br'er Wolf carved off a big piece of white meat and put it on his plate. 'Now old Mister Turkey's getting sort o' slim,' said he, 'reckon I'd better turn him over.' He turned him over. There was no turkey drumstick on the right side. Br'er Wolf was disgusted.

"'Br'er Rabbit! Where's that right drumstick?"

"'I don't know,' said Br'er Rabbit. 'I declare I don't.'

"Everybody was looking at Br'er Rabbit. By and by Br'er Wolf began to slice off some white meat for himself. 'All right, let's go on with the dinner,' said he, 'I'll find out who has that right drumstick yet.'

"Well, they finished their dinner and that same night they went to the dance. Br'er Fox took his left drumstick along, but Br'er Rabbit took along a drumstick, too—and it was the right one. The dance began. Old Br'er Bear was manager.

"'If any of you've had turkey today for your dinner,' said he, 'and got the right drumstick with you, you're entitled to call the figures for the dance tonight.'

"'I've got a drumstick,' hollered Br'er Fox.

"'But I've got the *right* one,' said Br'er Rabbit. And sure enough he pushed his hand under his coat and pulled a big turkey drumstick.

"'Well—well—well!' they all said. 'Br'er Rabbit's got the right drumstick, so he'll call the figures for the dance.' Now old Br'er Fox had to take a back seat. Br'er Rabbit strutted out in the middle of the floor and commenced to call the figures. And he sure did have a good time. Every now and then he'd call out figures that made old Br'er Fox change to some girl he didn't like. And then just for fun, Br'er Rabbit would holler right out to Br'er Fox's best girl: 'Now come stand by the caller! Now put your arms around him.' Of course all this made Br'er Fox very angry, so when the dance was over he said: 'Br'er Rabbit, you've got to prove it to me that a turkey ain't got but one drumstick. Come on, I'm going to take you to the place where I got that turkey today.' Old Br'er Rabbit tried to make a good excuse, but Br'er Fox pulled him along.

"Well, they started out and walked and walked until they came to the place where Br'er Fox had got his turkey. All the turkeys had gone to roost. Sure enough, everyone had the right drumstick tucked up out of sight. 'Ha! Ha! Ha!' laughed Br'er Rabbit, 'didn't I tell you Mister Turkey ain't had a right drumstick? Told you so, Br'er Fox; told you so.'

"'Wait a minute,' said Br'er Fox. 'Shoo! Shoo! Shoo!' Every turkey woke up and put down his right drumstick.

"'Now! What you got to say?' asked Br'er Fox.

"'Oh, pshaw, you can't fool me that way,' said Br'er Rabbit. 'You didn't say shoo to the one on the table today, 'cause if you had, he would have put down a right drumstick, too.'

"Now Br'er Fox just tucked in his tail and hung his head and went on home. And Br'er Rabbit hopped off just a-laffin' and a-yellin': 'Oh, pshaw, you can't fool old Br'er Rabbit like that. You didn't say shoo to the one on the table today.'"

This was the end of little Cless' story. He had told it just exactly as Granny had told it to him. The room was literally roaring with applause. The little brown boy took his seat. Not another child ventured to the platform. The story-telling contest was ended. Of course little Cless got the drumstick, but he didn't eat it at the school party. He wrapped it in a paper napkin and took it home to Granny. And Granny just hugged him and kissed him and cried: "Oh, Granny's little lamb, Granny's little man!—I just knew you were going to win that drumstick. And you brought it home to me, did you?—Bless your little heart!"

THE STORY OF THE LITTLE TIN HORN

Georgia Douglas Johnson

It was Christmas morning. Tommy Brown sprang out of bed and ran joyfully to his stocking, which hung by the fire-place, from the top of which pointed a bright tin horn, the goal of his wishes. He immediately began a wild triumphant tooting, but suddenly he stopped short in amazement, for there, seeming to glide from the very heart of the horn, was a tiny fairy who looked upon him with a smile.

Before Tommy could collect his scattered wits the fairy spoke thus: "The Fairy Queen wishes you to attend her at once in the Court of Fancy-clime. Shall we take the rainbow and obey?" With that she clapped her hands and

"What does the clear book say about the cheerful giver?"

Tommy saw a tinted rainbow appear at his feet.

As in a dream he found himself consenting, and they were soon whirling swiftly, far above the church spires, through the downy clouds that melted as they passed.

At length the rainbow settled in a field of blooming buttercups and the little fairy said, "Welcome to Fancy-clime."

Strains from far-away zithers came softly, and above them rose the shrill voice of children singing. The words were sweet but strange to Tommy.

He was ushered at once into the presence of the Queen who greeted him from her shell-like throne, her black eyes shining like stars from her red-gold face. Like a daffodil she seemed in her pale-yellow foam robe. "Welcome, little world-boy," she cried with quick glances. "What is that you hold so closely in your hand?"

"My new horn," was the stammered reply. "I only got it this morning. Santa brought it."

Then the fairy clapped her hands and Tommy saw a strange sight. Suddenly a cloud appeared and as swiftly disappeared, and Tommy gazed in amazement upon a poor, little, ragged girl. She was looking toward her empty stocking, which hung by the fire-place in a bare and cheerless room. Tommy gazed earnestly at the scene before him, forgetting the fairies and his strange trip—forgetting everything but the sorrow of the little girl. Finally she turned her eyes away from the empty stocking and saw Tommy, at the same time spying his little tin horn, as he thought. Her eyes widened, she took a step forward, and putting her thin brown finger in her mouth, stood waiting.

Tommy thought deeply for a moment, then, stepping forward boldly, said, "Oh, little girl, do take my Christmas horn; it makes beautiful music."

Smiles were rippling upon the little girl's face as she took from Tommy's hand—not a horn but a beautiful doll, her heart's dearest wish.

Then the scene faded and Tommy found himself looking into the pleased face of the daffodil Queen who spoke thus: "Where have you been, Tommy?"

"I do not know, Queen Fairy, but I thought I saw a poor little girl who had no Christmas gift. I gave her my horn but it turned into a doll. I do not understand."

The fairy nodded her thick curls and questioned further, "Are you sorry that you gave your horn away?"

"Oh, no!" cried Tommy, "I am glad I gave it to the little girl."

Just then a fairy bearing a book with glass leaves appeared. "Read," said the Fairy Queen. "What does the clear book say about the cheerful giver?"

"He who gives freely and joyfully becomes the child of all the fairies. Although he gives away, he keeps, and happiness is always round about him."

Here the fairy closed the book and disappeared. The Fairy Queen then said:

"Blow upon your horn,
And your wishes shall be born."

Tommy, to his great amazement, saw that he was still holding in his hand the little tin horn which he thought was lost to him. He was about to raise it to his lips when the Fairy Queen said, "Wait!"

She clapped her hands and immediately Tommy saw the self-same rainbow which had brought him to Fancy-clime, sailing gently to his feet. At the same moment appeared the little fairy who had attended him there. She took him by the hand and they seated themselves on the rainbow which rose softly, and in a trance Tommy found himself standing before his Christmas stocking, rubbing his eyes in wonderment.

His mother had come into his room and seeing Tommy so dazed said, "What ails you, Tommy-boy?"

"I've had a wonderful trip, mother dear, to Fancy-clime where the fairies live, and they gave me a strange gift. I can give to anyone whatever he wishes. Try me."

His mother laughed and waving her hands in the air sang:

"I should like a coach and four,
Standing, prancing, at my door."

Tommy flourished his horn and blew softly—then do you know a very wonderful thing happened—a fine coach with real horses, four of them, stood restlessly pawing the earth in front of their little cottage, and Tommy's mother gazed in astonishment. Tommy's eyes widened too as he saw it, but he said, "Wish on, mother dear."

And as she wished, Tommy blew upon his horn enough presents for themselves and all the village folk beside.

Part Four

Tell Me a Story

People all over the world and of all ages love stories. So in every issue of The Brownies' Book there were several stories. Many of these stories were folktales from different ethnic groups from the large continent of Africa. Some of the stories are Br'er Rabbit stories from the black South. Some were African-American versions of African stories. But sometimes these old tales took on new meanings in the New World. For instance, the Br'er Rabbit stories, beneath their amusing surfaces, often taught slaves how to survive slavery—how, for example, they could sometimes outsmart their masters. The Annancy stories from the Caribbean islands are related to the African stories and to the African-American stories, for Africans stolen from their homes were taken to the islands as well as to the United States.

Some stories from The Brownies' Book tell how something came to be—"How Mr. Crocodile Got His Rough Back," for example. "Old Man and the Bullberries" tells how Native Americans developed their method for picking berries. Others explain nothing but are just for the fun of telling a story. Still others try to teach a lesson to children about how they should behave. Some of the stories take place in the world we all live in. However, the storytellers don't always understand the people they are writing about. For instance, one writer says that some people on this earth are savages. But as we learn more about people around the world, we realize that nobody is a savage. We just have different ways of thinking and doing things that others don't always understand. So the people in some stories might seem strange to us even though they are real people. In addition to the stories about real people, there are other stories that happen in make-believe places with make-believe characters. Some stories are serious, some are mysterious, and some are funny. They can be told by one person or they can belong to an entire community.

"Once upon a time," in Uganda

FOLK TALES

The only thing that is nicer than telling a story is to listen to it. Did you ever stop to think that just as you sit very still in the twilight and listen to Father or Mother telling stories, just so children are listening, all over the world—in Sweden, in India, in Georgia, and in Uganda? I think you probably know where the first three countries are, but maybe it would be best for me to tell you that Uganda is in beautiful, far-off, mysterious Africa.

Some people are specially fond of telling stories about animals. About twenty-five hundred years ago a poor Greek slave, Aesop, told many and amusing tales about the fox and the wolf and all the rest of them. And you High School boys and girls probably have already read the clever animal stories told by Jean de la Fontaine in the seventeenth century.

Now here is a story about animals which African Fathers and Mothers tell to their little sons and daughters. The story is very old and has come down from father to son for many generations and has probably met with almost no changes. Such a story is called a *folk tale*. There are many folk tales to be gathered in Africa, and Mr. Monroe N. Work, of Tuskegee, has collected very many of them from various sources. This one, "The Hare and the Elephant," has been selected by Mr. Work from Sir Harry Johnston's book called "The Uganda Protectorate."

Folk tales, folk songs, and folk dances can give us—even better than history sometimes—an idea of primitive peoples' beliefs and customs.

THE HARE AND THE ELEPHANT

Once upon a time the hare and the elephant went to a dance. The hare stood still and watched the elephant dance. When the dance was over, the hare said,

"Mr. Elephant, I can't say that I admire your dancing. There seems to be too much of you. Your flesh goes flop, flop, flop. Let me cut off a few slices and you will then, I think, dance as well as I."

The hare cut off some huge slices and went home. The elephant also went home; but he was in agony. At length he called the buffalo and said,

"Go to the hare and ask him to return my slices."

The buffalo went to the hare and asked for the slices.

"Were they not eaten on the road?" asked the hare.

"I heard they were," replied the buffalo.

Then the hare cooked some meat—it was a slice of the elephant, and gave it to the buffalo. The buffalo found it very tender and asked him where he got it.

"I got it at a hill not far from here, where I go occasionally to hunt. Come hunting with me today." So they went to the hill and set up some snares. The hare then said to the buffalo, "You wait here and I will go into the grass. If you hear something come buzzing 'Zoo-oo-oo-oo-oo-oo-oo,' hang down your head."

The buffalo waited. Presently he heard, "Zoo-oo-oo-oo-oo-oo-oo—." He hung down his head. The hare threw a big rock, hit the buffalo's head and killed him. The hare then skinned him and carried home the meat.

When the buffalo did not return, the elephant sent an antelope to ask the hare to return his slices. But the hare disposed of him in the same manner as he had the buffalo and carried home his meat.

The elephant sent a succession of messengers for the slices, but none of them returned. At last the elephant called the leopard and said, "Go to the hare and ask him to return my slices."

The leopard found the hare at home. After they had dined, the hare invited the leopard to go hunting on the hill. When they arrived and had set up their snares, the hare said,

"Now you wait here and I will go into the grass. If you hear something come buzzing, 'Zoo-oo-oo-oo-oo-oo-oo,' hang down your head."

The hare then went into the grass and presently the leopard heard a buzzing, 'Zoo-oo-oo-oo-oo-oo-oo,' but instead of hanging down his head, he held it up and a big stone just missed him. Then he hung down his head, fell over and pretended that he was dead. He laughed to himself, "Ha! ha! Mr. Hare, so you meant to kill me with that stone. I see now what has happened to the other messengers. The wretch killed them all with his 'Zoo-oo-oo-oo-oo-oo-oo.' Never mind, Mr. Hare, just wait."

The hare came out of the grass and when he saw the leopard lying stretched out, he laughed and jumped and scraped the ground. "There goes another messenger," he said. "The elephant wants his slices back. Well, let him want them."

The hare then gathered some grass and vines and made the leopard into a bundle ready to carry. "If I had my knife, I would skin him here," said the hare. "As it is, I must carry him a little way, then hide him, and run home and get my knife."

Having said this, the hare hoisted the leopard on his head and walked off with him. The leopard enjoyed riding on the hare's head. After the hare had carried him a little way, the leopard put forth his paw and gave the hare a deep scratch. He then drew in his paw and lay quite still. The hare at once understood how matters lay and put down the bundle. He did not, however, pretend that he knew, but said,

"Oh, there seems to be a thorn in the bundle."

He then roped the bundle very firmly, taking care to tie the paws securely. He then placed the bundle on his head and went along to a stretch of forest. Here he placed the leopard in the woods and went off to get his knife.

As soon as the hare had gone, the leopard tore open the bundle and sat up to wait for the hare's return. "I'll show him how to hunt and to say, 'Zoo-oo-oo-oo-oo-oo-oo-oo, hang down your head!' I'll show him how to cut slices off my friend, the elephant." The leopard looked up and saw the hare returning with his knife.

When the hare saw the leopard sitting up, he ran into a hole in the ground.

"Come out," said the leopard, sniffing vainly at the hole.

"Come in," said the hare.

The leopard saw that it was useless to try to coax the hare to come out, so he said to a crow that sat on a branch just above the hole, "Mr. Crow, will you watch this hole while I run for some fire to burn out the hare?"

"Yes," replied the crow, "but don't be long away, because I will have to go to my nest soon."

The leopard went for the fire. After a while the hare said,

"I am certain, Mr. Crow, that you are very hungry."

"Yes, very," replied the crow.

"Are you fond of ants? If you are, I have a lot of them down here."

"Throw me up some, please."

"Come near the hole and I will."

The crow came near. "Now open your eyes and mouth wide."

The crow opened his mouth and eyes as wide as he could. Just then the hare flung a lot of dust into them, and while the crow was trying to remove the dust, the hare ran away.

"What shall I do now?" said the crow, as he finished taking the dust out of his eyes. The leopard will be angry when he finds the hare gone. I am sure to catch it. Ha! ha! I have it. I will gather some ntengos (poison apples), and put them in the hole. As soon as the leopard applies the fire to the hole, the ntengos will explode and the leopard will think that the hare has burst and died."

The crow accordingly placed several ntengos in the hole. After some time, the leopard came back with the fire.

"Have you still got him inside?" he asked.

"Yes, sir."

"Has he been saying anything?"

"Not a word."

"Now then, hare," said the leopard, "when you hear 'Zoo-oo-oo-oo-oo-oo-oo-oo,' hold down your head. Do you hear?" No reply. "You killed all of the elephant's messengers just as you tried to kill me; but it is all finished now with you. When I say, 'Zoo-oo-oo-oo-oo-oo-oo-oo,' hang down your head. Ha! ha!"

Then the leopard put the fire in the hole. There was a loud explosion. The leopard thought that the hare had burst and died. But instead, the hare was at home making a hearty meal of the last of the elephant's steaks. None of the other animals ever bothered the hare after that. They remembered what happened to the elephant's messengers.

He held the box to his ear.

CHRONICLES OF BR'ER RABBIT

Julia Price Burrell

Br'er Rabbit and Br'er Pa'tridge went hunting. They brought in a fine little sheep.

"Now," said Br'er Rabbit, "who will go get some fire to cook our meat?"

"You shall go, for you are larger than I, and you can carry more," declared the little Pa'tridge.

Said Br'er Rabbit, "You shall go, Br'er Pa'tridge, for you can fly more swiftly than I can run, and we will not wait so long for our feast."

Br'er Pa'tridge set off; soon as he was out of sight, Br'er Rabbit fell to work tearing the flesh into pieces convenient for him to carry off—and when Br'er Pa'tridge returned with the fire he found only a few scraggly pieces left. He fairly

"See all my brothers dying."

gasped: "Well! WHERE is our meat, Br'er Rabbit?"

Br'er Rabbit scratched his chin with his right forepaw—he stared hard at the spot where the meat had been—then with a sudden upward jerk of his naughty head he said:

"Why, Br'er Pa'tridge, I just turned my eyes towards a queer sound I heard in yonder brush and 'fore I turned me round again that meat been gone! Oh, what shall we do, Br'er Pa'tridge?"

But without seeming to notice the greedy Rabbit, Br'er Pa'tridge lifted his head and in answer to his call, "Bob-White!" a score of hungry partridges flew to him and they all ate the miserable fragments which Br'er Rabbit had not been able to steal away. As they all flopped over onto the ground, Br'er Pa'tridge cried. "O, Br'er Rabbit, that meat was surely poison. See, all my brothers dying!"

"Poison meat won't do for me!" thought Br'er Rabbit. "Let me go fetch that meat I hid away!" and he bounded over the ground, returning with the tender meat which he had meant to eat alone. When he had brought it all, Br'er Pa'tridge said quietly, "Now, Br'er Rabbit, let's divide equally!"

And they did.

BR'ER RABBIT WINS THE REWARD

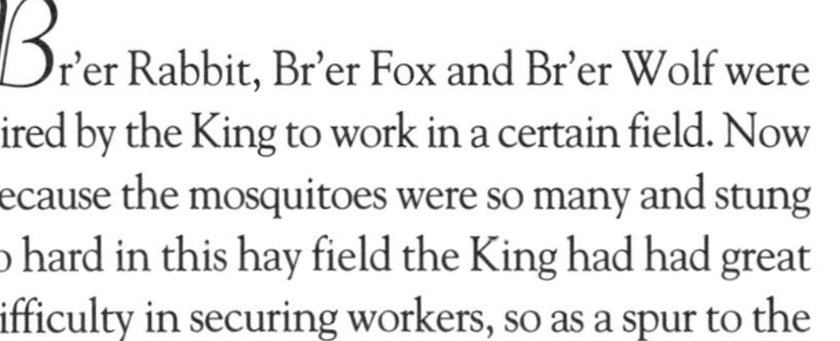

Br'er Rabbit, Br'er Fox and Br'er Wolf were hired by the King to work in a certain field. Now because the mosquitoes were so many and stung so hard in this hay field the King had had great difficulty in securing workers, so as a spur to the laborers he promised to him who should work longest without heeding the mosquitoes a special reward.

All three, Br'er Rabbit, Br'er Fox, Br'er Wolf, set to work, each determined to win the reward. How those mosquitoes did bite! Every half

He slapped his stinging legs.

minute Br'er Wolf stopped to slap one! Every five minutes Br'er Fox stopped to swat at the troublesome pests!

What of Br'er Rabbit? Oh, they were not sparing him either, but that little animal is a "schemy" creature! He worked away, and as he worked he talked. Said he, "My old Dad, he haves a plough horse; he black here and here," and as he said "here" each time he slapped his stinging legs where the mosquitoes were biting—"and," he went on, "he white all here"—slapping again at the enemy!

So he continued talking and slapping and working. It never occurred to the King that Br'er Rabbit was killing mosquitoes. It appeared to those who looked that Br'er Rabbit was not bothered.

He won the reward.

BR'ER RABBIT LEARNS WHAT TROUBLE IS

Br'er Rabbit approached the King. "O, King," he began, "teach me what is trouble. I hear the people talk of trouble, but I have never seen it."

Then the King said thoughtfully, "Br'er Rabbit, if you would always be happy, give up this desire of yours to know trouble—for it brings tears and much weeping. Return to the brier patch and be a good rabbit child."

But Br'er Rabbit was not so to be put off—and seeing that he was determined, the King slowly brought forth a small tightly covered box.

"Do not open it until you have almost reached the further end of the open field near the brier patch. There is trouble in this box," cautioned the King.

As Br'er Rabbit ran down the path he thought of his box—he ran faster; as his pace increased, so did his curiosity. He paused a second and held the box to his ear—what was it he heard? he thought. It must be a baby crying. "Hush, baby!" he said, but as the racket continued he thought he would take just the merest peep inside. He turned just to see if anyone were watching. The King was following him.

"Don't you open that box, Br'er Rabbit!" he cried.

"Oh, no! no! no!" Br'er Rabbit prevaricated. "I just only looked to see how close behind me you were!"

Br'er Rabbit ran on—again he paused to listen—and to peep—again the King shouted and Br'er Rabbit refrained. He had run now as long as he could—his curiosity burned him past endurance. He would raise the top and peep inside so quickly that even the King, as he followed, should not notice. His little paw scarcely moved the cover. Oh, wow! if you will excuse me for saying so. "Br-r-r! Bow-wow-wow-wow!!" and "Br-r-r!" Two hungry hounds burst out and upon poor little Br'er Rabbit, giving him a pretty chase over the fields until he finally reached the welcome brier-patch worn and breathless. The dogs did not catch Br'er Rabbit—but to this day just the sight of a dog means *trouble* to Br'er Rabbit.

Br'er Possum carried Mister Tortoise home on his back.

Little Cless had just returned to his apartment from an excursion to the famous Bronx Park in New York City. At last his wish to see the many wonderful animals in this zoo had come to pass. But somehow they didn't interest him quite as much as he expected. Perhaps this was due to the fact that there were countless other holiday attractions, or perhaps it was because Granny couldn't go along to tell him the wonderful stories that she knew about them. But this was no grown-ups' outing—this trip. It was a holiday excursion conducted by Cless' teacher—and for kiddies only! So poor Granny had to stay at home. However, as soon as Cless began his dinner he commenced to tell Granny all about the strange animals he had seen at the park. And what do you think he imagined the funniest creature in the whole zoo?—Br'er Possum!

"Oh, Granny! You just ought to see him," shouted Cless. "He's the cutest little thing in the whole zoo. And every time you go near his cage he just stretches out and plays dead. Granny, what makes him do that—was he born that way?"

"Why, of course not, Cless. Haven't you ever heard how Mister Tortoise taught Br'er Possum that trick? Well," added Granny quickly—she knew Cless hadn't heard this tale—"guess I'll have to tell you—but after dinner, honey."

Now Cless had a hurry-up dinner, pushed his chair away from the table, hopped into Granny's lap and indicated his readiness to her by a soft, sweet smile that fairly danced over his little brown face.

"Now understand, Cless," explained Granny as she began, "this was many years ago, long before you were born—or even Granny. Br'er Possum was living away down in old Virginia in the hollow of a cypress tree in Chuckatuck swamp. And on the side of this same swamp, away down in a dark, crooked hole, there lived Mister Tortoise. Now Br'er Possum was a particular friend of Mister Tortoise, and used to visit him every night to get some of the delicious carrots and beets and turnips that he kept in his hole. This made life very easy for Br'er Possum, so instead of working he just cuddled up in his hollow every day and slept till night. But one day a strange storm blew up. Big, rolling clouds hid the sun and after a while there was a heavy downpour of a mixture of sleet and snow. For three days and three nights this sleet and snow poured down so hard that neither Br'er Possum nor Mister Tortoise could go out.

"Now, Mister Tortoise was all prepared for this weather. He had already stored up his carrots and beets and turnips for his winter food, so the storm only stopped him from going fishing. Br'er Possum was not so lucky. He didn't have one bite in his hollow, so it wasn't long before he began to squeal desperately for something to eat. Naturally, just as soon as the storm lulled he crawled out of his hollow and went dragging over to Mister Tortoise's den to get something. He was hungry and weak and was therefore compelled to travel very slowly, and when he got there Mister Tortoise had just crawled out of his hole and toddled on down to the river a-fishin'. Br'er Possum wondered what to do. Should he go on down Mister Tortoise's hole and help himself to carrots and beets and turnips, or should he go down to the river and help his friend fish? He thought a while and then decided to go down to the river. But he had not gone long on his way before he met Br'er Fox.

"'Hello there, Br'er Possum,' says Br'er Fox. 'How do you do this morning, and where you going so early?'

"Br'er Possum replied that he was feeling pretty hungry and was going to the river to fish with Mister Tortoise, his friend.

"'Why,' says Br'er Fox, 'I've just come from the river a-fishin' with Mister Tortoise myself, and he's caught just one little minnow fish.'

"Then Br'er Fox went on to tell Br'er Possum how Mister Tortoise had been fishing since sunrise and how he had threatened to keep on fishing till sundown if he didn't catch a big fish. Furthermore, he told Br'er Possum that Mister Tortoise had promised him some carrots and beets if he'd stay and help him fish. 'But,' said he, 'it was too cold down there for me. I just couldn't stand it.'

"Nevertheless, he had promised to go back to the river that afternoon and carry Mister Tortoise home on his back. But, of course, he didn't mean to got back to the river at all. What he really meant to do was to find Mister Tortoise's hole and rob it of the carrots and beets and turnips. So after throwing one or two hints at Br'er Possum, Br'er Fox came right out and said: 'Seems like you ought to know where Mister Tortoise lives, Br'er Possum—he's your friend.'

"'I do,' says Br'er Possum.

"'And you claim you pretty hungry?' asked Br'er Fox.

"'Yes, hungry as I can be.'

"'Well, would you listen to a scheme to get something to eat?'

"'Maybe I would,' says Br'er Possum. 'What is it?'

"'Would you go and help me rob Mister Tortoise's hole while he's at the river?'

"'Oh no! no! no!'exclaimed Br'er Possum as he walloped his big, rough tail on the ground. 'I could never do that. He's my best friend.'

"'But how's he going to know it?' argued Br'er Fox. 'How's he going to know it when he's at the river a-fishin'?'

"Well, Br'er Fox kept on asking this question and saying, 'And yet you claim you so hungry!' till Br'er Possum got in the notion of going. So he said, 'Wait here, Br'er Fox, till I go home and get a basket and we'll go and rob Mister Tortoise.'

"Of course, Br'er Fox agreed to wait, so Br'er Possum started off to get the basket. But on his way home he began to think of the many kind things that Mister Tortoise had done for him. Now this worried Br'er Possum so much that before he got to his hollow he had completely changed his mind. So instead of going right back to Br'er Fox with the basket he took a short cut through the swamp to see if Mister Tortoise was still fishing at the river. And sure enough what did he see but a great big tortoise with his head chucked through the ice and his feet away up in the air, just a-going 'flippey-te floppey-te! flippey-te floppey-te!' He was struggling to catch a fish. Br'er Possum sneaked up behind Mister Tortoise, grabbed him by the hind legs and snatched him out of the ice.

"'Spe-u!' whistled Mister Tortoise as the cold water gushed from his mouth. 'My gracious alive, Br'er Possum, you liked to scared me to death—I thought you were Br'er Fox. Where in the world did you pop up from anyway?'

"'Just from Chuckatuck Hill,' says Br'er Possum, 'and I met Br'er Fox up there.'

"'Sure enough!—what did he say?' asked Mister Tortoise.

"'Said he'd been down here a-fishin' with you all the morning. Said you'd just caught one little minnow and—!'

"Right here is where Mister Tortoise cut Br'er Possum right short and asked: "Did he say I promised him something to eat?'

"'Yes,' said Br'er Possum, 'and you better watch him too 'cause he's just been trying to get me to go with him to your hole and steal all you got.'

"A low-down scamp!' says Mister Tortoise. 'How can we get him, Br'er Possum?'

"'Just you get on my back,' says Br'er Possum, 'and let me take you to your hole. Then I'll go back and get Br'er Fox and bring him there to pretend like I'm going to steal your carrots and beets and turnips, and when he comes down in your hole you just grab him and choke him to death.'

"Now both of them agreed to this trick and as soon as Br'er Possum had gulped down the little fish to give him enough strength to run, he took Mister Tortoise on his back and started to his hole by a round about way through the swamp. In about ten minutes they were home. Mister Tortoise slid off Br'er Possum's back and scrambled on down in his hole to wait for Br'er Fox. Now Br'er Possum started back in the same round about way to meet Br'er Fox. When he got back Br'er Fox was very angry and asked why he had stayed so long. Br'er Possum told him that he couldn't find the basket.

"'Well,' says Br'er Fox to Br'er Possum, 'how come you panting so hard like you been running a long ways?'

"'Oh, that's because I'm hungry,' says Br'er Possum, 'I didn't run a step.'

"'Hush up your mouth, Br'er Possum,' says Br'er Fox, didn't I hear you way through the swamp running *bookiter! bookiter! bookiter!* Who

Br'er Fox and Br'er Possum hold a conference.

you fooling? And how come your breath smells so much like fresh fish?"

"Of course, all this was enough to make Br'er Fox suspicious, but he was so hungry and Br'er Possum played so innocent that he still thought he would take a chance in Mister Tortoise's hole. So the two hungry creatures started out. But as soon as they came to Mister Tortoise's hole and saw all the fresh tracks around it, Br'er Fox balked and declared that he would never take the chance. Well, they stood in front of the hole and fussed and argued and argued and fussed till Br'er Possum was sure Mister Tortoise heard all they said. Then he hollered right out loud: 'Oh pshaw! Get out the way, Br'er Fox, you too scared to do anything! Get out the way! I'll go down; you stay up here and fill the basket as I bring the food up.'

"To be sure, Br'er Fox didn't object to this, so Br'er Possum crawled into the hole and slid on down to the bottom. Soon as he got down there he met Mister Tortoise and told him that they would have to think up a better trick to catch Br'er Fox.

"'Heard every word you spoke,' said Mister Tortoise. 'Just you leave it to me, and when I tell you to squeal—*squeal loud.* And when I tell you to lie down and play dead, don't squeal at all!—

Do you understand?' Br'er Possum said he did. Now Mister Tortoise grabbed him by the back and pretended that there was a mighty scuffling going on. My, there was such a-squealing and a-squealing and a-grunting and a-groaning that poor Br'er Fox way at the top of the hole was just shaking with fright. Finally there was a sudden hush. Then Mister Tortoise gave Br'er Possum a butcher knife and told him to go over in the corner and lie down just like he was dead. Br'er Possum obeyed. And about that time Br'er Fox thought everything was over, so he poked his head in the hole and hollered: 'Hello there, Mister Tortoise.'

"'Who's that darkening this hole?' says Mister Tortoise.

"'It's me—Br'er Fox—come for the carrots and beets and turnips you promised me this morning at the river.'

"'Oh sure! sure!—come on down,' says Mister Tortoise. 'You're the very one I'm looking for. I've just killed a great big possum. Come on down and help me skin him and I'll give you a piece.'

"Br'er Fox went down and sure enough there was Br'er Possum all stretched out just like he was dead. Now Br'er Fox was just as tickled as he could be. He began to strut about and say, 'Oh, what a fine supper I'll have tonight!' But his fun did not last long, for as soon as he turned his back, Mister Tortoise jumped on him, grabbed him by the throat so he couldn't squeal, and then hollered for Br'er Possum to come on with his butcher knife. Br'er Possum came. And while Mister Tortoise held Br'er Fox by his long mouth, Br'er Possum cut Br'er Fox's head clean off. That same night they skinned him and baked him and ate him for their supper. And after supper they talked much of this trick of playing dead. Br'er Possum liked it so well that he took it up, played it once or twice on Br'er Rabbit, and since that day he has played it on everybody but Mister Tortoise."

Granny's tale was finished. She tickled little Cless under his chin and asked him if he thought he could tell the story of how Br'er Possum learned to play dead. He assured her that he could. So now she pressed his little round face close to hers and literally smothered him with soft kisses. Then she slipped him from her lap and told him that he might join the romping holiday kiddies out in the street below.

How Mr. Crocodile Got His Rough Back

by

Julian Elihu Bagley

It was a bleak November afternoon in New York City. To be more exact it was in Harlem. The snow was falling fast, and between the long row of high dwellings on 135th Street thousands of flakes were whirling, swirling about much the same as goose feathers would whirl if dumped from some high building into a rushing wind. The sun had long since hid his face, while the white fleecy clouds of the morning were fast changing into a cold, cold gray. It was too cold for the kiddies to go out. So in the high windows dozens of them could be seen watching the grown-ups hurrying along the street below. Occasionally some one tripped on the sidewalk. Then the youngsters could be seen tumbling back into their houses in an uproar of laughter.

Among these children was a little curly headed boy named Cless. But Cless had a different purpose from the other boys and girls. He was looking for the letter carrier. For every day Cless received some pretty post card from his father who was then working in a hotel at Palm Beach, Florida.

"What will it be today, and why doesn't the mail man come on?" thought Cless. Finally the postman turned into 135th Street and made his way to the entrance of the building in which the little boy lived. Cless ran down to meet him. The postman handed him a card. On one side was Cless' address, on the other a picture of a little colored boy riding a big crocodile. Cless was both disappointed and frightened.

"Oo-ee! what an ugly thing this is," he shouted as he turned and walked into the elevator.

"Let me see?" asked the elevator boy.

Cless handed him the card.

"Sure is ugly! And that's the thing that eats little colored boys. See all them rough bumps on his back? Well, they are the toes of little colored babies sticking up under his skin. That's Mister Crocodile," concluded the elevator boy. "He used to have a smooth back before he began to eat little colored babies, but now it's rough."

Little Cless was very much frightened, and as soon as the elevator reached his floor he dashed out and went running to his apartment crying: "Granny! Granny! oh Granny, look what daddy

"They formed a big circle around the sleeping crocodile."

sent me today—a big ugly crocodile! And I hear he eats little colored babies. Granny, is it true? Is it true, Granny?"

"Why certainly not, Cless. Who in the world told Granny's little man such a story?"

"Elevator boy, Granny—elevator boy," answered little Cless between sobs. And a little later he stopped crying and told his grandmother the story just as the elevator boy had told him.

"It's no such a thing, it's no such a thing," said Granny. "Why don't you know frogs were the real cause of crocodiles having rough backs?"

"How's that, Granny? Please tell me—tell me quick, Granny, please," begged little Cless.

"All right, I'll tell you," promised Granny, "for I certainly don't want my little man scared to pieces with such ugly stories." Now little Cless felt relieved. He hopped into Granny's lap, huddled up close to her side and listened to her story of how the crocodile got his rough back.

"A long, long time ago," she said, "in Africa, down on the River Nile there lived a fierce old crocodile. And this was the first crocodile in the world. Before him there were no others. Now this crocodile lived in a cluster of very thick brush, and, although there were many other animals in the swamp larger than he, he was king of them all. Every day some poor creature was seized and crushed to death between this cruel monster's jaws. He was especially fond of frogs and used to crush dozens of them to death every day. Now the frogs could hop faster than the crocodile could run and he never caught them in a fair race. But he always got the best of them by hiding in the mud until some poor frog came paddling along and then he would nab him and crush him to death between his big saw-teeth. Of course this was easy, for at that time Mister Crocodile had a smooth, black back, and it was so much like the mud that the frogs could never tell where he was.

"But one day a happy thought struck Mister Bull Frog who was king of all the frogs in that swamp. He thought it would be a good idea to pile some lumps of mud on the crocodile's back, and then the frogs could always tell where he was. This plan was gladly accepted by all the frogs in the swamp. So the next time the crocodile crawled into the mud to take his winter nap, Mister Bull Frog and all the other frogs went to the place where the monster lay and daubed a thousand little piles of mud on his back. And when they had finished they could see him from almost any part of the swamp. Now they knew they were safe. How happy they were! They all joined hands, formed a big circle around the sleeping crocodile, and while Mister Bull Frog beat time on his knee the others shouted this jingle so hard that their little throats puffed out like a rubber ball:

'Ho, Mister Crocodile, king of the Nile.
We got you fixed for a long, long while.
Deedle dum, dum, dum, deedle dum day,
Makes no difference what you say!'

"They shouted this jingle over and over again. And the last time they sang it Mister Bull Frog got so happy he stopped beating time, jumped up in the air, cut a step or two, then joined in the chorus with his big heavy voice:

'Honkey-tonkey tunk, tunk, tink tunk tunk!
Honkey-tonkey, tunk; tunk, tink tunk tunk!'

And when all the singing and dancing were over the little frogs went home.

"But Mister Bull Frog chose to stay and watch the crocodile. All winter long the crocodile lay in the mud. Nevertheless the Bull Frog kept a close watch over him. Each day the lumps of mud that the frogs had stuck on his back were growing harder and harder.

"At last spring came. The sleepy creature awoke and immediately began to shake his back and flop his tail. But the more he did this the madder he became. Finally he was just whirling 'round and 'round in the mud, biting himself on the tail and groaning, 'Honk! honk! honk!' But the lumps of mud had done their work. They were there to stay. And finding it of no use to wiggle he crawled out on the bank of the river and began to look for something to eat. Nothing could be found on the shore, however, so he slipped back into the muddy water to see if he could catch some frogs. In this he failed, for no longer could he hide himself. No matter how much his skin looked like the mud, the little frogs could always tell where he lay by his rough back.

"So ever since that day little frogs have lived in perfect safety along the banks of the River Nile or any other place so far as crocodiles are concerned. And as for Mister Crocodile himself, he has gone on and on even down to this day with his rough scaly back. And this is how he got it, Cless," ended Granny, "and not by eating little colored babies."

Little Cless had followed every word of Granny's with eager interest. Now he smiled a smile of relief, thanked her for the story, jumped from her lap and skipped out to join the happy group of little children who were still peeping into the street from their windows. Here Cless showed his crocodile to as many children as were close enough to see it. And to those who were nearest he told the story over and over again of how the crocodile got his rough back.

ONCE 'TWAS A LITTLE PIG

Julian Elihu Bagley

Granny had promised more than once to tell Cless the story of the little pig, but somehow she had forgotten all about this tale until one June evening when her little boy sauntered into the house from his usual playtime in the street. It was long after twilight when he came in, and while Granny was not disturbed, she nevertheless disliked the idea of his staying out so late.

"Mind, you little scamp," she threatened as he came in, "mind!—you know what happened to the little pig who stayed out late one night."

Now of course Cless hadn't heard what happened to the little pig, so Granny took him by the hand and led him into the living-room, where they both sat down—Granny to tell the tale and Cless to listen.

"Once 'twas a little pig," began Granny, "who lived in a nice little pen near the banks of a river in the Land of Sunshine. Now this little pig had everything he wanted except a cover over his pen. So one day when the farmer who owned him came out to give him his dinner, the little pig asked him to put a cover over his pen.

"'Oh, sure!—sure!' promised the farmer, 'sure the little pig can have a cover for his house.' But the farmer kept putting the little pig off this way until one night a big rain came. And all that night the water fell *pitter-patter! pitter-patter!* in the little pig's face.

"The next day when the farmer came out naturally the little pig asked about his shed again and he got the same old answer—'Oh sure the little pig may have a shed over his pen.' Night came once more and there was no shed over the little pig's pen. So he stole out that evening by the moonlight to see if he could find something to make him one. He hadn't gone very far before he came to a big bunch of palmettos. Now palmettos are little palms that grow in the Land of Sunshine. They are about the size of a fan and make a fine covering for a shed. So the little pig gnawed off enough of these to serve his purpose, took them back to his pen and commenced to put up his shed. He worked hard all night and the next morning when the farmer came out he was surprised to find a nice cover over the pen.

"'Who made the cover for your pen, little pig?'

"The little pig said, 'Me.'

"'Well it looks mighty nice,' said the farmer as he started back to the house. But by and by he came back as angry as a lion. Some one had been in his cornfield that night and stripped off some of the best corn in the patch.

"'Little pig,' he hollered, 'it's you—nobody but *you* who's been in my cornfield last night. Get out, little pig—little pig, get out! I don't want you any more—wouldn't have you any more. Get out; get out and root for yourself the rest of your life.'

"Of course the little pig wasn't guilty but the old farmer was so very angry that he thought it best to leave. He left. Now he hadn't gone very far before he came to the same bunch of palmettos from which he had built the shed of his pen. Here again he got another load of palms and started down to the riverside to build him a house. On his way down he came upon Mister Crocodile. It was a very hot day and Mister Crocodile had crawled out of the mud and was cooling off under the shade of a big magnolia tree.

"'Heyo, there, little pig! Where you going this hot day with a whole load of palmetto fans?' The little pig told Mister Crocodile he was looking for a place to build a house.

"'Stop a while and fan me a bit, little pig, and I'll show you a nice, cool place to build a house—right by the riverside.' Now the little pig was almost scared to death. He didn't know whether he should take a chance on fanning Mister Crocodile, or whether he should run back to the angry old farmer. He finally decided to fan Mister Crocodile. And while he was fanning him he took the time to tell him about the corn which had been stolen the night before.

"'Why it's Br'er Bear who's been stealing that corn; didn't I see him passing by here last night with a whole arm full of green corn?' The little pig was so glad to hear this that he jumped up and squealed with delight. Now he could go back and make the old farmer understand who had been stealing all the corn.

"But Mister Crocodile begged the little pig to help him set a trap for old Br'er Bear. The little pig agreed. And that same night the crocodile sent him up in the cornfield to wait for old Br'er Bear.

"'Now,' said the crocodile, 'you go up in the cornfield and wait till old Br'er Bear comes. And when he does come you grunt like a hog and he'll take after you. Then you just run as fast as you can toward the river. I'll meet you half way up the road and I'll trip old Br'er Bear down and break his neck.'

"Well the little pig started out, came to the field and hid himself among the corn. Now he waited and waited, but old Br'er Bear didn't come. So presently he dropped off in a nap. And just about that time old Br'er Bear tipped into the cornfield and commenced a-snapping and a-popping off the ears of corn. The little pig was snoring with all his might, but as soon as old Br'er Bear got his arms full of corn the little pig commenced to dream that old Br'er Bear was choking him to death.

"'Whee! whee! whee!' he squealed.

"'Who's that squealing like a hog?' asked Br'er Bear.

"Of course the little pig didn't answer. He just kept right on squealing 'Whee! whee! whee!'

"Presently old Br'er Bear went over toward the noise and commenced fumbling 'round in the dark for the little pig. It wasn't long before he stumbled upon him. Down went old Br'er Bear's armful of corn and up jumped the little pig. Both started out for the river. The little pig was in the lead and was running with all his might. Old Br'er Bear, close behind him wasn't making many steps, but my, he was making such long ones! You could hear his big feet a-going *vip-vop! vip-vop!* And every now and then he'd get close enough to the little pig to make a swipe at him with his big, rough paw. But the little pig kept on running till he came to the place where Mister Crocodile had promised to wait for him and Br'er Bear.

Both started out for the river.

"Now what do you think?—Mister Crocodile had got tired waiting and had gone back to the river! So the little pig had to keep on down to the water. And just about the time he was almost to the river and out of breath and about to give up the race, Mister Crocodile poked his head up out of the water and hollered: 'Run, little pig!—little pig, run! Run, little pig!—run! run! run!'

"And the little pig was certainly getting over some ground too. It was a clear moonlight night and you could see the dust a-flying up behind his heels as plain as if it were day. At last he reached the river. *Ker chunk!* right overboard he went. Right behind him splashed old Br'er Bear—*ker chunk!* Now just as soon as Br'er Bear struck the water Mister Crocodile hit him such a blow with his tail you could hear it go—*ker pow!*—way up on the hillside.

"Br'er Bear was no more good after this one blow. Mister Crocodile grabbed him by the neck and kept on ducking him under the water till he drank himself to death. By this time the little pig had paddled ashore and was waiting for Mister Crocodile to push old Br'er Bear in. When he saw that old Br'er Bear was sure enough dead he asked Mister Crocodile if he might go home early the next morning and tell the farmer who had been stealing all the corn. The crocodile consented. So early the next morning the little pig started home once more.

"The farmer met him at the gate with the same old cry—'Go away, little pig; go away, I don't want you any more. Wouldn't have you. Go away and root for yourself the rest of your life. Somebody's been in my cornfield again last night and it's nobody but you. It *was* you 'cause I saw your tracks. Go away, little pig—go away.'

"But the little pig wouldn't go away, so the mean old farmer got a big stick and began to chase him away. And he chased him and chased him till he came to the river. And what did he see there but a great big bear—dead! The little pig ran right up to Br'er Bear and stopped and looked first at the farmer and then at Br'er Bear as much as to say: 'Here lies your corn thief!'

"The old farmer quickly saw that Br'er Bear was guilty, for the proof was there in the corn tassels that stuck to him while he was stealing the corn. They were still clinging to his hair. At last the farmer really believed the little pig innocent. And what do you think he did to show his belief? Why he simply skinned old Br'er Bear right there by the riverside and carried the little pig back to his pen. And by and by, when the old farmer was settled, he just stretched that nice big bear hide across the pen, and the little pig had a waterproof shed that lasted as long as he lived."

THE LITTLE PIG'S WAY OUT

Julian Elihu Bagley

Did the little pig ever do anything to pay Mister Crocodile for keeping old Br'er Bear from drowning him?" asked little Cless one evening.

"Oh, yes, honey—certainly; of course he did," answered Granny in rapid succession.

"Well, what did he do?"

"Oh, he did so many things I don't know what he *didn't* do," was Granny's evasive reply.

"Well, what was *one* of the things he did?" Cless demanded.

Granny was bemused. "I—I—I think," she said haltingly, "I think he saved Mister Crocodile's life once."

This was exactly what little Cless wanted his grandmother to say. "How did he do it, Granny? How did he do it?"

"Well, you know," said Granny, "after Mister Crocodile had drowned Br'er Bear in the river and saved the little pig, all the other bears in The Land of Sunshine had it in for him. Naturally, then he had to be very careful about his movements. Every time he crawled out on the banks of the river to cool off, he kept a sharp eye out for the bears. They were determined to get him. They didn't care at all about catching the little pig, but oh my, how they did want to catch Mr. Crocodile! Now it wasn't very long before Mister Crocodile found this out. Of course, he wanted to tell his friend, the little pig, but he didn't dare leave the water in the daytime. He was afraid the bears would catch him. One day, however, he made up his mind to leave the water, but just as he started out he looked up the road and saw two great big bears tromping down to the river to get a drink. Mister Crocodile ducked his head under the water and lay perfectly quiet. He wanted to hear what they were going to say.

"'Oh yes,' said one to the other as they lapped up the water, 'we'll get old Mister Crocodile yet. Any time we bears go after a thing, we're sure to get it. And we won't miss Mister Crocodile—I'll bet my life we won't.' Now when they had finished drinking they lay down on the bank of the river to rest and to talk about their plan to catch Mister Crocodile. The whole scheme was laid out by these two bears, who were the smartest in the Land of Sunshine. They meant to keep watch down by the riverside all day. This would stop Mister Crocodile from coming out to get his sun bath; and if he did come out they would catch him.

"Well, Mister Crocodile overheard their plan and therefore made up his mind to keep his head under the water. Now sunshine to a crocodile is what water is to us. They must have sunshine; we must have water. So, of course, he couldn't stay under the water forever. What should he do? He himself did not know, but he thought the little pig could find a way out for him. But to get to the little pig was another question. How could he do it? An idea struck him that the safest time to go was at night when the two bears were off guard. So one dark night he crawled out of the water and toddled out to see the little pig and to tell him his trouble.

"'Heyo! there, little pig,' said Mister Crocodile as he jumped up on the pen. 'I haven't seen you since the night I drowned old Br'er Bear. And what do you think, all the bears in The Land of Sunshine have heard about my drowning Br'er Bear and they're trying to kill me. They don't want you—said so, but they'll give anything in the world to catch me. Now, little pig, I helped you out when you were in trouble, what are you going to do to help me? I've got to have sunshine, you know, and I can't possibly get it with two big bears guarding the river all day.'

"The little pig was thinking. And while he was thinking, he heard a heavy tromping down the road. Presently two big bears loped up to the pen, sniffed around the outside a time or two and then went galloping away. But they had found what they wanted. They knew Mister Crocodile was in that pen. And Mister Crocodile knew that they knew too. He was almost scared to death. 'Little pig, what shall I do? What shall I do, little pig? Tell me—tell me quick. How can I get back to the river before moonrise?'

"The little pig was thinking. At that moment, however, he could not upon his life think of a scheme that would get Mister Crocodile past the bears and back to the river before the moon rose. Presently the moon came up and with it came a big bright idea. Out in the field near the little pig's pen stood a scare-crow which a farmer had put up to frighten the crows away. This was just the thing to do the trick, thought the little pig. 'I'll just undress that scare-crow,' said he, 'and dress up Mister Crocodile like a sure-enough man.' And I wish you could have seen the little pig dressing up Mister Crocodile! Took that old scare-crow's coat, slung it round him, pulled an old derby hat down over his eyes, handed him the scarecrow's wooden gun, and then Mister Crocodile looked like a sure-enough man a-going hunting.

On guard

"'Now,' said the little pig as he handed Mister Crocodile the gun, 'you just take this gun in one hand, keep that derby hat pulled down over your eyes, and go on back to the river. If you meet the bears they'll never know you. But mind, keep a level head. If you don't they'll certainly find you out.'

"Well, Mister Crocodile started out. Everything went all right till he was about half way to the river. Here he met the two bears. Both Mister Crocodile and the bears were almost scared to death, but Mister Crocodile held his head and kept right on advancing like a real hunter, while the bears became frightened, whirled around and went galloping back to the swamp as fast as they could. Now Mister Crocodile was safe. He went toddling on down to the river just a-laughing and a-thinking about the cunning trick he had played on the bears. But this wasn't the only time the old scare-crow served his purpose so well. For that night before Mister Crocodile jumped overboard he pushed a big stick into the ground and dressed it up with the scare-crow's clothes. The next morning when the two bears started down to the river to get some water and to look for Mister Crocodile, they spied the old scarecrow. Back to the swamp they went. And for three weeks they tried again and again to get down to the river, but every day they found the old scare-crow on guard. At last they gave up the watch, and Mister Crocodile, no longer afraid, came out each day and took his sun bath without being troubled.

"Of course, this was a long, long time ago," concluded Granny, "but if you go to The Land of Sunshine this very day you will still find the old scare-crow on watch down by the river. And the belief is yet common among the bears that he is some mysterious hunter put there to protect Mister Crocodile forever."

ANNANCY AN' TIGER RIDIN' HORSE

This Folk Tale is one of the famous Annancy stories, which came from the West Indies, particularly from Jamaica, St. Kitts, Antigua, Trinidad, and Barbadoes. Annancy is a fantastic character, usually the hero of the tale. This story is taken from the collection by Pamela Colman Smith, but all the versions are practically the same.

In a long before time, Annancy an' Tiger was both cortin' de same young lady. An' dey was bery jealous ob each oder. So one day Annancy, him go to de young lady house, an' him say:

"You know Breda Tiger is not'ing else dan an ole ridin' horse?"

An' de young lady was bex (vexed).

An' so de nex' time Tiger come fe see her, she say:

"Go away wid you! How you can come cortin' me, when you know you is not'ing but an old ridin' horse!"

An' Tiger, him bawl out:

"Who tell you dis one great big lie?"

An' she say Annancy tell her, an' she didn' tink it was a lie at all! So Tiger, him say him would bring Annancy to prove it! An' him hurry go Annancy house. But Annancy see him comin', out ob de window. An' him run an' get 'pon de bed an' play him was sick. An' Tiger come to de door, an' knock, an' say bery sof'ly:

"Breda Annancy, is you in?"

An' Annancy say, as dough him was bery sick:

"Yes, me Breda, I is in."

An' Tiger, him go in. An' Annancy say:

"Oh, me Breda, I so sick wid feaver!"

An' Tiger say:

"Breda Tiger is not'ing else dan an ole ridin' horse."

"You tell de young lady dis one great big lie, dat I is not'ing but you fada's old jackass ridin' horse? Now you is to come an' prove dat I is not a ridin' horse!"

An' den Annancy say:

"Oh, me Breda! How you tink I can come wid you? I just tek de doctor medecine an' two pill! How you tink I can come to de young lady house tonight?"

An' Tiger say:

"You mus' come! I tell you what I wi' do, Breda; I will carry you 'pon me back!"

So Annancy say, all yite! An' him get up, an' tek him saddle down from de' rafter, an' put it 'pon Tiger back, an' Tiger say:

"Wha' dat for?"

An' Annancy say:

"Dat is so I can go sof'ly 'pon you' back, fe me head hurt me so!" An' den him go an' tek down him bridle an' rein, an put dem' pon Breda Tiger.

An' Tiger say:

"Wha' dat for?"

An' Annancy say:

"Dat is so when you walk too fas', I will pull you back, me head hurt me so!"

Den Annancy, him go and tek down him spur an' ridin' whip; an' den him mount up 'pon de table, an' den 'pon Breda Tiger, an' say:

"Now, me Breda Tiger, you mus'n' walk too fas'."

An' Tiger walk off. An' when dey get a mile an' a little, Annancy tek him ridin' whip an' give Tiger a lash! An' Tiger jump an' say:

"Warra! Wa' dat?"

An' den Annancy say:

"Oh, me Breda, de flies, dey boder you so, I is lickin' dem off!"

And den Tiger say:

"Nex' time doan lick so hot!"

So dey go anoder mile an' a little; an' den Annancy tek him ridin' whip an' lash Tiger 'pon de ear! An' Tiger say:

"Warra! Wa' dat?"

An' Annancy say:

"De flies, dey boder you so, Breda Tiger!"

An' Tiger say:

"Nex' time you mus'n' lick so hot, Breda Annancy!"

An' den dey go anoder mile an' a little, an' at las' dey get to de young lady house, far as de yard mouth.

An' when dey get dere, Annancy see de young lady standin' in de door mouth, an' him stan' up in him stirrup, like how jockey do, a' Kin'ston race cou'se. An' him lash Tiger, an' use him spur till Tiger gallop! When dey get to de door where de young lady was standin', Annancy take off him hat an' wave it, an' him bawl out:

"Me no tell you so, Missus! Dat dis old Tiger was not'ing but me Fada's old long-ear jackass ridin' horse?"

An' him jump off, an' Tiger was so 'shame dat him gallop away into de bush, an' was neber seen any more!

OLD MAN AND THE BULLBERRIES

Grey Wolf

Old man was walking along, very thirsty, so the first river he came to, he flung himself down to drink. Right after he had filled up, he noticed a branch full of bullberries, lying under the water.

"Say, that is fine," exclaimed Old Man. "Berries! I guess I'll dive in and get 'em."

He dived in, swam around under water, and felt for the berries; but not one could he find.

"That's queer!" he gasped, coming to the surface. "I'll look again."

When the water cleared, he stared into it again. Sure enough, there were the berries.

Old Man dived a second time, and the poor fellow nearly suffocated, trying to stay under water long enough to find the berries. Finally he came up and blew a long breath and climbed out on the bank. After a minute, he turned to look and the berries were there as before!

"I don't stay under long enough, that's the trouble!" exclaimed Old Man. He found a stone and tied it around his middle and jumped in. He went down, like a stone, and flopped on the hard bottom of the river. Once there, he thrashed his arms about, looking for the berries. It was no use. At last, choking and bubbling, he tried to rise, but could not. The stone held him down.

"Do I die now?" he wondered.

"No," answered his tomahawk—"cut the cord!"

Old Man cut the cord, and the rock fell on his toes.

"OUCH!" he gurgled.

He shot to the surface. Now he was so exhausted that he had to lie on his back to recover breath. Suddenly he noticed, right above him, a berry bush, leaning out over the river. It was the reflection of this bush that Old Man had dived for!

"So!" cried Old Man to the berry bush, "you fooled me, did you!" He jumped up and picked out a stick and attacked the berry bush, beating it until he had knocked off all its berries.

"There!" he cried, as he ate the berries, "that is your punishment for fooling Old Man. After this, even the women will beat you!"

It was so. From that time, whenever the Indian women wanted berries, they beat the bullberry bushes with sticks, having first spread blankets to catch the berries. Old Man taught them that.

Wolf and His Nephew

Elsie Clews Parsons

Do you know where the Cape Verde Islands are? No? They are off the most western point of Africa—Cape Verde, the green cape. In those islands now and for several centuries some of the best story tellers, I believe, in the world have been telling one another stories which once travelled, some of them, from the African mainland, some of them from the Hispanic peninsula. For stories, you know, travel like people, from one end of the world to the other. How? Guess.

We catch the stories somewhere on their travels, but we seldom learn where they started from. The stories I am going to tell you I caught in Rhode Island, after they came over to this country from the Cape Verde islands, and, as I said, some of them reached the Islands from Portugal and some from Senegambia or Sierra Leone; but whence they came to those countries, who knows? Perhaps from Arabia, perhaps from India, perhaps from some old, old African kingdom. At any rate, they have been moving about the world a long time, a very long time.

After you have read about these tricks which Wolf, the big, greedy, slow fellow, and Peter, his quick and sly little nephew, play on each other, tell the story in your turn to somebody who likes stories. Remember, these tales are tales not to write but to speak. I have written them down for you only because I can't reach you with my voice for which written words are only a makeshift, a lifeless sort of makeshift. But if you tell the story to somebody in your own words, you will make it come to life again.

Peter had a place in the country, where the food was good. One day he met his Uncle Wolf. Wolf said to him, "Ah, Nephew, where have you been and what have you been eating to make you so fine and fat? Your Uncle has been around here without being able to find a thing to eat. Do take me where you get your food."

"Uncle, I won't take you where I get my food. You're too greedy. They'd catch you and kill you."

Wolf begged. "No, I won't be greedy. Take me! Take me!"

"All right. Tomorrow at dawn I'll take you."

That night Wolf did not sleep at all, and at midnight he knocked at Peter's door. Peter said, "Oh, Uncle Wolf! Go home. It's still the middle of the night. Nobody would go at this hour."

At one o'clock Wolf began to crow like a cock—"Cocorico! Cocorico! Cocorico!" Then he went and knocked at Peter's door. Peter got up and said to him, "It's too early yet. Go home! Do go home! It's too early yet. It's you crowing like a cock. I know you. Go home!"

Wolf had a little house. He went back to it and waited a little while, then he set the house on fire. He went back and knocked again on Peter's door. Peter got up and saw the light of the fire. Wolf said to him, "See the light? It's dawn. Time to go. See the light?"

"Uncle Wolf," said Peter, "I don't know what to do with you. Here you are setting fire to your house. Now you will have to live on the street. Well, let's go."

They went to the house of Aunt Goose. On the way Peter said to his uncle, "Uncle Wolf, if Aunt Goose catches us, she will kill us. We must work quickly. Eat only one egg to every fifty you put in your bag."

"All right, Nephew," said Wolf. But to every fifty eggs Wolf ate, he put only one in his bag. Peter put into his bag one hundred eggs to every one he ate.

"Time to leave, Uncle Wolf," said Peter.

"I have still an empty place in my stomach," said Wolf. "I have still to eat for my grandmother and for my mother and for my father and for my wife and for my children."

But Peter would not wait. "I am going, Uncle," he said. "When you are ready to come out say 'Cushac! Cushac!' for the door to open and when you are outside say 'Cubic! Cubic!' for the door to close."

"All right," said Wolf, and he went on eating. After he finished eating all he could and wanted to leave he called out, "Cubic! Cubic!" The door shut tight. "Cubic! Cubic" he shouted. The door shut tighter. "Cubic! Cubic! Cubic!!!" The more he shouted, the tighter it closed.

Aunt Goose was coming. Away on a little hill stood Peter. He saw her and sang:

"Little stick, little stick.
Are you going to beat Sir Wolf?
Aunt Goose comes from gathering wood."

Inside the door, Wolf heard Peter singing and sang back:

"Nephew, my nephew,
You are a sly one!
Into someone's house you bring me to feed.
When you know I am unlucky.
Cubic! Cubic!"

Outside Aunt Goose sang:

"Wan! Wan!
Dew falls, sun shines,
And I am coming."

Peter sang again:

"Little stick, little stick,
Are you going to beat Sir Wolf?
Aunt Goose comes from gathering wood."

Now Aunt Goose came up to her door with her bundle of wood. She put it down and said, "Cushac! Cushac!" The door started to open when from inside Wolf called, "Cubic! Cubic!" and it closed again. Again Goose said, "Cushac! Cushac!"—"Cubic! Cubic!" said Wolf. Goose sat down before the door. "Door," she said, "why don't you open? Other days you open when I say, Cushac Cushac!" The door flew open.

Wolf ran under the bed. Then Aunt Goose made herself some coffee. She drank it and lay down to rest. She belched.

"You pig!" exclaimed Wolf under the bed.

Aunt Goose looked around everywhere. She couldn't see anybody. She went back to bed. She belched again.

"You dirty pig. Don't you see a man is under the bed?" called out Wolf.

This time she saw him. She dashed at him. He jumped out and caught hold of the roof truss. "Come down so I can kill you," said Goose. But Wolf held on until he grew tired.

"I'm tired hanging here, Aunt Goose," he said.

"If you're tired hanging by your hands, hang by your feet," she said.

"I'm tired hanging by my feet," Wolf called out again.

"If you're tired hanging by your feet, hang by your belly," said Goose. Wolf let go with his feet. He fell into a pile of ashes by the fireplace and was lost to sight.

Just then Peter passed by. "Peter? Oh, Peter! Come in here," said Goose. "Your uncle was here, but now I can't see where he is. He fell down. He must be dead."

Peter called out, "Our yellow race never dies without belching."

Wolf heard him. He belched. The ashes scattered and there was Wolf in full sight. Aunt Goose began to beat him. She beat him almost to death.

There was a Goat that had three kids, named Melo, Maria, Sané. She raised them in a house she could lock up, and every day she would come in from the fields to suckle them. She sang:

"Melo, Maria, Sané,
Open the door for me to suckle you."

One day Wolf heard this song and while Goat was away, he came to the door and sang in a gruff voice:

"Melo, Maria, Sané,
Open the door for me to suckle you."

"Oh, Sir Wolf! We're not going to open to you," cried the kids. "You're not going to get us to eat."

So Wolf went to the doctor to ask him how he could make his voice soft like a goat's. "Get a woolen blanket, a pot of water, and a bundle of wood,' said the doctor. "Make a fire and heat the water. Jump into the pot and tell your nephew to cover it with a blanket. In this way your voice will become soft." Wolf did this and stayed three days in the pot. Then he went to Goat's house and sang:

"Melo, Maria, Sané,
Open the door for me to suckle you."

They opened the door, and he swallowed them down, all three of them.

Then he went to the well for a drink. "Sir Wolf," the Well asked, "what have you eaten to make you so thirsty?"

"I have eaten goose-eggs," answered Wolf.

Mistress Goat was going along, crying for her children. She met a Donkey. Donkey said to her, "Mistress Goat, how is it that every day I meet you singing and dancing, but today you are in tears?"

"I have reason to cry, Sir Donkey; Wolf has eaten up my three kids."

"Come along with me," said Donkey. "I'll turn Wolf over to you."

When Wolf saw Donkey coming towards him he said, "Come here, Donkey old boy. You're the very fellow I am looking for to eat." Donkey ran away.

Goat met an Ox. Ox said to her, "Mistress Goat, how is it that every day I meet you singing and dancing, but today you are in tears?"

"I have reason to cry, Sir Ox: Wolf has eaten up my three kids."

"Come along with me," said Ox. "I'll turn Wolf over to you."

When Wolf saw Ox coming towards him he said, "Come here, Big-neck. You're the very fellow whose blood I want to drink."

Ox ran away.

Goat met a horse. Horse said to her, "Mistress Goat, how is it that every day I meet you singing and dancing, but today you are in tears?"

"I have reason to cry, Sir Horse; Wolf has eaten up my three kids."

"Come along with me," said Horse. "I'll turn Wolf over to you."

When Wolf saw Horse coming towards him, he said, "Come here, Horse, old fellow. You're the very one I want to wrestle with." Horse made towards Wolf, but as soon as Wolf came on, too, Horse kicked up his heels and ran away.

Goat met an ant. Ant said to her, "Mistress Goat, how is it that every day I meet you singing and dancing, but today you are in tears?"

"I have reason to cry, Mistress Ant; Wolf has eaten up my three kids."

"Come along with me," said Ant. "I'll turn Wolf over to you."

"I don't think you can turn Wolf over to me," said Goat. "Big fellows like Donkey, Ox and Horse couldn't; how can a little creature like you?" Ant sang:

"I am a little ant.
Smoke doesn't blacken me.
Sun doesn't burn."

She went on up to Wolf and Wolf swallowed her. Then she bit into Wolf's guts. Wolf cried, "Ant, let me alone!"

"I won't let you alone until you let out the three children of Mistress Goat."

Wolf let out one. "That's all," he said.

"Mistress Ant, I have three children," said Goat.

Ant bit Wolf again. Wolf said, "Ant, do let me alone!"

"Not until you let out all the kids," said Ant. Wolf let out the last kid. Goat took the three kids and went off to the fields.

From this, you see that you must not disparage anyone because he is little, for Ant, little though she was, gave back to Goat her three kids.

Wolf and Peter, his nephew, went into the country and stole a pig. They took it to a cave and made a fire and put on the pot. Wolf was sitting on one side of the fire, and Peter on the other. When the pig was almost cooked, Peter took a little stone and threw it up to the roof of the cave. As the stone was falling down he said, "Look, Uncle Wolf, look! The cave is falling down on us. Get up and hold it up." While Wolf went to hold up the cave, Peter took the pot outside and ate up the food. He went away, leaving Wolf holding up the cave.

For three days Wolf stood there holding the cave up, then he jumped aside and fell and cut his head. He went home and asked his wife if she had seen Peter.

She said, "No, I haven't seen Peter. You better leave that boy alone and stay home. He'll kill you yet."

"I'm the one who's going to kill him! Isn't he my nephew?"

Next day Peter smeared his head with molasses and went to see his uncle. When he came in he said, "Mistress Isabel, where's Uncle Wolf?" Wolf was hidden under the bed. He wanted to catch Peter. As Peter took off his hat, Isabel saw the molasses and thought it was blood, so she screamed.

Wolf came out from under the bed. He cried out, "Oh, Peter, my nephew! Who has done this to you?"

Peter answered, "Oh that's nothing, my uncle. I told a man to hit me on the head with his axe, and that came out."

Wolf touched Peter's head and then he put his fingers in his mouth. My! but it was sweet! "Isabel! Isabel!" he called to his wife. "Get the axe and hit me, too, on the head." She hit him and drew blood. He cried, "Hit me again, hit me again! It isn't sweet yet. Hit me again!!" She almost split his head in two. Then she had to go and get herbs to make a plaster to cure it.

After his head was healed, Wolf started out to the beach to find Peter. Peter was a fisherman. On the beach Wolf began to pick up snails and crabs to eat. A claw stuck in his teeth. Peter was at the other end of the beach when he saw his uncle. He came up to him and said, "Uncle, I'll get that claw out for you." Peter had a needle in his hand.

"No, Nephew, not with that," objected Wolf. "Don't you remember that the shroud of your mother was sewed with a needle?"

Peter got out a pin. "No, Nephew. Don't you remember that pins were used for nails in the coffin of your mother?"

Peter picked up a straw. "No, Nephew. Don't you remember it was a straw that choked your mother to death? Why don't you take it out with your fingers?"

Peter started to take it out with his fingers and Wolf snapped his teeth on his fingers and bit a piece out.

"Nephew, you are a smart fellow, but I am smarter than you. Remember I am your uncle."

Peter said, "Uncle Wolf, I came to tell you where you could get something good to eat. Now you've bitten a piece out of my finger, I won't tell you."

"Oh, Nephew, do tell me. I'll put the piece back on your finger, even if I have to take a piece out of my own finger."

"Well, Uncle Wolf, I'll take you there," said Peter, "but you've got to learn the rule."

It was a fig-tree. You could not reach the tree, it was too high up. You had to say, "Come down! Come down! Come down!" and the tree would come down, and you could climb on it and say, "Go up! Go up! Go up!" and it would go up as far as you wished. Then you said, "Stop!" When you got enough to eat you would say, "Come down! Come down! Come down!" and it would come down.

Wolf said to the tree, "Come down! Come down! Come down!" and the tree came down and he climbed on it and said: "Go up! Go up! Go up!" He said, "Stop," and he began to eat. He ate so much that he forgot the rule and when he wanted to come down he said, "Go up! Go up! Go up!" and the tree kept going up: It went all the way up to Heaven.

When Wolf got there God said to him, "What are you doing here? How are you going to get down again?"

"I don't know," said Wolf.

"Well, take this piece of leather," said God, "go to the river and wash it and bring it back to me. I'll make a drum for you and I'll tie a string on you and let you down. When you reach the bottom, play your drum and I'll know you're there and cut the string."

When Wolf went to wash the leather, he was so hungry that he ate it. When he came back he told God the current had carried away the leather while he was washing it. God gave him another piece of leather. He was still hungry and he ate it and told God again that the current had washed it away. God gave him another piece of leather and this time God sent Saint Peter along with him to watch him and see if he was telling the truth. Every time Wolf started to carry the leather to his mouth, Saint Peter said, "Pst! What are you doing?"

I'm just smelling it!

"Oh! I ain't eating it, I'm just smelling it," said Wolf.

God made him the drum and tied him to a string. "When you get down, play the drum and I'll cut the string," said God.

On the way down Wolf saw a Bluejay. He called out, "Eh there, Bluejay! Give me a piece of your meat." (Bluejay has a red mouth and it looks like meat.)

Bluejay said, "Play your drum for me, and I'll give you a piece."

Wolf was hungry, so he began to play his drum. He played "St. John of God" in double quick time. God heard him playing and cut the string. As Wolf was tumbling down over and over, he kept hollering to Peter, "Nephew! Oh Nephew! Put some mattresses and straw down for me to fall on." Bluejay laughed at him and flew away, and when Peter heard him he took all his knives and forks and razors and pins and all the sharp things he could find and put them there for his uncle to fall on.

There was a famine in the land and people were looking about for something to eat. The day Wolf reached the king's house, the king was

marrying off his daughter. For three days Sir Wolf had had nothing to eat. At the king's house he started to cry. The king said to him, "What is the matter with you?"

He said, "I'm not crying for myself, I'm crying because your daughter is going to ride to her wedding on an old pack saddle, just a straw saddle, and I who know how to make leather saddles—"

"Good," said the king. "I'll put off the day of the wedding, and I'll give you a week to make saddles for us all to ride on to the wedding. Go into my store-house and make up all the skin which is there into saddles."

Wolf said, "All right! I'll make it all up in a week." Every day for a week they passed food and water in through the window of the storehouse for Wolf. He ate up the food and drank the water, three buckets each day, and each day he ate up a skin. On the seventh day, when the king went into the store-house, he found only a cow's tail.

The king invited Peter to the wedding, to be the best man. He knew Peter would invite his uncle to go with him, and in this way he could catch Wolf and give him a beating. Peter did invite Wolf. "There is no one to go with me but you, Uncle Wolf. You are my uncle."

But Wolf said, "I can't go. I stole all his skins from the king. I ate them up. I'm not going to his house."

Peter said, "You better go. The king is a rich man. He won't bother about the skins. He's forgotten all about it."

"Well, I'll go with you," said Wolf, "but I'll have to go as your horse, so the king won't know me. The only thing I ask of you is not to forget me when you get there—send me out a bucket of bones."

Peter agreed and started to put a saddle on his uncle.

"Don't put that on me, I don't like it!" shouted Wolf.

"But every one has a saddle on his horse. If I don't put one on you, the king will know it's you." After Peter put the saddle on, he started to put the bridle in Wolf's mouth.

"Don't put that thing in my mouth! I can't eat with that thing in my mouth!"

"But I'll take it off when we get there."

"All right, but be sure you take it off."

Then Peter started to fasten on his spurs. "But you will rip me up. I won't be able to hold my food," grumbled Wolf.

"I won't touch you with my spurs. Everybody wears spurs. If I don't, it will look queer."

"All right, put them on, but if you use them to me, I'll kill you when we get back home."

Wolf was a good runner. When Peter dug the spurs into him he ran so fast that in fifteen minutes he was at the king's house. Peter tied him to the foot of a tree at the street door. The other guests arrived, and Wolf pawed the ground to make them think he was a horse. Then the servants began to pass by with food. Wolf begged,

Wolf was a good runner

"Give me something to eat! Oh! do give me something to eat!"

The servants said, "What's that? If that isn't a horse talking! We are going to tell the king."

"No, no, don't say anything, don't mention it!" cried Wolf. But they went and told the king. The king loaded his gun and shot at Wolf. He hit him in the eye. Before he could shoot again, Wolf pulled back on the rope and broke it and ran away.

After the wedding the king gave Peter twenty cows. Peter took them out to pasture and within six months he had thirty head. As his pasturage was too small, he moved to another place. It was just where Wolf happened to be. When Peter saw his uncle he called out, "Uncle Wolf, I've been looking for you. Here are the cattle the king has sent you. That shot was not aimed at you. They were just shooting a gun off for the wedding."

"Very well," said Wolf. "I accept the cows and I'll make you my cowherd. I'll give you one cow out of every thirty to milk for your self." But Wolf was so greedy that he had milked all his twenty-nine cows before Peter began to milk his one cow. So Wolf began to beg him, "My nephew, give me that cow of yours to milk today and tomorrow I'll give you two cows."

Peter was afraid of Wolf, so he gave him back the cow. Next day Wolf gave Peter two black cows; but before Peter began to milk, Wolf had finished milking his cows and he said, "My nephew, give me those black cows because black cow milk is very sweet; tomorrow I'll give you three cows."

Next day Wolf gave Peter three white cows; but before Peter began to milk them Wolf had finished milking his cows and said, "My nephew, give me those white cows, because white cow milk is just like cream; tomorrow I'll give you four cows."

Peter said, "For three days I have had nothing to eat. I'm hungry. I won't give them to you."

Wolf said, "All the cows are mine anyhow," and he began to beat Peter.

Peter ran away to a hill and Wolf began to milk the white cows. There on the hill Peter yelled out, "If you are looking for that blind horse, you'll find him down there in the ravine milking a white cow, one of the cows you sent him."

Wolf stopped milking. He looked up. He called out to Peter, "Is it that king asking for me?"

Peter did not answer but yelled again, "Run, run, if you want to catch him. He's a good runner. If you don't run fast you won't catch him!"

Wolf left the cow and started to run. Peter yelled again, "Better run fast after Wolf! If he gets to the sea down there, you'll lose him! He's a good swimmer. You won't be able to catch him in the sea, he's too good a swimmer." Wolf ran down to the beach. He was not able to swim, but he heard what Peter said, and so he believed that he could swim and he jumped into the sea and was drowned. Peter came down from the hill and took the cows and enjoyed his life without his uncle.

Yesterday I came from there and left Peter having the happiest time in the world.

Little shoes run up the hill and down.
Bee kidney, mosquito liver,
Who runs the quickest can have it.
Who can tell a better one, tell it.

THE TWO STARS

AN INDIAN LEGEND

Aaron Jeffery Cuffee

On certain clear nights in midwinter, two unusually bright stars shine in the western sky between the time the sun sets and the moon rises. If you should ask an old Indian what two stars they are, he would tell you "The Lovers," and he might tell you this story.

Okoya—tall, straight as a hickory sapling, was in love with Weyana, the most beautiful girl in all the great tribes of the Prairie Country. Wrapped in his blanket, Okoya used to stand on the hill above the camp and play love songs to Weyana on his flute. As if in answer to the sweet strains, Weyana used to come out of her father's wigwam, stand for a minute, and then go back again. Okoya, his heart happy, would go back to his own wigwam.

The families of the two were glad of their mutual love and planned a great marriage feast for the spring. But the winter was very severe and there was much illness in the tribe. Weyana became so ill that her father called in the medicine men, who are the doctors of the Indians. They came into the wigwam where poor Weyana lay and chanted prayers to Gitchi Manitou, the Great Spirit; they muttered curses on the evil spirits of disease; they drummed fiercely on their tom-toms; and in spite of it all, Weyana died.

Okoya was grief-stricken. He went without food for days. He sat in his wigwam, or went out into the forest alone for weeks at a time. No one ever saw him give way to his sorrow, but his heart was dead within him.

One night, sorrowful, he stood gazing at the sun, its great big eye half closed; and he saw a bright little star which he had never seen before, shining in the sky above the sun, and then he heard a voice speaking to him; it was the voice of his lost Weyana coming from that tiny star!

"I am thy beloved Weyana. Pray do not grieve for me. I shall be here to greet you until you, too, are called by Gitchi Manitou to Shipapu, the land of our fathers."

When Okoya heard these wonderful words, all sorrow left him; he was comforted. With arms outstretched to the fast-disappearing sun, he chanted this prayer:

"O Sun, thou red and flaming God,
Thy long, light-fingers beck'ning,
Pray summon me with just a nod,
To the Land of Happy Hunting."

After that he used to come out every night and stand for a long time talking to the little star until, like the sun, it sank in the west and Okoya had to bid it "Good night."

With spring came the time of war parties, as well as planting. War dances were held, bows and arrows made ready; men chosen. Okoya, who had shown his bravery before, was made a full-fledged warrior now and allowed to wear a single eagle feather in his hair. He was very proud of his new honor and at dusk he went out into the cool air to give thanks. Shawan, the south wind, rustled about heavy with the odor of leafing trees and newly turned earth; faintly throbbing with the beat of the war drums down in the camp; shrill with the "peeping" of the frogs in the marshes. Okoya lifted up his arms and gave thanks to Gitchi Manitou for having been made a warrior. Then he turned to tell his little star of his good fortune, but he could not find the star. Had he made some mistake in direction? No, Indians do not do that. The star was not there any more, and in his despair Okoya cried to all the stars,

"Tell me, O stars, I beseech you,
Where is thy sister Weyana?"

In their tiny, far-off voices the stars answered him.

"The Gods of the Storms and the Winter,
Have taken her with them forever."

And as if in mockery of his grief the war dance began with wild cheers and the regular beat of tom-toms down in the camp.

Lonely and with heavy heart, Okoya put on his war paint and set out with the war party before daybreak next day. He felt that Gitchi Manitou in anger had turned his face away from him. Life was no longer a joy; it was a burden. He spoke to none of his companions and they in turn left him to himself, thinking that he was growing afraid of the danger ahead of him.

Silent as shadows, the warriors sped toward the country of the hostile tribe. Had you been near them, you could not have seen them because they hid themselves so carefully.

Towards dark, the band heard the bark of a wolf behind them. The bark was repeated at short intervals and each repetition was closer than the last. Now the bark of the wolf was a signal of the tribe, so the party stopped and hid in the woods. Soon an exhausted runner staggered into view and fell before he had reached the war party. The whole party ran towards him in alarm, because he was one of their own men left at home to guard the camp.

The first to reach him were told of a raid on the village by a hostile band of Indians. Even the women and children had helped defend their wigwams, and he had been wounded in trying to escape with the alarm to the war party. With the

Weyana used to come out of her father's wigwam

delivery of his message the runner's voice grew fainter, and after one convulsive shudder, his body grew rigid; he was dead.

Grief and rage filled the hearts of the warriors. In haste they buried their fallen comrade, and spurred on by the thought of the danger of those at home, they traveled back all night, at a very tiring pace.

In the dawn of the next day they saw smoke ahead of them, and dismay made them hurry faster. Were they too late? Was the village in ruins? They surprised the raiders' sentinels, and saw that only a few of the wigwams had been burnt; the remainder were safe. So they scattered and hid behind stumps, trees and rocks, and started their deathly game of hide-and-seek. All day long the fighting lasted, and as the day drew to its close it was evident that, due to the fatigue of the rescuers and the superior numbers of the raiders, defeat and the massacre of the people in the camp seemed certain.

Suddenly with a cry of defiance, Okoya sprang from behind the stump which had hidden him, electrified his tribesmen by throwing down his bow and arrows, and, with knife and tomahawk alone, dashed toward the hiding places of the hostile band.

The enemy was terrified by Okoya's boldness. Their hands were unsteady, so all of their attempts to hit him with arrows were futile. They were sure that he was some god who had come to help the other tribe, a god whom neither arrows nor knives could harm. So when Okoya's men followed him in his dash, the enemy fled. The village was saved.

Then, just after sunset, his work finished, the day won, Okoya fell, pierced by an arrow. As his followers reached him, he managed to raise himself on one elbow, and with the other arm to point toward the western sky above the fading light of perfect day. Then with a smile as of content, he sank back dead. When his men looked up where he had pointed, they saw a single very bright star; and even as they gazed at it in wonder, another small star appeared, close to it, and grew and grew in brilliance until it was equal to the first.

The old wise men of the tribe say the Storm Gods and the Gods of Winter always admire great bravery, and that when they saw how brave Okoya had been they gave him his heart's desire. They returned Weyana to him unharmed, and then Gitchi Manitou made them two bright stars.

What do you think? If you go out some clear, cold night, and ask them, maybe the stars will tell you.

THE TWIN HEROES

AN AFRICAN MYTH ADAPTED BY

Alphonso O. Stafford

In that far-off time when the world was young, there lived in a town of a powerful king, a widow whose name was Isokah, and whose husband, a brave warrior, had fallen in battle.

She had two baby sons, called Mansur and Luembur. They were twins, with bodies round and shapely, the color of dull gold.

At their birth an old man, known for his gift of prophecy, had said, "Twins are a gift of Anambia, the Great Spirit, and they have been sent to us for a special work."

Everyone in that town, knowing how true were the sayings of the old man, believed thereafter that the twin babes of Isokah would grow into manhood and become warriors of note and possibly heroes of great renown.

When they were six weeks old, their mother planted in her garden, a short distance apart, two seeds. With great care she watered the earth about and when the seeds sprouted and became tiny plants, her care for them did not cease.

As the years passed, Isokah's two sons grew tall, strong, and pleasing to the eye, like the graceful pine trees around their home. In play, in the hunt, and in deeds of daring, these two boys always took first place among their companions.

Meanwhile, the two plants grew into fine trees with beautiful spreading foliage. When Mansur and Luembur were old enough to understand, Isokah took each of them to one of the trees, and said,

"This, my son, is your life tree. As it thrives, withers, or dies, so you will grow, be in peril, or perish."

After that day, Mansur and Luembur watched his own tree with increasing interest and felt for it a loving tenderness when resting under its spreading branches during the heat of the day, or in the cool of the evening, while listening to the strange cries in the jungle; or gazing with wonder at the clear sky with its brilliant stars, and the silver crescent changing nightly into a great golden ball.

How happy was Isokah as she watched her boys grow into early manhood, and the life trees thrive in strength and beauty with them.

During this time, Mansur had many strange dreams—dreams of great perils in the jungle, dreams of different lands—but more often he had visions of Yuah, the daughter of Zambay, who was Old Mother Earth, the first daughter of the first father.

Yuah was said to be beautiful. Her beauty was like the dusk at twilight, when the stars begin to twinkle in the afterglow of the western sky.

One day, after Mansur had passed his twentieth year, he said to his mother, "The time has come for me to marry and I am going in search of Yuah, the daughter of Old Mother Earth."

Though her sorrow was great when she heard these words, Isokah knew that she could not always keep her sons near her. So she called upon Muzimu, a wizard of strange powers, and asked him for some magic to help her son, Mansur, in his quest.

When this was given, she returned and gave it to him, saying, "My son, this is your magic. I shall guard your life tree while you are away and Luembur, your brother, will watch over me."

Mansur then put his strong arms around his mother's shoulders, bowed his head upon her cheek, and gave her his farewell kiss. Then, taking from her the magic, he touched some grass he had plucked from the ground. One blade was changed into a horn, another into a knife, and still another into a spear.

Before leaving, he called Luembur, saying, "Brother, be ever near mother Isokah, and let no harm befall her."

For days and days Mansur travelled. What a picture of natural beauty met his eye everywhere! How verdant was the foliage of the trees, shrubs, and plants of the African plains and highlands; how sparkling the streams that foamed over rocky beds of granite and sandstone, how beautiful was the coloring of the flowers, how gay was the plumage of the birds, how graceful and striking in size were the animals that fled before him as he pushed his way onward to the land of Zambay, the mother of his desired Yuah. When overcome by hunger, Mansur called upon his magic for food.

At last, the far country of Zambay was reached. Whenever a stranger entered it, he was escorted at once to Zambay, the queen, the all powerful ruler of that land. The usual custom followed, when Mansur was seen striding forward with his spear in hand, horn across shoulder, and knife at side.

Standing near her mother, Yuah saw the stranger—saw him in his strength and in his early manhood, so lithe in movement and so fearless in bearing. Straightaway her heart warmed to him. How happy was Mansur when he beheld this dream-girl as a reality and saw in her eyes, a look of friendly interest that passed into admiration when he recited the story of his travels and the purpose of his visit.

Three days later, they were married. A fine feast was held, followed by joyous singing and a merry dance. The finest house in the town was given to the bride and groom, where for many months their happiness was complete.

One day, while idling in his new home, Mansur opened the door of a strange room which he had never noticed. In it were many mirrors, each covered so that the glass could not be seen. Calling Yuah, he asked her to remove the covers so that he might examine them. She took him to one, uncovered it, and Mansur immediately saw a perfect likeness of his native town; then to another, and he saw his mother and his brother, Luembur, sitting in peace beneath his life tree. In each mirror he saw something that carried his memory back to his past life and the country of his birth.

Coming to the last mirror, larger than the others, Mansur was filled with a strange foreboding. Yuah did not uncover it. "Why not let me look into it, Yuah?" asked Mansur.

"Because, my beloved one, in it you will see reflected the Land of Never Return—from it none returns who wanders there."

Now this remark made Mansur very curious, and he longed as never before, to see this mirror

"Do let me see it," urged Mansur.

that could picture so strange a land or so mysterious a scene.

"Do let me see it," urged Mansur. Yielding at last to his entreaties, Yuah uncovered the mirror, and her young husband saw reflected therein that dread land of the lower world—that unsought place of cruel King Kalungo, of which all men had heard. Mansur looked in the mirror a long time, then he said,

"I must go there; I must leave you, my dear."

"Nay, you will never return; please do not go, my beloved one," pleaded Yuah.

"Have no fear," answered Mansur. "The magic of Muzimu will be my protection. Should any harm befall me, my twin brother, Luembur, will come to my rescue."

Now this made Yuah cry and she was very, very sad, but her tears did not move Mansur from his desire and his purpose.

In a few hours he had departed for the Land of Never Return.

After travelling many days, Mansur came upon a weird old woman working in the fields. In her eyes, there was mystery; in her presence, there came to him a feeling of awe. Though he knew not then, she was the never sleeping spirit that guarded the secrets of the Land of Never Return.

Approaching her, Mansur said, "My good woman, please show me the road to the land whence no man returns who wanders there."

The old woman, pausing in her work, looked at him as he stood there, so tall and straight. A smile passed over her wrinkled face as she recognized in Mansur one of the true heroes for whose coming she had waited many years.

Much to his surprise, the old woman, after a long and deep gaze, said,

"Mansur, I know you and I shall direct your way, though the task before you is one of peril. Go down that hill to your right, take the narrow path, and avoid the wide one. After an hour's travel, you will come to the dread home of Kalungo, the Land of Never Return. Before reaching his abode, you must pass a fierce dog that guards his gate, fight the great serpent of seven heads within the courtyard, and destroy the mighty crocodile that sleeps in the pool."

These impending dangers did not frighten Mansur. Following the narrow path, he came within a short time to a deep ravine. Through this he walked, head erect, eyes alert, and spear uplifted. Suddenly he observed the outer gate of the Land of Never Return.

By means of his magic, he passed the fierce dog, and after a severe battle he succeeded in destroying the serpent, that seven-headed monster. Near the pool, he saw the mighty crocodile resting on its bank, and rushed forward to strike him. Then, by accident, Mansur's magic fell upon the ground, and immediately he was seized by the crocodile and disappeared within his terrible mouth.

At home, his mother, Isokah, and brother, Luembur, noticed with fear that the life tree of Mansur had suddenly withered.

"Mother, my brother is in danger. I must go at once in search of him," cried Luembur.

Rushing to Muzimu, the wizard, Isokah procured some more magic, returned home and gave it to Luembur and besought him to go immediately in search of his twin brother.

As he departed, a great weakness seized her, and supporting herself for awhile against the trunk of Luembur's life tree, she slowly sank to the ground, with a foreboding that she would never again see her sons.

When Luembur reached the town of Zambay, she was much struck with the resemblance he bore to his brother, and Yuah was overjoyed that he had come to go in search of Mansur. She noticed with pleasure that Luembur also carried the same kind of spear, horn, and knife that Mansur had.

Yuah showed him the magic mirrors, reserving for the last the fateful one that had caused Mansur to depart for the Land of Never Return.

After resting awhile, Luembur continued his journey and, as in the case of his brother, came after many days to the weird old woman working in the fields.

The story of his quest was soon told. After it was finished, she said, "I know you, also, Luembur." She then gave him the same directions.

When he reached the gates of the land of Kalungo, the fierce dog fell before the magic spear of Luembur. Then rushing to the bank of the pool where the mighty crocodile was dozing in the sun, Luembur with one great blow of his spear slew him. Then taking his knife he cut along the under side of the dead crocodile, and strange to state, Mansur jumped out, well and happy.

Swift as the wind, the twin brothers left the gates of the dread Land of Never Return and travelled upward to the place where the weird old woman worked in the field, under the rays of the glinting sun.

When she beheld them, she stood erect, a deeper mystery flashed into her age-old eyes, and in her presence, there returned to the brothers, that same feeling of awe, but now more intense.

Finally she spoke, "Brothers, by slaying the fierce dog, the terrible serpent, and the mighty crocodile, you have released the spirits of the

"Mansur jumped out, well and happy."

brave, the wise, and the good, who were prisoners in the realm of cruel Kalungo. They may now return to Mother Earth when they desire, and visit the abode of their mortal existence. Your task here below is now finished.

"You, Mansur, shall be lightning, that mortals may ever see your swift spear as it darts through the clouds; and you, Luembur, shall be Thunder, that mortals may ever hear and know the power of that flashing spear."

With these words, the sleepless spirit of the Land of Never Return touched each of the brothers, and Mansur went to the East and became the swift, darting lightning; and Luembur went to the West and became the loud, pealing thunder.

In the land of Zambay, when Yuah, through her magic mirrors, saw what had happened to the brothers, she cried with much grief. Neither by day nor by night would she be comforted.

At last her mother, Zambay, said in a gentle and sad voice, "My daughter, when your husband, Mansur, and his brother, Luembur, are angry in their home, amid the clouds, and have frightened men and beasts, here in my land, your beauty and your smile will bring them joy. At such times, your body clothed with many colors, will bend and touch me, your Mother Earth. Go hence, and live with them.

With these words, Yuah went away from the home of her mother, and we see her now as the beautiful Rainbow, after the storm clouds of Mansur and Luembur have passed on their way to the home of The All Father, the Great Sky-Spirit, Anambia.

THE LADDER TO THE SUN

AN AFRICAN FAIRY TALE

Alphonso O. Stafford

In the olden times, long before the white man came to Africa, there was a great chief whose oldest son Kee'mäh was regarded as a youth of rare promise.

In the arts of war as practiced by his people Kee'mäh took a leading part and in the assemblies of his tribe where questions of interest were discussed or laws enacted, he became a speaker of force and skill.

In form he was tall, his carriage free and graceful, his eyes dark and full of fire and his color that of old bronze. No father or mother passed him without a feeling of admiration and no maiden saw him without a look of interest. But to Kee'mäh the emotions which his appearance and fine character aroused in others meant nothing, so intent was he in preparing for the day when he would take up the rule of his father.

Like all fathers, Kee'mäh's wished before he died to see his son happily married. So on several occasions the old chief had hinted to Kee'mäh that the time had come for him to select a wife but to these hints the son had turned a deaf ear.

Finally Kee'mäh said to his father: "I will not marry any girl on earth, but for bride I must have a daughter of the Sun and Moon."

The astonishing wish of his son seemed to the old chief a very foolish one—one that could not be realized—one that he dared not discuss with the elders of his tribe, as it would indicate to them that his eldest son, regarded so highly as a youth of courage and wisdom, was somewhat unbalanced in mind.

But no argument changed this strange wish of Kee'mäh. At last, more to humor his son, the chief called one of his men, famed for his writings on pieces of bark, and told him to write a letter to King Sun and ask for one of his daughters to be the bride of Kee'mäh.

To his son the chief then gave the letter, believing that would be the end of this fanciful wish—but Kee'mäh felt that some way would be found to deliver the letter to King Sun.

As no man of the tribe could make the journey it was suggested that some animal or bird would undertake the unheard of trip. At that time man could converse with the creatures of the jungle and the birds of the air. So the deer was called and asked to deliver the letter.

"On earth I can run with the wind, but without wings I cannot go to the land of the Sun," returned the deer when he heard of the wish of Kee'mäh.

"Call the hawk," replied the anxious youth. But when the hawk heard the message that bird answered, "I fly above trees and rivers, but the land of the Sun is beyond me."

Then the eagle was given the task but his reply was—

"Though I fly above the clouds on mountain peaks, the home of the Sun is farther than the dwelling place of the thunder and lightning; there I cannot fly."

Now the sorrow of Kee'mäh was great when he heard these answers. He felt that his letter would never be delivered and he brooded much alone, far away from the home of his father, in the silent fields and near the woodland streams.

One day while in this mood Kee'mäh was near a brook, standing under the shade of some tall pine trees. Ma'nu, the frog, hopped near and spoke. "Think no more of your messenger, Kee'mäh. Give me your letter. I will deliver it."

"What! You carry a letter to that far off world?" returned the surprised youth.

"Yes, I, Ma'nu the frog, will carry your letter to the home of King Sun."

"Should you fail, you and your family can never croak again, and death will come to them all," remarked Kee'mäh.

"But I shall not fail," returned the frog, blinking his great eyes.

In much doubt but with hope the young man gave the letter to the frog and under the slope of a hill in a spring that little fellow dropped, holding in his mouth the bit of bark on which the letter was written.

With new hope Kee'mäh returned home and soon there was heard near the spring a faint sound made by two quaint little girls who carried a jug fashioned of clay. The jug was put down into the spring of water. When it was drawn up, Ma'nu, the frog, was hidden in it. One of the little girls lifted the jug upon her head, then both of them mounted a ladder of cobweb made by Anancy, the spider. As soon as they touched the ladder, they travelled faster than the wind blows—up, up into the air, never stopping, never speaking, until they reached the home of the Sun, in the land of dazzling light.

The two little girls before returning to their rooms placed the jug of water on a table in the great hall of the palace of King Sun. As soon as they left, Ma'nu, the frog, jumped out of the jug, put the letter on the table and hopped on the floor where he found a corner in which to hide. That night when King Sun returned to rest from his long journey across the sky he went into the great hall which was lighted by the golden beams of his wife and queen—the Moon.

Near the jug of water brought from earth by his water girls, he saw a letter which he read with wonder and surprise: "I, Kee'mäh of earth, eldest son of Chief Kee'mahnah, wish to marry a daughter of the Sun and Moon."

Again and again the King read the strange letter, wondering all the time how any one living on earth—far, far below, could send a letter to the far off land of his Kingdom, there beyond the clouds.

But sleep called the King and the mysterious letter was forgotten. When all was quiet Ma'nu came from his hiding place, jumped upon the table and was soon at the bottom of the jug.

In the early morning, after King Sun had begun his day's journey to the far west, the two water girls came to the hall for the jug. Down, down the cobweb ladder almost as fast as a flash of light, they descended, never stopping, never speaking, until the spring on earth under the slope of the hill was reached. When they put down the jug into the cool water to fill it, Ma'nu, the frog, hopped out and hid himself from their sight.

After the departure of the water girls the frog went to the village of men and found Kee'mäh who asked at once, "Ma'nu, what became of the letter I gave you?"

"Prince Kee'mäh, I placed the letter on King Sun's table in the hall of his great palace," replied the frog.

"Nonsense, Ma'nu; how could you go to the Kingdom of the Sun?"

"Listen, my Prince; you shall hear the story of my trip to the far off land of King Sun."

Ma'nu then related the story of his ascent with the water girls by way of the cobweb ladder to the land of the Sun and Moon. Each described incident increased the surprise of Kee'mäh, and his admiration for the cleverness of the frog was expressed again and again in words of praise. Taking courage from the recital of Ma'nu, Kee'mäh asked his father to have another letter written, to be delivered the same way.

The next night King Sun was again surprised to read another letter with these words: "I, Kee'mäh of earth, eldest son of Chief Kee'mahnah, wrote you asking for a daughter in marriage. Why did you not answer?"

At once the water girls were called and asked. "From what place do you bring such strange letters?"

The astonished girls replied, "We know of no letters, mighty King; from earth we bring only cool, sparkling water." The Sun made no comment but thought that he would write an answer to the letter and place it upon the table where he had found the other two. So early the next morning, after the King of day had gone forth, Ma'nu came from his hiding place, took the letter and made ready to return to earth in the water jug.

The two girls came merrily into the hall, dancing and singing a little song:

"Down, down Anancy's ladder we go,
Through the cloudland to earth below,
To the spring so cool and clear;
Then up again its water we bear,
For our loved King, so great, so bright,
To slake his thirst in the calm of the night."

As before, Ma'nu was carried down to earth by the water girls—though those elfin creatures knew not that the frog was hidden within their jug with a letter from King Sun to Kee'mäh.

In due time the letter was delivered and great was the joy of Kee'mäh when he read: "You on earth, the eldest son of Chief Kee'mahnah, who wishes to marry a daughter of the Sun and Moon, first send to her a suitable present."

In a few days a very dainty and handsome necklace of gold and ivory, made by the most skillful goldsmith of Chief Kee'mahnah's tribe, was ready. Then it was given to Manga, one of the wisest of wizards, to touch it with a potent charm. Afterwards Kee'mäh carried the necklace to Ma'nu, the frog, and placed it around his throat as he sat watching under the slope of the hill for the coming of the water girls.

Now King Sun in his daily journeys across the skies had seen many strange sights upon earth and had often wondered at the singular acts of men, but never before was his surprise so great as when he saw on his table in the palace hall, the beautifully carved necklace that had come so mysteriously as a present for one of his daughters.

He admired its beauty for several minutes, then called his youngest daughter, Lâ-mô-le, by name. When she appeared in the arch of the door King Sun approached and gently placed the gift of Kee'mäh around her neck. The eyes of Lâ-mô-le twinkled with pleasure as her fingers ca-

"Father, when may I see this gift of beauty?"

ressed the gold and ivory links. Then observing the exquisite carving of the ivory and the delicate tracery of the gold, her joy increased and her lips kept repeating, "O father, how beautiful; how beautiful!"

King Sun listened to the words of his daughter and smiled. When her words ceased, he noticed on her face the expression of wonder quickly change into one of desire. "Father, when may I see the one who sent this gift of beauty?" asked Lâ-mô-le.

As soon as the question was asked the expression of desire had passed into one of great eagerness, followed by a tinge of expectancy when her father said:

"That's impossible, my daughter, as the necklace came from earth and I know not its sender except by name of Kee'mäh, eldest son of Chief Kee'mahnah."

These words seemed to affect Lâ-mô-le in a strange way. A feeling of great joy, thrilling and pleasurable, came over her though she knew not the cause—neither at that time did her father, King Sun.

But Ma'nu, the frog, hidden in the corner of the palace, knew. He knew that her feeling was that of love, love that the charm placed on the necklace by Manga had aroused. When King Sun observed the strange effect of the necklace, he told her of the mysterious letters that had come from Kee'mäh in such a mysterious manner.

This story of wonder and surprise moved Lâ-mô-le to exclaim, "O father! let him marry me; please let Kee'mäh marry me."

"Tomorrow I will give my answer, daughter," returned her father.

Never did Ma'nu return with such pleasure to earth and never was Kee'mäh so happy as when he heard what had followed, after the necklace had been placed around the slender throat of King Sun's daughter.

Now he knew that Manga was the wisest of men, the most wonderful of wizards.

The next day King Sun in his journey across the sky looked down with great care upon the land of Chief Kee'mahnah. He was pleased with its beauty, the industry of the men and women, the grace and symmetry of the thatched huts, the dignity and poise of Kee'mahnah and his eldest son as they passed among their people.

That night King Sun said to his expectant daughter: "Lâ-mô-le, I am delighted with what I noticed today on earth in the land of Chief Kee'mahnah. Since his son Kee'mäh found such a clever way to deliver a letter asking for one of my daughters in marriage and then sent a present which has aroused in you such a love for him, I will now find a way for you to go to earth and become his bride."

Then he called Anancy, the spider, and had him weave, stronger than ever, the ladder used by the water girls, as his daughter, Lâ-mô-le, was to be borne down to earth.

Anancy departed to call to his aid a host of his fellow workers and a few nights later reported that the ladder was strong enough.

Then several water girls were called and kissing his daughter tenderly, King Sun touched her eyes with sleep. The girls then bore her gently to the ladder—down, down the cobweb steps, now strong as strands of silver, never speaking, never stopping, until they had placed her near the spring and returned to their home in the land of the Sun.

In the morning when Lâ-mô-le opened her eyes from sleep she looked around her with delight at the green grass, the brilliantly colored flowers, the tall, tapering trees; then to her ears came the hum, chirp and twitter of insects and birds.

How strange and yet how lovely! Then as she touched her necklace there returned that feeling of joy and longing which moved her so strangely when her father first clasped it around her throat.

But these new scenes and fancies were suddenly interrupted as she saw coming toward her with outstretched arms a tall, handsome youth saying, "O beautiful daughter of the Sun and Moon, I am Kee'mäh, eldest son of Chief Kee'mahnah; come be my bride." She shyly held out her hand and as her face lighted with a smile of great charm she said gently,

"I, Lâ-mô-le, youngest daughter of King Sun and Moon, have come from the land of the sky to wed thee."

Thus we are told by our elders how in the olden times Kee'mäh, the oldest son of Chief Kee'mahnah, took as bride a daughter of the Sun and Moon, and why the image of Ma'nu, the frog, was carved upon the spears and war horns of his people.

THE THREE GOLDEN HAIRS OF THE SUN-KING

Adapted by John Bolden

A king once went hunting and was lost in the forest. Toward evening he came to a charcoal burner's hut and asked if he could spend the night there.

In the middle of the night he saw three ladies dressed in white standing by the cradle in which lay the charcoal burner's baby.

One of them said, "Bad luck go with this child!"

The second said, "He may turn it to good."

And the third, "He shall marry the king's daughter."

The king was very angry at this, but he said nothing. The next day, when the charcoal burner had shown him the way to his city, he said, "Give me your child. I will take him to court, where he shall make his fortune."

But instead of doing this, the king told a servant to put the boy in a basket and fling him into the river. The basket floated down the stream until a fisherman drew it ashore and took the child to his wife. The boy lived with them until he was twenty years old; they called him Nameless.

One day the king passed by and saw him, and said to the fisherman, "Is this handsome youth your son?"

"No," said the fisherman, "I fished him out of the river twenty years ago."

The king was terrified to find the charcoal burner's child was still alive, and said, "Let him take this letter from me to the queen."

In the letter he wrote, "Dear wife, have this youth put to death at once or he will bring us all great harm."

John Bolden

Nameless took the letter, but lost his way in the forest. Presently he met a lady in white, who said to him, "Come and rest in my hut awhile. Then I will show you the way to the queen."

While the boy slept, she burned the letter and put in its place one that read, "Dear wife, let this youth marry our daughter at once or great harm will come to us."

When Nameless reached the city, he was greatly surprised and pleased to find that he was to marry the princess. When the king came back, he found that the wedding was over, but he concealed his anger and only said, "You must prove yourself worthy to be my son-in-law. Go and get me three golden hairs from the head of the Sun-King; then shall you be king and rule with me." In this way, he hoped to be rid of him.

Nameless set out very sorrowfully for he and his wife loved each other.

As he wandered, he came to a great black lake, on which a white boat floated. He called out, "Boat ahoy! Come and ferry me over."

The old ferryman said, "I will, but you must promise when you come back to tell me how to escape from this boat."

Nameless promised. Presently he came to a great city. There he met an old man who asked, "Whither away?"

"To the Sun-King," said Nameless.

Then the old man led him before the king of that place, who said, "Twenty years ago there was a fountain in our city that made everyone young who drank of it. Now it is dry, and only the Sun-King knows the reason. You must ask him why this is so."

Nameless promised and went on.

He arrived presently at another city where an old man asked him, "Whither away?"

"To the Sun-King."

Then this old man led him before the king, who said, "Twenty years ago stood a tree that bore golden apples. Whoever ate of them grew young and healthy and never died. But the tree

"She twitched out a hair!"

has ceased to bear fruit, and only the Sun-King knows why this is so."

Nameless promised and went on. Soon he came to a great mountain, where he saw an old lady in white sitting in front of a beautiful house.

She asked him, "Whither away?"

"To the Sun-King."

"Come in," she said, "I am his mother. Every day he flies out of this house as a little child, at midday he becomes a man, and in the evening he returns a graybeard."

She made Nameless tell her all his story, and said she would ask her son the three questions.

"But now," she added, "you must hide; for if he finds you here, he will burn you up."

She hid him in a great vessel of water and bade him keep quiet.

In the evening, the Sun-King came home, a feeble old man. When he had eaten his supper he laid his head in his mother's lap and fell fast asleep. She began to comb his golden hair.

When she twitched out a hair, he said, "Mother, why won't you let me sleep?"

She answered, "I dreamed of a city in which a tree of golden apples bear no more fruit; and I am troubled because I cannot think what the people should do."

The Sun-King said, "They should kill the serpent that gnaws at the root of the tree."

Presently she twitched out another hair, and he said, "Mother, why can't you let me sleep?"

She answered, "I dreamed of a city in which the fountain of youth has run dry; and I am troubled because I cannot think what the people should do."

The Sun-King said, "They should kill the toad that blocks the source of the spring."

After a time she twitched out the third hair, and he said, "Mother, do let me sleep."

She answered, "I dreamed of an old ferryman on the black lake; and I wonder how he can escape so that he can die in peace."

The Sun-King said, "Let him hand the oars to another and jump ashore; the other must stop in his place."

Then she let him sleep.

Early the next morning he arose and flew away as a little child.

The white lady gave Nameless the three golden hairs and kissed him saying, "Now I have done all I have promised. Go back to your wife and be happy."

When he came to the city of the golden tree, and the fountain of youth, he told the two kings what they should do, and received a rich reward. When he reached the black lake, the ferryman rowed him over gladly for the news that he brought.

He arrived at home and gave the king the three golden hairs. The king was furious in his heart, but he said to himself, "I must go and drink of that wonderful spring and eat of those wonderful apples."

When he reached the black lake, the ferryman handed the king the oars and jumped out so that the king had to stay in his place.

As he never came home again, Nameless and his beautiful wife ruled the land in peace and prosperity.

THE LAND BEHIND THE SUN

Yolande Du Bois

You didn't know that there was such a place, did you? No, neither did Madalen, until she went there. Madalen looked like a little Japanese girl, with a dimpled face, golden-brown in color, and soft jet-black hair. Her pretty almond-shaped eyes usually sparkled and danced with mischief. In fact, one afternoon these black eyes held too much mischief for her own good, and after she had succeeded in breaking two saucers, teased the white kitten, eaten the sugar on the sideboard and tangled her grandmother's knitting, her mother decided to put her to bed. I forgot to tell you that Madalen was a very little girl.

"But, Mamma," she protested, "I'm not sleepy, not a bit," and she opened her eyes very widely indeed.

"You've been a very naughty little girl, and if you don't behave, the Brownies will come and carry you away."

"Are the Brownies bad fairies?"

"Well," replied her mother, "they are little brown elves who catch naughty little boys and girls and carry them away until they promise to be good."

"Oh-oh," gasped Madalen, "and where do they take them?"

"Oh, somewhere down behind the sun," laughed the mother. "Now, Madalen, you really must close your eyes and go to sleep."

"Yes, Mamma," said the little girl, "but I wanna know—is it dark behind the sun?"

"Um-m, perhaps. I've never been there," and her mother closed the nursery door hastily. For quite a while Madalen lay perfectly still, with one chubby brown finger in her mouth.

"I wish"—she said aloud after a few moments, "I wish I could peek behind the sun, just to see what it is like."

"Do you really want to see behind the sun?" piped a small sweet voice.

"Oh," squealed Madalen, "who was that?"

"Look behind you," continued the voice. The words were no more than spoken when Madalen whirled around and there, on her very own bedpost, sat the prettiest little figure you ever saw. It looked like a doll, about eight inches high, but Madalen had never seen a doll who could laugh and swing her feet as this one did. Moreover, this minute figure was entirely gold. Her little hands and face were a dull golden-brown, her eyes were like a topaz, her filmy draperies seemed to shimmer with sunlight, and her hair shone like pure gold spun into threads. As for her wings, have you ever seen a bubble in the sunlight? Well, that's what her wings were like. When Madalen could recover from her astonishment she asked:

"Who are you, and where did you come from?"

"From behind the sun," gaily replied the little figure. "I'm one of the ladies-in-waiting, and my name is Topaz."

"Oh," said Madalen, "do you really live behind the sun—what is it like back there?"

"It's a very beautiful land," said the little creature soberly. "Would you like to visit it for a little while?"

"Yes," hesitated the child, "but how shall I get there? Besides, Mamma would spank me for running away."

"Just hold on to my hand tight and shut your eyes—when I say, 'Open,' then you'll be there; and as for your mother, she'll never miss you from your crib."

Madalen obediently shut her eyes and clasped the hand of the tiny fairy. For a second she heard a rushing noise, and some voice, only much louder, bade her open her eyes. Looking around, she was astonished to see that Topaz was now the same size as herself.

"Oh," she cried, "you've grown up."

"No," laughed the fairy, "you've grown down."

"Do you mean," demanded the little girl, "that I'm as small as you were?"

"Yes indeed—you had to be to get behind the sun. Now take my hand and come along if you want to see the court of the Queen."

Madalen placed her hand in the fairy's and to her consternation, they rose in the air.

However, as she seemed to float along quite easily and without any effort, she soon gathered up courage to look about her. First of all, she noticed that although the sky above her was a deep blue in color, there was no sun. She couldn't tell where the light came from, but everything seemed enveloped in a silvery glare as though a full moon were shining over them. The next strange thing that she noticed was that the ground was blue; they were floating swiftly over hills and valleys, and the smooth velvety grass, the swaying trees and dainty cottages—all were delightful shades of blue.

"Why is everything blue?" she inquired of her guide, "and where's the sun?"

"Silly!" exclaimed Topaz with a smile, "you're behind it, so naturally you can't see it, and the back of the sun always gives a silver light. Everything is blue because it's our Queen's favorite color. Her name is Sapphire, and all her ladies-in-waiting are called after precious stones."

Madalen replied to this explanation with a nod because she was so busy looking she just couldn't speak. They were approaching what looked like a crystal city. As they drew near, Madalen could see that each little house was a single sapphire, carved into delicate tunnels and pergolas. The little city spread out, and in the very center stood the palace. It was an immense structure, entirely of blue stones set in silver. At the gate of the city they dropped back to earth, and Topaz touched a tiny bell on the lacy silver gate before them. Almost immediately the gate flew open and they beheld a little brown man dressed in a soldier's suit of blue velvet trimmed with silver.

"Greetings—Lady of the Topaz," he said, bowing low before the golden fairy.

"Gatekeeper, this is Lady Madalen from the Land in Front of the Sun."

At this the quaint little man bowed so low that he nearly tumbled on his nose, and the two girls were obliged to hurry on to keep from laughing and hurting his feelings. That never would have done, you know—it's awfully unkind to hurt people's feelings.

As they passed through the winding streets of

the little city, Madalen noticed the cheerful faces of the inhabitants, which were all different shades of brown.

"Why!" she exclaimed, "everybody's brown."

"Yes," smiled Topaz, "didn't you know we are the Brownies—we are all brown, even our Queen."

"Why are the ladies-in-waiting named after stones?" inquired the little visitor.

"Because each one looks after the children born in the month her stone represents. What month were you born in?"

"October," replied Madalen.

"Oh," cried the fairy, "that's Opal's month. She is the most beautiful of us, except the Queen—her wings and her dresses are all changeable just like the Opal. Well, here we are. Now, Madalen, follow me and do exactly as I do."

Madalen obediently followed Topaz, gazing meanwhile with awestruck eyes at the structure which they were entering. Her eyes were dazzled by the light from the innumerable blue stones. Crossing the moat over a high arched bridge, Topaz paused and raised her arms. Madalen did likewise and the gate swung open. They ascended a wide, blue carpeted stairway, with a vast reception room also carpeted and hung with blue. At the far ends Madalen could see two blue thrones cut out of single sapphires.

"This," explained the fairy, "is the throne room. It is nearly time for the Queen to receive, so we'll wait."

She had hardly spoken when the vast doors on each side swung open and the ladies-in-waiting appeared. It would be impossible to describe them all, but they were very beautiful. There was the Amethyst in her robe of royal purple, the Ruby in rich red, the Turquoise in delicate blue, and the Opal, resplendent with her rainbow wings and draperies and flaming hair. Looking at the others, Madalen noticed them eagerly watching the throne, so she gazed also. Suddenly it became enveloped in a puff of smoke and as this cleared away she saw the Queen on the throne. When all the ladies had curtsied, Madalen stood before her.

"Lady Madalen," said a voice like a silver bell, "greetings and welcome, my dear."

The Queen's cordiality and beauty soon quieted the child's fears. She looked like a mere girl, about Madalen's color, wrapped in sheer blue chiffon. Around her plump brown neck was a necklace of blue. Even her sandals were blue and the blackness of her hair seemed to reflect blue lights.

Madalen watched the court proceedings with interest and afterward the Queen turned to her and inquired how she liked their land.

"Oh," cried the visitor, "I think it's just wonderful—but I thought you punished naughty children here."

"No," replied the Queen, "but sometimes we bring them here to show them how nice it is to be good."

"Oh, I see," replied Madalen, "and what *does* become of the bad ones?"

"Well, if they insist on being naughty, the Wicked Witch of Bogland gets them."

At this juncture the Queen looked very sad.

"Sometimes," she continued, "we can buy them back as the Witch is very fond of gold and silver, and we have plenty of that because whenever anyone in your world does a kind act a piece of gold drops into our treasury."

The Queen went on to tell how the Wicked Witch of Bogland had captured the young King. He was so handsome that she refused money for him but determined to marry him herself. Her eyes filled with tears as she murmured.

"We've tried lots of earth-children but they've all failed and you're too small."

"Well," offered the little girl, "if you tell me what to do I'll try to help you."

Then the Queen sent for Opal and charged her to direct Madalen on her way. As they went out of the Palace, Opal said:

"I know you don't know me but I've often sung you to sleep."

Soon they came to a hedge of thorns and Opal placed a little blue cap on Madalen's head and bade her good-bye, saying:

"Good luck, little one, I would come also but the fairies of this country may not enter Bogland."

Then she clapped her hands and Madalen found herself in a dark wood. Seeing a dim light in the distance, she followed it and soon found a tiny cabin. By this time she was awfully scared but she managed to knock on the door. A hump-backed dwarf opened it and motioned her to enter and turning to the other figure in the room, he squeaked:

"A tasty morsel, eh, mother?"

Looking past the dwarf, the girl saw the Witch, a bent figure in black with a white distorted face and hard gray eyes.

"Hee-hee," she cackled, "a very fine supper, my son; here, fetch me some water to boil her in."

Madalen looked around her in terror. There was no way of escape, she would be cooked alive!

The elf returned and setting down the pail, motioned her to get in it. As she hesitated, the Witch started toward her in a rage and in a panic of fear the child grasped the pail and flung the water over her.

"Oh, oh, oh," screamed the Witch. "Just look what you've done. I'm melting! Didn't you know any better than to wet me?"

Sure enough she was melting before their eyes. The dwarf fled into the darkness as she sank into a shapeless mass. Almost immediately bells began to ring everywhere and people of all shapes and sizes appeared to thank Madalen for their rescue. After a moment of astonishment she recovered herself enough to ask for the unfortunate "King of the Brownies." After a long search they found him hidden away in a dark garret, weak with hunger. Curtsying, Madalen exclaimed joyously:

"The Witch is dead, your Majesty."

Of course his surprise and joy knew no bounds. He was a handsome little king in spite of his rags, with a clear, kind eye. Bidding the others follow, they hurried through the wood to the thorny hedge where the King clapped three times and they were on the other side. When they reached the court, everyone went positively wild with joy and gratitude and determined to give a magnificent ball in honor of Madalen; but when they went to look for her she wasn't there at all!

And far away, in the land of the sun, Madalen was just waking up.

That night at supper her father looked at her strangely, saying:

"I never noticed that little star-shaped mark on your forehead before, daughter."

"No," replied Madalen, "that's where the Queen of the Brownies kissed me."

"What!" cried her astonished parents, "you've been dreaming again."

"Perhaps," said the child.

But she knew quite well it wasn't a dream and we knew it too, but we aren't telling all we know.

THE MELODY MAN

James Alpheus Butler, Jr.

I

When the autumn leaves whistle down to the ground, and Old Man Winter promises his arrival, the whole atmosphere of the forest seems to take on a golden aspect, and one finds it unnecessary to await the golden glow of the sunset to notice this. The reddish-yellow of the falling leaves, the dark branches of the trees fast becoming bare, the industriousness of the little denizens of the woods preparing for the long, bleak months to come, are all familiar sights. Yet only a visitor might enjoy the picturesque autumn of the little town of Avondale to the fullest extent, only a stranger might perceive and thoroughly enjoy the wonderful autumn atmosphere which envelops the entire town itself—even to the snug houses—for all of this was familiar to the inhabitants of the village.

Two little children—a boy and a girl—sat upon the porch of one of these snug little houses.

"I'm dreadfully tired of these old piano lessons," Emily Thomas said as she swayed back and forth in her little rocking chair. "Every Monday and Wednesday and Friday—Paul, I think that's too much, don't you?"

"Yes," said Paul, a robust little boy of twelve, "and I'm awfully tired of that old violin professor. He makes me tired with his 'do this, an' do that.' And he always wants me to count aloud. I think that is very silly."

"That's just the way it is with Miss Van Ness."

"And there's old Jack Smith—always guying me about playing ball whenever he sees me going to take my lesson. Always braggin' that he doesn't have to bother with any old stuck-up professor. It makes me angry to have to go in there with him—the professor, I mean—and all the other fellows are out having a good time."

Just then their mother's voice was heard from within.

"Children," she called, "you had better begin your practicing now. You know your teachers say you must devote at least one hour an afternoon to practicing."

Paul said "Pshaw!" but they both went in, for they were both obedient children, and Paul immediately began playing the scale of C Major on his violin, while Emily began her piano finger exercise.

II

One typical autumn day, not very long afterwards, there came into the little village of Avondale a tattered old man, almost dressed in rags. Yet from those garments shone a most benevolent old countenance which seemed to be kindness, and gentleness itself. The hat which he wore was minus a crown, and his shoes were much too large for him. His coat seemed mere drapery around him, for the sleeves were torn into shreds. Still this seemed not to alter in the least the impression which he gave to the few people he met as he came into the town. For, upon looking into his eyes, a strange, intense feeling seemed to come over you, it seemed as if you were gazing into the deep blue of a soul as mighty as the sea, as clear and pure as crystal, as humble as the Dove of Peace. And under his arm he carried a wooden box wrought in the semblance of an ancient violin case. Who knew what compelling melodies might emerge from the instrument which one was confident that the box contained!

At first no one paid very much attention to this little old man with the strange looking box which he held so tightly. It was true that whoever chanced to gaze into his eyes was struck with wonder and awe and often with a strange embarrassment—he gazed so sadly, his stare was so haunting. But these villagers, busy with other affairs, promptly forgot the torn old man, and gave their attention to their own pressing affairs.

No one knew from whence he came nor cared to take the trouble to find out. No one knew his purpose in entering the village, and no one knew where and how he lived while there.

On the second day of his stay in the village he chanced to be walking up Poplar Street, and his step was slow and uncertain. He seemed to be glancing at the houses as if trying to find out who lived in there by merely looking at them. Twice he stopped and seemed as if he would sit down, and twice he shook his head and moved sadly on. Then suddenly a rock came sailing with intense speed from an alley and struck the violin case. Almost at the same time there came a "Yee—ho!" from the same alley and a boy with a sling-shot scampered away. The old man stopped and opened his violin box. And then he withdrew his old instrument, with four patched strings.

Now it was just about time for a school to dismiss. The children, happy at the thought of freedom, emerged in a joyous, boisterous crowd and came down the street in a jolly throng. Among them, leading in the laughter and play, were Paul and Emily Thomas.

Suddenly the crowd spied the old man looking fondly at his violin. Paul ran ahead and shouted in glee:

"Hark, hark, the dogs do bark,
The beggars are coming to town.
Some in rags, some in jags,
And some in velvet gown."

The crowd was elated. Every one shouted in glee. "Oh, look at the rag man." "Say, mister, want a coat?" "What a fine derby he has on. No crown!" "Ain't that head bald though." "He's got on rags now. His velvet gown must be in his fiddle-box."

But this did not last very long. Suddenly the old man put his violin under his chin and made several long strokes with his bow. Then he launched into a melody—the most wonderful melody the children had ever heard. They became quiet in an instant. They stared at him with large and incredulous eyes. Paul and Emily hardly knew what to think. A ragged man like that playing such wonderful music!

The old man seemed to have the charm of the Pied Piper. From one and two blocks around the children swarmed around him to hear the wonderful music. He seemed to carry their little minds off into the land of far, far away. It was as if some good wizard had come to them and suddenly crowded them into a crescent boat and sped them to the Land Where Dreams Come True.

But good things must end, and at last the old man finished his melody. When he stopped, it seemed as if the children had been released from a spell. As if awakening from a dream which ended too soon, they clamored around him and cried "More—more—oh, please, just one more piece."

But the Melody Man shook his head and, placing his violin back in his box, silently, sadly went his way.

III

Emily and Paul saw no more of the Melody Man that day. Paul was rather quiet and thoughtful all of the afternoon. When he took his violin from his box he looked at it a long time before beginning to play. When he did finally begin practicing he drew long bows, and wondered if his violin, too, were capable of bringing forth the melodies which the old man had played.

He thought of the way he had led the crowd into making fun of the old man at their first sight of him. And something seemed to tell him that he had done wrong in doing this—he was almost sorry. All that afternoon he thought of the old man with the violin playing for the enchanted children. All afternoon there was before him the vision of the kindly old face, the bent, but firm, body covered with tattered clothes.

He did not rush out today to play with his little chums, as he usually did as soon as the hour which he was compelled to give to his daily practice ended. Instead he went to his mother who was sewing upon the front porch.

"Mother," he said, "I heard a most wonderful man today."

"Is that so?" asked his mother. "Who was he, Paul?"

"An old man, and he played a violin."

"A violin!"

"Yes, mother. All of the children were just coming from school and they met him, too. He was dressed almost from top to bottom in rags, and he had a violin that must be a hundred years old, and he played in the street for us. I liked it so very much!"

"And I thought my little boy didn't like a violin."

"When I heard the old man play I was sorry I had objected to practicing. If I could just play as he did! Oh, mother, do you think it will ever be possible?"

"Why of course, Paul."

"Will I be able to make people dream as he made us dream?"

"Of course."

"Will I be able to make people cry?"

"Yes, if you practice each day."

"And laugh, too?"

"Why, of course, Paul."

The little fellow jumped up and clapped his hands in glee.

"Oh, mother, I'm going to practice every day—every day! I'm never going to miss one. Maybe some day I can do just like the Melody Man!"

The next day was Saturday and since there was no school Paul set out to look for the Melody Man. Jack Smith had told him just that morning that he had seen him playing a "fiddle" further down the street, and Paul was anxious to hear him again.

He walked down Poplar Street and then turned down a sort of alley that led to the part of town where the poor little boys and girls lived.

He hardly expected to find the Melody Man in that part of town, yet it seemed as if something guided his footsteps in that direction. About a half an hour later he was glad he had come into that part of the town. For suddenly there came to him the soft notes of a violin!

With quickened footsteps Paul headed towards the spot from which the notes came. He turned a corner and seemed to burst upon a gathering which almost startled him.

For there, in the midst of a crowd of poor little girls and boys, was the Melody Man playing his violin. It was a beautiful and inspiring sight even though it was in the poor part of the town. The Melody Man was the center of the group and sat upon the dilapidated steps of an old house. His gray, long hair seemed to wave back and forth as he nodded to the rhythm of his music. He seemed to be in exactly the right atmosphere, and seemed to be filled with indescribable joy at the cheer and diversion he was bringing to the people in this crowded street. Even the grown people were listening to the notes which arose from the soul of the Man. From many windows wearied heads were thrust out, in many shop doors there suddenly appeared faces and bodies transformed and enthralled by the music of the Melody Man. Those notes of the Melody Man, seemingly so gentle and modest, rang out as trumpets in the environment of the slums so unaccustomed to such things.

Paul approached and watched and drank in the notes, until suddenly the man stopped and laid his fiddle aside.

"Little children," he said in a strange, feeble voice that gave the impression of being cracked, "do you want to hear a story?"

Everybody cried out as one, and the Melody Man, nodding his head, began his narrative. All the children settled around in comfortable attitudes.

"I am going to tell you a story," began the Melody Man, "that is not unlike my music. It is going to be a tale of one who set out on a noble mission and of what befell him. It is going to be a tale of cheer, and of sorrow." And the Melody Man stared ahead and seemed to be looking backwards into the past.

"Boys and girls," he continued, "there was once a youth, a fine lad, who had neither mother nor father. But his voice was as fresh as the morning, his brow was massive like the mountains and gave hint of a soul as big as life itself. When he smiled it was as if a thousand fairies cast a spell of joy upon you.

"The greatest ambition of the lad was to bring joy to people who knew not what joy was, to cheer those whose shoulders were laden with worry. And the Almighty had blessed him with a Gift with which he might carry out his noble desires. And this gift was a passionate understanding of the soul of music and its relation to human beings.

"So one day, with the light-heartedness of youth, the lad set out to serve humanity with a violin under his arm. It must have been that the very birds recognized in him a friend, for whenever he happened along the road they would always pour forth their most beautiful songs, and they even seemed not to fear him. And to reward them the lad would sit by the side of the road for hours playing for them and imitating their songs with his magic bow and fiddle.

"Time passed and the lad traveled far and wide with his fiddle playing for all and everyone he met, and especially for those who were poor and downcast and despondent. And there was many a heart which he raised from the mire and muck of despair and worry.

"The lad became an old man. He had traveled all over the land of his home and had seen foreign countries—even to the most remote corners of the earth where savages dwell. And during this time he had made friends with Princes, and Kings, and the Rulers of the earth, and even gathered enough of the world's riches to suffice him for the rest of his life. So he decided to build him a big house in which there could be seen the most splendid things man could make, and live in it for the rest of his days.

"But when the old man went to live in his house a strange thing happened. He never felt at home in it. He had no people around him—no open-eyed children to play for, no worn and worried people of the slums to cheer and bring joy to. In his large, dreary house there was nothing but evidence of worldliness, of gold, and all of his life he had been a vender of dreams. It seemed to the old man that he would go crazy if he had to live there.

"So this old man went into his attic where he had thrown his ragged garments when he came to live in the big house and donned them again. And he found his old violin box which had accompanied him on his journeys, and once more he set out as he had done throughout his life. And to this day he has never returned to the big house that he built for himself."

At the end of his tale the Melody Man arose. His kindly countenance lit up in an all-embracing smile. The children clapped in glee. Then he spoke again. "And, now, my little children, I will have to go on my long journey again. For in some other town there are children just like you waiting on a Melody Man to come into their lives."

The children were sad when he said this. They clung to him and begged him with all the ardor of childhood not to go. But the Melody Man was firm, and sadly shook his head.

IV

That evening Paul and Emily sat on their porch with their mother and father. Paul was relating to his father the tale which the Melody Man had told that morning. His father was very interested.

"Well, Paul," he said, at its conclusion, "do you think the tale which the Melody Man told you might be true?"

"Why, no sir," answered Paul, "I thought he just told it for fun."

Mr. Thomas leaned back in his chair and smiled. And then he spoke. "As a matter of fact," he said, "the Melody Man is a great violinist. I knew of him when he was young and famous. At that time his name was on the lips of the world." Mr. Thomas paused. "Throughout his life," he said, "he loved to play for the poor folks who cared to listen. This was what brought him fame and fortune, and besides he seemed to enjoy influencing the poor, unlucky people. Recently, I heard, he left his mansion to continue his work—his great work. And that is your Melody Man, though few people recognize in him the great violinist of the last century."

"Why—" began Paul.

But just then he stopped. For, trudging up the road, there was the Melody Man himself.

It was dusk. In the deepening gloom there could only be distinguished the bent figure of an old man, with a case clasped tightly under his arm. He held a staff in his hand with which he helped himself along. A hollow reverberation emanated from the violin case, because there were no plush linings within it and the violin was moving about because it did not fit. As he walked, the thump of his stick was followed by the thump of his boots on the pavement.

He passed under a glowing street lamp, and what the light revealed was an inspiration.

There was first of all the splendid figure—that of a man old but still possessing poise—the poise of one who is distinguished. And there was the countenance—a countenance radiating all that savors of the pathos of life, the joy of service, the grandeur of a life given to humanity and the uplift of children who have scant opportunity for witnessing the most beautiful creations of the mind of man. It was a countenance of contentment brim full of the noble happiness which comes from the consciousness that one has done something for his brother who hasn't had the same opportunities he has had. It was a countenance filled with the expectancy of the greater services which lay ahead to be performed, and which seemed to look forward to the performance of them with an eagerness to serve unparalleled.

And as his figure passed away into the dusk of evening and on, on into the distance, the Thomases felt as if something divine had passed before their vision.

Emily broke the silence.

"Mother," she said sweetly. "I'll never refuse to practice again in all my life."

Paul said, "I wouldn't miss another day of violin lessons for all the gold in the world."

And they all were soon silent with thoughts of the Melody Man who brought joy to inhabitants of this world of sordidness.

May they, too, be as faithful to humanity as the Melody Man!

THE GOLD PIECE
A PLAY THAT MIGHT BE TRUE

Langston Hughes

CHARACTERS

A Peasant Boy
A Peasant Girl, his wife
An Old Woman

Scene
The interior of a hut by the roadside. It is twilight. A boy and a girl are lying before the fireplace, a gold piece on the floor between them. There is a door at the right of the fireplace and a window at the left. During the play the twilight deepens into darkness.

THE GIRL *(Looking at the coin)*—Just to think that this bright gold piece is ours! All ours! Fifty whole loren!

THE BOY *(Smiling happily)*—The ten old pigs were fat ones, Rosa, and brought us a fine price in the market.

THE GIRL—Now we can buy and buy and buy.

THE BOY—Sure we can. Now we can buy all the things we've wanted ever since we've been married but haven't had the money to get.

THE GIRL—Oh! How good, Pablo! It seems we've been waiting an awfully long time.

THE BOY—We have, but now we shan't wait any longer. Now we can get the wooden clock, Rosa. You know—the one that we've wanted since we first saw it in the old watch-maker's window. The one so nicely carved, that strikes the hours every day and runs for a whole week with a single winding. And I think there is a cuckoo in it, too. It will make our little house look quite elegant.

THE GIRL—And now you can buy the thick brown boots with hob nails in them to work in the fields.

THE BOY—And you may have the woolen shawl with red and purple flowers on it and the fringe about the edges.

THE GIRL—O-o-o! Can I really, Pablo? I've dreamed of it for months.

THE BOY—You surely can, Rosa. I've wanted to give it to you ever since I knew you. It will make you look so pretty. And we'll get two long white candles, too, to burn on Sundays and feast days.

THE GIRL—And we'll get a little granite kettle for stewing vegetables in.

THE BOY—And we'll get a big spoon to stir with.

THE GIRL—And two little blue plates to eat from.

THE BOY—And we'll have dried fish and a little cake for supper every night.

THE GIRL—And—but Oh! Pablo—It's wonderful!

THE BOY—Oh! Rosa! It's fine!

THE GIRL AND THE BOY *(Rising and dancing joyously around and around the little gold piece which glistens and glitters gaily on the floor before the open fire as if it knew it were the cause of their joy)*—Oh! How happy we are! Oh! How happy we are! Because we can buy! Because we can buy! Because we can buy and buy and buy!

(Just then an old woman's figure passes the window and there is a timid knock at the door. The dancing stops. The Boy picks up his shining gold piece and clutches it tightly in his hand.)

THE GIRL *(With a little frown of annoyance)*—Who's there?

(The door opens slowly and a bent old woman leaning on a heavy stick enters.)

THE BOY *(Rudely)*—Well, Grandmother, what do you want?

THE OLD WOMAN *(Panting and weak)*—I've come such a long way today and am very tired. I just wanted to rest a moment before going on.

(THE GIRL brings her a stool and she sits down near the fireplace.)

THE GIRL *(Sympathetically)*—But surely, Old Woman, you aren't going any further on foot tonight?

THE OLD WOMAN—Yes, I am, child, because I must.

THE GIRL—And why must you, Old Lady?

THE OLD WOMAN—Because my boy is in the house alone and he is blind.

THE GIRL—Your boy is blind?

THE OLD WOMAN—Yes, for eighteen years. He has not seen since he was a tiny baby.

THE BOY—And where have you been that you are so late upon the road?

THE OLD WOMAN—I've been into the city and from sunrise I have not rested. People told me famous doctors were there who could make my blind boy see again and so I went to find them.

THE GIRL—And did you find them?

THE OLD WOMAN—Yes, I found them, but *(her voice becomes sad)* they would not come with me.

THE GIRL—Why would they not come?

THE OLD WOMAN—Because they were great and proud. They said, "When you get fifty loren, send for us and then perhaps we'll come. Now we have no time." One who was kinder than the rest told me that a simple operation might bring my boy's sight back. But I am poor. I have no money and from where in all the world could a worn out old woman like me get fifty loren?

THE BOY and THE GIRL *(Quickly)*—We don't know!

THE BOY *(Keeping his fist tightly closed over the gold piece)*—Why, we never even saw fifty loren!

THE GIRL—So much money we never will have.

THE BOY—No, we never will have.

THE OLD WOMAN—If I were young I would not say that, but I am old and I know I shall never see fifty loren. Ah! I would sell all that I have if my boy could only see again! I would sell my keepsakes, my silken dress that I've had for many years, my memories, anything to bring my boy's sight back to him!

THE GIRL—But, Old Lady, would you sell your dream of a wooden clock, a clock that strikes the hour every day and need not be wound for a whole week?

THE OLD WOMAN—Yes, Child, I would.

THE BOY—And would you sell your wish for white candles to burn on feast days and Sundays?

THE OLD WOMAN—Oh! Boy, I would even sell my labor on feast days and Sundays were I not too weak to work.

THE GIRL—And would you give up your dream of a woolen shawl with red and purple flowers on it and fringe all around the four edges of it?

THE OLD WOMAN—I would give up all my dreams if my son were to see again.

(There is a pause. THE GIRL, forgetting for a moment her own desires, begins to speak slowly as if to herself.)

THE GIRL—It must be awful not to know the sunshine and the flowers and the beauty of the hills in springtime.

THE BOY—It must be awful never to see the jolly crowds in the square on market days and never to play with the fellows at May games.

THE GIRL—And the doctor says that maybe this boy could be made well.

THE BOY—And the Old Woman says that it would cost but fifty loren.

THE GIRL—*(Suddenly)*—I have no need of a gay shawl, Pablo.

THE BOY—We have no shelf for a wooden clock, Rosa.

THE GIRL—Nor vegetables to cook in a granite kettle.

THE BOY—And a big spoon would be such a useless thing.

THE OLD WOMAN *(Rising)*—Before the night becomes too dark I must go on. *(She moves toward the door.)*

THE BOY—Wait a moment, Mother. Let us slip something into your pouch.

THE GIRL—Something bright and golden, Mother.

THE BOY—Something that shines in the sunlight.

THE GIRL—Something from us to your boy.

(They open THE OLD WOMAN'S bag and THE BOY slips the gold piece into it. THE OLD WOMAN does not see what they have given her.)

THE OLD WOMAN—Thank you, good children. I know my boy will be pleased with your toy. It will give him something to hold in his hands and make him forget his blindness for a moment. God bless you both for your gift and—Good-Bye.

THE BOY and THE GIRL—Good-Bye, Old Woman.

(The door closes. It is dark and the room is lighted only by the fire in the grate.)

THE GIRL—Are you happy, Pablo?

THE BOY—I'm very happy. And you, Rosa?

THE GIRL—I'm happy, too. I'm happier than any wooden clock could make me.

THE BOY—Or hob-nailed shoes, me.

THE GIRL—Or me, a flowered shawl with crimson fringe.

(They sit down before the fireplace and watch the big logs glow. The wood crackles and flames and lights the whole room with its warm red light. Outside through the window a night star shines. THE BOY and THE GIRL are quiet while the curtain falls.)

"But, Old Lady, would you sell your dream of a wooden clock?"

The Dragon's Tooth

Willis Richardson

CHARACTERS
Julius
Thassan
Illea
Antonella
The Soothsayer
PLACE—The ancient world
TIME—When the coming of Christ and the fall of the Roman Empire were dreams of the distant future.

The scene is a rocky place bare of trees, grass or anything growing from the earth. At the right is a pile of rocks, beyond which is a great cliff. Out of sight and below the cliff is a rocky valley to which a road at the right leads. A wide plateau stretches to the rear and to the left. Two boys and two girls are rolling a pretty ball from one to the other, and by accident the ball passes one of the girls and rolls down the path which leads to the valley. All four children go to the side of the cliff and watch the ball roll down.

Julius—There it goes rolling down the hill.

Illea—It will not stop until it reaches the bottom.

Thassan—It's at the bottom now. Let's go for it.

Antonella—The great wolf may get us.

Illea—The monster down there is not a wolf, it's a lion.

Julius—How do you know it's a lion and not a wolf?

Illea—It roars like a lion.

Thassan—So does it howl like a wolf.

Antonella—And it screams like an owl at certain times.

Thassan—Let's go down anyway. It may not hurt us.

Julius—No one has ever come from there alive.

Illea—I'd hate to lose the ball.

Antonella—It's better to lose the ball than lose your life.

Thassan—What will we have to play with then?

Julius—We'll have to find another, or something else.

Illea (Looking around on the ground)—There's nothing here to find but old rough stones.

Julius—We can go back to the city.

Antonella—Yes, we may find something there better than a ball to play with.

(They all start to the left and Julius sees someone coming.)

Julius—Here comes the king's soothsayer. Let's ask him about the monster that lives down there.

Illea—How would he know about it?

Antonella—He knows all things. He tells the prince the meaning of his dreams.

Thassan—We'll see what he will say about the monster.

Illea—Who will ask him?

Julius—I will.

Thassan (In a whisper)—Ask him everything you want to know.

(The Soothsayer appears. He is a tall, thin man with long white whiskers. His back is bent and he leans upon his rod.)

Julius (Addressing him)—Are you the Soothsayer to the king?

The Soothsayer (In hollow tones)—Yes.

Julius—You tell the prince the meaning of his dreams?

The Soothsayer—Yes.

Thassan (Pointing towards the cliff)—Can you tell us about the monster that lives down there?

The Soothsayer—Yes.

(His monotone embarrasses the boys so Illea talks to him.)

Illea—We rolled our ball down there and cannot get it. We want to know if the monster is a wolf or a lion. Does he kill men? Would he kill little children? Tell us all about him!

(Not being able to reply to this volley of questions with the same monotone, The Soothsayer sits on a rock to talk to them.)

The Soothsayer—The monster below is neither a wolf nor a lion.

Antonella—What is it, then?

The Soothsayer—A dragon, a wonderful strange dragon.

Julius—How is he strange?

Thassan—How is he wonderful?

Illea—Sometimes he howls like a wolf; sometimes he roars like a lion; and sometimes the sound he makes seems like the two combined. What is he like?

The Soothsayer—His body is like a lion's and his head is like an alligator's; his teeth are like a shark's—but most wonderful of all are his blazing eyes.

Thassan—What are they like?

The Soothsayer—Like two blazing suns. They blind who looks in them, and the looker dies of fright.

Julius—Have you ever seen him?

The Soothsayer—No, I have not seen him.

Julius—How do you know so well how the monster looks?

The Soothsayer—I know that as I know all other things; but what I've told you is not half the wonder.

Illea—Tell us all of it!

The Soothsayer—Years ago, when I was young and strong, there lived two dragons in the cave below, with many young ones. At that time a spirit whispered in my ear that the female dragon had in her mouth a tooth on which was written the secret of the future good of the world. I told the king and he, in spite of my warning, sent two of his warriors down to kill the dragons; but these warriors never returned.

Antonella—What happened to them?

Thassan—You knew what would happen to them?

The Soothsayer—I knew what would happen to them and warned the king, but he was too determined; so they died, although they killed the female.

Julius—How did they die?

The Soothsayer—After they killed the female, they were frightened to death by the other dragon's eyes.

Illea—If you know so many things why don't you know the secret on the tooth?

The Soothsayer—Only the gods know that. I know the secret is there and I can read it, but it must be brought to me.

Julius—Which monster has the wonderful strange tooth?

The Soothsayer—The female one, the one the warriors killed.

Thassan—And so the tooth is still in the monster's mouth?

The Soothsayer—Not now; that has been years and years ago. Since then the wolves and vultures have eaten the flesh and scattered the bones so that there only remains the dragon's skull and teeth. Since then the little dragons have grown strong; and now, along with the older male, they watch the skull and teeth by turns as if these remnants of their mother's were sacred. No minute passes in the day or night when two large blazing eyes are not on watch. They watch more closely than Argus could have watched.

Antonella—How will the secret of the future good of the world be gotten then and brought to you?

Illea—If the warrior covered in armor cannot do it, is it possible to do it?

The Soothsayer—There are few things that are not possible. This is not one of them.

Julius—How can the thing be done, and who can do it?

The Soothsayer—A child can do it better than a man. An innocent child, unarmored and weaponless, can bring the secret of the future good of the world. You can bring it if you are bold and careful.

Julius—I? You think that I could do so great a thing?

The Soothsayer—Any child could do it who would be bold and careful.

Julius (Eagerly)—If I should bring the secret of the future good of the world then I should be great forever throughout the world?

The Soothsayer—Do not be selfish. If you should bring the secret of the future good of the world, all children would be great forever throughout the world; for to all children this secret belongs by right of youth and hope and innocence.

Julius—Tell me what I may do to bring it to you.

The Soothsayer—You say your ball has fallen over the cliff?

Julius—Yes.

The Soothsayer—Then you and Thassan go down by the path and find the ball. When you find it, play about with it. Roll it here and there. Roll it close to the mouth of the dragon's cave and near the skull, then pull the longest, loosest tooth and bring it here to me. On it is written the secret of the future good of the world.

Julius—But how are we to outlive the blazing eyes that have destroyed so many?

Thassan—How shall we escape the powerful paw?

The Soothsayer—Keep your eyes on the ground, upon the skull and tooth. Do not look into the blazing eyes or you will be destroyed. He will not harm you otherwise. He will not strike you with his powerful paw. He will not notice you. He looks for warriors armed and clad in armor.

Julius—Come, Thassan.

The Soothsayer—Do as I have said and you cannot fail.

Thassan—We'll get it, Julius.

(They go down the path to the left.)

Illea—Suppose they fail to bring the dragon's tooth?

The Soothsayer—Then the secret must remain hidden until it is brought.

Antonella—I cannot see how anything could be written on a dragon's tooth.

The Soothsayer—It was written there by the gods.

Illea—In what language is it written?

The Soothsayer—In a language not known to you. In a language known to the gods and known to me.

Antonella—It must be strange to know so many things.

The Soothsayer—Look over the cliff and see what they are doing.

(The girls go to the edge of the cliff.)

Illea—We cannot see them.

Antonella—I hope the dragon has not captured them.

The Soothsayer (His eyes closed)—You cannot see them, but I can see them.

Illea (Turning to him)—How can you see them?

The Soothsayer—As I see all things.

Antonella—What are they doing?

The Soothsayer—They are near the mouth of the cave, close to the skull.

Illea—And the dragon, what is he doing?

The Soothsayer—The dragon does not notice them. They have the tooth! They are coming! Watch for them!

(The girls look over the cliff again.)

Antonella—They are running this way. I know one of them has it!

Illea—Run Julius! Run Thassan! Here they are!

(Julius and Thassan appear. Julius has the tooth in his hand.)

Julius—I have a tooth, the largest I could find; but it has nothing on it.

Thassan—Nothing but a few scratches.

The Soothsayer—Give the tooth to me.

(Julius gives him the tooth.) This is the one and the secret is written here.

Illea—I do not see it.

The Soothsayer—You see it, but you do not understand it.

Antonella—Interpret it for us.

The Soothsayer (Reading from the tooth)—"The secret of the future good of the world depends upon the growth of Love and Brotherhood. Liberty, Equality and Fraternity must rule the world in place of Inequality, Envy and Hate."

Julius—How can this future good be realized?

The Soothsayer—Children such as you must bring this good about. It must grow in your hearts until you are men and women, and as you grow you must spread the truth abroad.

Thassan—Let's go back to the city and tell what we have learned.

The Soothsayer—Yes, go back to the city and tell the news.

Julius—What of the dragon?

The Soothsayer—When he misses the tooth he'll call the younger ones and tell them what has happened. Then they will set up such a howl as you have never heard.

Illea—How can he tell them? Dragons cannot talk.

The Soothsayer—They have a language all their own, the same as all other things.

Antonella—Let's go back to the city before they howl!

(All start out towards the left, and as they are going, a great noise comes up from the right.)

Part Five

For All Little Folk: An International Community

The editors of The Brownies' Book felt that it was very important for their readers to know about current events all over the world. So every issue had a section called "As the Crow Flies." That means that this column was about all kinds of things, for a bird could see a lot flying through the sky all around the globe. But there were many other ways the editors used to tell the readers about the wide world of which they were a part. Most issues had a section that gave directions for playing games from different countries. Often, writers who traveled to cities in foreign countries—Mexico, Spain, Cameroon—would write about those places for The Brownies' Book's readers. Some of the children who read The Brownies' Book lived in other countries and wrote letters to the magazine either in English or in their own languages. These were printed along with English translations. Some American readers only dreamed about the time when they would be able to travel to some of the places they read about.

Once in a while you may be confused by what you read. For example, in the story entitled "The Gypsy's Finger Ring" the gypsy says that she is from Africa but is not a Negro. The story simply reflects the bigger problem of people not realizing that Egypt, where the gypsy is from, is a part of Africa. Just as importantly, this statement makes us realize how difficult it is to understand the real meaning or importance of racial groups, an idea raised also in "Over the Ocean Wave." Few of us know what a "gypsy" actually is. Many of us don't know that the Egyptian civilization is built upon the "Negro" civilizations of the Upper Nile region of Africa. In this story the gypsy may mean simply that she is not African American, like the children with whom she is talking.

Perhaps the most important reason for the editors' including pieces about the entire world is that they wanted African-American children and young adults to know that at the same time they studied and worked for the benefit of black people, their talents would contribute to a world community. The brownies needed to know about the lives of others, just as others should know about them—the children of the sun.

Filipino school girls

Spring Songs

Jessie Fauset

The Runaway Kite

My kite broke loose on a windy day,
And 'way, 'way up in the air it flew;
And though I've sought for it, far and near.
It has never come back from the lofty blue.
Now where does it stay, and what does it see,
And what all day long does it find to do?

I think that it floats on a snowy cloud
Or jauntily rides on a saucy breeze;
And when it gets weary it flutters down
To the shelter of tall and stately trees;
Or the fairies may use it as a sail
For their fairy barks that patrol the seas.

The Singing Top

On sunny days I spin my top
From morning until noon;
It whirls in rings,
And hums and sings
This little pleasant tune—
"Sweet April comes, then leafy May,
And then comes golden June!"

The Teasing Hoop

My hoop goes trundling down the street
And I go skipping after.
And as it bounds along so fleet,
It says with elfin laughter:
"Make up your mind that in this race
You're bound to have the second place,
No matter, child, how hard you try,
You cannot run as fast as I."

SALT! VINEGAR! MUSTARD! PEPPER!

Spring evenings after supper
When we're all dressed up so neat,
We children take our skipping-rope
And play out in the street.
You never heard such noise and mirth,
Or saw such nimble feet.

We jump all sorts of fancy ways—
"High water, water low,"
And some of us jump "Double Dutch"—
We do it fast or slow;
But "Vinegar, mustard, pepper, salt,"
Is the favorite, you know.

ADVENTURES ON ROLLER SKATES

On April afternoons I say,
"Mama, I'd like to skate today."
She thinks I'll play out in the street
With Maude and Harold Jones and Pete—
But really I go far away.

Sometimes I skate in Switzerland,
With ice-clad hills on every hand;
Sometimes I'm off in Russia far—
(They still talk there about the czar!)
I'm *never* here, you understand!

I skate in Greenland; Norway, too,
And skim its fjords of icy blue,
When I get back my mother calls,
"Come in before the dampness falls!"
She'd wonder if she really knew!

CHINESE NEWS

Annie Laurie McCary

Our recent government census approximates the population of the United States at one hundred and twelve million people. The words "Red," "Bolsheviki," "Sovietism," the names of Lenin and Trotsky have turned our attention to Russia and we see there a country larger than ours in area and with more inhabitants, but think of a country teeming with so many people that they cannot be counted! A country where in one of the least densely populated provinces the average number of persons is five hundred and thirty-one to the square mile, and where in the more crowded sections an estimate of from one thousand to fifteen hundred to the same area is not exaggerated! Such a country is China—a country with a total population conservatively supposed to be four hundred and fifty million.

In our bold assumption of superiority, we Westerners send missionaries to China as though it were some new, uncivilized portion of the globe. How absurd—what upstarts we must seem to the calm, stolid yellow men of that far eastern empire whose clan records date back to 2800 B.C.! Some three thousand years after the beginning of their records, before America was even discovered, Marco Polo, well known friend of our history days, writes in his travels of a Chinese financial system so far advanced at that time that paper money was in circulation, and of astrologers who consulted an astrolabe to forecast the weather, thus anticipating our modern Weather-Man.

Some claim that this vast empire has been welded together by oppression, by the series of conquests to which it has submitted; but the Chinese themselves assert that it coheres rather by the almost universal acceptance of the ethics of Confucius, whose wise precepts, given forth five hundred years before our Christ was born, inculcate all the cardinal virtues and include love and respect for parents, respect for an allegiance to authority—symbolized by allegiance to the ruling prince—respect for and obedience to all superiors, respect for age, and courteous manner to all. These are the people to whom we send missionaries—whom we would civilize!

The foundation of China rests upon the family life. Parents really rule their households; children have reverential respect for mother and father. A child gravely kowtows (makes a formal bow) to his parents upon entering their presence. No youth would eat or drink in the presence of his father or mother until invited to do so. Among the nobility, etiquette is so rigid that if a son is addressed by his father while at his meal, he must stand before answering. The power of parents is practically unlimited—extending even to life or death. The mother, who is theoretically inferior, is the real controller of

the family, extending her authority even to the wives of her sons. One incident, while cruel and apparently heartless, shows how absolute is a mother's power. A wealthy young Chinaman, who had come under "civilized" influences in Hong Kong, was leading a wild life—motor cars galore, reckless gambling and all the rest. To his mother's remonstrances he turned a deaf ear, so she had him locked up in chains and fetters. The boy, however, escaped and when he was finally returned to her, his mother had the tendons of his ankles cut, thus permanently crippling him. Thus do the Chinese treat the prodigal son.

Nearly all geographies show the Chinese ladies with their piteous, bound feet. The origin of this custom is lost in antiquity and to our Western minds seems incomprehensible, but it is considered over there a badge of a free and reputable family. In recent years some of the Imperial family have stopped this practice and edicts forbidding it have been issued, but a custom so deeply rooted cannot be abolished in a day.

Apparently a Chinese lady's dress is unchanging—a beautifully embroidered jacket, long pleated skirt, and wide trousers. The general cut, the lines, remain the same for it is considered immodest and indelicate for a lady to show the lines of her figure. The colors are usually bright crimson or yellow with the delicate shades of all other colors. We suspect the styles change with the differing intervals of embroidery. Wives of officials are entitled to wear all the insignia and regalia of their husband's rank.

The preliminaries to a social call are as rigid and formal as that of all social intercourse in China. The scarlet visiting card, three or four inches wide and sometimes a foot long—depending upon the social rank of the visitor—is first sent in and returned with an invitation to enter. The hostess, meantime, dons on her latest "gown" and according to the rank of her caller meets the latter at the first, second, or third doorway, as the caller's rank demands.

Three-fourths of the Chinese population is rural. There are few important Chinese cities. Hong Kong—practically a European commercial center in an Oriental setting—Shanghai, Canton and Pekin, the capital, are best known to us. Our largest interest is in the villages as really representative of Chinese life. The houses are made simply of the soil, molded into adobe bricks, dried until they cease to shrink. The roofs are mostly flat—supported by timbers—and serve as a storage place for crops and fuel. Instead of numbers the houses may have a name over the door. The sill is moveable with a hole cut in it as an entrance or exit for the family cats and dogs. In the small yards the babies, chickens, geese, ducks, cats, dogs, all play together in merry confusion.

The principal cultivation is that of rice. The first crop is sown about April and reaped early in July. The second, later in July, and reaped at the end of September. Other crops are of fruit, vegetables and mulberry trees in the silk regions. Tea and poppies (for the opium contained therein) are the other mainstays.

The Chinese are expert quarrymen—stonecutters—and sawyers. The lowest form of labor is the work of the coolies who carry coal and building materials. The hours are long, the work most taxing, and the pay almost nothing! After the day's work, however, the workmen dearly love games—or rather gambling. Though gambling houses are forbidden by law, no official supervision could circumvent betting—for instance, on the number of seeds in a melon, and such wa-

gers! Besides gaming, cock-fights are the next popular amusement.

Chinese education is based upon the wisdom of the ancients and to the young student is set the task of *memorizing the Classics!* Book after book is stored away in the pupil's memory. As official positions are awarded to those who pass the governmental examinations, boys spend years preparing themselves, committing to memory the works of Confucius, commentaries upon the same, and mastery of Chinese characters. The whole system is one of cramming. In the principal cities within recent years American and European schools have been introduced and the type of education with which we are familiar is being established.

All that we have just said about education refers almost entirely to boys, for girls are not given much education and never go anywhere to speak of. One Chinese woman said that she hoped in her next existence she would be born a dog, so that she could go where she chose! Betrothed at the earliest possible date, a girl's period of unmarried life is spent in merely caring for her body.

Says the Chinese father, "Why should I teach her how to read, write and reckon, when it will never do me any good?"

"But she is your daughter."

"Not after she is married."

With the exchange of ideas between China and women of Western lands, it is to be hoped that the girls will some day soon come into their right of a free and untrammeled girlhood as we Westerners conceive of girlhood and its joyousness.

"OVER THE OCEAN WAVE"

Betty and Philip went with Uncle Jim to the "movies" that rainy afternoon, and there they saw a picture of two young colored girls.

"Look, Phil," whispered Betty, "there are some colored folks just like us. Who are they?"

"It tells underneath the picture," said Philip, "but the words are so hard and long. Quick, tell us what it's all about, Uncle Jim."

So Uncle Jim read obediently, "Left and right: Beautiful Princess Parhata Miran, eighteen year old daughter of the Sultan of the Island of Jolo, and Carmen R. Aguinaldo, daughter of the former Filipino bandit, who are now enrolled as students in the University of Chicago, Illinois."

By the time Uncle Jim had finished, the picture had passed on, and the feature picture began. The children were very much interested in this, for it was a Wild West Show, and Uncle Jim thought they had forgotten all about the two Filipinos. He was rather glad of this, for the children could ask a great many difficult questions. Of course, Uncle Jim knew lots of answers, but it

is not easy to know something about everything, and if it were not for children's magazines, Uncle Jim would hardly know what to do.

As it was, Betty and Philip had hardly stepped out into the pleasant, silver rain, before they began.

"Where did you say those girls came from?" asked Betty. "Were they really colored? They looked a little odd, though the fat girl looks like Mabel Ross who sits next to me in school."

"They're from the Philippines," said Uncle Jim with a slight groan, for he knew he was in for it now. "And they are colored—that is their skin is not white; but they belong to a different division of people from what we do. You see, we colored Americans are mostly of the black, or Negro race; whereas these girls belong to the brown, or Malay race. Do you know anything of the different races in the world, Betty?"

"Yes," said Betty promptly, and standing still in the pattering rain, right in the middle of the street, she began. "There are five races: the red, or Indian; the yellow, or Mongolian; the white, or—"

"Oh, make her stop that, Uncle Jim!" interrupted Philip. "She got a hundred in an examination on the different races once, and she's been talking about them ever since. Tell us where the Philippines are."

"Well," said Uncle Jim, "let me see if I can make you see them plainly without the map. Do you know where China is?"

"Yes," said Philip, "it's in Asia, right on the Pacific Ocean."

"Good," said his uncle; "now the Philippine Islands are a large group of islands lying in the Pacific Ocean, south and east of China, directly east of French Indo-China, and north and west of Borneo. The China Sea is on the west of these islands, between China and the Philippines, and to the north and south and east lies the wonderful Pacific Ocean. Do you get the picture, Betty?"

"Yes," said Betty, "I do. Aren't the names pretty—Borneo and the China Sea. It seems to me I smell all sorts of good things. Tell us about some more places with the queer, pretty names."

"I'm not so sure I can remember," said Uncle Jim. "Let's see now, the Philippines form a sort of a capital S, with very shallow upper and lower curves. At the top of the letter is Luzon, and at the bottom Mindanao, and right through the center is a group called the Bisayas. I've forgotten the names of the islands that form the group, but I'll tell you some day."

"Well, here we are right at home, so look it up now," said the children. So they went into the little sitting-room and got out the atlas, and there were the Bisayas, with names that delighted Betty more than ever: Panay, Negros, Leite, Cebu, Samar, and Bohol. Off to the west, and not belonging to the Bisayan group, but still one of the Philippines, lies long, slim Palawan.

"And down here in the corner is Jolo," cried Philip, who had been looking industriously through the pages of his little geography.

"Show it to me," said Uncle Jim, much relieved to find out where it was before the children had forced him to admit his lack of knowledge. So Philip showed him with a pudgy, brown finger, which nearly blotted out the island, for Jolo was so tiny. Sure enough, there it lay, a little speck of an island quite to the southwest of the extreme south-western point of Mindanao. It seemed to be a very important island, however, for to the north and west of it lay the Jolo Sea, and to the south and east of it lay a group of tiny islands called the Jolo Archipelago.

"Archipelago is the name for a lot of islands all jammed up close together," Betty told her uncle.

Princess Parhata Miran and Carmen R. Aguinaldo

"Now," said Uncle Jim, "you kiddies have had a fine time of it. Get out and give me a chance to read the paper."

"Just one thing more," begged Philip. "Do tell me what the picture meant when it spoke of the bandit Aggy-Aggy—what was his name, Uncle Jim?"

"Aguinaldo, you mean. Oh, that was the name of a great Filipino leader," said his uncle. "You see, the Philippines used to belong to Spain, but in 1898, as the result of a war between Spain and the United States, the islands were given to us. Aguinaldo, a brave and spirited Filipino, resented American rule and waged warfare for a long time against the Americans. He was finally captured and banished by the new-comers in authority.

"Of course, according to them he was a bandit, or outlaw—a person who breaks the laws. But in the eyes of his own countrymen he was probably regarded as a patriot. It all depends," said Uncle Jim, "on how you look at it. As it is, the United States has finally promised the Filipinos their independence, and there is a delegation of Filipinos in Washington this minute to remind us of that promise. I shouldn't be surprised if the influence of Aguinaldo were back of it all. Now I shall not answer another question. Get out."

"It's too bad you're a boy," said Betty, turning to Philip, "because both the people in that picture were girls. I shall play first at being the 'Beautiful Princess,' whose father is Sultan of the funny little island, and then afterwards I shall be the daughter of the bandit."

"Oh," said Philip, "you don't suppose I care. I am going to be the bandit!"

THE JURY

When the inhabitants of Chambéry heard that their town was going to have American soldiers, it was a great joy. Everyone was eager and impatient to show to these brave soldiers our gratitude and our admiration.

About a year ago the first boys arrived. It was on a spring day; all nature was in feast to welcome them. In the streets, the little babies who knew only one English word were crying very loudly, "Good-bye, good-bye," and the American soldiers sometimes answered with a smile or sometimes took the babies in their arms or caressed their faces. Men and women came near the soldiers and shook hands with them and said to them words of welcome.

The homes of the French families were open to them and those merry men were received like children of France. They passed sweet moments and everyone was anxious to make them a nice stay.

Among all, the happiest were the colored boys. They were unhappy in America, and for that reason they were particularly cherished among us. They were eager for a good word and glad to see that the French made no difference between them and the white—and when time came for them to return to America, one of them wrote—

"My stay in Paradise is over."

And he wrote, also—

"I shall hold the dream forevermore of those glad moments found in Chambéry."

If the black Americans shall hold forevermore the dream of the glad moments found in Chambéry, we, also, shall keep forevermore the remembrance of their self-sacrifice. They gave their blood for France.

We shall remember, also, forevermore, their affection and we shall not forget that in America they are unhappy, and on this side of the ocean we shall do all that we can to help them.

The old world must help a part of the new to conquer their liberty and rights.

Gabrielle Gonay, *Chambéry*, *France*

(A little French girl writes the following letter to an American who served in the Y.M.C.A. overseas. We have made no changes in her English. How many Brownies can write French equally well?)

Dear Mister Seldon,

Just this morning I received your nice letter, and I will'nt wait for ansyer you. I pardon easely your delay, and I accept your excuses. I was sorry you had been sick and I sincerely hope you are quite well now. It is quite funny, is it not, my letters in English? You are too much indulgent indeed when you say I write better in your language. But English is so awfully difficult you know. Meantime I have very often the opportunity for reading English or American magazines, *Saturday Evening Post* and *Cosmopolitan* especially. Some time I have *Life* too but not often. I like very much all these magazines and *Life* is very funny. I thank you very much for the little story you send me. Pictures some time make better work than a long speech. Don't you think so? Once Madame Carpentier has given me two numbers of *The Brownies' Book*. They were very interesting indeed and I have had a great pleasure when I have read them. If once you write to the editor give him please, my congratulations will you?

Amli, *Bordeaux, France*

I live in the Philippines, but I have an aunt in the United States, and some times she sends me magazines. Last time she sent me a number of *The Brownies' Book*. I was very pleased and delighted. I showed it to my teacher and friends. We had never seen a magazine with pictures of pretty colored children in it. I have told my aunt that I should like all *The Brownies' Books* I could get. I am eleven years old and am in the sixth grade.

Minnie V. Kelly, *Philippine Islands*

It is a full year since I am reading *The Brownies' Book* and it pleases me so much that I can't stay still.

Now my dear *lectores* (readers), I have all as my best friends. I am a Cuban born, but my parents are natives of St. Kitts. Think for one instant and then answer these few words: Would you like to have me as friend? Tell me what would please you to know of Cuba.

Now I am looking out in the next number to see all my friends and if there is any that can read and write Spanish. I will finish dedicating these simple verses to *The Brownies' Book* in Spanish. I want to see who is going to be the translator or translators of it in the next.

A Ti

Eres *Brownies' Book*
Grandioso laud
Brindandole al niño
Refulgente alegría.

Llegaste *Brownies' Book*
Desplegando plenitud
Viva, viva para siempre
Tu gloriosa "entente!"

Claris Scarbrough, *Nuevitas, Cuba*

To Thee

(*This is the translation of* "A Ti")

You are, O *Brownies' Book*
A wonderful charm,
Bringing overflowing joy
To childhood.

You arrived, O *Brownies' Book*,
Scattering plenty;
May your glorious "entente"
Live, live forever!

CUEVA ONDA

Hallie Elvera Queen

Cueva Onda is situated in Aguadilla, Puerto Rico, on the western coast near where Columbus landed on his second voyage.

It was the eve of El Inocente Maripose (the innocent butterfly), which in Puerto Rico falls on the 28th of December. It was during the Christmas recess and the youngsters had decided to take me on an outing. You must know that it is very warm in Puerto Rico in December, so we got into our thinnest clothing and our broadest sombreros.

"Where shall we go?" cried out many voices. Rosario, who is indolent and does not care for exertion, suggested El Canto de las Piedras. Edelmiro, who is practical, said that there was nothing to see at El Canto except Cofresi's stone. Now Cofresi was a pirate who, with his companion Silvia, sailed up and down Mona Passage. Edelmiro explained that on the site of one of the Piedras (rocks) they had cut the number 10,000, supposed to represent a number of dollars buried beneath, and had fled. They never returned and until today no one has been able to move the stone. "There's nothing else to see there and you have to go by boat and it's dangerous for girls," he added.

I liked the romance of the story but I agreed with Edelmiro as to the danger and asked them to think of another place. Suddenly Ramon called out, "Can you climb—let's go to Cueva Onda." If I could not climb, I thought it was time to learn as there was a general acclaim of "Cueva Onda—Cueva Onda!" I could not get them to tell me what it was but only knew that I must climb. Puertorican children love a secret and I could not rob them of its joy. So we decided to take Ramon's suggestion.

They came for me next morning bright-eyed, gayly dressed and very mysterious. Several of the boys had large rolls of twine. There were baskets of provisions, but no drinking cups. I asked Rosa Maria about these but she said they were not needed. We started off through La Calle Nueva and thence reached a winding mountain pass where we traveled one by one. Carlos and Edelmiro led the way. Benito, Diego and Luis stayed at the rear to help any stragglers along. About half way up the pass we met two little boys coming down to the city market. One carried a live pig strapped over his shoulder while with his free hand he covered its mouth to keep it from squealing. The other one bore on his head a basket of tomatoes and eggs. Neither wore shoes. We stopped just long enough to get their pictures.

All along the way mysterious hints were thrown out as to what I was going to see. However, I had no idea what Cueva Onda was until Carlos suddenly called out from the head of the procession: "Chain!" and each one on the line offered his hand to the one behind him. I heard the rippling of water. We were at the mouth of a natural cave beneath which flowed one of the many "lost rivers" found in the tropics. There were two single board walks from end to end and no supporting sides. Overhead, in graceful canopy, were marvelous mineral formations festooned with hanging ferns and moss. Dangerous as it seemed one could not resist the beauty and not a child was afraid.

"Is this Cueva Onda?" I asked. "No, just the entrance," said Rafael, and our voices sounded unearthly in that silence. As we wound, in our chain, through the long tunnel, all feeling of fear left me. I was Alice in Wonderland. Edelmiro was the White Rabbit and I knew that I should soon see greater wonders. I think I still believe in fairies and I should not have been surprised to have found myself suddenly growing shorter or taller, or to have heard fairy bells ringing amid the rippling of that lost river. Gradually we began to note bits of light in the mossy grove.

"See," said Josefita, "the fairies have caught some rays of the sun and put them in the tunnel to light our way." So we followed them to the outerworld.

Without breaking the chain, the boys started uphill and from Fairyland came to the end of our journey. I noticed that the boys ahead of us, on reaching the top of the pass, did not go on, but spread out as in a circle; when I reached the top Argentino, who was always half mystic, said to me in awe: "Cueva Onda, senorita." And there it was before me. Cueva Onda—the Deep Cave, an extinct volcano with open crater and arching sides from which there was a constant seepage of water. The broad pit seemed bottomless. "Lie down with your faces to the ground," said Carlos, and as we did so, with our heads over the crater, we could hear the rushing, rushing of the lost river beneath us.

The Spaniards have a disease which they call "Nostalgia"; "Homesickness" say the English dictionaries. It is not just that and though we have no word for it I know that I felt it then—a longing to be a part of Nature, to climb down into that cave and follow that lost river on to its source, or else to lie there forever and listen to its singing. But the boys were more prosaic. Suddenly Diego threw a large rock into the center of the cave. We could hear it bounding, knocking, dashing as it went along, but we never heard it strike the water. Then the boys helped us up. "Come on, senorita," said Rafael, "let's see how deep the cave is."

We moved sideways in a circle along the narrow ledge, holding with one hand to the wall of the cave and keeping the chain with the other. Juan Batista and Federico unwound the cords to which they attached large rocks. Then lying flat on their faces, they let the cords into the cave. Argentino and Luis assisted in drawing them up from time to time, but never did the stones or cords get wet, though we still heard the water rushing on.

Suddenly Amalia noticed something coming up the mountain pass. Edelmiro became a scout and called out "Aguadores" (water bearers). Sure enough we saw an old man and woman coming up the pass, bearing water vessels. Both were barefooted. The woman had no head covering and the man wore as a hat a roll of cloth tightly twisted to look like a conventional life-saver. Each bore on his shoulder a tin vessel like an empty gasoline can. Like most Puertorican peasants, they were silent. I was glad of this, for I knew they were fairy people of the Cave and did not wish my illusion spoiled. Sure-footed, they wound their way to that point where the seeping water flowed freest and placed their vessels there. Then they squatted on the ground and waited

"Cueva Onda, senorita!"

for the "latas" to be filled. We could not get a picture for the overhanging walls of the crater made too much shadow, but I see it now: those two mystic old people out of Fairyland or Bible lore, seated fearlessly on the edge of an extinct volcano, waiting for Nature to fill their water vessels, while a lost river flowed beneath them and a new generation sat watching them. The tune of a familiar hymn came to my ears: "Day by day the manna fell," as the old man and woman lifted the filled vessels to their heads and went down the pass.

Ana Maria suggested that we go down the hill for lunch, but Carlos thought it romantic to dine on the top of the crater. Carmen and Marcola, practical souls, spread the repast, then we "chained" again and went round the crater for water. I could see now why no drinking cups had been provided. With our hands we caught the water which fell in crystalline streams and tasted like nectar. Argentino insisted that we were not in Fairyland but on Olympus and that the old man and woman were really gods and goddesses. And indeed the food had a delectable taste.

Josefita, who is timid, suggested home all too soon, and reluctantly we descended the pass. We passed the little barrios where tumble-down thatched houses stood side by side; we bordered streams where women washed their clothing on the rocks, milkmen rinsed their cans and horses paused to drink; we went down groves of royal palms and now and then had a "lift" on an ox-cart. As we neared the town, Carlos and Edelmiro, who were still ahead, called out. "Listen! a serenata!" We heard the voices of a group of strolling musicians; weird, native instruments were thrumming out their plaintive music, and now I knew:

Puerto Rico is Fairyland, Olympus, and the land of chivalry; and those who journey there may be fairies, gods, or knights, as they will.

"Setting-up" exercises in a Puerto Rico school.

The Legend of the Aqueduct of Segovia

Julia E. Brooks

Segovia has been spoke of as "a dead city, still serenely sleeping in a dream of which the spell has been broken neither by the desecrating hand of the tourist crowd, nor the inrush of commercial activity, nor by any native anxiety for self-exploitation." The only really living thing in poor, dead Segovia is the aqueduct.

This mighty structure which brings the cold, sparkling water of the Rio Frio from the Guadarrama Mountains, ten or twelve miles away, was built by Trajan, the Roman emperor whom the Spaniards claim as their countryman. It is constructed of large blocks of stone laid one upon another without cement or mortar. Upon close inspection one would say that these blocks seem to have been laid at haphazard, since some of them jet out daringly and hang over so as to cause one to fear that some day the whole structure may collapse. But, seen at a proper distance, this bridge is a model of symmetry and balance and the traveler gazes in amazement at the gray and purple tints of its granite blocks as they glow in the deep blue of the Castilian sky.

The aqueduct of Segovia

The whole length of this aqueduct, which has been standing for perhaps 2,000 years, is 1,615 feet. It consists of 320 arches which begin single and low but which, in order to maintain the level, rise gradually and become double, one row over another, as they span the valley, the stream, and the highway. The three central arches rise to a height of 102 feet. The lower row of these is surmounted by three stone steps over which, in one of the pillars of the upper row, are scooped out two niches. In the niche looking toward the town there is a statue of the Virgin; and in the other, at the back, is a figure which the people of Segovia call the image of the Satanic architect of the bridge. For the Segovian fancy has created an interesting legend concerning the origin of this aqueduct.

Many years ago, they say, Satan fell in love with a beautiful girl of Segovia. This maiden lived with her family in a neat little house in the mountain, and every morning she had to go to the spring in the valley to get water. On a certain day the Evil One came out to meet her and said to her gallantly: "You are very beautiful. I love you very much; and if you will promise to marry me, I will do whatever you ask of me to please you."

Now, the young girl was very frightened, so she ran to the church in order to ask the advice of the old priest, who was her friend. "It is a dangerous thing to displease the devil," the old man said to her thoughtfully, "we must use tact in dealing with him." Then after thinking a long time he added, "I have it! Beg him to do something impossible and he will not worry you any more."

The young girl went away encouraged because of this advice, but all that night she thought over what the good priest had said to her. "What shall I ask of him?" she asked herself again and again. By and by a happy idea struck her. She was tired of going to the spring in the valley for water—"Why not ask Satan to build an aqueduct that would carry the water from the neighboring river to the mountain and to the city there on the top of the rock? That was, indeed, unreasonable."

The next day when Lucifer appeared to her, the trembling maiden said to him: "I wish that in one night you build for me an immense aqueduct that will cross the valley and the lower part of the city and bring to us the fresh, cool water of the Rio Frio."

The devil left her and the maiden went home with a light heart. She had asked of Satan something that was impossible; now he would not molest her any more. But scarcely had the maiden fallen asleep when she was awakened by dreadful noises. "What could they be?" She grew cold with fear. "Could it be possible that Satan was attempting to comply with her request?"

Indeed, through all Segovia the people heard the roaring of Satan, and the groans of the thousands of wicked spirits who were with great difficulty tearing enormous granite stones from the depth of the earth, and helping their chief in the superhuman construction of the colossal aqueduct. At dawn the work was completed and Satan, smiling with satisfaction, awaited impatiently the arrival of the maiden.

When the Segovian maiden saw the wonderful aqueduct and Satan looking at her with that malignant smile, the poor girl trembled with astonishment and fear. As Satan approached to claim his reward, she began to cross herself. On seeing the sign of the cross, Satan fled swiftly across the mountain and over the valley—and the people of Segovia say that he is still running, for he has never since been seen in Spain.

A BULL-FIGHT
(UNA CORRIDA DE TOROS)

Julia E. Brooks

Before I reached Madrid I read in my guide-book, "Perhaps the only unadulterated Spanish article in the now almost entirely Europeanized Madrid is the bull-fight." Immediately I determined that I should see at least one fight. Accordingly, as soon as I became settled in my hotel I began to cast about for an *aficionado* (one fond of the bull-fight). This was an easy task since all Madrid loves this sport. The difficulty then lay, not in finding an expert *aficionado* who was willing to take me to the bull-fight—for all Spaniards are obliging, charming of manner, and the embodiment of politeness—but in selecting one whom I considered the best companion for a woman who was quite alone in this great Spanish metropolis. I finally decided that it would be best for me to take as my guest the *portera*, a woman who showed me many kindnesses while I was in Madrid. Her good *esposo* (husband) bought the tickets and in a fever of excitement I awaited the appointed hour.

ANNOUNCEMENT
(Program)
PLAZA DE TOROS DE MADRID
Corrida Extraordinaria

If the weather does not prevent, there will take place an extraordinary Bull-fight. Six Bulls, from 4 to 5 years, with the white and black divisa of the ancient and accredited establishment of His Excellency—

MARQUES DE GUADALEST
OF SEVILLA
LIDIADORES
(Those who take part in the bull-fight)
PICADORES
Salustiano Fernandez (Chano) Rafael Marquez (Mazzaratini), etc.
ESPADAS
Louis Freg—Jose Roger (Valencia)—Bernardo Munoz (Carnicerito)
BANDERILLEROS
Mariano Rivera, Alfredo Freg, y Antonio Seguda (de Valencia), etc.

The corrida will begin at 3:30 sharp. The doors of the Plaza will open two hours before.

The selection of the bulls will take place at 12:00. Tickets of admission one peseta.

The famous band of Hospicio will enliven the spectacle, playing the best known pieces of its repertoire.

The laws governing the corrida will be rigidly enforced.

I read the circular over and over. This was to be a rare treat. "I am going to see not one bull, but six bulls killed," I said to myself one moment; but the very next, I asked myself if after all I was going to find any real enjoyment in this brutal and cruel sport. Then too the *corrida* (fight) was held on Sunday and I had been taught—well, this was my only chance to see a bull-fight. It was

Going to the bull-fight

my duty to go. Yes, I was sure of that. It was not only my duty to go but to stay until I had seen at least one bull killed, no matter how repulsive the spectacle was to me. Accordingly, at the appointed hour we hailed a coach, and after some little discussion as to whether we should engage it by the trip or the hour, started out. Down *Calle Principe*, a short ride through the *Puerta del Sol*, and there we were in the *Calle de Alcala*. As the little streams empty into the great river, so streams of human beings poured from all sections of Madrid into the *Calle de Alcala*. They came on foot, on the street cars, in coaches, in automobiles. They crowded the various entrances of this beautiful *Plaza de Toros* (bull-ring). They jostled each other in their anxiety to get in early, in order that they might miss nothing that was to be seen.

The *Plaza de Toros* of Madrid was erected in 1873–74. It is built in the Moorish style, with a huge archway at the entrance, and has a diameter of 112 yards. The arena (*redondel*) is separated from the seats of the spectators by a wooden barrier about six feet high. In front of this barrier there are at intervals additional barriers with sufficient space for a man who is hard-pressed to run behind, but not large enough for a bull to get through. Behind the first mentioned barrier runs a narrow passage. The rows of seats next to this passage are called *Asientos de Barrera*, *de Contra Barrera* and *de Tendido*. The upper and protected rows, which are divided into *Delanteras* and *Asientos de Grada*, are called *Gradas*. Above the *Gradas* are the *Palcos* (boxes) and the *Andanadas*. Gentlemen who attend the function alone often sit in the *tendidos* or *gradas*, but when there are ladies in the party they usually sit in a *palco* or in the *delanteras de grada*, as exit is then possible at any moment without attracting attention.

"The Spaniards are always very careful to advertise the *ganaderia*" (establishment where the bulls are bred), my friend was explaining to me as we were jostled by the crowd. "The best bulls come from Andalusian *ganaderias*. The bulls of the Duke of Veragua and Senor Miura for years enjoyed the greatest reputation. "*Por aqui, Senorita*" ("This way, Miss"), she said, indicating the seats we were to occupy. She secured the leather cushions which everybody uses on this occasion and when we were comfortably seated she continued—"A bull of four years from one of these establishments has brought as high as 1500 *pesetas* ($300). They are sent from their pastures to their destination by railway in cages or they are driven along the highroad with the aid of *cabestros* (trained oxen). When they reach the ring they are kept and fed in open *corrales* (yards) until a day before the *corrida* (fight) takes place. The bulls are then placed in the dark *Toriles* adjoining the arena, from which they are driven into the ring after being goaded into as great a state of excitement as possible."

"And from what section of the country do the best *espadas* (swordsmen) come?" I asked.

"The *espadas*, too, are Andalusians," she replied, "and are recruited almost altogether from the rural population. Prior to the 16th century, bull-fighting was a prerogative of the aristocracy, but since the construction of the first great *Plaza de Toros*, here in Madrid, this once chivalrous sport has been changed into a public spectacle in which trained *Toreros* take part. Indeed Spain offers nothing else for a son of the people without political influence except to become a *torero*."

I looked at my program. On that day there were scheduled to appear three distinguished *espadas* concerning whose prowess there had been no little talk among the *aficionados*. "This Freg," said a man wearing a hat shaped like a chimney-pot, to my companion, "is without a doubt a very wonderful fellow." "*Claro!*" she responded, her pretty black eyes beaming with happiness, making radiant that sweet face framed in a mantilla of rich black lace.

"*Pero, mira, mira, ud, Senorita!*" ("But look, look, Miss!") she cried, touching me on the arm and directing my glance toward the president's box. For at that moment the president was giving the signal for the function to begin. The band played a military march and the *cuadrilla*, which has been called the procession of the dramatis personae—entered. There were *alguarriles* (policemen) dressed in ancient costumes and mounted on fine horses; *espadas* (swordsmen), vulgarly called *matadores* (slayers) with capes of various colors; *banderilleros* (men who throw the barbed darts into the bulls' necks) in satin suits; *picadores* (men who vex the bulls with thrusts of their lances) mounted on old hacks; attendants on foot *(chulos)* with the team of gaily decorated mules which is used to drag off the dead bulls and horses. They saluted the president, who on this occasion was a distinguished visitor, marched once around the arena and disappeared. Then a policeman *(alguacile)* dashed up to the box of the president from whom he received the key of the gate through which the bulls entered the arena. He rushed back to the gate, which, by the way, was not locked. It was thrown open, there was a loud blast from a trumpet, and out rushed a bull wearing the badge *(divisa)* of his breeder, his Excellency Senor Marques de Guadalest of Sevilla. The fight was on.

You have been told that the bull had been kept for hours in the dark without food. Imagine, then, his bewilderment when half blinded by the sun, he dashed into the arena. The excited screams of 14,000 spectators maddened him. He saw just in front of him a man waving a red cloak *(capio)* and he made a lunge for the cloak just as the man jumped gracefully aside. Immediately the bull espied a *picadore* dressed in yellow, wearing a broad brimmed hat, mounted on an old worn out horse and holding in his hand a lance. The next moment the bull's horns had pierced the horse's stomach and the *picadore's* lance had plunged into the bull's back. The *picadore* jumped from the falling horse and ran to safety behind the barrier, while the bull continued to gore the dying horse. The waving of cloaks in another direction lured him away. For ten long minutes the clever *capadore* thrilled his spectators with his skillful maneuvers. Then the furious bull charged a horse with such force that the *picadore's* leg was crushed between the horse and the barrier. He clung to the barrier until friends came to take him to the infirmary. The horse, with his bowels protruding, galloped riderless around the ring until another charge of the bull brought him to the ground. Thus ended the first act of the fight.

Now, when the bull had been sufficiently wearied *(castigado)* by the picadores, the *banderilleros* in gorgeous livery entered, bearing barbed darts ornamented with colored papers which must be artistically planted in the bull's neck. The bull, fresh from his encounter with the horse, was met in full charge by the *banderillero* who jumped quickly to one side and stuck two *banderillas* (barbed darts) in his neck as he passed. The bull darted after another *banderillero*, who escaped by jumping over the barrier. He then turned to the man in the center of the arena, only to receive two more *banderillas*. The bull, now vexed almost to the limit of his endurance, charged a dead horse. He took him on his horns, lifted him in the air, then dropped him on the ground. Once more he returned to the *banderillero* who, standing still in front of the bull, sent the third pair of finely aimed *banderillas* into his neck. A storm of applause greeted the *banderillero*. He was acclaimed a hero. Then the president gave the signal, for the *Suerte de Matar*—the third and last act of the drama—was about to begin.

The *espada* (swordsman) with his hair done up in a pig-tail and gorgeously arrayed in a velvet suit embroidered in silver, and wearing white silk stockings and black slippers, approached the president's box and dedicated to him the death of the bull. By dexterously handling the red cloth *(muleta)* under which the sword *(estoque)* destined to deal the death blow was concealed, the *espada* "coquetted" with the bull a few moments. He knelt daringly before the bull, he stood erect and struck a tragic pose. The bull's horns seemed to pierce the man's loins. I lowered my head and closed my eyes as the *espada* reeled backward into the arms of two attendants, but thousands of Spaniards jumped to their feet. "*Dios!*" groaned my companion. The next moment she pulled me to my feet. "*No, no, Senorita; Mira, ud, mira!*" ("No, no, Miss, look, look!") I opened my eyes in time to see the wounded man plunge the sword downward through the animal's neck into his heart. Up from 14,000 throats there went a scream. Men threw their hats in the air, women waved their handkerchiefs, people were pushed from their places in the general excitement. The supreme ambition of the *espada* had been realized. He bowed to the spectators and then made his way painfully to the infirmary. In the meantime, the *coup de grace* was given to the fallen animal by a *puntillero* who pierced his spine with a dagger. Then the team of mules with jingling bells carried off the dead bull and horses. The traces of blood were covered up with fresh sand and the show was ready to begin again with a fresh bull.

A murmur of discontent ran through that vast throng, followed by *"Que vaya el presidente!"* ("Away with the president! Hiss! Hiss!") Over in a corner some men began to fight and the policemen rushed in to separate them. Cushions were thrown into the arena, and men and boys jumped into the arena and started toward the president's box shouting: *"El Presidente, el Presidente!"*

"They are angry because the president did not give the honor to the wounded *espada* that was due him," my companion told me. But the president remained totally oblivious of the general confusion. He sat unmoved while the policemen drove the people out of the arena. Upon the arrival of the second bull the *aficionados* returned to their places and order reigned. Six bulls were killed that day, but I was ready to leave after the first one had been dragged out and I think that I could never be induced to attend another bull-fight.

But the Spaniard would say with a shrug, *"Vaya que gente!* What does it matter if a few old hacks that would soon fall dead themselves are killed to make sport for the *aficionados?* As for the bull, *Carrajo hombre!* You, yourself, if you were in such a rage as the *toro*, would no more feel the thrust of a sword than the prick of a gadfly!"

God's Children

Carrie W. Clifford

Elizabeth was English,
Rebeckah was a Jew,
Eileen was an Irish lass,
And very pretty too.

Carmen was a Spaniard,
And French was sweet Marie,
Gretchen was a German,
And tidy as could be.

Juliet was a Roman,
Minerva, Greek, you see,
Wenonah was an Indian,
And lived in a tee-pee.

Beatrice was Italian,
Yum-Hum was Japanese,
Pale Vera was a Russian,
And San Toy a Chinese.

Dark Dinah was a Negro,
Fair Hilda was a Swiss;
More maids were there, including
Scotch Jane, a charming miss.

Now all of these dear children
Are cousins you can see,
And though they may not look alike,
Are like as like can be!

For all have souls and minds and hearts,
Image of God above;
And all must keep His great command
To trust, to hope and *love*.

English Indoor and Outdoor Games

I
Nuts and Hay

The players pick sides and form into two parallel lines facing each other. One of the lines dances with joined hands towards the other line singing:

"Here we come gathering nuts and hay, nuts and hay, nuts and hay

Here we come gathering nuts and hay, on a cold and frosty morning."

When they sing the second line they dance back to their places.

Then the other line dances forward and then backwards singing:

"Whom will you have to take her away, take her away, take her away,

Whom will you have to take her away, on a cold and frosty morning."

The first line then sings:

"We'll have little Ruth Anna to take her away, take her away, take her away,

"We'll have little Ruth Anna to take her away, on a cold and frosty morning."

The two people who have been chosen from the two different lines, advance. A handkerchief is placed on the floor between them. They place one foot at the edge of it and at a given signal join hands and pull. The one who succeeds in pulling the other over to his side wins the game. This goes on until one side has nearly all the children of the other side on its side.

Note—1. American children will find the tune of "Here we go round the mulberry bush" suited to these words.

2. Any name may be used in the place of Ruth Anna.

II
Ring a Ring of Roses

This game is for very young children. They join in a ring and dance around to the following words:

"Ring a ring of roses
A pocket full of posies,
Tishoo, tishoo, we all fall down."

At the end they all fall down.

III
TOM TIDDLER'S GROUND
(OUTDOORS)

A part of the ground on which the children are playing is marked off as Tom Tiddler's ground. One of them is chosen to be Tom Tiddler and he is placed in the middle of his ground. The other children keep dashing over, and onto his ground shouting "I'm on Tom Tiddler's ground." He chases them; when he catches one it is that child's turn to be Tom Tiddler.

IV
SARDINES (INDOORS)

This is on the same lines as hide and seek except that it is reversed. Two players go away and hide. After a while all the rest set off in a body to look for them. When one, by chance, finds them, he does not shout out joyfully "I've found them," but puts the others off the scent and goes back and joins the hiders. This goes on until there is only one searching. Then the game is begun afresh. It must be played absolutely in the dark.

V
GHOSTS (INDOORS)

This game must be played in an absolutely dark room with only one door. A ghost is chosen among the players. He goes out of the room leaving the door ajar, while the other players hide themselves in various corners of the room, or lie flat on the floor. Presently, when everything is quiet the ghost must enter the room, but so quietly that the others do not know. When they do know, because he will probably stumble, they try to escape from the room. The last person to be caught is the next ghost.

Students at Freetown, Sierra Leone

The Gypsy's Finger-Ring

Willis Richardson

At the left we see a clump of trees, at the rear a green field where violets and buttercups are growing, and at the right a porch where the mother and her son, Leon, are sitting. Leon, a boy of ten, is sitting on a low stool at his mother's feet reading a child's story book. His mother, who is sitting in the chair behind him, is leaning forward reading over his shoulder from the same book. After they have sat in this position for a few moments the silence is broken by the sound of girls' voices in the house. They are happy, laughing voices, and presently the owners of them appear in the doorway. They are Rose and Eleanor, girls of eleven and twelve. They stop chattering and look at their mother and brother intently for a few moments before Rose speaks.

ROSE—Mother, can we go out to gather violets?

THE MOTHER (*Looking up*)—May we—

ROSE—May we go out to gather violets?

THE MOTHER—You and Eleanor?

ELEANOR—And Leon.

LEON (*Looking up from his book*)—I don't want to gather violets. That's girl's business.

(*Rose and Eleanor each go over and take Leon by a hand.*)

ROSE—Come, Leon, put that old story book down.

ELEANOR—You wouldn't read your grammar half so much.

LEON (*Looking up at his mother appealingly*)—Mother—

(*But the mother is amused by the scene and decides not to interfere.*)

ROSE (*Pulling him up*)—Come on, it's Spring! We've been cramped in the house all winter.

ELEANOR—Stop frowning, Leon, smile! Look

at the sky and sun, how bright they are. Look at the trees and the fields.

ROSE—Everything is happy and bright; come on, Leon.

(He reluctantly allows himself to be led from the porch.)

THE MOTHER *(Picking up Leon's book)*—How far are you going, children?

ROSE *(Pointing towards the field)*—Just across the field to gather violets and buttercups and whatever else we find.

THE MOTHER—Don't get your dresses dirty; Leon, don't walk in wet places or crawl upon your knees.

ELEANOR—We won't let him, Mother.

THE MOTHER—And don't stay away too long.

ROSE—We'll be back in half an hour.

(They begin to gather flowers a few yards away and move farther and farther away as they gather them. And now we must follow them across the field as we follow the characters of a photo-play. Leon has begun to take interest in the expedition.)

ROSE—Leon, don't you feel better in the open fields than you did sitting cramped up on that old porch?

LEON—Yes, I like it now. The air is so fine I feel like running and jumping.

ROSE—Don't run and jump, we haven't time for that, and besides you'll mash the flowers.

ELEANOR *(Busily adding to her store)*—Do fairies drink the dew from the buttercups?

ROSE—I've heard they do.

LEON *(Pointing across the field)*—Who is that?

ELEANOR—Where?

LEON—See, there among the trees, the woman in the dress of many colors.

ROSE—Oh, a gypsy, a fortune teller, I suppose.

ELEANOR—A fortune teller?

ROSE—Yes, a woman who tells fortunes and reads minds.

LEON—*(Doubtfully)*—Reads minds how?

ROSE—She can look in your hand and tell what's in your heart.

LEON—She cannot look in *my* hand and tell what's in *my* heart.

ROSE—Some say she can.

ELEANOR—Let's go and speak to her.

ROSE—Yes, and let her read our hands.

LEON—She shall not read my hand.

ELEANOR—Let's speak to her anyway.

(They move forward and we see at last where they are going. In a clear space among the trees sits a gypsy knitting a shawl. She is sitting on a camp stool in front of the van and around on the grass several fine rugs are lying. The children move to the edge of the space and stop.)

THE GYPSY *(Looking up from her work)*—Good morning, little people.

THE CHILDREN *(Together)*—Good morning.

THE GYPSY—Do you want anything?

LEON—Rose says you can tell fortunes and read minds.

THE GYPSY—I can.

ELEANOR—And look in one's hand and tell what's in one's heart?

THE GYPSY—Yes, come, let me read your hands.

LEON *(Closing his hand and putting it behind him)*—You cannot read my hand.

THE GYPSY—Come over anyway and talk with me. *(The three go over to help.)*

The Gypsy—Three little colored children. I love children.

ROSE *(Noticing her dark complexion)*—Aren't you colored, too?

THE GYPSY—I am in a way but not the same

What a pretty finger-ring!

as you. I was born in Africa, but I'm not a Negro. I was born in Egypt.

ELEANOR *(Looking at her ring)*—Oh, what a pretty finger-ring.

THE GYPSY—Do you like it?

ROSE—It's beautiful!

LEON—Where did you buy so strange a ring?

THE GYPSY—I did not buy it.

LEON—You found it, then?

THE GYPSY—When I was a little girl like your sisters here I found a piece of pearl on the banks of the Nile in Egypt, and my father, a magician, carved this ring and shaped it to my finger. It has a wonderful power.

LEON—What kind of power?

THE GYPSY—Whoever goes to sleep wearing this ring may dream or see whatever he wishes of the past or present.

LEON—I'd love to see the future.

THE GYPSY—I'll read your hand and tell the future to you.

LEON—You shall not read my hand, I want to dream of the future by the ring.

ELEANOR—What can I see of the past?

THE GYPSY—Whatever you wish to see. Put on the ring and sleep but a few moments and you can see as many years of the past as you wish to see.

ROSE—See a year pass in a moment?

THE GYPSY—Yes, dreams are strange things; one can dream of the passing by of many years in a moment's time.

ELEANOR—I want to see the slave days before the war, how the slaves lived and how they toiled and suffered.

THE GYPSY—Why choose such a dreary time, such a cruel place?

ELEANOR—A look back now and then to where we came from will urge us on.

THE GYPSY *(Taking off the ring)*—Hold out your finger till I put it on. *(Eleanor holds out her finger and the ring is put on.)* Now lie upon the grass and dream for a moment. *(She lies upon the grass and sleeps while the gypsy and the other children watch her. Presently she awakes weeping and Rose goes to her.)*

ROSE *(Putting her arm around Eleanor)*—What's the matter, Eleanor?

ELEANOR *(Wiping away her tears and handing the Gypsy the ring)*—I saw such awful things.

LEON—What did you see?

ELEANOR—I saw women and children beaten and driven about; I saw half-naked children walking barefoot on the cold, hard ground, carrying burdens heavy enough for men. I saw wives sold from their husbands and mothers sold from their children, men beaten upon their backs with knotted whips—things far too cruel to tell.

ROSE *(Stopping her)*—Don't tell them then. You'll frighten me and I will not want to dream.

THE GYPSY *(To Eleanor)*—Why did you want to see such cruel things?

ELEANOR—I wanted to see how much we had attained. I want to know how much more it will take of time and strife and pain to make us great.

THE GYPSY—You want to be great?

ELEANOR—To be great as a people, so that the people of a thousand years from now will read their histories and know that we were as great as other people.

THE GYPSY *(To Rose)*—What do *you* wish to dream of?

ROSE—I want to dream of the Jews and their sufferings now.

THE GYPSY—Of the Jews in Russia?

ROSE—The Jews do not suffer in Russia any more, the Czar has gone.

THE GYPSY—Of the Jews in Germany?

LEON—The Kaiser has gone and all the Germans are freer now.

ROSE—I want to see the Jews in the east of London, to see how they live.

THE GYPSY—What do you know of the Jews in the east of London?

ROSE—They suffer, too. We heard our mother and father talking of them.

THE GYPSY—But England is a prosperous country, no one suffers there.

ELEANOR—So is America a prosperous country, but we Negroes suffer here.

LEON—All toiling people suffer in all countries.

THE GYPSY—You are wise children. You have heard and remembered much.

(To Rose.) Put on the ring and dream.

(She slips the ring on Rose's finger and Rose lies on the grass and sleeps. They watch her silently until she wakes.)

THE GYPSY *(As Rose wakes up)*—What did you see?

ROSE—I saw things nearly as bad as Eleanor saw. The Jews are not bought and sold, they are not beaten, nor are they forced to bear too heavy loads. The thrifty Jews, the buyers and sellers of things, the makers of money, live harsh and bitter lives. They live on crusts in dark, cold, filthy places and only get a pittance for their toil. The rest, the people of power, steal from them. I saw a dozen people sleeping in one room. I saw mothers, fathers and children working side by side through long dull hours.

LEON *(To the Gypsy)*—Let me wear your ring and dream a dream.

THE GYPSY—You cannot dream of the future by this ring.

LEON—Have any tried and failed?

THE GYPSY—No, none have tried. Let me read your hand and I will tell you the future.

LEON—I do not want my hand read.

THE GYPSY—Then you cannot know the future.

LEON—Let me try, and if I fail to see the future by the ring, I'll let you read my hand.

THE GYPSY *(Handing him the ring)*—I know you'll fail, but put it on your finger, you may try.

(Leon puts the ring on his finger and lies down and sleeps. The others watch him until he wakes. He wakes smiling.)

ROSE—Did you see anything of the future?

LEON—Yes.

THE GYPSY *(Surprised)*—You saw the future when you slept there?

LEON—Yes, I saw wonderful things.

THE GYPSY—Give me back the ring.

LEON *(Giving her the ring)*—You said I could not see the future by the ring.

THE GYPSY—It's strange, it's more than I can understand.

ELEANOR—What did you see, Leon?

LEON—I saw men and women and children happy at last. None of them were so poor that they were suffering, none were so rich that they were overbearing. The whole five races were in harmony, all working side by side for the good of all. *(He gives the Gypsy his flowers.)*

You may have my flowers for letting me wear your ring. I must run and tell my mother what I saw.

(He goes.)

THE GYPSY *(To the girls)*—Your brother there is bold and resolute; he should make a good, strong man.

ROSE—We hope he will.

ELEANOR—We shall be proud of him.

ROSE—You may have my flowers for letting me wear your ring.

ELEANOR—And mine too.

(Both give their flowers to the Gypsy.)

ROSE—Now we must catch Leon; good-bye.

THE GYPSY—Good-bye.

(They run and catch Leon and we follow them across the field until they come to the porch where their mother is sitting as they left her, reading the book which Leon dropped.)

THE THREE—Oh, mother, we saw wonderful, strange things!

THE MOTHER—Where are the flowers?

ROSE—We gave them to a Gypsy for letting us wear her ring.

THE MOTHER—What did you see?

ELEANOR—I saw the past; the cruelty and hardships that were heaped upon the slaves.

ROSE—I saw how the Jews of East London live in the present.

LEON—I saw the future full of happiness and hope.

THE MOTHER—How did you see these things?

ROSE—A Gypsy let us wear her ring and dream them.

THE MOTHER—You saw the condition of men divided into three periods—chattel slavery, wage slavery and freedom.

LEON—I hope we'll live to see what I have seen.

THE MOTHER—You are all young and you may live to see it. The future is your great promise, your great hope, it's all you have to live for. Work to make it happy, wait for it, and be patient while you wait.

The End.

THE KOLA

Colonel Charles Young

Africa has many nut-bearing plants and trees. Among these is the ground-nut, which is known in our country, the United States, as the peanut. In Africa, thousands of tons of these nuts are raised and exported to Europe for making both edible and lubricating oils. The ground-nut is roasted in Africa and used for making a very acceptable soup. A "ground-nut chop" well seasoned, into which hard-boiled eggs are put, constitutes a fine Sunday dinner among both civilized and native peoples.

Then there is the oil-palm nut which is refined and sent abroad for food. Much of our butter, both here and in Europe, is made from this oil-palm nut. The oil-palm tree bears a kind of nut after the fashion of a bunch of bananas. Each nut is enclosed in a sheath containing oil which surrounds a kernel, itself having a fine white oily meat, which, when crushed, yields a still finer grade of oil very similar to that coming from the meat of the coconut.

But the most precious of nuts comes from the Kola tree. These nuts are seldom sent out of Africa, for, when eaten, they take away fatigue from the traveler and furnish him strength upon the weary way, at the same time being thirst and hunger killers. These nuts, in the regions where the tree does not grow, command a very high price and are much sought after by the natives. By the way, our Coca-Cola of the drug stores in the United States does not come from this kola nut.

The kola nut has many social uses in Africa; for example, if a traveler staying all night in a town should chance to find a red kola nut in the water brought him for his bath, this would be secret warning from a friend that danger is near him; to be on guard. A white kola nut in the bath is either a sign of friendship or an offering to the Great God-Spirit. No African man offers a white kola nut and then betrays the one to whom he gives it.

Nothing can be more beautiful than to see the kola groves in bloom at Dolasan, on the far off Liberian Hinterland.

The following rhyme on the kola tree is offered to *Brownies' Book* readers by a lover of his little black and brown brothers both in Africa and America.

THE KOLA TREE

Take your gleaming cutlass blade,
With heart and arm a-thrill,
Go into the forest shade
And swing it with a will;
Fell bush and bough at liberty,
But never cut a kola tree!

REFRAIN

Never cut the kola tree,
Sign of Trust and Friendship free;
It stands for Peace on land and sea,
So never cut a kola tree!

In the fragrant kola grove,
Mid leaves and blossoms bright,
Peace and Friendship ever rose
In search of kolas white,
Which "far more precious than the red
Are given, not sold," Sadana said.

UP TO THE CRATER OF AN OLD VOLCANO

Langston Hughes

Near Toluca, Mexico, is an old volcano, Xinantecatl. The fires which once burned within its bosom have long ago gone out and now, in the deep crater that in past centuries held boiling lava and red hot ashes, two calm blue lakes sparkle like dainty jewels in a rough setting. No one knows when the last eruption of this volcano took place but some say that it was long before the time of Christ, and when the Aztec Indians came down from the North to found their powerful empire, Xinantecatl, for so they called it, had long been sleeping. Now, like a dead giant at rest, it is still great and majestic. Rising above the puny cities and little low hills that cluster about its base, it is as some nature king rising above a subject people. The ancient Indians thought it a god and climbed its steep sides carrying gold and jewels and precious gifts on their backs as an offering to the mountain deity. Even today the rural Indians say that when shots are fired in the crater or stones thrown into the blue lakes, the mountain becomes angry and calls the clouds to hide its peaks and send rain down upon its disturbers. We in Toluca, however, are not afraid of Xinantecatl. It is like a well known friend to us and one whom we see every day. On clear mornings its peaks are sharp and distinct in the blue sky; at evening the whole mountain makes a great black silhouette against the twilight colors.

When the boys of the Instituto, Toluca's high school, began to plan a two-day walking trip to the crater, and invited me to go with them, I accepted eagerly. They, with the customary Mexican politeness, put my name first on the list of those who were to go and several of the students went with me to aid in choosing the proper kind of "trumpeate," a sort of bag for carrying food. It is woven from marsh grass and is light of weight. They also saw that I bought a wide Mexican hat, as protection from the sun, and told me all the things that I would need to carry. First, plenty of lunch; then, two warm blankets because we were to sleep in the open mountains; my camera for pictures; a bottle for water; a small amount of cognac or some other liquor in case of mountain sickness in the high altitude; and a pistol. "But above all," they said, "take onions!" Those who had been up to the volcano before claimed that they were the very best things to smell if one began to feel ill in the thin air near the summit. I thought to myself that if I should get sick, the scent of onions would only make me worse. Nevertheless I took them and when the time arrived for their use I found my mind completely changed about their smell.

It was a beautiful sunny morning when we left Toluca. From the platform of the small station, where we were to board the seven o'clock train for Calimaya, we could see the white, sparkling

snow peaks of the volcano and they seemed very high and far away. There were forty of us going on the trip and, before leaving time, the first coach of the tiny train was completely filled with Instituto boys. The aisle of the car was one jumble of blanket rolls and fat "trumpeates" of food, and the windows were crowded with faces—mostly brown faces of laughing young fellows, all talking at once and watching the late comers hurrying down the platform. These dark faced, friendly school boys were about like other dark skinned boys of my own race whom I had known in the United States. They made me remember a hike that the colored Y.M.C.A. fellows, in Chicago, took out to the sand dunes one summer. There the car windows were crowded with dark faces, too, and everybody talked at once. The only difference was that in Chicago they were speaking English and when a late member of the party reached the platform, every one cried out, "Hurry up!" while here, when Rudolfo, the tardy, came running through the gates, every one in the window shouted, "Apurese!" which means the same in Spanish.

The little train went click, click, click, down the pretty valley. We passed several small villages: Metepec, with its great church large enough to hold its whole population; San Francisco, a collection of small huts, and a white temple; Mexicaltzingo, where the country bullfights are held; and then Calimaya, where the road to the volcano begins.

We found Calimaya a small, clean town with cobblestone streets and a stream of water running down the center of each one, where the cows and long horned oxen stopped to drink.

We piled our blankets and bags in one corner of its arched "Portales" to wait while two of the boys went for the guide and the burros—patient little beasts of burden—who were to carry our things. After a long while the burros came. There had been some disagreement in regard to the money to be paid, so we learned, the guide having set a price and then suddenly changing his mind, saying that he could not risk his animals in the cold mountain air for such a small sum. But finally an agreement was reached and we had three burros, a boy and two men to drive them, and a guide—all for a price that would amount to but five American dollars, and this for a two-day trip!

When the word "Vamanos" was given, the three small animals were almost hidden under their loads of blankets and lunch-bags, but being strong, sturdy little beasts, they did not seem to mind. They started off down the road with a trot, the two drivers and the boy running behind

shouting, "Burro! Burro!" to make them go faster. The members of the hiking party, freed of their luggage, had nothing to pack now except the canteens or water bottles and their guns. Very few having pistols, there was an unusual variety of fire-arms in sight, from a modern rifle to ancient carbines. The reason for so many shooting machines was that we might meet bandits on the road, and, though it was only a *might*, every one should be prepared. During the revolutions and until a year or so ago the hills were full of robbers, who, not content with taking travelers' money, would ofttimes take their clothes, even to their shoes, leaving the robbed ones to get home as best they could. Now, though such robberies are infrequent, no one goes far into the country unarmed. The boys of the Instituto, going through the quaint streets of Calimaya, looked like a small militia.

The road leading to the foothills was quite bare of trees. High in a cloudless sky, the sun beat down upon our heads without pity, while the dust rose in clouds from under our feet. On either side the road was lined with maguey and cactus plants which served as a sort of fence around the fields, where lazy, slow-moving oxen were pulling wooden plows yoked to their horns, and wide-hatted peons pricked them languidly with sharp-pointed sticks. After about an hour's walking we passed Zaragoza, a small village which, like all Mexican villages, had its tall old church towering sad and beautiful above the miserable little huts. By this time all our water bottles were empty and our throats were dry. The guide promised us that we should come to a river soon and when we finally reached its friendly banks, after what seemed like an eternity of tramping in dust and sun, we lay on our stomachs like dogs and drank the cool clear water that came rippling down from the hills.

Soon the road began to ascend and we found ourselves climbing a slope covered with little pine trees. Before us, when we reached the summit, we saw only pine clad hills and then more hills, hiding the volcano from us. Looking back, we saw the wide valley of Toluca below, dotted with red roofed villages and the white towers and domes of old, old churches. At its opposite side we saw the mountains rising like a wall about the valley, shutting it in from the rest of the world and protecting it with their grey and purple strength.

The road now led upward, and it was not easy climbing through the forest of stunted trees with the sun like a hot ball overhead. About one o'clock, when everybody was aching and tired, the guide showed us a little cañon at one side of the road and said that here was the last water to be found before reaching the crater, the next morning; so he advised us to stop for lunch and to fill our water bottles. The burros were unloaded and everyone searched in the pile of "trumpeates" for his lunch-bag. As each woven sack looked just about like another, there was much opening and exchanging and inspecting before each one had his own. Then we scattered about the slope and prepared to eat. One of the boys from each group went down to the spring for water, and it was deliciously sweet and cool. After lunch we decided to rest a while. The guide said we had made good time and in three hours we could reach the timber line, where we were to make camp on the edge of the woods.

At three o'clock we climbed up to the road, loaded the burros and were off again—up, up, up. We had left the foot-hills behind us now and were on the very slope of the volcano itself. Here the trees, taller and thicker, made what we call a real forest. Perhaps we had eaten too much lunch, or perhaps we were tired, but anyway the trail seemed difficult. Then, too, we had begun to notice the lightness of the air and at every hundred yards or so we had to stop for breath. Some of the boys began to feel ill and at this juncture the onions put in their appearance. I felt none too well, so I began to search in my pockets for my onions, too—and when, with a dull ache in my head and a breathless feeling in the lungs, I pressed them to my nose, all the former aversion to their scent disappeared. I kept them under my nose all the way to camp.

And whether due to the onions or not, I didn't feel any worse while some of the fellows had to walk so slowly that they were left behind the rest of the party.

In the late afternoon we passed through a part of the forest where it seemed as if more than half the trees had been torn up by the roots. Great tree trunks, so large that we could hardly climb over them, lay across the path. Looking down, I could see whole hillsides strewn with these fallen members of the forest. Some of the boys explained to me how, two years before, a hurricane had swept across the mountains and tried to carry the whole forest off with it. The fallen trees were a bad impediment to our progress because, in an atmosphere where one cannot walk without getting out of breath, to climb over a gigantic trunk is an exercise that is not taken with pleasure.

It was almost six o'clock when we arrived at the spot chosen for camp, just below the timber line, where the trees of the mountain end. We were close to the peaks now and one of them, that looked very near, loomed between us and the sinking sun so that all the mountain-side was in shadow. Down below we saw the valley—far, far beneath—bathed in a twilight mist of rose and purple; the little river, that had been a winding, silver thread all day, had now turned golden in the sunset.

We began to make camp. Some unloaded the burros and tied them fast to trees. Others searched for the dry limbs and branches of the pine in order to make the fires. And still others, too tired and out of breath to do anything, sank down upon the ground to rest, for the last hour of the ascent had been the hardest of all.

The shadows on the mountain-side deepened and the sunset colors faded from the sky. For me, the evening passed quickly. There was supper around the blazing camp-fires, of which each group of fellows had its own; then songs and stories and more songs, to which the two burro drivers contributed a love ballad which they said they had learned down in the "hot country." At nine, the first guards were posted and the camp became still. The only noise to be heard was the occasional sob-like "hee-hooing" of the burros and the strong "Alerta" of the watchers, crying to each other from the four corners of the camp.

At two o'clock, when my turn came to stand guard, the moon had gone down behind the mountain and the forest was in inky blackness. The low burning camp-fires gave a little light. A long way off and deep down in the night-covered valley, we saw the white lights of Toluca, shining like a cluster of sunken stars in the darkness.

The next morning, at sunrise, we were off for the crater. A half hour's walk took us past the timber line, out of the forest, and to the open mountain-side. In a little while we found ourselves at the foot of one of the volcanic peaks, which, if we chose to climb it, would give us a view down into the crater. About half the party chose to go up; the others took the burro path which led around the side of the peak, entering the crater at the lowest opening. The peak, which near the top was covered with large patches of snow, did not appear to be very high. But we soon found that the steepness of its slope and the lightness of the air made the ascent more laborious than we thought it would be, and at every eight or ten steps we had to stop for breath. It seemed as if we would never reach the summit. The rocks and sand and gravel, of which the mountain was made, slipped beneath our feet and made us slide half-way back at every forward movement. We had to cross the snow covered spaces on our hands and knees—they were so slippery. When we finally gained the summit, it seemed as if our last breath had gone. We were very high and, between us and the hills below, the white clouds drifted by.

As we turned to look down into the crater, we saw it as a sort of double one, divided into two parts by a long hump-backed hill. On each side of the hill there was a blue lake with a rocky shore. The sides of the crater were steep and many colored, and the three highest of the tall, jagged peaks that formed its ragged edge had snow upon them. We, on top of our laboriously climbed summit, had an excellent view down into that part of the volcano where La Laguna Chica (The Little Lake) sparkled in the morning sun. Those who had taken the burro path were already resting on its shore and the height from which we saw them made them appear very tiny. Feeling the pangs of hunger, as we had not yet eaten breakfast, and knowing that the burros carrying the lunchbags were waiting for us below, we began to descend. Half running, half sliding in the loose sand and gravel of the inner slope, we reached the bottom much more quickly than we had ascended. On the sandy shore, scattered with big boulders taller than a man, we ate our breakfast and drank the cold, refreshing water of the clear blue lake.

After breakfast we decided to see La Laguna Grande (The Big Lake), and so, circling around the side of The Little Lake, we began to climb one of the low ends of the hump-backed hill. In a short while, from the top of its rocky ridge, we saw below us the deep blue waters of La Laguna Grande, so beautiful and lovely and calm that it gave one a thrill of surprise at finding it buried in this old volcano's burnt, scarred walls. Some people say that this pretty lake has no bottom and that swimmers who venture far into its cold waters may be drawn down into unknown depths. Its smooth, innocent surface, however, gives no indications of such treachery, and the charm of its beauty makes one think it is a good fairy lake and not the wicked old witch with the pretty face, which reputation has given it.

We walked all around the rocky shore, stopping now and then to pick up small queer-colored stones or the sulphur coated rocks found on the beach. To reach the other end of the lake's long oval required more time than we had expected, for distances are deceiving in the high clear air. We stopped often to rest, sitting down on the large boulders and admiring the beautiful colors in the sides of the crater whose walls were sometimes deep crimson capped with jagged peaks, sometimes bright red or soft orange streaked with purple, and sometimes just gray rock covered with snow patches near the rim. And the blue lake was always like a jewel in a rough setting. At the other end of the oval we found erected on the sandy shore, a large wooden cross which a band of religious people had carried up the steep trail some years before. They held a mass in the crater. Behind the cross rose "El Pice de Fraile," the highest of the Xinantecatl peaks, glittering snow white in morning sun. From its tooth-like summit on a clear day, one who has a pair of strong binoculars can see, off the coast of Guerrero, more than a hundred miles away, the silver waters of the Pacific.

When we climbed back over the hump-backed hill and down to the wider shore of the Little Lake, the burros were already packed with our blankets and much diminished lunch bags. Before we reached the spot where we had eaten, the first ones started off. We filled our water bottles and canteens from the lake and started after them. When we came to the highest point in the narrow road we turned for a last look at the little blue lake below, the hump-backed hill and the opposite red and purple walls of the volcano. Then we turned and followed the path which curved, at a dizzying height, onto the steeply sloping outer sides of the crater, where a false step too near the edge would have sent one tumbling down a mile or so into a green tree-covered valley. We took care not to make the false step.

When, at sunset, we unloaded the burros in the clean little "Portales" of Calimaya, although stiff and footsore and weary, everybody was happy and agreed that it had been a fine trip. A few minutes later, sitting on the platform of the country station, awaiting the last train for Toluca, we could see, high and far away, the sharp, jagged peaks of the old volcano faintly outlined against the sunset sky. They seemed so very high and so very far from us we could scarcely believe that just ten hours before we had visited them and drunk the cool snow water of their clear blue lakes.

A Kindergarten Song

Carrie W. Clifford

Little babies in a row,
Little dresses white as snow;
No hair, crinkled hair, straight hair, curls—
Lovely little boys and girls!

Little children in a ring,
Hear them as they gaily sing!
Red child, yellow child, black child, white—
That's what makes the ring all right.

Lad and lassie, youth and maid.
Born in sunshine, born in shade;
Zulu, Esquimaux, Saxon, Jew,
United, make the world come true!

God's big children all at work,
Not one dares his task to shirk;
"All for each, and each for all"—
White man, red man, black man, tall.

THREE SCANDINAVIAN GAMES

Nella Larsen Imes

Dear Children:

These are some games which I learned long ago in Denmark, from the little Danish children.

I hope that you will play them and like them as I did.

I
CAT AND RAT

Those playing join hands, forming a closed ring. One child is chosen for "cat" and another for "rat." The game starts with "rat" outside the ring and "cat" inside. "Rat" is helped by those inside the ring who raise their hands to help him to run either out or in between them, but when "cat" tries to follow, those forming the ring stand still without raising their hands.

As soon as "cat" manages to touch "rat" the two in the ring between whom cat and rat last ran become new cat and rat, and so carry on the game.

II
HAWK AND PIGEONS

Boundaries are marked. One child in the middle of the space represents the hawk.

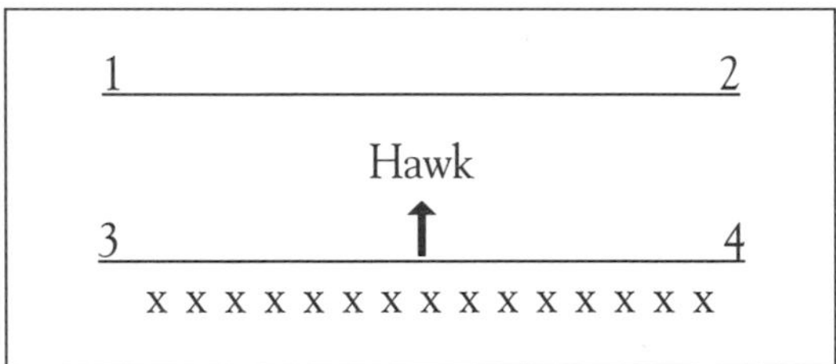

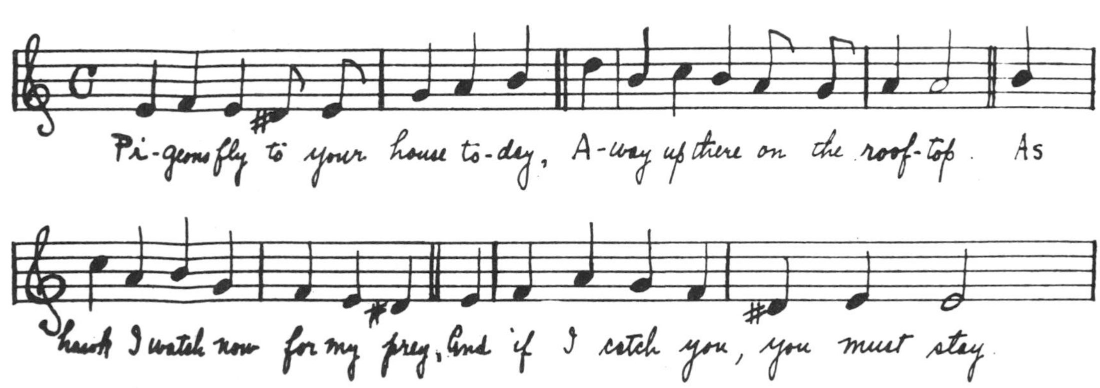

The pigeons are arranged along boundary line 3–4 and face toward the hawk. The hawk begins the game by singing the following song:

> Pigeons, fly to your house today
> Away up there on the roof-top;
> As hawk, I watch now for my prey,
> And if I catch you, you must stay.

At the last word sung the pigeons run across the space to the other boundary, 1–2, while the hawk tries to catch one of them. The captured pigeon becomes a hawk. The hawks, now holding hands, call out the signal "Run!" and all the pigeons run across the space. All those caught become hawks and the game proceeds until all the pigeons are caught.

III
TRAVELERS

> I took a walk along the sand,
> The sea-side sand;
> And there I met an old, old man
> With staff in hand.
> He spoke to me so,
> He spoke to me so:
> And asked me the name of my country, Ho!

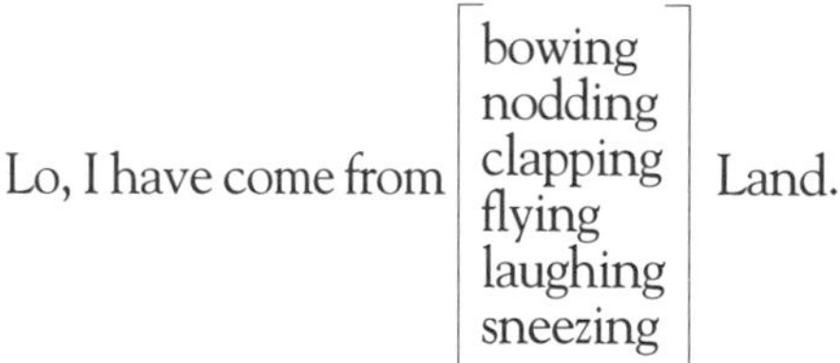

Lo, I have come from [bowing / nodding / clapping / flying / laughing / sneezing] Land.

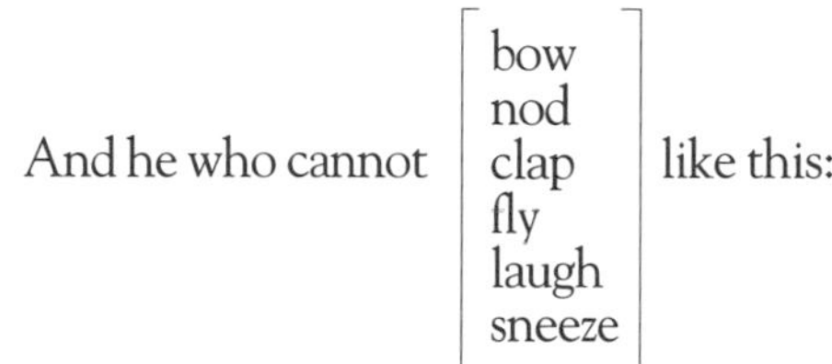

And he who cannot [bow / nod / clap / fly / laugh / sneeze] like this:

came not, I know from [bowing, etc...] Land.

A child in the center with a stick represents the old man. The others form a circle and march around until "met" is said, then stand still. At "spoke to me" all bow to the old man. At "bowing land" all begin to bow. With other verses all nod, clap, laugh, sneeze, as the case may be. At "flying" all march around with arms waving.

DANISH FUN

Nella Larsen Imes

Dear Children—These are pleasant memories of my childish days in Denmark.

N.L.I.

THE FOX GAME

One player represents the fox. If outdoors he sits on a stone, if in the house, on a stool or box. Another player represents the goose and the rest are goslings.

The goose stands in front with the goslings in single file behind her, each having his hands on the shoulders of the one in front of him. They circle, still in this position, around the fox chanting the first verse of this song:

Our goslings fly to the meadow
To eat the bright green grass,
Shame on the wicked fox
Who watches as they pass
In the summer-time.

Is the old fox at home today?
And what is he doing pray?
He sits upon a stone
And crunches on a bone
Till the evening gray.

"And who is to be your prey?
Oh come now, foxie, say?"
"*You*, goosie, goosie gander,
As fat as fat can be;
Also goslings three!"

At *summer-time* the goose stands in front of the fox with the goslings behind her. The second verse has the same action as the first. The third verse is sung by the goose and fox alone. At *goslings three* the fox rises and tries to catch one of the goslings, while the goose with out-stretched arms tries to prevent him.

The first gosling caught is the fox next time; but the fox must keep on chasing until he has captured three.

HIDE THE SHOE

The players sit in a circle and one player brings the shoe and says:

"Shoemaker, shoemaker, mend my shoe,
Have it done by half past two!"

Then he goes out and the shoe is passed to each one and finally hidden. When he comes back he must hunt for it. Occasionally the shoe is tapped on the floor. The person who has the shoe when found is, of course, "it" for the next time.

THE KING IS HERE

All sit in a circle except one, who stands and is called the jester. He is supposed to begin a story, inventing it as he goes along. Frequently without warning he uses the words "*Change places*." The players however pay no attention at all to this, but when the jester adds the information "*The King is here!*" all jump up and change places and the jester endeavors to get a seat. If he succeeds the one without a seat becomes the jester. No change is to be made unless the jester says plainly "*The King is here!*" If, for instance, he says "*The King is coming!*" the players are not to change. This uncertainty adds to the excitement and fun.

DANISH RIDDLES

When has a man four hands?
When he doubles his fists.

At what time was Adam born?
A little before Eve.

When the clock strikes thirteen,
what time is it?
Time to repair the clock.

What is the color of a winter fruit?
Orange.

What is the national color of France?
Tricolor.

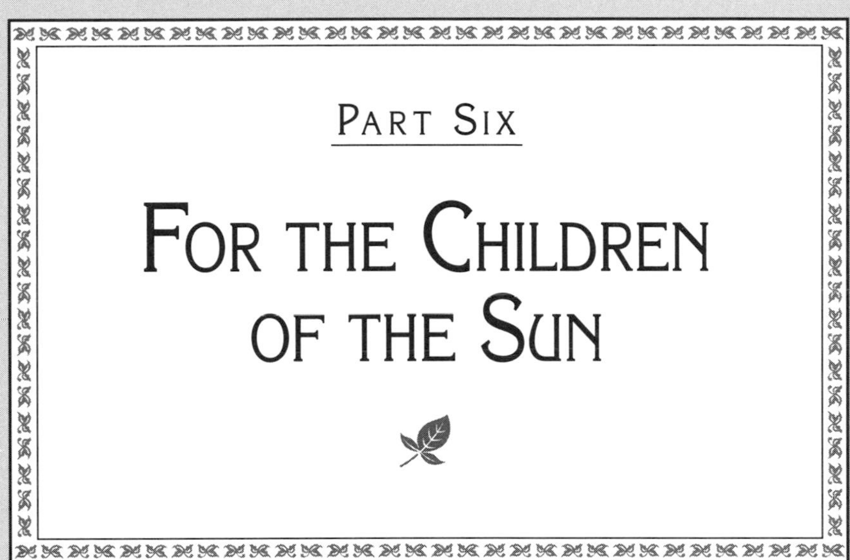

Part Six

For the Children of the Sun

On the following pages you will find a facsimile, or an exact, photographic copy, of the April 1921 edition of The Brownies' Book. In these pages you will see many different things. There is an announcement for a contest to see who could sell the most subscriptions for the magazine. The grand prize was a scholarship of $50 a year for four years, a large amount of money in 1921. You will see the table of contents. In the small writing on the bottom of the page you notice that the editors ask for submissions of writing and art "relating to colored children." There are several photographs of "true brownies" as well as drawings by illustrators such as Laura Wheeler and Marcellus Hawkins, whose art appeared in almost every issue of the magazine.

This April 1921 issue is typical in several ways. For example, it includes a Br'er Rabbit story and puzzles in the "Playtime" section. It includes a travel story. This one, about a Mexican village, is by the poet Langston Hughes. But before he was a famous poet, he was a high school student who often contributed poems and stories to The Brownies' Book. The story "Chocolate Cake" was written by another reader, Pocahontas Foster, who often sent in her stories and letters. Contributor James Alpheus Butler, Jr., was another reader who went on to be a published writer as an adult.

There is no issue in which poetry and fiction are not featured. Neither is there an issue in which "The Judge" column, written by Jessie Fauset, does not appear. This is a column in which several young characters have discussions with the Judge about all kinds of topics—education, their relationships with their parents, what they want their lives to be like when they grow up, or how they act with their friends and brothers and sisters.

Like most issues, this one has a story that teaches the young readers about historic people and places and times, ranging from the abolitionist movement in the North, to the South Carolina sea islands, to famous musicians and heroes. The column called "As the Crow Flies" made sure that at the same time that readers were learning about the past, they were also keeping well informed about current events both in the United States and around the world. You will notice, too, that "The Jury" section shares letters from readers who live all over the United States, along with a letter from Cuba. You can learn even more about the young people who read The Brownies' Book by reading "Little People of the Month," which gives news about the things they are doing, no matter how big or small—performing well in school, being polite children, participating in track and field events. You can learn about the parents of the brownies by reading "The Grown-ups' Corner."

At the end of this issue you'll see advertisements for books written by both black and white writers. The editors of The Brownies' Book thought their young readers and their parents might be interested in these books because they were related to Negro life. There is also an advertisement for The Crisis, the magazine published by the NAACP (the National Association for the Advancement of Colored People), an organization to which many brownies' parents belonged.

Many people contributed to making The Brownies' Book a wonderful magazine: editors, writers, parents, artists, and most of all, the young readers themselves. It was their magazine more than 75 years ago: they wrote in letters and stories and sent in pictures of themselves. It was their magazine because they loved it. It is your magazine now.

THE BROWNIES' BOOK

APRIL 1921

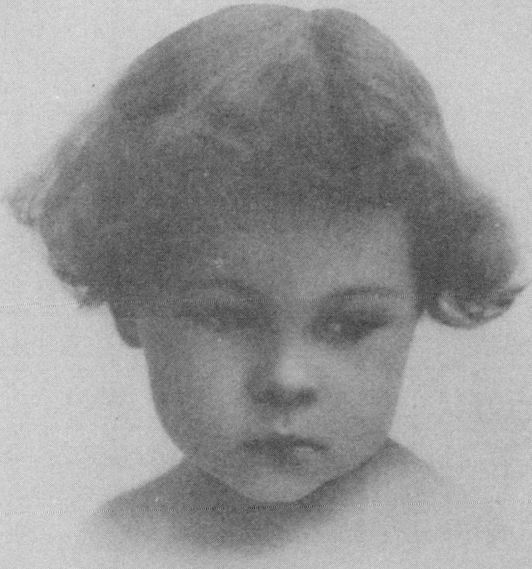

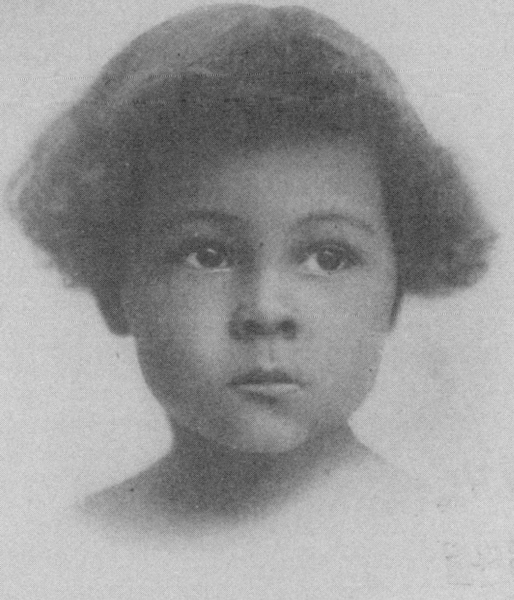

SPRING NUMBER

15 CTS A COPY

$1.50 A YEAR

A CHAMPIONSHIP CONTEST

THE BROWNIES' BOOK should have a hundred thousand subscribers and should be read by a million children who especially need its inspiring pictures, stories and news of colored youth.

To introduce this magazine to many new readers we are launching a SPECIAL CIRCULATION CAMPAIGN and, in addition to regular liberal commissions to agents, we offer championship medals on the following terms and conditions:

100 Championship Medals

50 GOLD MEDALS

To the person in each State or Territory of the United States who sends us the largest number of subscriptions to THE BROWNIES' BOOK mailed to or delivered at our office on or before July 1, 1921 (provided the highest is not less than 25 annual subscriptions), we will send a beautiful Championship Gold Medal, besides paying the usual agent's commission. The subscription price is $1.50 a year. Foreign subscriptions $1.75 a year.

50 SILVER MEDALS

To the person in each State or Territory of the United States who sells the largest number of copies of THE BROWNIES' BOOK bought on or before July 1, 1921 (provided the number of copies totals not less than 250), we will send a beautiful Championship Silver Medal, besides allowing the usual agent's commission. The sale price is 15c a copy.

The contest is open to any man, woman, boy or girl.

In case of a tie for any prize, each tieing contestant will receive a prize identical with that tied for.

$50 Scholarship for Four Years

To the person who makes the best showing in this Championship Contest a scholarship of Fifty Dollars a year for Four Years is offered by Mr. Thomas J. Calloway, a business man of the race, who is anxious to see THE BROWNIES' BOOK widely read and who desires to encourage the youth in industry and zeal. To win the scholarship it is necessary to win a gold or silver medal. The $50 a year will be paid to the school to which the winner goes for education.

Write at once for agent's terms, subscription blanks, sample copies and current copies to sell.

DU BOIS and DILL, *Publishers*

2 West 13th Street **New York, N. Y.**

THE BROWNIES' BOOK

Published Monthly and Copyrighted by DuBois and Dill, Publishers, at 2 West 13th Street, New York, N. Y. Conducted by W. E. Burghardt DuBois; Jessie Redmon Fauset, Managing Editor; Augustus Granville Dill, Business Manager

VOL. 2. No. 4. APRIL, 1921 WHOLE No. 16

CONTENTS

FIFTEEN CENTS A COPY: ONE DOLLAR AND A HALF A YEAR

FOREIGN SUBSCRIPTIONS TWENTY-FIVE CENTS EXTRA

RENEWALS: The date of expiration of each subscription is printed on the wrapper. When the subscription is due, a yellow renewal blank is enclosed.

CHANGE OF ADDRESS: The address of a subscriber can be changed as often as desired. In ordering a change of address, both the old and the new address must be given. Two weeks' notice is required.

MANUSCRIPTS and drawings relating to colored children are desired. They must be accompanied by return postage. If found unavailable they will be returned.

Entered as second class matter January 20, 1920, at the Post Office at New York, N. Y., under the Act of March 3, 1879.

"The Captain of Plymouth"
Scene from the play of that name, written and staged by Katheryn M. Campbell at Paris, Texas

The Brownies' Book

Vol. 2—No. 4 APRIL, 1921 Whole No. 16

HEN springtime comes with her sparkling April days, little New York kiddies are not much inclined to study, especially if it be at night-time and away up stairs in an apartment house. This is the rule and little Cless was no exception. Naturally, then, when Granny made him study under such trying conditions he kept constantly on the alert for some way out. It was one night in flipping over the leaves of an old geography that he hit upon the scheme that promised him some relief. He had come to one of those animal maps, I'm sure you have seen one with its buffaloes rushing headlong across the plain; its turkeys with outstanding wings and fan-shaped tails strutting around with all the pride of a peacock; or a puma or a jaguar sinking his teeth into the back of a fleeing deer. Cless saw all these and many others, but none caught his attention so solidly as the little creature that swung down by his tail from the limb of a tree in the far corner of the map. This was Br'er Possum.

"Look! Granny," shrieked Cless as he took up the geography and rushed over to show his grandmother. "Look!—here's Br'er Possum swinging from the limb by his tail. See how cute he is! And, Granny, you never did tell me about the trick he worked on Br'er Rabbit. Won't you tell me now? Please, Granny, 'cause I'm so tired reading my lesson."

Granny had been so cunningly led up to the story that she couldn't possibly refuse. So she threw aside her evening paper, took off her spectacles and, while little Cless lay back on the sofa, she began another tale of Br'er Possum.

"You remember how Mister Tortoise taught Br'er Possum to play dead, don't you?"

Cless assured her that he did.

"And you remember how he worked the trick on Br'er Fox?"

"Yes'm."

"Well since Br'er Fox was killed and there

was no one else so cunning as he, Br'er Rabbit decided that he just had to get this new trick from Br'er Possum. So he set out to learn it. Of course Br'er Possum wouldn't tell Br'er Rabbit anything about it, but Br'er Rabbit felt sure he could get all the information he wanted from Miss Possum, Br'er Possum's sweetheart, who lived about five miles away from Chuckatuck, at a place called Crown Hill. So all that winter Br'er Rabbit tramped over to Crown Hill every Friday night, pretending to be in love with Miss Possum. But he wasn't in love with her at all. The truth of the matter was that he simply went to see her with the hope of some day coaxing her to tell him Br'er Possum's trick. Now Br'er Possum was on to all this and that's why he hadn't told any one—even his sweetheart—about his new trick.

"But there came a time when Br'er Possum had to either try his new trick or lose his love, for Br'er Rabbit was so cute and wore such good clothes that he was about to make Miss Possum forsake her old lover. The test came one Easter Monday night. There was an Easter Party on Chuckatuck Hill to which every creature was invited. Br'er Possum, of course, expcted to go over to Crown Hill and get Miss Possum and bring her to the party. Br'er Rabbit had the same hope. And Miss Possum was cruel enough to promise each one that she would go with him—*alone*. Br'er Possum heard of her plan, but he was not disheartened. He was determined to show her that he was just as clever as Br'er Rabbit. The night for the party came. Br'er Possum dressed up in a brand new, blue suit, put on a big Buster Brown collar and decorated it with the reddest and widest tie that he could find. But all this fine dressing did not count, for when he went over to Crown Hill to get Miss Possum she said: 'Why I'm going to the party with Br'er Rabbit. Sorry you took the trouble to come over to-night.'

"Br'er Possum was astonished.

"'All right,' said he as he sank his head into his handkerchief and began to cry. 'Can I stay and see you off?'

"'Certainly,' she agreed.

"The two sat down and began to talk. Now I think Miss Possum mentioned everything except her love for Br'er Possum, and I think he told her everything he knew except his new trick. At eight o'clock, in strutted Br'er Rabbit. He was dressed in the finest suit imaginable and was puffing a big cigar and swinging a carved walking-cane. All this, of course, made him look like a *real* sport. He was very much surprised to find Br'er Possum there, but he tried hard to keep from getting excited. He sat down, crossed his legs, told a few jokes, talked a little about the weather and then got up and said: 'Let's go to the party, honey.'

"Miss Possum got up and made ready to go. But as soon as she started out, Br'er Possum fell violently ill. 'Whee-a! whee-a! whee-a!' he began to cry. 'Send for Mister Tortoise.'

"Now Mister Tortoise was not a real doctor, but his sassafras tonics were a positive cure for any pain imaginable. So Miss Possum begged Br'er Rabbit to go and get him. Br'er Rabbit went. Meanwhile Miss Possum exerted every possible effort toward keeping Br'er Possum alive until Br'er Rabbit returned with Mister Tortoise. At last Mister Tortoise toddled in. He flung open his satchel of roots, crawled up to Br'er Possum and laid his head upon his breast to listen for his heart thumps. And sure enough it was going: *'Thump! Thump! Thump!'*

"'Where's the pain?' asked Mister Tortoise.

"'Oh-ee! Oh-ee! everywhere,' cried Br'er Possum. 'I can't live. Leave me! Leave me! Leave me and let me die.' Then he turned over on his face, uttered a plaintive cry and in another moment he was apparently dead. Immediately Miss Possum began to wring and twist her hands and cry, 'Ee-hee! Ee-hee! I'm so sorry I treated Br'er Possum so mean. Ee-hee! I'm so sorry—so sorry. Poor me—poor me!'

"She was almost scared to death, for it had already been rumored on Chuckatuck Hill that Br'er Rabbit was layin' for Br'er Possum, and she knew if he died that night, there would be some excitement in Chuckatuck the next day. Well, for her, the party was over. Once more she begged Br'er Rabbit to go over to Chuckatuck Hill and tell Br'er Possum's folks that he was dead. And she kept on moaning and sighing and sniffing till Mister Tortoise had pity on her and let the secret out. 'Don't you know Br'er Possum ain't dead?'

"'Isn't he?—Isn't he?' she asked nervously.

"'Why, of course, he isn't. I taught him to do that trick last winter. He played it on Br'er Fox and got by with it and now he thinks he's got to play it on everybody. But he shan't play

At eight o'clock in strutted Br'er Rabbit

it on you.' By this time Br'er Rabbit was well out of sight, so Br'er Possum hopped up from the floor and began dancing and shouting:

"'Oh goodee gar!
I've fooled old Br'er Rabbit,
And now that he's gone
You and I can have it.
Going to take you to the party
Or know the reason why,
'Cause I've fooled Br'er Rabbit—
E-ee! E-ee!——I!'

"'Oh but I thought you were dead,' cried Miss Possum as Br'er Possum stopped singing.

"'No, indeed,' he answered. 'I was just playing dead! It's a new trick Mister Tortoise taught me the first of last winter.' And then for the first time he told her all about the trick he played on Br'er Fox. As soon as she heard this story she became very proud of Br'er Possum, for if he had outwitted Br'er Fox last winter he had certainly outwitted Br'er Rabbit now. Therefore, he must be the slyest creature in the whole woods. 'Come along, honey, let's go to the party,' begged Miss Possum.

"'Sure!' chuckled Br'er Possum. 'You'll excuse us, won't you, Mister Tortoise? Thank you for your medicine!' Mister Tortoise assured them that they were welcome to his services and within a few moments he was on his way to his hole, and Br'er Possum and Miss Possum were on their way to the party.

"When they reached the party everybody was laughing and dancing and having a good time. But as soon as the rabbits noticed that it was Br'er Possum and Miss Possum, instead of Br'er Rabbit and Miss Possum, they quit dancing and began to ask, 'Oh where's Br'er Rabbit, Miss Possum—where's Br'er Rabbit?' But before she could answer, Br'er Possum was dancing a jig and singing his same old song over and over again—

" 'Oh goodee gar!
I've fooled old Br'er Rabbit,
And now that he's gone
You and I can have it.
Brought my Honey to the party—
You know the reason why,
'Cause I've fooled Br'er Rabbit—
E-ee! E-ee!——I!'

"Well he kept on singing this way till the dance started again. Nobody could get any sense in him till then. Now he took Miss Possum and danced and danced till it was time to go home. When they got back home they found Br'er Rabbit lying in front of Miss Possum's den. He had got lost over in Chuckatuck Swamp and had come back and cried himself to sleep. 'Br'er Possum got well again,' said Miss Possum as Br'er Rabbit got up and began to rub his sleepy eyes, 'and we decided to go to the party.' Br'er Rabbit didn't believe this tale but he didn't dare say so, for it was a disgrace for a rabbit to admit that he had been outwitted by a possum. It was almost day now, so Br'er Rabbit and Br'er Possum told Miss Possum good-night and each started for his den. But Br'er Possum never told Br'er Rabbit, and Br'er Rabbit," concluded Granny, "never has been able even up to this day to find out just how Br'er Possum turned the trick on him that Easter Monday night."

Granny had consumed half an hour or more in telling this tale, for she included a number of minor details that I have purposely omitted. All this, of course, had given little Cless ample time to get rested from his books. And now it was bed-time, so he rolled down off the sofa, ran over and kissed Granny good-night, and hurried on off to bed where the sandman soon had him dreaming dreams of how Br'er Possum outwitted Br'er Rabbit.

IN A MEXICAN CITY

LANGSTON HUGHES

TOLUCA sits in the highest plateau of Mexico at the foot of the old and long extinct volcano "Xinantecatl", which is said to be named after one of the ancient Indian kings. All around us there are mountains and our valley is broad and fertile. Here the climate is cool and often cold, but the poor folks never have shoes to wear nor do the rich use stoves in their houses. In summer it is the rainy season and every day brings long showers and misty clouds that hide the mountains. In winter the sky is clear and the sun shines warm at mid-day, but in the shade it is always cool.

The house where I live faces a little plaza or park and from my window I can see many interesting things. Every morning a bare-footed old woman in a wide straw hat and long skirts drives a little flock of white sheep down the street, and sometimes she has a tiny baby lamb in her arms. They go to the country to graze all day and in the evening they come back again. Often I see a funeral procession passing through the plaza on the way to the Panteon and as they do not have hearses here, the men carry the casket on their shoulders while the mourners walk behind them. On Sundays the park is full of black-shawled women and men wrapped in *serapes* or blankets who come in the early morning to say mass in the quaint old church in front with its pretty tower and its most unmusical bells.

There are many churches here and all of them are very old. Some were built before the Independence, when Mexico was still under Spanish rule, and have beautiful domes and tall, graceful towers. Practically every one is Catholic and they keep many feast days. On the day of the Innocent Saints there is a custom that reminds one of our April Fool. On this date things should never be loaned and if you forget, the article is sure to be sent back by the joking friend who borrowed it, accompanied by a tiny box full of tiny toys and a note calling you a "poor little innocent saint". On the second of November, which is a day in honor of the dead, they sell many little cardboard coffins and paper dolls dressed as mourners, and if a person meets you in the street and says "I'm dying", you must give him a gift unless you have said "I'm dying" first; then, of course, he has to treat you to the present. On a certain day in January the people take their animals to be blessed and in the church-yard one sees everything from oxen to rabbits. Each is wearing a bit of gay colored ribbon and they wait patiently for the priest to come.

The houses here from the outside all look very much alike and are but a succession of arched doors and windows with small balconies facing the sidewalk. They often have lovely court-yards and verandas but these are hidden from the passers-by behind high walls, and the fronts of the houses never tell anything about the beauty that may be within them. When one enters a house the door usually leads directly into the court-yard or sometimes into the long open corridor from which every room has its entrance. In the *patio* or court-yard there are flowers the year round and if it is a large one, there may be a garden or trees. On the railing of the long veranda, too, there are many pots of red and pink geraniums and fragrant heliotrope. Inside the house there will probably be little furniture. Only a few of the well-to-do people have a great deal, so most of the homes use chairs as their principal space fillers. In a friend's parlor I counted twenty-seven one day and the only other articles of furniture were two small tables. Most of the parlors of the middle-class folk show the same emptiness but perhaps it is a good idea, for on holidays there is plenty of room to dance without moving anything out.

The kitchens here are very different from American ones, for they do not use stoves or gas ranges. The fuel is charcoal and the stoves are made of stone or

Market-day in Toluca

brick, built into the wall like a long seat, except that they have three square grates on top for the fire and three square holes in front for removing the ashes. Some are prettily built and covered with gaily colored tiles. To make the fire several splinters of pine are lighted in the grate and then the black pieces of charcoal piled on top. Then one must fan and fan at the square holes in front until the charcoal on top begins to blaze, and in a little while you have a nice glowing fire ready to cook with.

The shops here in the portals, which is Toluca's "uptown", are much like the American stores, but in the little *expendios* in the side streets one can buy a penny's worth of wood or a tablespoonful of lard or a lamp full of oil. The poor here do not have much money. These little shops paint themselves all sorts of colors and have the funniest names. One I know is called "The Wedding Bouquet". Others are "The Light of America", "The Big Fight", "The Fox", and so on, and one tinner's shop is even called "Heart of Jesus". The last store on the edge of town, where the road leads off to San Juan, has the very appropriate name of "Farewell". One who did not know Spanish could acquire a whole vocabulary just by reading the store names which are painted in large colored letters across the front and are often accompanied by pictures or decorations to illustrate their meanings. For instance, the meat market called "The Bull of Atenco" has the animal's picture on one side of the door and a bull-fighter's on the other, painted over a background of bright blue.

Friday is market-day in Toluca and the square outside the market-house is one sea of wide Mexican hats, as buyer and trader jostle and bargain. The surrounding streets are lined with Indians from the country who squat behind their little piles of vegetables, or fruit, or herbs, which they have to sell and which they spread out on the ground before them. One old woman will have neat little piles of green peppers for a cent a pile. Another will have beans and another wild herbs for seasoning soup or making medicine. The fruit sellers, of course, always have a most gorgeous and luscious display. Under a canopy created from four sticks and some sort of covering to make a spot of shade, are piled all sorts of strange, delicious fruits. There one finds creamy alligator pears and queer-tasting mangoes; red pomegranates and black zapotes; small, round melons and fat little bananas and the delicately flavored granada, which feels like a paper ball and has a soft seedy pulp inside. Then there are oranges that come up to us from the hot country, along with limes and juicy lemons that are not sour like the ones we know up North.

Here people never buy without bargaining. If the price asked for a thing is two cents, they are sure to get it for one. These price arguments are always good-natured and the merchant, knowing that he will have to come down, usually asks more than he should in the first place. Everyone going to market must carry his own baskets and sacks and even the paper for his meat, as everything is sold without wrapping.

A market-day crowd is composed of all sorts of people. A rich señorita with her black scarf draped gracefully about her shoulders is doing the family buying, while the servants carrying baskets follow behind. Indian women with sacks of vegetables on their backs; others with turkeys or chickens in their arms; little ragged brown boys seeking a chance to earn a few cents by carrying a customer's basket; and beggars, numberless beggars, blind, lame and sick beggars, all asking patiently for pennies or half-rotted fruits; these are the folks one sees on market-day pushing and elbowing their way through the crowd which is so thick that nobody can hurry.

On one side of the plaza are the sellers of hats and the large yellow mats that the Indians spread down on the floor at night for sleeping purposes. The Mexican straw hats have wide round brims and high peaked crowns and, though cheap, most of them are prettily shaped. The Indian, upon buying a new hat, will not take the trouble to remove his old one, but puts the new one on top and marches off home with his double decked head gear. Sometimes a hat merchant, desiring to change his location, will put one hat on his head, and as each peaked crown fits snugly over the other, he then piles his whole stock on top of himself and goes walking down the street like a Chinese pagoda out for a stroll.

Here everything that people do not carry on their backs they carry on their heads. The ice-cream man crying *nieve*, balances his freezer, and the baker-boys carry a shallow basket as big around as a wagon wheel. This basket has a crown in the center and when filled with bread it fits over the head like a very wide Mexican hat, while its wearer underneath is as insignificant as the stem of a mushroom. Sometimes we see fruit sellers, too, with great colorful mounds of fruit piled upon their wooden trays and balanced gracefully on their black-haired heads. When a thing is too heavy or too unwieldy to put on the head, then it is carried on the back, and the Indians bear immense burdens in this way. Men, women and even small children are often seen with great loads of wood or charcoal, or sacks of grain, on their backs, and the only carriage that the little Indian baby ever knows is its mother's back, where it rides contented all day long, tied in her *rebosa* or shawl.

PLAYTIME

PUZZLES

Arranged and Answered
by
C. LESLIE FRAZIER

EVERY child likes to solve puzzles, so here are a few original ones for the Brownies. Study them and forward your answers to the Editor with your name and age attached. Send in your own puzzles so other Brownies can work on them. Always enclose the solutions to the puzzles you submit. Answers to this month's puzzles will be published next month. Send in your answers by the tenth of April.

REMEMBER, all puzzles submitted *must* be original, and, while it isn't necessary, we would like for them to be of racial nature.

The letters in this poem are all mixed, and it is called "printer's pi". What poem is this and who wrote it?

Read citric, how ym giltnhges os resopled,
Ldwuo I imthg dutys ot eb cnepir fo serob,
Ghirt seylwi luowd I uler ahtt llud taeste—
Tub, ris, I yam ton, lilt oyu etadbaic.
—Ulap Neecraul Uarbnd.

BEHEADINGS

The beheaded letters, placed in the order here given, spell the name of a famous Negro astronomer.

1. Behead staff of life, and leave to understand writing. 2. Behead total cost, and leave to ascend. 3. Behead at no time, and leave at all times. 4. Behead none, and leave any. 5. Behead flushed with success, and leave tardy. 6. Behead an ancient warrior, and leave sleeping time. 7. Behead act of sending out, and leave a delegation. 8. Behead a contest in running, and leave an illustrious aviator.
EXAMPLE: 1. B-read.

TWISTED QUOTATIONS

Too many cooks breed contempt.
When poverty comes in at the door, honest men get their own.
To play the dog out of joint.
Two heads seldom agree.
Too much familiarity spoils the broth.
To send one away in a stack of hay.
When rogues fall out, love flies out of the window.
Two of a trade are better than one.

WORD SQUARE ARRANGEMENT

When the words here selected are placed one over the other, the same words will be given across and down.

My first is a male parent; my second is to stick; my third is to steal; my fourth is having been cautious; my fifth is a family name; my sixth is consisting of reeds.

EXAMPLE:

F A T H E R
A * * * * *
T * * * * *
H * * * * *
E * * * * *
R * * * * *

A CONUNDRUM

If conductors on cars had animal mascots with them while on duty, what would put you in mind of the mascots when you entered a furniture store?

LETTER-WORDS

Place two letters together and make words.

EXAMPLE: 1. NV (Envy).

1. To grudge. 2. Not difficult. 3. A number. 4. To rot. 5. A bird. 6. Whoever. 7. Place of confinement. 8. A loud sound. 9. A vine. 10. A tree. 11. A tower in France. 12. A tract.

NEGRO HISTORY

1. Who was Attucks?
2. Who was Dunbar?
3. When did Booker T. Washington die?
4. What date is Emancipation Day?
5. What Negro helped to survey Washington city?
6. Where is Frederick Douglass buried?
7. Who made the first clock made in America?
8. What story is "Topsy" a character in?
9. Did Negroes fight on the Confederate side in the Civil War?
10. How long did the Civil War last?
11. What was the Carrizal incident?
12. Who is Bert Williams?

THE GIRL RESERVES

AT our meeting on January 22, we held our semi-annual election of officers. We were fortunate in having with us as visitors, Mrs. Boyce, President of the Washington Y. W. C. A., and Miss Clayda Williams, of the National Board, who, with Miss Florence Brooks, our Girls' Work Secretary, assisted with our election. Mrs. Boyce presided and Misses Williams and Brooks kept record of the votes. Elizabeth Morton, our former president, had been so faithful and had performed the duties of her office so well, that had our rules allowed it, she would have been unanimously reëlected. But we want to give each a chance.

Our new officers are: President, Julia Delany; Vice-President, Elaine Williams; Recording Secretary, Hortense Mimms; Corresponding Secretary, Lillian Smith; Treasurer, Sylvia Wormley; Reporter for THE BROWNIES' BOOK, Annette Hawkins.

The officers of the High School group of the Dramatic Club are: President, Ida May Hall; Vice-President, Eudora Keyes; Recording Secretary, Dorothy Craft; Corresponding Secretary, Edwina Simpkins; Treasurer, Estelle Welch; Reporter for THE BROWNIES' BOOK, Avis Spencer.

In order to give a better idea to the officers and board members of our Y. W. C. A., it was decided that they be invited to a model initiation and Girl Reserves meeting. The ladies selected Saturday, and this being the meeting day of the Dramatic Club, it fell to our lot to conduct the exercise.

Under the direction of Miss Brooks, the initiation ceremony took place, led by President Julia Delany. Seven members were initiated and received light from the red, white, and blue candles of Health, Knowledge, and Spirit.

We were honored by the presence of Miss Hallie Q. Brown, who was introduced to the girls by Mrs. Boyce, and who complimented the exercise and gave us much encouragement. Perhaps at some time THE BROWNIES' BOOK may tell us and the other Girl Reserves more of Miss Brown and what she means to our race.

The third Sunday of each month has been given over to the Girl Reserves by the Religious Committee for Vesper Services. On February 20 the Dramatic Club had charge, but owing to the very bad weather they postponed it until the following Sunday, when they were invited by the Junior Endeavor of the Lincoln Congregational Church to hold the service at their church.

February being the birthday month of so many noble men, the Dramatic Club held a service of Great Memories in honor of those who gave their lives to the betterment of the world by serving others.

They revived the great memory of Abraham Lincoln, Frederick Douglass, Henry Wadsworth Longfellow, and George Washington. The club sang the hymn, "Still, Still With Thee", the words of which were written by Mrs. Harriet Beecher Stowe. Mrs. M. I. Hill gave a helpful talk on the topic, "Ready for Service", a line of the Girl Reserve Code, which expresses a summary of their efforts, and the girls rededicated themselves by repeating the Code.

Our Little Friends

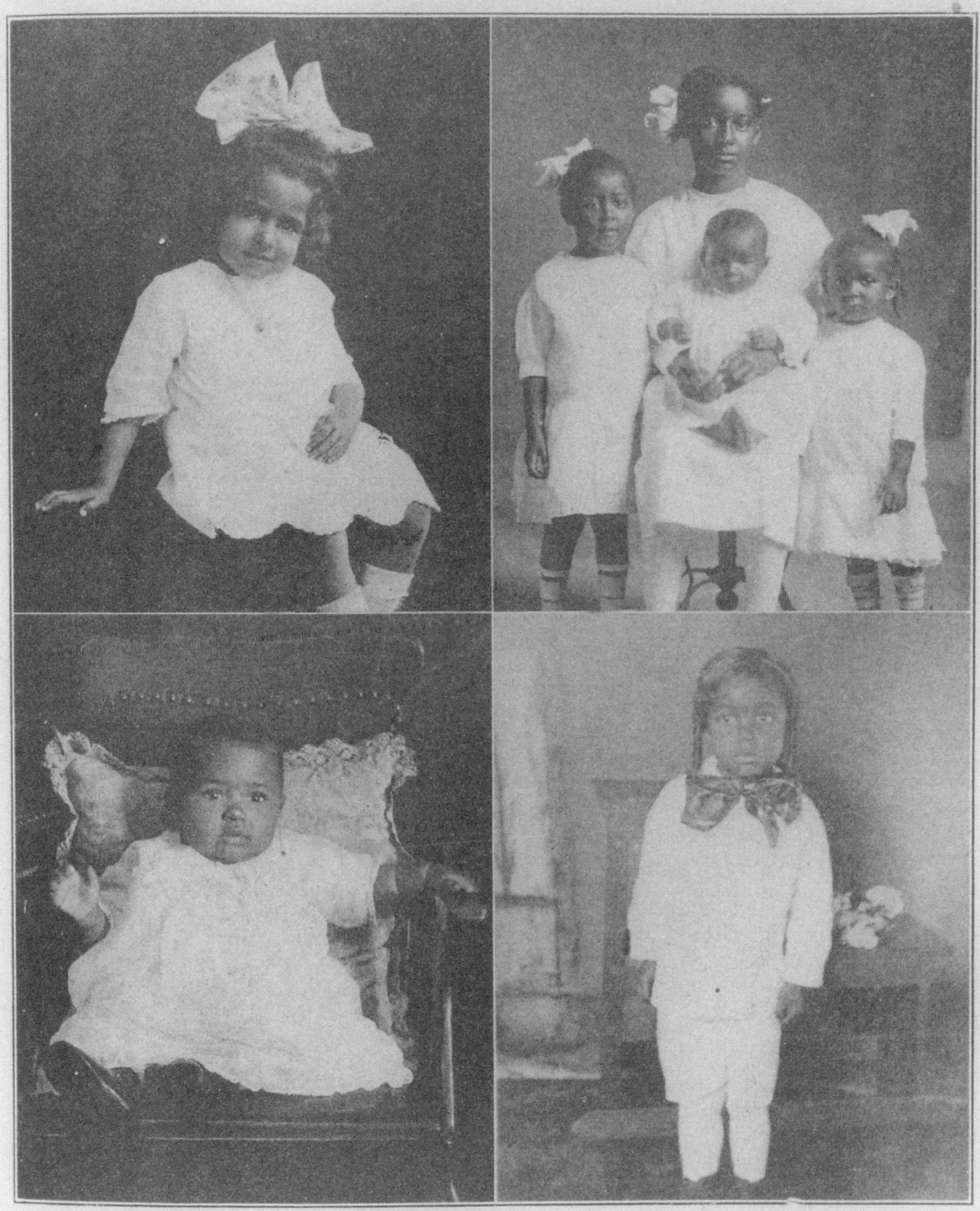

THE JUDGE

"I WISH," says Billy looking disconsolately at a long line of fractions, "that a fairy would come along and give me three wishes."

"What would you do with them?" Wilhelmina wants to know.

"I'd wish first, that children didn't have to go to school, and second, that children didn't have to go to school, and third, that children didn't have to go—"

"My goodness!" William interrupts, "you'd certainly mean to get your wish."

"As a matter of fact, some children don't have to go to school," says the Judge, "but if they haven't a certain amount of training and knowledge when they get to be men and women, they're mighty sorry for it just the same."

"Well how can they get the training if they don't go to school?" asks William.

Wilhelmina looks thoughtful. "There must be some way though. Don't you remember Maude and Jimmie Keating? They'd never been in a school in their lives, until they came here. And they were smart, they knew all sorts of things. I never saw anybody know so much geography and history as Maude—all about such funny places, too, South America, and—and Guadaloupe,—or something."

"Well she ought to," William reminds her, "she'd lived in those places for a long time. Don't *you* know a lot about this town? You've lived here forever."

"You see," says the Judge, "all education is for, is to produce knowledge. Your friend Maude, although she had never been to school, happens to be the child of parents who for one reason or another have travelled a great deal and have done it in all sorts of odd places,—that is odd to our notion. Consequently, Maude knows about those foreign countries and that means geography to you. She also may have learned just what combination of former events has made those people decide to live according to certain laws and to adopt certain customs,—and that is your idea of history."

"Oh," says Billy in surprise, "is that the way history and geography are made? I never thought they had anything to do with people that you know about."

"Of course that's the way. Some child in France is reading about New York State this minute and thinking how wise he is because he has collected facts which are a part of your every day life. But to go back to the business of getting an education. All children can't get their training like the Keating boy and girl by visiting new people and places, so that is the reason why they must learn them from books, which are short cuts to the knowledge gained by actual experience. If Billy were a clerk in a grocery now, he'd learn all about fractions in a short while, because he'd be selling people a fraction of a pound, or of a peck, or of a quart of something, and would be making change for a fraction of a dollar."

"And because he isn't in a position like that," says Wilhelmina with sudden understanding, "he has to learn how to do it in school out of a book—"

"So that if he should ever be in such a position he'd know how to act. Precisely," nods the Judge. "We go to school to fit ourselves as far as we may for all the possibilities of life. Learning things by actual experience is often pleasanter, but it takes a great deal more time."

"Books *are* wonderful things," says William almost reverently. "Why we'd never get anywhere without them, would we?"

"They are probably the greatest *single* blessing in the world," the Judge tells him. "If we didn't have them, and schools, and teachers, it would take a whole lifetime to learn geography, and another one to learn history, and still another to understand arithmetic,—"

"Just the same," pipes Billikins, who has been an attentive listener, "I'd like to learn how to do sums in a candy-shop."

GIRLS TOGETHER

LILLIE BUFFUM CHACE WYMAN

Sketches from Life

Part I

WHILE slavery existed, it created evil and sorrowful feelings, and when it ceased to exist, it left behind it a terrible trail of pain, passion and prejudice. Still, all the while, there has been a great deal of love and kindliness between white and colored Americans; and, moreover, there has always been a special bond of affectionate sympathy between those white people who, for more than a hundred years, have been trying to help colored people. I am going, therefore, to tell you a little about girls who worked together and loved each other, in some way connected with racial difference.

It must have been about the year 1800, that little white Sarah Grimké began to be "girls together", playing with slave children in Charleston, South Carolina. Her family were wealthy slave-holders. She used to pray to God that the slaves might not be beaten. Once, when she was less than six years old, she saw a woman very cruelly whipped, and that wee mite of a creature fled in childish terror from her own home,—from her slave-holding mother's home,—down on to the Charleston wharves. She begged a sea captain, whom she found there, to take her away where people did not do such dreadful things to each other! How the pitiful infant had ever come to suppose there were any such blessed places of refuge, I cannot tell you.

Later, Sarah was forbidden to teach the slave children to read. But a little slave girl had been assigned as her waiting-maid, so they became "girls together" in an innocent rebellion. At night they used to put out the light in Sarah's room, carefully screen the keyhole in the door, and then, as she wrote long afterwards, "flat on our stomachs before the fire with the spelling book under our eyes, we defied the laws of South Carolina." In that State, it was then a penal offence to teach slaves to read.

Sarah had a sister named Angelina, who was twelve years younger than herself. When Angelina was a child, she kept some soothing lotion among her hidden treasures, and at night she would creep secretly out of the house to annoint the wounds of the slaves who had been beaten. Heroic little girl in the darkness! When she was grown up, she tried to make an Abolitionist of her mother, and to influence her brother not to be harsh with the servants. Failing in both these efforts, and half broken-hearted, she went North, where Sarah had gone before. Neither of them ever again saw their native city or their mother. In 1835 Angelina and Sarah became the first women in America who addressed secular public meetings in behalf of the slave. Theirs were like angelic voices calling far and wide: "Pity the Slave, free him and do right by him." In one of his poems, Whittier spoke of the Grimké sisters as "Carolina's high-souled daughters".

I think it did often happen, in that sad and bad old time of slavery, that white children taught the slaves what they had themselves learned at school. Now and then, doubtless, they did so in a spirit of kindly comradery, and perhaps, in other cases, from childhood's innocent desire to show off. So childhood did help to soften the lot of the dark race, and to keep generous the heart of the white. Blessed be childhood!

I knew, long ago, a Maryland woman, whose parents had been slave-holders. She said that as a little girl, she had played a great deal with slave children, and that she used to feel sorry because they never could be white and live as white people did. When she was asked if she had ever thought that her playmates, although they never could be white, ought still to be free,—"No," she answered, "I never thought of that."

William Lloyd Garrison founded in 1832 the New England Anti-Slavery Society, which demanded the immediate abolition of slavery. All previous anti-slavery societies, in the country, had advocated a gradual liberation of the slaves, and by such methods slavery had been, by that time, abolished in most of the Northern States of the Union. I wonder if my readers all know what were the gradual emancipation methods. They were like this: the Quakers discouraged slave-holding by their members, and finally forbade it entirely, and commanded all persons in their fellowship to free any slaves they possessed. The separate states began to make laws forbidding the sale of slaves into other states, and requiring all slaves who had attained to a certain age to be set free on an especial date, and others at a later date.

Mr. Garrison and his followers felt that to work for such gradual action, though better than doing nothing, did still imply that the slave-holder had a sort of moral right to hold human beings as property for a time. So he and eleven other men formed this New England Anti-Slavery Society, to declare, to all America, that it was a sin for anybody to treat a fellow human being as property for a single hour. The Abolitionists (as Garrison and his followers were called), did not bring about immediate emancipation by demanding it, but they did establish the principle that slavery was wrong then and there, and they did largely create the feeling which led to the final destruction of the institution.

There were two great men in the country then, who stood for two opposing ideas, and each typified his own for all future students of American history. C. Calhoun, in the South, said: *"Slavery is right."* Garrison, in the North, said: *"Slavery is wrong."* Other people, except the close followers of each of these men, said practically, on the one hand, "Slavery is convenient and we must have it"; or, "Slavery is a burden that the white man must carry for the good of the black man, and so we whites have a right to get all the ease we can out of it, till it shall please God to institute some other system." But also, and mostly in the North, men said: "Slavery works badly, but if we can get rid of it, in the course of one or two hundred years, it is better to be patient with its existence for a while, than to disturb everybody now about it. Meanwhile, we'll help a little, one way and another, to make it more likely that the thing will end of itself, by and by."

Twelve *men* had formed the Immediate Emancipation Society, but *women* and *girls* began, at once, to work for its object. There were half-grown children, in Plymouth, Mass., where the Pilgrims first settled in 1620, who went without butter or something else good to eat, so as to save money to give to the anti-slavery cause. If they were like the children in my father's family, they adored the anti-slavery men and women, who spoke in public meetings. And they promised, if their parent should be sent to jail for helping fugitive slaves, that they would be "very good," while left alone at home. Abby Morton, afterwards Mrs. Diaz, the story writer, told how she and other Plymouth girls "nudged each other" with delight, when a minister, in church, made an unexpected allusion to the duty of freeing the slaves.

Now, with the kind permission of my readers, I am going to tell some of my own family history,—because it bears on the general subject of this paper, and because I know more about my own relatives, as to slavery, than I do about many other people.

Arnold Buffum, my mother's father, was the first President of the New England Anti-Slavery Society, and he was one of the first lecturers, which it sent out to proclaim its doctrines. He had five daughters, all grown up, but all still young enough to be "girls together" in their zeal for Abolition. The youngest daughter, Lydia, then about twenty years old, taught a little private school in Fall River, probably in the house of her sister, Mrs. Chace, for the latter wrote to their father, that Lydia had three colored children among her pupils, saying that they were "Hannah, and a little boy and girl, part Indian and part Negro, — cunning looking enough". Lydia went once to Philadelphia and wrote back, that when she returned to Fall River, she would bring with her a young colored girl, who was an escaped slave and did not dare to stay any longer, so near the slave-holding states as Philadelphia.

There was a sixteen year old niece of Arnold Buffum's named Hannah Shove. She was a pretty, little, brown-eyed creature, with short, dancing curls and dainty mannerisms. She seemed made just to have a good time with girls and boys. Such small maidens do not like to do unpopular things, but Hannah was willing to do almost anything to help the slaves. So she bought at an anti-slavery fair a little basket, which must have been covered with some fabric, for it is on record, that the "cover" bore a printed picture of a slave, kneeling and praying for freedom. Heaven only knows where the child got the money to pay for it! In a letter to her cousin, Mrs. Chace, (who many years later became my mother), she said she carried her kneeling slave everywhere she went (to make its silent appeal, I suppose), but that everybody laughed at her for doing it. It may seem a little thing, but I think Hannah was plucky to brave all that laughter.

I came on this earthly scene a dozen years after Hannah had carried the emblem of the slave's wrongs, and I, as a very small child, used to see, in my mother's best parlor, a little box made of pasteboard, covered with drab silk. I gazed at it with holy awe, for the picture of a kneeling and chained Negro was printed on the silk. The slaves in this country had not then been freed. There were English and Scotch women, who regularly sent things over the ocean to be sold at anti-slavery fairs, and this box had been made and sent to America and sold at such a fair. Probably Hannah's basket had also come from England. It may be that my mother's box, and its purchase by her, dated back to the same general period in the 1830 decade. Certainly my mother had something like it, in her house, at that same time, for I find, among her papers, an allusion to it, in a tender record about a little girl of hers named Susan, who was scarcely three years old when she died.

In those early anti-slavery days, some of the Abolitionists had a habit of speaking of each other as Brother or Sister So-and-So. I tell this to explain something in the quotations, I am about to make from my mother's journal. I also want to ask my readers to notice that these little stories show how constantly and lovingly she taught her children to remember the bondman as bound with him. It went on altogether, family love and love for humanity.

Here they are, the records the young mother made of her baby Abolitionists after two of them had died.

"When George was two years old we had a black woman to clean house, who brought with her a baby about eleven months old.

"The first time George saw her, he asked me what it was, and I told him she was a little girl. He looked at her with some surprise and then exclaimed, very tenderly, 'Pippy, pippy' (pretty). When he was carried into the bedroom, he wanted to 'kiss little girl', and he was permitted to kiss her."

After Susan's death, the mother made this entry in her record:

"I have omitted to say that she felt a sympathy for the poor slave without, it is true, being able to understand his condition, knowing only that he was poor and suffering. When permitted to look at the articles belonging to the Sewing Society she would say of the kneeling representation, 'Poor save, muvver, poor save'; and, I believe it was the day before her sickness, when I was dressing her in the morning, her sister asked me why I called Amos Dresser, who was then there, 'Brother Dresser'. I replied, 'Because he is an Abolitionist and so am I'. Susan said 'So I'."

The articles referred to in the passage above were some which the Sewing Society was preparing for sale at anti-slavery fairs.

George died before he was quite nine years old, and a notice of his death, probably written by his mother, appeared in Mr. Garrison's paper, *The Liberator*. I quote one paragraph: "Although young in years he was the devoted friend of the slave and gave early promise of being one of the firmest advocates of the rights of the oppressed." That was what Abolitionists trained their children to become,—the friends of the oppressed.

(To be Continued)

An April Rain Song

LANGSTON HUGHES

LET the rain kiss you.
Let the rain beat upon your head
With silver liquid drops.
Let the rain sing you a lullaby
With its pitty-pat.

The rain makes still pools on the sidewalk.
The rain makes running pools in the gutter.
The rain plays a little sleep tune
On our roof at night,
And I love the rain.

LOLLY-POP

A POEM BY

O COME with me to Lolly-pop Land,
  To the land where the lolly-pops grow!
There cats have wings, bees have no stings,
  And the rivers up-hill flow!

The birds all talk in Lolly-pop Land,
  As plain as plain can be!
The birds all talk and the trees all walk!
  Just come with me and see.

O come with me to Lolly-pop Land,
  To the land where the lolly-pops grow!
Fish climb the trees with the greatest ease,
  And the lobsters with them go!

In Lolly-pop Land strange things you'll see!
  Now this is all quite true.
I saw a cow being chased by a bunny!
That seemed to me so very funny,
  That I wrote it down for you!

I saw a rat that was chasing a cat,
  In Lolly-pop Land so fair!
  I saw a hare that was chasing a bear!
And the bear was—Oh! *so* fat!

I saw a dog being chased by a frog,
In dear old Lolly-pop Land!

I saw a hen being chased by a wren!
(They both played in the band!)

In the fields there grow fine things to eat,
In Lolly-pop Land, I know.
Cakes grow on stems, with muffins and gems,
And pies on bushes grow!

I'd like to live in Lolly-pop Land,
In Lolly-pop Land so fair.
I'd wear old clothes and go with bare toes!
O *don't* you wish *you* were there?

I'd live under trees and take my ease,
In Lolly-pop Land so funny.
If the trees went walking, I'd keep on talking,
And stay where it was sunny!

The birds will tell such strange, strange tales,
Such tales as you like to hear,
Of giants and fairies, of cats and canaries,
Of lions and camels queer!

Then fly with me to Lolly-pop Land,
To the land where the lolly-pops grow,
We'll have such fun, and, when day is done,
We'll come right home in a row!

HE world,—the sad and bad and beautiful world,—is full of promise today. For Spring is here and sweet April, and just as all the bleakness and bitterness of the Winter have passed, so, too, must all the evils and unrest of the war change to harmony again. Caw! Have faith poor world! All will yet be well!

❡ Germany has refused to fulfill her obligations to the Allies and as a result French, Belgian and British troops are occupying Düsseldorf and other towns on the Rhine. The Allies have not been so much interested in the amount of money which Germany was to pay, or her methods of paying it, as in Germany's refusal to recognize her obligations under the Treaty or her responsibility for the war, and in her disregard for the Paris terms. But Germany's attitude throughout has been of such a nature that finally Lloyd George declared at the meeting of the Supreme Council in London that German public opinion as represented through Minister Simons was clearly not prepared to pay.

❡ In Italy the peasants have been seizing large tracts of land. This has happened particularly in Sicily.

❡ A little island in the Pacific Ocean, about 80 miles square, is causing a great deal of controversy between the United States and Japan. This little island, called Yap, is a great cable center and belonged to Germany before the war. Then the Paris Conference assigned it to Japan, who now insists that the United States must keep out of Yap and cable by means of Manila. Almost the last act of President Wilson's administration was formally to object to awarding the island to Japan because this gives her control over an "international center of communication". Japan says that we did not sign the treaty of Versailles or join the League of Nations, so we have no voice in the matter.

❡ Premier Dato, leader of the Liberal-Conservative Party in Madrid, Spain, has been assassinated.

❡ The Prince of Wales while on a visit recently to Glasgow, Scotland, was met by a large band of unemployed men bearing banners, "We want the prices of 1914." Labor members of the Town Council objected to giving a dinner to the Prince saying it was a shame to feast royalty when hundreds of families were starving.

❡ After the Armistice, France sent black soldiers among others to Germany in her "army of occupation", but later withdrew them. Now Germany, in order to stir sentiment against France among nations which are not friendly to black people, declares that these soldiers are still in her cities. But Marshal Ferdinand Foch, of France, has issued a statement saying: "For several months there has not been a single black soldier on the left bank of the Rhine."

❡ Australia has for the first time elected a woman, Mrs. Cowan, to membership in parliament.

❡ Germany is preparing to re-enter the struggle for world trade. She is to make 119 locomotives for railways in Spain.

❡ Poland is planning to build a radio station at Warsaw which will compare with the best in the world. It will cost between $2,000,000 and $3,000,000. Poland desires to get in closer communication with America because about 20 per cent. of her people are here, and she has never been able to get in touch with them without having her messages censored.

❡ In Rome the Benedictine Commission, including Cardinal Gasquet, Fathers John Chapman, Henri Quentin and Abbot Emelli, are revising the old Latin Version of the Bible, known as the Vulgate.

LTHOUGH my heart goes out to the East, I caw with relief when I get back to America, my home. For though there are many ills here, at least I am not saddened as I was in Austria and China by the sight of

starving, helpless children, and broken, discouraged grown-ups; the wrecks of War and Famine. Oh little Children of America give of your plenty to feed the poor abroad, and resolve to grow up lovers of Right and of Justice, so that Pain and Pestilence may no more stalk through the world.

¶ On March 4th Warren Gamaliel Harding became the 29th President of the United States. His inauguration stands out as being marked by extreme simplicity. Mr. Wilson escorted Mr. Harding to the Capitol but was unable on account of his poor health to engage in any further ceremonies. A remarkable feature of this occasion was that Mr. Harding's address, due to a new invention, the "Amplifier", could be heard by all the thousands who thronged the huge space about the Capitol. Mr. Harding's speech was really a sermon based on the text from Micah, chapter VI., verse 8: "What doth the Lord require of thee, but to do justly, and to love mercy, and to walk humbly with thy God?"

¶ Champ Clark, former Speaker of the House, died just before the Inauguration. He was seventy-one years old and had been in political life for forty-five years.

¶ The Sixty-Sixth Congress has sat for the last time. Some of its enactments are well worth mention. For example, it made a provision for fixed residences in certain foreign cities for our diplomatic representatives. It also passed the Transportation Act, Merchant Marine, Mineral Leasing and Water Power Acts, and the Edge Act, which permits corporations to be formed to finance export trade.

¶ The United States loses several million dollars a year from forest fires alone.

¶ The galleries of the American Fine Arts Society in the Fine Arts Building, on West Fifty-seventh Street, New York, which were destroyed by fire, January 30, 1920, have been rebuilt. They follow the main lines of the original plan, but are more substantial and better lighted. They were reopened March 5, 1921.

¶ For a little while this country feared the possibility of an epidemic of typhus, a terrible disease, communicable almost solely through body lice, and brought into this country by immigrants who on account of the war had been living in bad and unsanitary conditions. But now medical and health experts have the centers of infection so well in hand that the disease cannot spread.

¶ New York is having great trouble over the breakdown of her transportation lines. Some of them are bankrupt, others are threatened with bankruptcy, and the service is consequently very poor. Two remedies are suggested. Governor Miller proposes a consolidated system to be owned by the city but leased to a private corporation for operation on a higher but reasonable fare. Mayor Hylan insists on city ownership and city operation at the present fare, with deficits paid out of the general tax fund. Meanwhile the public suffers.

¶ A coin-operated machine for polishing shoes has been designed by Herbert Oliver, of Baltimore. All the customer has to do is to put a nickel in the slot, push down a lever, and the machine does the work; it dusts, applies polish, and finishes the polishing process, with the aid of polishing cloths. Both shoes may be done at the same time within a minute and a half.

¶ Charles Gilpin, the Negro actor who has won so much fame in the portrayal of the title rôle in the "Emperor Jones", was one of the ten honor guests at the dinner of the Dramatic League, March 6. For a time quite a controversy raged as to whether or not Mr. Gilpin in spite of his ability should be invited because of his color. Mr. Gilpin's attitude throughout this trying situation was marked with a fine dignity which brought him increased admiration and respect.

¶ As a rule the names of nominees for the President's Cabinet are submitted to the Senate at a special session called "extraordinary session", on the day after inaguration. But on March 4, 1921, immediately after having been inaugurated, Mr. Harding appeared at the executive session of the Senate, read, himself, the names of his nominees and asked for immediate action. The Senate without any opposition confirmed the list submitted. A rule permitting the president to take such a step was adopted in 1806, but it is believed that this is the first time it has been put into action.

¶ Judge Kennesaw Mountain Landis recently accepted a post as arbiter of baseball disputes, at a salary of $42,500. But Representative Welty, of Ohio, has moved that the Judge be impeached on the ground that he has neglected his official duties for another gainful occupation.

CHOCOLATE CAKE

POCAHONTAS FOSTER

UNT CARROWAY, who lives in the country, was coming to our house to spend a week, so Geraldine and I were going to sleep on the third floor. We just love to sleep on the third floor because the storeroom is up there and there are loads of old books with queer pictures that we like so much to look through. We could stay up until perhaps ten o'clock at night looking at these books and mother would think we were in bed.

We were so busy the day before Aunt Carroway came, fixing her room. We had to bring down extra covers for her bed because Aunt Carroway is very cold natured. "I wouldn't have a furnace for anything," she'd say. "Just give me my fire-places and a frontroom stove." She has lots of queer ways. She won't drink cocoa like the rest of us—she just has to have her coffee with malted milk in it. Who ever heard of putting malted milk in coffee! Geraldine and I just look at each other and try to keep from smiling when we see Aunt Carroway fixing her coffee.

The very first night Aunt Carroway got to our house she started in with directions. "I don't know what time you city folks get up," she said, "but I don't stay in bed all day myself. And I must have a cup of coffee by six o'clock in the morning or else I'll have a headache all day." Now, of course, we didn't want her to have a headache, but just imagine six o'clock in the morning! I don't remember ever getting up at six but once before then, and that was the time Uncle Jackson took us to Milburn in his car. I just thought mother would have me make Aunt Carroway's coffee, even though it would mean my getting up before day, and sure enough mother said:

"Gwendolyn, I think I'll give you that job. You can set Big Ben to alarm at quarter after five and that will give you just enough time to get the coffee made."

"Mazie," said Aunt Carroway, "can Gwendolyn really make coffee? You know I want *real* coffee. If it isn't but a half cup I like that good."

"Oh, yes," said mother, "she knows how. She made it for her father every morning when I was sick with the grippe that time. Gwendolyn, remember—one tablespoonful of coffee to a cup of water."

"Yessum," I said, "I know."

That night Geraldine and I had planned to look through the old family Bible. It has so many nice pictures, but when I thought of that five o'clock time I thought I had better go to bed. It was much colder on the third floor than in the other part of the house, so Geraldine and I slept in our bathrobes. Weren't they nice and warm, though! Geraldine hates to pull the window down at night, although I don't mind so much—in fact, I sort of like it.

"Don't lower that window!" said Geraldine. "There's enough air in this cold storage, and mother will never know."

Well, I'd hardly got warm and stretched out good in bed when Big Ben alarmed. I had meant to shut it off quickly and make believe I didn't hear it, but it alarmed so loudly I knew mother heard it and I had to get up. This was in January and you know how dark it is at five o'clock in the winter. And it was so cold I was really glad I hadn't lowered the window. I got dressed and was downstairs by half-past five. Just as I was about to commence the coffee Aunt Carroway called down, "Geraldine, Gwendolyn, —oh goodness, which one is it? I don't know why on earth your mother named you two so much alike. I always wanted one named after me." (But I've thanked my stars a thousand times that mother didn't name me Carroway. What a name!) "Don't make my coffee in that percolator," she continued, "use a sauce-pan if your mother has no coffee pot. I don't believe in those things."

"Yessum," I said. All that talk so early in the morning, I thought. Aunt Carroway should have known better than to holler like that at that hour. Well, I got the coffee pot,—mother had one which she used before Cousin Fan gave her the percolator—and I washed it good, put exactly one cup of water in the pot and one tablespoonful of coffee. When I had put it on the gas I went in and fixed a place on one side of the table. At six o'clock the coffee was ready and Aunt Carroway came downstairs.

"You needn't have fixed the table in the dining-room," she said. "I could have had my coffee in the kitchen just as well.

Then Aunt Carroway never said another word. Didn't even say how the coffee was and if there is anything I like it is to be praised when I've done something. So when mother came downstairs I wishpered to her to ask Aunt Carroway how it was.

"Good morning, Sister." Mother always calls her sister. She says it's because Aunt Carroway is the older, but I don't see any reason for that. I'm older than Geraldine and still Geraldine doesn't call me sister. "How was the coffee?" she asked.

"It was all right, I suppose; but gracious, it does seem that I could have had a full cup of coffee. And, too, it wasn't black enough. I guess maybe Ger—Gwendolyn didn't use enough coffee."

Now Aunt Carroway had just said the night before that she'd rather have a half cup of good coffee than a lot of "coffee water", as she calls it. And I certainly had tried to make that coffee right. Well, I was so hurt that I just cried right out loud. I couldn't help it. But father said it was all right and that I mustn't feel so badly about what Aunt Carroway said because she was old and apt to be a little queer. Father is so nice about things like that. Mother explained that that wasn't real black coffee and that even though it was strong it would hardly be real black.

"Oh, yes," said Aunt Carroway, "it was strong enough, but I do like my coffee to be black."

Of course, I had measured an exact cup of water and when the coffee boiled, some of it boiled away.

"I'll tell you what to do," Geraldine said, "make two cups of coffee and let it boil down and if there is any left just pour it in the sink."

I thought that a pretty good plan so the next morning I used two cups of water instead of one. Of course, I used more coffee, too, I was so determined to have it right. I was all ready for Aunt Carroway about ten minutes before six. Then I poured out a little coffee to see if it was black enough. Just as I went in the closet to get the coffee strainer I spied the vanilla. "That's just the thing!" I thought. It was quite black and I was sure it wouldn't hurt because mother uses it in almost everything. So I put some in the coffee. When Aunt Carroway came down she said, "My, the coffee smells good. If it's as good as it looks I know it's all right."

I knew I had struck the right idea then. It was the vanilla that made it smell and look so good. But when Aunt Carroway tasted it she shouted so she brought everybody downstairs.

"Great heavens, child!" she exclaimed. "What on earth have you done to this coffee? Yesterday it was bad enough, but I declare this morning it's worse!"

"Maybe it's that malted milk," I said, although I knew perfectly well it wasn't.

"No, it isn't," said Aunt Carroway. "Malted milk nor no other kind of milk tastes like this, and I know it. That's just the way with children raised in the city. They don't know a thing about the things they should know. There neither you nor Gwendolyn (she really meant Geraldine) know the first thing about cooking, and you ten years old. It's a shame!"

Just then mother spoke up—mother is so different from Aunt Carroway. Mother says it's because Aunt Carroway has no children of her own and therefore she has no patience with children. Well, if that's what makes the difference I'm certainly glad mother has children.

"Never mind, Sister," mother said. "I'll have some coffee for you in ten minutes."

I was glad things happened as they did because after that morning I never got up again at five o'clock.

It was the morning before Aunt Carroway went back home when she and mother were talking and I heard her say, "Mazie, it certainly is a shame to bring two girls up the way you're bringing up these children. It's what I've always said about children raised in the city. They never know a thing about housework." Really, Aunt Carroway knows more about city folks and their way of living for never having lived in the city herself than anyone I know of. "If you'll let Gwendolyn—I don't know if I have the name right now, but I mean the oldest one, that youngest child is too spoiled."

"That's right," said mother—"Gwendolyn."

"Well, if you'll let her spend her vacation with me I'll teach her some of the things she ought to know. She's plenty old enough to learn to do something now."

"All right," said mother.

Well, when I heard that, I was too sick and excited to listen any longer. I just hustled off to tell Geraldine.

"The pleasure's all yours," she said. "I'm glad I am spoiled. You can have the trip."

Well, as soon as vacation time came Aunt Carroway wrote for me and mother started me to the country. Father had cautioned me to be very careful about everything and to do just as Aunt Carroway told me and he was sure I'd like the country.

Aunt Carroway met me at the station in a little buggy. When she saw the large bag I had she said, "Great heavens, child,"—that's her regular saying—"anyone would think you were going away for a year with all these clothes! Your mother makes you children too many clothes. City folks and their manner of dressing—there's no sense in it!"

It took us about an hour to get to Aunt Carroway's house. It really isn't so far from the station, but Aunt Carroway doesn't believe in having the horse trot. "We've nothing to hurry for," she said, "so we'll let the horse walk. It's too hot for him to trot."

It was about five o'clock when we got to the house and as I was hungry Aunt Carroway started to fix some supper.

"We'll just have some nice fresh apple sauce and some biscuits. I don't believe in a heavy supper. I have my main meal at noon."

Now all my way down there I had dreamed of nothing less than a nice fried chicken and apple sauce for dessert. I do like apple sauce, but not alone with nothing but cold biscuits. I ate it, though, and made believe it was just what I had wanted for supper. Before it got dark good, Aunt Carroway said, "Well, Chunk,"—she says she calls me "Chunk" because I am so fat, but I believe she gave me that name because she couldn't remember which one I was, Gwendolyn or Geraldine.

"Well, Chunk," she said, "I guess we'll be going to bed. You must be tired from your trip and tomorrow I want to show you how to darn stockings. I have a good many here that need mending and it will be good for you to learn how to darn."

"Yessum," I said and off I went to bed.

Aunt Carroway lives in the country where there aren't so many people, and there are no children near her at all. Her house has five rooms, three downstairs and two upstairs. It looks as though the kitchen had been built after the other part of the house. It looks sort of added on like. The two rooms upstairs are smaller than those downstairs, with low ceilings. A flight of narrow, winding stairs leads to the second floor. Her bed was so white and feathery looking that I hated to muss it up to get into it. I was to sleep in the front bedroom and Aunt Carroway had the backroom so she could hear if anything got at her chickens.

It was a long time before I could go to sleep. I couldn't help thinking of home and how Geraldine had said when I left, "You can have your country and fried chicken, but give me my home, sweet home." And now if she only knew that I hadn't had my fried chicken, wouldn't she laugh!

Aunt Carroway let me stay in bed the next morning until seven o'clock. When I came downstairs she was frying the loveliest spring chicken and she had biscuits in the oven. I had to rub my stomach because it seemed as though I could taste it already. Then she said, "Look out in the well, Chunk, and you'll see a pail hanging there. Bring it to me. The butter is in it."

You know people in the country where Aunt Carroway lives, don't have ice boxes. They put all their food in pails and hang the pails in the well. I went outside to get the butter. Now I didn't know I should pull the pail up—I thought I should untie the string. Just as I had the string untied it slipped from my fingers and there went the butter to the bottom of the well. What to do I didn't know. I just stood there and tried to think.

"Can't you draw it up?" Aunt Carroway asked.

"Oh, yessum," I stammered, "but I don't see it."

"What?" she asked, and came outside to the well. I hated not to tell the truth, but I just couldn't get myself in bad. With mother it would have been different, but with Aunt Carroway—oh, no!

"Well," she gasped, "if that isn't the limit! I know, some of those boys who came here to farm this summer have just stolen that butter. It's outrageous! But it's good I have some more."

Breakfast was lovely and I was proud to think how slick I got out of that butter scrape. Sure enough Aunt Carroway did start me darning. I knew something about darning before that, but I didn't tell her so. I did the darning so nicely that Aunt Carroway really praised me. "Imagine Aunt Carroway praising me," I told Geraldine when I got home.

The next day was the awful day. I was to have my first lesson in cooking. I was to make a chocolate layer cake because I liked that and as I had done so well with the darning I was allowed to say what I wanted to make. I did everything just as Aunt Carroway told me, and

What on earth have you done to this coffee?

the cake turned out fine. Then for the chocolate icing. Aunt Carroway told me exactly how to make the icing and then she went out to see about her hen that was hatching some baby chicks.

"You understand just how to mix it, don't you?" she asked.

I assured her that I did so she went on out. Now Aunt Carroway uses sweetened chocolate and if there is anything I like it is sweetened chocolate. I'd much rather have it than candy. I tried my best not to eat any of the chocolate, not even the smallest crumb, but somehow I did taste a little tiny piece and before I knew it over three-fourths of the chocolate was gone. I don't know why I ate it, but I did. Then what to do I didn't know. Then I remembered one time when Mrs. Hinton, who belongs to mother's club, was coming to call on mother and we didn't have any more chocolate, mother used cocoa and the cake was so good that Mrs. Hinton asked how to make it. There was my way out and Aunt Carroway had a great big can of cocoa that she had bought at a sale and was going to send to the Good Saints Orphanage. I just reached down in the can and used two cups of cocoa. It didn't look quite black enough so I used another cup. Now you'd think I would have learned from my first experience with making things black, but I hadn't. I didn't know I should have put sugar with the cocoa and you can just imagine how that filling tasted. I don't know how I ever got it to look as nice as I did, but between the milk and water it did turn out to look all right. That night Aunt Carroway cut the cake for supper.

"It looks good, doesn't it?" she said.

Since then I've decided that I don't want the things I make to look so good and maybe they'll taste better.

I can't tell you what Aunt Carroway did when she tasted the cake. She knew right away what I had done. That night she wrote mother to come and get me. Two days later father came for me. I thought he would scold me when Aunt Carroway told him what I had done. But he didn't. When we were on the train he said, "I don't believe I want you to be a cook any way. I think I'd rather have you study music," and I think so too.

When Comes the Wavering Spring

MARY EFFIE LEE

O THRASHER brown,
And shy slight Thrush in suit of russet,
When spring spreads splendidly around,
Sprawls wantonly to challenge and fill—
With scents and sounds steeped deep in magic—
The sense of every dreamer, of every bird;—
Aye, even the wood thrush, shy and thoughtful,
Even the wood thrush, shy and simple,
Who hides away at the foot of the hedges
On the black, moist earth,
And sings in hidden places, pipes and sings
All that a heartful can,
In trembling, wavering tone
That is the spirit of wavering spring.

I would sing if I could;
I know that feeling.
I know that feeling of ten thousand things,
That throbbing of the heart,
That troubling stirring of thought
That wakens wistful memories,
When comes the wavering spring.

THE JURY

I HAD heard so much about Aiken, I was very anxious to get there. After I was on the train I was hunting for my berth which I expected to be a room, but afterwards found it was not.

I saw many very interesting sights. But at the most interesting part it grew dark and I could look out no longer. This was just when we were crossing the Potomac River.

At Washington we had a half-hour wait. Most of the people got out and looked around, but I did not know my way around so I stayed in the car. It was then 7 o'clock. At 10 o'clock I retired. When I arose the next morning I went and sat by the window again. I did not have to change until I reached Trenton, S. C. I was somewhat surprised at the looks of the roads which were not paved at all, but were of red clay.

When I reached Aiken I was so very tired that I vowed I would not go on the train again for quite a while.

Do you not think I spent a very pleasant trip?

HAZEL MARSHALL,
Aiken, S. C.

I AM going to tell you about Castle Island, for the children who read THE BROWNIES' BOOK. It is a place in the Atlantic Ocean. A long time ago, in the Revolutionary War, colored men threw up earth there so they could help to fight the British; their General was Washington. The island is a part of South Boston. I have done my best on this letter. I hope you will like it. I am nine years old and am in the fourth grade in the Agassiz School. Miss Maria Baldwin is the principal.

LAURA CARROLL,
Cambridge, Mass.

PLEASE allow me space in your paper to tell how I enjoy reading THE BROWNIES' BOOK. I have received three copies and they are the most interesting books that I ever read, and I love them because they tell about my own race. I am fond of the little Brownies that I read of in these books and I wish them great success.

I am in the sixth grade and very much interested in my books and music also. I am eleven years old. I have two other little sisters, Althea and Virginia.

ANNIE ELIZABETH MCADEN,
Reidsville, N. C.

IT is a full year since I am reading THE BROWNIES' BOOK and it pleases me so much that I can't stay still.

Now, my dear *lectores* (readers), I have all as my best friends. I am a Cuban born, but my parents are natives of St. Kitts. Think for one instant and then answer these few words: Would you like to have me as friend? Tell me what would please you to know of Cuba.

Now I am looking out in the next number to see all my friends and if there is any that can read and write Spanish. I will finish dedicating these simple verses to THE BROWNIES' BOOK in Spanish. I want to see who is going to be the translator or translators of it in the next.

"A TI"

Eres BROWNIES' BOOK
Grandioso laud
Brindandole al niño
Refulgente alegría.

Llegaste BROWNIES' BOOK
Desplegando plenitud
!Viva, viva para siempre
Tu gloriosa "entente"!

CLARIS SCARBROUGH,
Nuevitas, Cuba.

I RECEIVE THE BROWNIES' BOOK every month and I am always glad when it comes, for it is a very interesting book. Not only do I enjoy reading THE BROWNIES' BOOK, but my mother and uncle like it also and I am sure every little boy and girl must enjoy reading it.

VIOLA MURRAY,
Pittsburgh, Pa.

TOMMY AND THE FLOWER FAIRIES

A One Act Play

EULALIE SPENCE

CENE: Living-room in Tommy's home. Spring flowers on table.

Time: Afternoon in early spring.

Note: Eight year old Tommy is the much spoiled and petted only child of wealthy parents. When the scene opens he is in an armchair, reading fairy tales.

Tommy (*Petulantly*)—"What silly stories! I'm tired of reading anyway! (*Closes book*)—Oh, how I wish something nice would happen! I wonder if any really, truly person ever saw a fairy or a giant?" (*Drops book on floor—snuggling down deeper in his chair—sighs deeply—falls asleep.*)

(*A faint rustling is heard. The Fairy Queen of the Land of the Spring Flowers appears. She tip-toes over to Tommy, waving her magic wand.*)

Queen—

"Open your eyes, O Tommy dear,
The Queen of Flower Land is here!"

Tommy—"O, I must be dreaming! Why who are you? A real fairy?"

Queen—"Your wish has come true, Tommy. You are not a very happy little boy, are you?"

Tommy (*In a shamed tone*)—"Well, I was sort of tired of everything. Nothing exciting seems to happen except in my story books. (*Picks up book.*) Are you from one of my stories?"

Queen (*Shaking her head and pointing to the flower-laden bowl on the table*)—"These are my children who come up out of the earth to carry joy messages to tired hearts, Tommy. Would you like to hear some of them?"

Tommy (*Eagerly*)—"Yes, yes!"

Queen (*Waving wand*)—

"Hasten over dale and hill,
To do my bidding, Daffodil!"

(*Daffodil—all golden—appears dancing lightly. She bends in a low curtsey at the feet of the Queen.*)

Queen—"Arise! Now Tommy, you shall hear what Daffodil has done this day."

Daffodil (*Bowing once more*)—"O Queen, this day I have cheered the bedside of many a sick mortal. Tired hearts beheld me and knew that Spring had come. Eyes long closed in pain, drank deep of my golden glory. Even the weakest fingers gave a tender, loving caress. O Queen, the message I left was hope!"

Queen—"Thou couldst not have done a better day's work."

Daffodil (*Bowing low, stands aside.*)

Tommy—"O, wonderful Fairy, tell me! Are there any daffodils in this bowl?"

Queen—"Yes, Tommy."

Tommy—"But I never saw them! I never heard the message!"

Queen—"Your eyes, Tommy, have always been shut to the beautiful about you. But be cheerful, Tommy. You shall hear what my crocuses have been doing." (*Waves wand*)—

"Come forth, O bravest Child of Spring!
And give us of the joy you bring!"

Crocus (*Dances merrily into view, bowing low before the Queen.*)

Queen—"Arise, brave heart! For the sake of this mortal child, give us again your story of the day."

Crocus—"O Queen, I have brightened the gardens of the world. I have brought joy into the note of the singing birds, and courage to my timid, weaker flower mates of the garden. I have given the poet a new spring sonnet. I have brought joyous memories of other days to the hearts of the old and to the youth of the world have I brought the knowledge of love."

Queen—"O Crocus, without thee surely we might wait the Spring forever."

Crocus (*Bowing low*)—"Not so, O Queen! What are we without Your Majesty to inspire our best efforts?"

Tommy (*Wonderingly*)—"O, wonderful Queen, have you any other Spring flowers in your land?"

Queen—"Yes, many. Behold!"

(*She waves her wand and a troop of flower fairies appear, each one bows before the Queen.*)

Fairies—

"We are the flowers
Who herald the Spring.
From fairy bowers,
Come we to sing!
Joy, love and hope is

Daffodil dances before the Queen.

The message we bring,—
Harken, oh, harken,
Welcome the Spring!"

Tommy—"Thank you, dear flowers! I shall never forget you!"

Queen (*Waving wand*)—
"O, flowers of Spring, away, away,
New duties await the coming day."
(*Fairies dance merrily away.*)

Tommy—"O, Fairy Queen! You have taught me so much! Surely you will not leave me too?"

Queen—"No, Tommy! I shall be always near you. In the heart of each one of my children you will see me again. Now, Tommy dear, return to your chair and finish your dream."

(*Tommy obeys her command.*)

Tommy—"Good-bye, O Queen!"

Queen—"Good-bye, Tommy. You will not soon forget me!" (*Disappears.*)

(*Tommy starts up rubbing his eyes.*)

Tommy—"Why where is my Fairy Queen? O, I must have been dreaming!" (*Sees flowers on table*) "O, Flowers of Spring, I shall always keep your messages in my heart. Joy! Love! Hope!"

CURTAIN

Little People of the Month

OF course, there are many little Brownies who are ever so polite; but out in Chicago, a little Brownie boy has won a prize of $50 for his politeness. His name is Paul Rayfield Johnson and he is six years old.

You see, the Chicago *Tribune* awarded daily $50 prizes to the politest person discovered by its "Polite Editor". On the third of January, our little Paul was discovered at the corner of Wabash Avenue and 35th Street. Paul is a newsboy and his politeness "overwhelmed" the editor. Our little friend says he's going to use the money for his education. His only relative in Chicago is an aged grandmother, to whom he gives the credit for his fine manners.

Ivan Premdas has been awarded a scholarship by Queen's College in Demerara. He will get free tuition for four years and $10 a quarter for books. There were five children who passed the examination—four boys and one girl. Ivan, who was the youngest of the children, made the highest average. He is a pupil from Christ Church School. He was not eleven years old—since the examination was before his birthday—so he won the scholarship at the age of ten, and started to college at eleven.

This Brownie baby is S. D. Middleton, Jr. The Baby Welfare League declared him the healthiest baby in the city of Meadville, Pa. He has never required medicine of any kind. The Rev. S. D. Middleton, who is President of the Meadville Branch of the N. A. A. C. P. and Pastor of the Baptist Church, and Mrs. Sarah Hewin Middleton, his wife, have received many congraulations on having such a fine baby boy.

DeHart Hubbard is an athlete, and he's won *some* prizes! Don't you agree? He says:

"I entered competition in the spring of 1919. I was very succesful during my first season, winning all events entered in except one. During this season I won the all around championship of Cincinnati, and the broad jumping championship of the A.M.A. of the A.A.U.

"In the season of 1920, I again won the all around championship of Cincinnati and the B.J. championship of the A.M.A., setting a new district record of 22 feet 6 inches in winning the former.

"During the summer I was considered as an Olympic possibility, but was prevented by sickness from making the tryout.

"During my two years of competition I have won 15 first prizes, 3 second prizes, and 5 third prizes.

"I am at present affiliated with the Morgan Community Club of Pittsburgh."

Isn't this fine?

Last year was G. Francis Bowles' senior year at the Rindge Technical School at Cambridge, Mass. A silver loving-cup was offered as a prize to the student who wrote the best words for

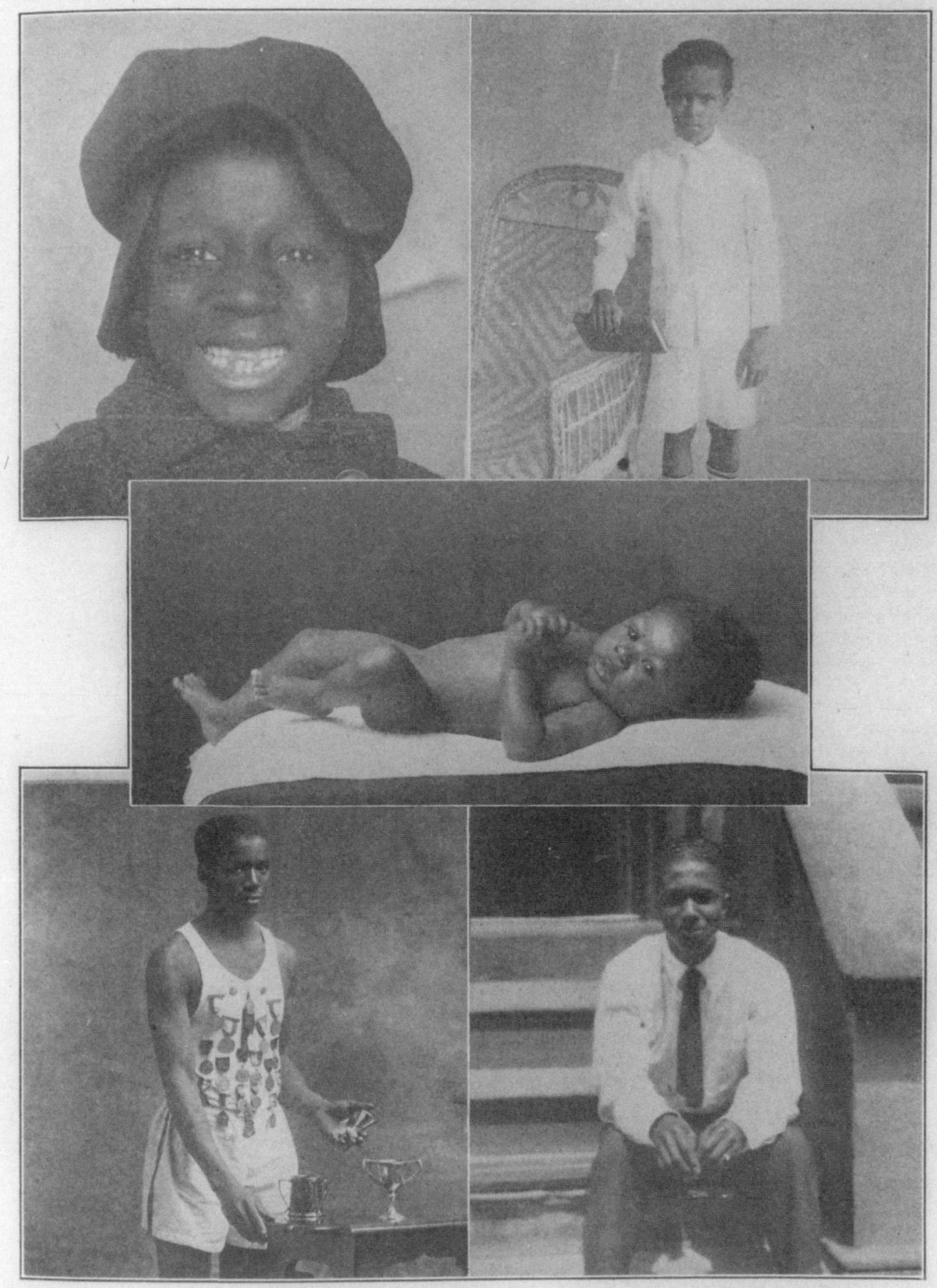

Paul Rayfield Johnson
De Hart Hubbard
S. D. Middleton, Jr.
Ivan Premdas
J. Francis Bowles

a school song or the best song, including both words and music. The contest was open for two months, during which time over one hundred songs were submitted. The cup was awarded to Brownie Bowles! He wrote the words and music of what was considered the best contribution. He is now a post-graduate of the Rindge School.

He is very unselfish, too, for his letter says: "I may add, that honorable mention was given to a colored boy named Edward Simms, for writing the words to a song for the school."

THE GROWN-UPS' CORNER

I AM sending, in behalf of the Negro Women's Federated Clubs of this state, one yearly subscription to THE BROWNIES' BOOK, to be sent to the State Training School for Negro Girls, J. R. Johnson, Superintendent, Taft, Oklahoma.

We are anxious that this magazine be placed in the hands of the girls of this school. Its interesting articles, pictures and games, together with its high moral tone, will, we feel, do much to brighten the daily life of those confined there and at the same time exert an influence for good which will be felt perhaps in all their after life.

Please start the subscription with the January number.

HARRIET P. JACOBSON,
Director, Legislative Department of the Oklahoma State Federation of Negro Women's Clubs,
Oklahoma City, Okla.

WILL you please let me express my appreciation of the value of THE BROWNIES' BOOK and of the great service it is rendering my little girl? It is teaching her that little girls that look entirely different from herself like just the same things and so are like her, although they do look different. That is a pretty important thing for a little American girl to learn. I think there are many thousand American fathers and mothers who would like their boys and girls to learn that lesson and would subscribe for THE BROWNIES' BOOK if they knew about it.

It is teaching some little Americans that indispensable lesson of "self-respect", and other little Americans that other equally important lesson of "respect for others".

Two or three of my friends are subscribing for it for these reasons, and I think others would if it could be brought to their attention.

GEORGE G. BRADFORD,
Cambridge, Mass.

WITH the largest sincerity in your efforts, it may seem to you that the child has come with a character of such strange complexity, of good and not-good mixed together, because of heredity and other touches which you cannot now measure, that it is difficult to make him understand, either through wise words of beautiful example, what you actually know of right, and what you could easily teach to a differently constituted child. Your certain knowledge of the clean and pure, the great, the excellent and the strong, he meets with indifference. He will not accept your teaching. What are you going to do? He is your child, and if you fail to implant the seeds of this very knowledge which he most needs to have, what of his future?

Will you not begin searching for new methods of inculcation; for new ability to teach? Will you not try to find out how far down into the soil of your own being the roots of your knowledge have struck? Is it so firmly your own, this knowledge, as to have brought perseverance and patience and a new kind of loving painstaking into blossom?

How much can you teach? What you know and nothing else; but the limits of knowledge in the human mind have never been set. We all progress to higher wisdom, you and the little learning child at knee, along with the acknowledged *savants* of the age. Teach him, Mother-heart, all that you can while he is with you; but remain humble and feel your way carefully ahead, lest in some moment of over-confidence you and the child may miss some lovely opportunity for growing that should have belonged to you.

YETTA KAY STODDARD.
San Diego, Cal.

TIP-TOP O' THE WORLD

ETHEL CAUTION

BERYL sat in the luxuriously cushioned, low chair before the fireplace, chin cupped in her hands, brown eyes fast on the flame-swept log. Not that she was thinking about the fantastic capers of those little tongues that leaped and played and disappeared; she was wondering why she had been so rash as to accept Helen's invitation to the month-end party. She might have known she wouldn't fit—they were all so jolly and self-assured, both the men and the girls. Of course, they should be, for did they not belong? Weren't their fathers all successful business and professional men, and were they not all used to large homes and luxury? She had always had these things, too, in her mind, but in reality had lived in two rooms all her life until she came to school. And then many times when her classmates were having fun, she was busy with the tasks that helped to pay her tuition.

Aside from always being busy, she was very timid and shy and hid behind an assumed mask of indifference and coldness a very human heart, hungry for companionship and understanding. Helen Lane had singled her out early in their freshman year and had been her very dear friend ever since. She had repeatedly offered Beryl the hospitality of her home, but Beryl had as repeatedly refused. But now that college days had come to an end and many dear ties were to be broken, she at last yielded and together with fourteen other folks just realizing the bigness of life, she found herself at Helen's home, high up on a pine-clad foothill from the top of which one commanded a view of miles of evergreen hills and fertile valleys.

As she sat now before the fire in her own room, she was thinking over everything, trying to decide whether or not she was really having a good time. She was just deciding that she enjoyed every bit of it—even the evenings when the others paired off, for it was fun to her to watch the capers and manoeuvres of the rest of the party. Besides, they had become used to her during their four years of association and she knew they were not unselfish or unkind, but had tacitly agreed that she preferred being let alone. It was worth it all just to be here among these wonderful hills and valleys, and the gorgeous sunsets and afterglows, and—just then an impish little flame stuck its tongue out at her and fled in glee. She heard it chuckle. In a few minutes another little flame winked its wicked eye at her and was then convulsed with mirth.

"Oh!" she cried, pushing her chair quite out of the way. "What a wonderful dance that would be—The Dance of the Flames!" She ran to her dresser, snatched up her scarf, and was soon lost in the composition of her new dance.

Next morning just as dawn was drawing aside the curtains of night, Beryl let herself noiselessly out of the house and sped away to the hill-top—"tip-top o' the world" she called it.

First she gave a long, low, musical call, followed by a series of intermingled notes till it seemed the whole hill was alive with singing birds. And soon it was. For in the few days she had been there she had made fast friends of the feathered folk who had learned that when she called it was worth while to answer. They fluttered around her now, perched upon her head and shoulders, and uplifted arms. Folks who were rather slow in approaching her because of her aloofness would have marveled at the intimacy with which these helpless songsters ate from her upturned palms and picked dainty morsels from between her smile-curved lips. In fact, they might have been suprised to discover that her lips could part with pleasure and her eyes dance with glee.

When her friends had finished their early meal, she raised her arms and sent them back to their nests with a gay little laugh. Then she tossed aside her cape, slipped off her shoes and stood poised as if for flight. Not so, for soon to the whistled accompaniment of "To a Wild Rose" her slender body swayed to and fro in rhythm with the music. As the spirit of the dance possessed her more and more she broke into words of her own making:

Little flower, slender flower,
Swaying in the moonlight;
Fragrance rare scents the air,
From thy petals white.
Flush of rose sometimes goes
O'er thy petal tips,

When the angels bend
To kiss thee with their lips.
O thou thought of God,
Sent to me from Heaven above,
Pray teach me all of love,
Teach me all of love, I pray,
Little rose, slender, snow-white rose.

Breathless she flung herself down on the soft pine needles while her eyes roved over the hills and she watched the path the sun made from Heaven to earth. "Life is a wonderful thing," she said and slipping into shoes and cape she hurried back before anyone should miss her.

Next daybreak found her again speeding with light feet and lighter heart to the hilltop. Excitement showed in every movement, for was she not to try out her "Flame Dance" this morning? And if it worked, would she not have five beautiful dances to put into book form? And would they not begin to bring true some of her life long dreams? She had an extra feast for the birds and chatted with these winged songsters as she never would have dared with any human being.

This morning instead of the soft white dress she usually wore, there was one of clinging yellow which caught the sunbeams and held them captive. The dance began. At first she lay a resinous section of pine on the grass. Soon a little spurt of flame played about one side; then an impish little one stuck its tongue out at the trees and hills; and another winked its eye gleefully at the sun. Soon the log was a mass of flames dancing, capering, darting out and disappearing, the sunbeams helping to perfect the illusion. At last, one by one the little flames flickered out and the log lay prone again in the fireplace.

"It worked, it worked!" she cried and slipped down to her shoes and cape. She became dimly conscious of another presence. Rising quickly to her feet she turned to face Jack Perrin, cap in hand, and admiration written all over his face.

"Oh!" she said. She was still too surprised to slip on her mask of aloofness and stood staring back at him.

"I hope you will pardon the intrusion, but each morning I have watched you speed up this hill and have wondered what took you abroad so early. No one seemed to be in the secret but yourself, so I determined to find out. Here I find you the embodiment of poetry and rhythm, the soul of music and beauty. We have all learned to think of you as stiff and cold, whereas you are warmth and feeling itself. You are wonderful."

And looking deeply and steadily into his eyes, she said "Oh!" and after a pause, "Life, you are indeed a wonderful thing."

Common Things

JAMES ALPHEUS BUTLER, JR.

I LOVE to sit in forests green
'Mid tufts of grass in splendor seen,
And scent the flowers in the air,
And gaze with wond'ring, raptured stare
On common things.

I love to haunt the woodland stream
Where water-lilies paint the scene,
Where meadow-sweet and water-cresses
Add color to the stream's recesses,
Where poppies red, in glory swaying,
Are with the yellow loose-stripes playing;
And then I pause, and think, and ponder,
And soon my heart is filled with wonder
At common things.

I love to hear a passing bird
Trill notes the sweetest ever heard!
I love to hear the night-bird's screeches,
Or watch the squirrel in the beeches;
Each sight, each sound a new joy teaches
In common things.

THE GIFT OF THE GOOD FAIRY

ONCE upon a time there lived a Good Fairy whose daily thoughts were of pretty little boys and girls and of beautiful women and handsome men and of how she might make beautiful those unfortunate ones whom nature had not given long, wavy hair and a smooth, lovely complexion. So she waved her magic wand and immediately gave to those who would be beautiful a group of preparations known from that time, fifteen years ago, until to-day and at home and abroad as

MADAM C. J. WALKER'S SUPERFINE PREPARATIONS FOR THE HAIR AND FOR THE SKIN

Wonderful Hair Grower
Glossine
Temple Grower
Tetter Salve
Vegetable Shampoo

Vanishing Cream
Cleansing Cream
Cold Cream
Antiseptic Hand Soap
Complexion Soap

Superfine Face Powder (white, rose-flesh, brown)
Floral Cluster Talcum Powder
Antiseptic Dental Cream
Witch Hazel Jelly

Results from the use of our preparations especially noticeable in the hair and skin of children.

Very liberal trial treatment sent anywhere upon receipt of a dollar and a half.

THE MADAM C. J. WALKER MFG. CO.

640 North West Street *Dept. 1-X* **Indianapolis, Indiana**

AFTERWORD

Dianne Johnson-Feelings

To Children, who with eager look
Scanned vainly library shelf and nook
For History or Song or Story
That told of Colored Peoples' glory—
We dedicate THE BROWNIES' BOOK.

This verse was written in 1920 by Jessie Fauset. She, along with W. E. B. Du Bois, was one of the editors of *The Brownies' Book*, the first substantial magazine designed especially for African-American young people. Technically an independent venture, it functioned as the children's counterpart to the NAACP's magazine, *The Crisis*. It was published by Du Bois and Augustus Granville Dill from January 1920 through December 1921. Du Bois is credited on the masthead as the conductor of the publication. Fauset served as its literary editor from January to December 1920 and as managing editor throughout 1921. The publication folded because it did not sell well enough to survive.

One of the first critics to give attention to the history of *The Brownies' Book* was Elinor Sinnette, a Washington, D.C., librarian and champion of African-American children's literature. Sinnette calls attention to some of the differences between this magazine and *St. Nicholas*, the best-selling American children's magazine from 1878 to 1945. During the two years of *The Brownies' Book*'s publication, poems such as "Ten Little Niggers" routinely appeared in the pages of *St. Nicholas*: "Ten little nigger boys went out to dine / One choked his little self and then / there were nine..." Cartoons, stereotypes, and all kinds of misrepresentations of the Negro were legion in *St. Nicholas*, and its tone, when it came to blacks, was harsh and condescending. Sinnette observes that when it came to covering political events, *The Brownies' Book* reflected "a more mature attitude." For example, on the issue of the revolutionary war in Mexico, *The Brownies' Book* tells its readers: "There has been a revolution in Mexico. President Carranza has been expelled and General Obregon is at the head of most of the opposing forces. The trouble seems to have been that Carranza was not willing to have what his rivals considered a fair election." For *St. Nicholas*, on the other hand, it was enough to report in conventionally smug terms that "those restless people beyond the Rio Grande spent the month of April in their favorite pastime—Civil War."

In the estimation of W. E. B. Du Bois, young black readers needed information that was interpreted and reported from a radically different perspective than that offered in *St. Nicholas*. At the very least, African-American children needed some kind of reading material that did not refer to them by the casually violent term "niggers."

Because of the preponderance of negative black images in the American mass media, the creators of *The Brownies' Book* were concerned that "all of the Negro child's idealism, all his sense of the good, the great and the beautiful is associated with white people. . . . He unconsciously gets the impression that the Negro has little chance to be great, heroic or beautiful." So, quite consciously, the editors went about their mission of presenting alternative images to Negro youth. Moreover, all of the artwork in the 24 issues of the magazine, with very few exceptions, was created by Negro artists and was explicitly concerned with the power and beauty of "negroness" or "blackness."

The creation of *The Brownies' Book* was, in essence, an experiment in pedagogy and propaganda aimed at African-American youth. In fact, Du Bois's well-known statement on the relationship between art and propaganda, part of his "Criteria of Negro Art" address at the 1926 Chicago conference of the NAACP, speaks specifically about young people:

> We black folk . . . have within us as a race new stirrings; stirrings of the beginning of a new appreciation of joy, of a new desire to create, of a new will to be; as though in this morning of group life we had awakened from sleep that at once dimly mourns the past and dreams a splendid future; and there has come the conviction that the Youth that is here today, the Negro Youth, is a different kind of Youth, because in some new way it bears this mighty prophesy on its breast, with a new realization of itself, with new determination for all mankind.

Certainly, *The Brownies' Book* was more than mere propaganda. As a children's magazine, part of its focus was on entertainment. But in the October 1919 issue of *The Crisis*, the "Children's Number" for the year, Du Bois outlines some of the complex issues involved in writing and publishing for children—specifically, questions of what information to present and how to present it. To what extent, he wonders, and in what ways, does an editor take into account the "peculiar situation" of the readership? Then comes the resolve for a new magazine. He says:

> There seems but one alternative: We shall publish hereafter not ONE Children's Number a year, but TWELVE! Messrs. Du Bois and [Augustus] Dill will issue in November, in cooperation with *The Crisis*, but as an entirely separate publication, a little magazine for children—for all children, but especially for *ours*, "the Children of the Sun."

> It will be called, naturally, *The Brownies' Book,* and as we have advertised, "It will be a thing of Joy and Beauty, dealing in Happiness, Laughter and Emulation, and designed especially for Kiddies from Six to Sixteen."
>
> It will seek to teach Universal Love and Brotherhood for all little folk—black and brown and yellow and white.
>
> Of course, pictures, puzzles, stories, letters from little ones, clubs, games and oh—everything!

What follows this account of the basic ideas undergirding the magazine is a more detailed outline of the new project's seven objectives, introduced with the words, "Deftly intertwined with this mission of entertainment will go the endeavor:

> (*a*) To make colored children realize that being 'colored' is a normal beautiful thing.
> (*b*) To make them familiar with the history and achievements of the Negro race.
> (*c*) To make them know that other colored children have grown into beautiful, useful and famous persons.
> (*d*) To teach them delicately a code of honor and action in their relations with white children.

These are peculiar endeavors indeed—to teach a child to be comfortable with his or her own physical reality, defined only or largely in terms of skin color. On the other hand, perhaps, they are endeavors to be expected in light of African-American history up to that point. In an essay in *Racism and Mental Health* (1973) the psychologist Gloria Johnson Powell asserts that "being a White person in a White society appears to mean very little to the development of self-concept but that being Black in a White society seems to be one of the most important factors in such development." Thus, those who set out to educate (in the broadest sense of the word) the African-American child must design their pedagogy with concepts of race and color taking on significant, and sometimes disproportionate, import. Writing more than 50 years after the publication of *The Brownies' Book,* James Comer, director of the Yale Child Study Center, and Harvard psychiatrist Alvin Poussaint lend further force to this approach, arguing in *Black Child Care* (1975) that the rearing of black and white children is not the same endeavor:

> We believe there is a difference.... The black awareness movement of the past few years has brought these problems out into the open. Increasing numbers of people are conscious of the need to prepare black children to deal with the questions and issues of race in a way which will be most beneficial to their overall emotional, social, and psychological growth and development.

This statement by Comer and Poussaint is not a version of a Negro pathology argument. Acknowledging that black Americans live in a racist, hostile society does not imply that they are, as a group, the embodiment of the concept of self-hatred. Rather, such an acknowledgment comprises a realistic assessment of the society of the United States, one that sets the stage for a black child's healthful outlook and maturation. Accordingly, as the October 1919 issue of *The Crisis* made clear, several of the objectives of *The Brownies' Book* were stated in explicitly racial terms, reflecting this reality. For example, one of the new magazine's endeavors was "to make them know that other colored children have grown into beautiful, useful and famous persons." Other objectives appear, upon cursory reading, to have more to do with being a person, regardless of race. In the words of the editors, these goals are:

> *(e)* To turn their little hurts and resentments into emulation, ambition and love of their own homes and companions.
> *(f)* To point out the best amusements and joys and worthwhile things of life.
> *(g)* To inspire them to prepare for definite occupations and duties with a broad spirit of sacrifice.

What becomes apparent immediately, however, is that even these objectives—which do not mention race explicitly—still have racial undertones. The "little hurts and resentments" may imply racial slurs and frustrations with societal constraints. These children are called upon to pursue careers that involve sacrifice—namely, careers directed toward improving the plight of African Americans as a group. For the creators of *The Brownies' Book,* these two enterprises, becoming a whole human being and becoming a responsible member of an African-American community, are distinguishable yet intimately related.

Du Bois and Fauset organized the magazine to have several regular departments, including "The Grown-Ups' Corner" and "The Judge." "The Grown-Ups' Corner" served as a forum for exchanges between adult readers and the editors.

Fauset, who wrote "The Judge" column, creates for this character the function of responding, indirectly, to parents' questions about child rearing. Directly, the Judge responds to the discussions and questions of his young friends, Billikins, Billie, William, and Wilhelmina. Fauset sets up the Judge as a kind of grandfather figure who is carrying out an assigned duty:

> "I AM the Judge. I am old, very old. I know all things, except a few, and I have been appointed by the King to sit in the Court of Children and tell them the Law and listen to what they have to say. The Law is old and musty and needs sadly to be changed. In time the Children will change it; but now it is the Law."

This introduction is fascinating for several reasons. The image of the "King" functions to transport the young reader to a realm somewhat removed from the ordinary, a magic place that captures the attention while the Judge addresses plain facts of everyday black life. Assuming the air and authority of a grandfather, the Judge takes his place in the long tradition of instructive storytelling. This Judge does not solely lay down the law; he also acknowledges that the Law is in need of profound revision. And the Judge makes it clear that children will be a part of this process of civic activity and legal change.

The place and importance of children are reinforced in the children's own section of the magazine—"The Jury." This term, of course, continues the legal metaphor and implies that the children have a valid and significant, even a deciding, voice in the discussions. And it suggests that children have a part in redresssing large-scale criminal acts that affect them. The Judge promises "to listen very patiently while the *children* speak to me and to the world." This grandparent Judge figure is fair, and he listens to children—perhaps more so than parents do. The magazine's creation of "The Judge" cleverly allows the editors to address the concerns both of parents and of young people, and to do so in a manner that might make both groups receptive.

A sample discussion from "The Judge" communicates the general tone of this regular column. The following excerpt appeared in the first issue of the magazine. These words are in reply to Wilhelmina's reasoning earlier in the column about buying new clothes and her complaints that her parents treat her like a child. The Judge answers:

> How do you *know* you like that hat? Is it suited to you? Does it really set off your figure and your smooth, brown skin? Or—and here I have a deep suspicion—do you choose it because Katie Brown has one like it and the Ladies of Avenue K, and—but hold! Who are K.B. and the L. of A.K.? Are they persons of taste, or simply of power? Do you imitate them for love, or fear? Does the choice of this hat represent your freedom of thoughtful taste, or your slavery to what the flamboyant Kitty does or to what rich white folk wear?
>
> Mind you, I'm not answering these questions—I'm just asking. We will assume that the hat is becoming and suits you and you want it. Now comes that awkward question of money. What is the question of money? Simply this: Of the 1,000 ways of spending this dollar, which is best for me, for mother, for the family, for my people, for the world? If the "best" way of spending it for you makes mother starve, or the family lose the home, or colored folk be ridiculed, or the world look silly—why, then, no such hat for you, and that, too, by your own dear Judgment.
>
> On the contrary, if nobody is harmed and you want the hat and have the dollars and cannot get more pleasure in any other way, get the hat and be happy. You see, dear Wilhelmina, all that is asked of Fifteen is to stop and think when hats call. And one more thing: Ask your best chum's advice. Who's she? Mother.

Again, it is clear that the Judge considers the authority and wishes of parents of primary significance, while he still accords full consideration to the sentiments of young people. Indeed, he makes the point to Wilhelmina that she can trust her own judgment, her own powers to think and to reason.

This response from the Judge is remarkable for several reasons. Most important, it calls attention to and draws connections between numerous issues that might seem, to a young person, completely peripheral to the immediate desire for some material possession. The first question the Judge asks Wilhelmina to think about is why she likes what she likes. To whose influences and to what kind of influences is she reacting? He points out to her that people sometimes wield power that society ascribes to them for the wrong reasons; for example, Katie Brown is by nature flamboyant; by accident of birth some people are rich and white. The wonderful thing about this portion of the Judge's gentle "lecture," as he calls it, is that while admonishing Wilhelmina to consider the hat's suitability for herself, he includes strong compliments for her own mind and culture.

Especially impressive is the Judge's treatment of "that awkward question of money." He makes it unremittingly clear that, in broad economic terms, every individual is responsible to herself or himself, the family, the community, the world. This sense of interconnectedness is an abiding concern of *The Brownies' Book*. One of the reasons for this, certainly, is Du Bois's commitment to a pan-African vision and a kind of world citizenship. At the same time, however, the magazine's format makes room for young readers themselves to raise questions about their relationships with others: "The Jury" is composed solely of the words of young readers. In "The Jury" section, young readers themselves are featured as full members of an African-American community in language that is clear and often eloquent; they express concerns parallel to those of the adults and the Judge.

Excerpts from the three separate columns illustrate this similarity of concern. First, from "The Grown-Ups' Corner"(February 1920):

> I have been waiting with some interest for the appearance of *The Brownies' Book*. . . . I am sure you have many good plans in mind for our children; but I do hope you are going to write a good deal about colored men and women of achievement. My little girl has been studying about Betsy Ross and George Washington and the others, and she says, "Mamma, didn't colored folks do anything!"
>
> When I tell her as much as I know about our folks, she says: "Well, that's just stories. Didn't they ever do anything in a book?". . .
>
> Our little girl is dark brown, and we want her to be proud of her color and to know that it isn't the kind of skin people have that makes them great.
>
> —Bella Seymour, New York City

The author of this letter highlights several interesting issues. She observes that immigrants to the United States are taught no African-American history. And she acknowledges that she herself is ill-equipped, as a working-class parent, to guide her daughter's education about that history. The closing paragraph underscores the preoccupation with physical appearance, and it tells of concepts of beauty that are more profound than meet the eye. Likewise, many young writers also make note of this issue of how how they look. Young James Alpheus Butler, Jr., writes to declare his pride in his brown skin. At the other extreme is a young girl from Seattle "who has never known of a father's love" and who feels that she is "not a very pretty girl, and for that reason I have not been able to get anyone to help me in my little plan [to go to a boarding school]. I have tried and tried to do something in Seattle, but the people are very down on the Negro race. In some schools they do not want colored children."

In a poignant way, this letter speaks to the issues of sexism (and its special relationship to the matter of physical beauty), racism, and the unfortunate link between these phenomena and the goal of attaining an education.

Bella Seymour's letter in "The Grown-Ups' Corner" adds to the dilemma of having access to an education the problem of being offered a curriculum that is Eurocentric. A young reader echoes this concern, saying:

> But since I read the stories of Paul Cuffee, Blanche K. Bruce and Katy Ferguson, real colored people, whom I feel that I do know because they were brown people like me, I believe I do like history, and I believe that it is something more than dates.

A final but crucial issue raised in Seymour's letter is that of the power of the written word in comparison to "just stories." Seymour's daughter is part of a literate culture and generation that, to some extent, dismisses and discounts the value and even veracity of tales not told in books. It is no accident that it is Du Bois, Fauset, and Dill, all people of letters and of the academy, who were the driving force behind this first successful African-American magazine for youth. More than most people, they recognized the ways in which words could be manipulated and the danger of such manipulation, in light of the mystique of authority held by the written word. In Fauset's persona of judge, she takes on this important issue, simultaneously addressing the recurring question of African-American identity and history. The following exchange illustrates the editors' understanding of this problem:

> "My teacher wants to know which is the greatest continent," said Billikins.

What follows is the naming of every continent except Africa.

> "And I," said the Judge, "would say Africa."
> They all stared at him.
> "Are you joking?" asked Billy.

"No."

"But you really don't mean it," protested William.

"I suppose," pouted Wilhemina, that you're just saying Africa because we are all of African descent. Of course—"

"No-o oh no!—but how on earth can you say that Africa is the greatest continent? It is stuck way in the back of the Atlas and the geography which Billy uses devotes only a paragraph to it."

"I say it because I believe it is so. Not because I want to believe it true—not because I think it ought to be true, but because in my humble opinion it is true."

"And may we know the reasons?" said William.

"Certainly: They are seven."

("O Master, we are seven," chanted Wilhelmina.)

"First: Africa was the only continent with a climate warm and salubrious enough to foster the beginnings of human culture.

Six additional reasons relating to matters such as industrial arts, cultural arts, the mastery of ironworking, and agriculture, follow.

"Gee!" said Billy.

"Don't understand," wailed Billikins.

"Few people do," said the Judge.

"I was just wondering," mused Wilhelmina, "who are the guys that write our histories and geographies."

"Well you can bet they're not colored," said William.

"No—not yet," said the Judge.

"Do they tell lies?" asked Billy.

"No they tell what they think is the truth."

"And I suppose," said Wilhelmina, "that what one thinks is the truth, *is* the truth."

"Certainly not," answered the Judge. "To tell what one believes is the truth, is not necessarily to lie, but it is not consequently true."

"Then one can tell falsehoods and not always lie."

"Certainly."

"I'm going to try that," said Billy.

"I wouldn't," warned the Judge. "You see it's this way: there are lots of things to be known and few to know them. Our duty is therefore not simply to tell what we believe is true, but to remember our ignorance and be sure that we know before we speak."

With humor and intellectual humility, the Judge impresses the listeners/readers not only with a knowledge of their legacy but also with an appreciation for the concepts of truth and ambiguity. This passage is part of a series of discussions on African civilizations. As such, it provides a good synopsis of the larger points that are elaborated upon in various ways in subsequent columns, in stories, and in illustrations.

There is a constant interchange in *The Brownies' Book* among the Judge, the grown-ups, and the young people. The excerpt above speaks in a special way to reader Alice Martin, a most perceptive observer of the manipulation that Du Bois addresses. She makes the following shrewd comment on how her geography is conceptualized in regard to race:

> . . . all the pictures are pretty, nice-looking men and women, except the Africans. They always look so ugly. I don't mean to make fun of them, for I am not pretty myself; but I know not all colored people look like me. I see lots of ugly white people too; but not all white people look like them, and they are not the ones they put in the geography.

Alice goes on to draw a further connection between herself and the pictures, noting that her white classmates look at the pictures, then at her, then whisper and laugh.

The Judge's column speaks not only to Alice Martin but to the parent who asks, "Now, the difficult problem for us is: What shall we tell him to do, and how best for him to answer [name-calling from white children], and instill in him race love and race pride?"

The Judge's comments also reinforce the resolve of young George Max Simpson, who asks the Judge to suggest a small library for him, as he is concerned about obtaining a well-rounded education. He declares his interest in learning about colored peoples all over the world and in someday working in Africa. Columns such as "The Judge" and parental involvement help to create attitudes such as George's: "My father is always saying that a great many wonderful things are going to happen to Negroes within the next twenty-five years, and I want to be able to understand and appreciate them."

In response to this letter and to the general need for reinforcing black identity, Alvin Poussaint reminded *Ebony* readers of the words of Barbara Sizemore, former superintendent of schools in Washington, D.C. She warned: "Identity is never complete. It is open ended and thereby subject to threat. The new black must discover ways to preserve the black identity, or he may be forced to surrender it again."

Poussaint cautioned that not only do our communities need the black awareness movement but that "our psyches require it." In these terms, Du Bois qualifies as a "new black."

Significantly, also, Du Bois understands that the identity of the modern black American citizen—and this includes us, today—is ultimately tied to Africa and to her people around the world. Additionally, the editors acknowledge the necessity of cultivating a global perspective. Du Bois urges adult members of the community to

> consult with us about the child that has some special gift or talent. Ask us to furnish figures and names to prove that it does pay...spiritually as well as materially, to educate our boys and girls up to the finest that is in them. Tell us what colored heroes and heroines you would like us to

> talk about, what foreign countries you would like described, briefly what dark children—and white, too, for that matter, for we colored people must set the example of broadness—are doing all over the glorious world.

The Brownies' Book section called "Little People of the Month" introduces readers to individual youngsters and recognizes their achievements. "As the Crow Flies" reports newsworthy events from all over the world. "Play Time" recorded the games of children worldwide and gave directions, making it possible for the "true brownies" to reenact them. And finally, the fiction and the poetry integrated all of the magazine's objectives, sometimes providing entertainment, sometimes instruction, and sometimes both.

"As the Crow Flies" enhanced children's understanding of the interrelatedness of events occurring in different parts of the globe. For example, it might contain an entry like this:

> This year was two things: it was the year of the Great Peace and the 300th year since our black fathers settled in America. Perhaps the good God remembered both these things when he made this year.

The crow reports at various times the number of colored students in northern colleges, the number of states that have ratified the amendment giving women the right to vote, the first meeting of the International Labor Conference, an annual meeting of the NAACP, the birthday of Frederick Douglass, and a wealthy Indian's gift to charity of $1.5 million. The news is always relevant to "people of color" in some context:

> The brown people of India have been given a share in their own government by the English. It is a small share but it marks the beginning of Justice to 315,000,000 colored people.

Or at home, for example:

> Congress is trying to frame a bill to keep people from advocating violence and riot. So far, the bills proposed would stop folks from thinking.

This news item demonstrates what is perhaps the single most important aspect of *The Brownies' Book:* Du Bois and the other editors always encourage the youngsters to think, even while grounding the magazine in a very particular philosophy.

"Little People of the Month" recognizes Mildred Turner of Brockton, Massachusetts, for being chosen to write the ode for her high school class because "by the election she achieved a signal honor for her race, since she is the first Negro to win this distinction at the school." However, at the same time that it celebrates black achievements, *The Brownies' Book* also tries to stress to the youngsters that they are fully black *and* fully American. One of the most striking

Brownies' Book covers is Paolo S. Abbate's "I Am an American Citizen," a bust of a black boy exhibiting pride and composure. In some instances, the magazine refers to its readers as patriots: "But we're especially proud of our girl patriots—for girls do have such a weary time trying to prove that they have brains and can be inspired and have ambitions."

The overall message is clear: All people, regardless of nationality, religion, gender, or race, deserve respect. Consider the following passage from "The Judge," which addresses this kind of universal respect and also alludes to the ethnic diversity of American society. In this scene, Billikins has been taunting the local Chinese laundryman and attempts to justify his actions:

> "But I'm an American. I'm better than they are. I'm the way *they* ought to be."
>
> "Billy," says the Judge gravely, "Do you know that what you are saying is the kind of thing that sets the world by the ears, that makes war, that causes unspeakable cruelties?"
>
> Billy says he doesn't understand. "I don't either," says William, "I wish you'd explain."
>
> "Consider. Suppose you, William, and a man from India, and a man from Ireland, and one from Venezuela, one from France, and one from Liberia were all wrecked on a desert island. Suppose not one of you possessed a single thing, which one of you would be the best man?"

Unfortunately, the implication of the last sentence is that possessions confer some kind of value upon their owner. But this kind of insinuation is counteracted by the totality of the magazine. The selection continues:

> "No one," Wilhelmina answers for him promptly.
>
> "Which one would own the island? The Hindu, the Frenchman, the—?"
>
> "There wouldn't none of us be owning that island, if it was me on it," says Billy ungrammatically. "We'd all of us have to have it together if there was going to be any peace. Why each one of us would have as much right to it as the other."
>
> "Even though William was an American?"
>
> "Why, yes, why should he own it all?"
>
> "That's just it. Well think of the world as a huge desert island, and all the people as being just wrecked on it. Hasn't each one of us a right to everything on the island—joy, light, love, 'life, liberty, and the pursuit of happiness'?"
>
> "That's from the Declaration of Independence," says William. "You know it Billy; you recited it at the school picnic."

The Brownies' Book as a whole strove to practice the values espoused in this passage. It regularly featured fiction from a variety of cultures, African to Native American to European. In addition, the "Playtime" column taught its young readers an international set of games and songs. Two of the most frequent contributors to this section were Nella Larsen Imes, who shared material from Denmark, and Langston Hughes, who sent stories and games from Mexico. It was a magazine for American black children, but the frame of reference was large. No wonder, as letters to the editors prove, correspondence came in from Cuba, the Philippines, and elsewhere around the world. Indeed, the magazine makes a commendable effort toward accomplishing its stated goal: "To teach Universal Love and Brotherhood for all little folks—black and brown and yellow and white."

Notably, in his autobiography, Du Bois says that *The Brownies' Book* is one of the two efforts of his life on which he "look[s] back with infinite satisfaction." (The other was the writing and producing of a pageant entitled "The Star of Ethiopia," first performed in 1913 in New York in commemoration of the 50th anniversary of the Emancipation Proclamation.) Fortunately, *The Brownies' Book* made it possible for many African-American young people to look ahead equipped with clearer self-identities and broader understandings of their world. Fortunately, too, the very existence of *The Brownies' Book,* and the objectives and themes it addressed, played a key part in sparking the development of African-American children's literature.

The Brownies' Book

DECEMBER, 1921

This is the last Brownies' Book. For twenty-four months we have brought Joy and Knowledge to four thousand Brownies stretched from Oregon to Florida. But there are two million Brownies in the United States, and unless we got at least one in every hundred to read our pages and help pay printing, we knew we must at last cease to be. And now the month has come to say goodbye. We are sorry---much sorrier than any of you, for it has all been such fun. After all---who knows---perhaps we shall meet again.

$1.50 A YEAR 15cts. A COPY

INDEX OF AUTHORS

INDEX OF TITLES

DIANNE JOHNSON-FEELINGS is associate professor of English at the University of South Carolina, specializing in children's, young adult, and African-American literature. She is the author of *Telling Tales: The Pedagogy and Promise of African American Literature for Youth* and *Presenting Laurence Yep*. She holds a Ph.D. in American Studies from Yale University.

MARIAN WRIGHT EDELMAN, the founder and president of the Children's Defense Fund, has been an advocate for disadvantaged Americans for her entire professional career. A graduate of Spelman College and Yale Law School, she was the first black woman admitted to the Mississippi Bar. During the mid-1960s she directed the NAACP Legal Defense and Educational Fund in Jackson, Mississippi. Mrs. Edelman has received many honorary degrees and awards, including the Albert Schweitzer Humanitarian Prize, and was a MacArthur Foundation Prize Fellow. She is also the author of several books, including *Families in Peril: An Agenda for Social Change*, *The Measure of Our Success: A Letter to My Children and Yours*, and *Guiding My Feet: Meditations and Prayers on Loving and Working for Children*.

ROBERT G. O'MEALLY is Zora Neale Hurston Professor of American Literature at Columbia University and previously taught English and Afro-American studies at Wesleyan University and Barnard College. He is the author of *The Craft of Ralph Ellison* and *Lady Day: Many Faces of the Lady* and editor of *Tales of the Congaree* by E. C. Adams and *New Essays on "Invisible Man."* Professor O'Meally is coeditor of *History and Memory in African American Culture* and *Critical Essays on Sterling A. Brown*.

THE IONA AND PETER OPIE LIBRARY
OF CHILDREN'S LITERATURE

The Opie Library brings to a new generation an exceptional selection of children's literature, ranging from facsimiles and new editions of classic works to lost or forgotten treasures—some never before published—by eminent authors and illustrators. The series honors Iona and Peter Opie, the distinguished scholars and collectors of children's literature, continuing their lifelong mission to seek out and preserve the very best books for children.

ROBERT G. O'MEALLY, GENERAL EDITOR